technical analysis 201
Formu

The 2012 SEASON	2
Chassis HISTORY	6
Car TABLE	8
2012 REGULATIONS	10
Controversies 2012	13
New DEVELOPMENTS	16
Talking about COCKPITS	24
Talking about BRAKES and TYRES	28
ENGINES 2012	32
Talking about SUSPENSIONS	40
Team's technical development 2012	
RED BULL	44
FERRARI	56
McLAREN	72
LOTUS	81
MERCEDES	86
SAUBER	92
FORCE INDIA	97
WILLIAMS	100
TORO ROSSO	105
CATERHAM • MARUSSIA • HRT	108
The 2013 SEASON	110
PIRELLI TYRES	110
2013 REGULATIONS	111
NEW DEVELOPMENTS	113
CONTROVERSIES 2013	116
EVOLUTION	118

The 2012 SEASON

Without doubt, this was the best Formula 1 season of recent years, both on the sporting and technical fronts. It had been a long time since we last saw no fewer than eight different drivers on six different cars stepping onto the top of the podium – only three in 2011 – with the battle for the world title ending in a heart-stopping finale in Brazil. All credit to the cars and the teams, which substantially evened out the general technical standards. And all credit to Pirelli, which supplied tyres that were different than those of 2011, tyres that required a special approach by the team technicians and drivers, bringing to life a situation that created a kind of uncertainty, especially during the earlier part of the season.

Although they won both world titles, Red Bull didn't dominate as they did in 2011, when they scored 12 victories of which 11 were Sebastian Vettel's. They had to be happy with seven wins including two by Webber.

In 2011 they also achieved 18 pole positions, all of them by Vettel, while in 2012 they "only" managed six.

In fact, if one had to create a table of the most competitive cars of the season, top prize would go to McLaren which, while equalling Red Bull in its number of wins, was overtaken by Ferrari in the constructors' championship due to an incredible lack of reliability. Ferrari must take the credit for having fielded the most original development of the season with its F2012, which produced good reliability. Rather like Adrian Newey did with the rear end of the RB5 in 2009, Maranello also brought back the pull rod suspension layout for the front end, which had not been seen in Formula 1 since 2001.

It was a decision taken for aerodynamic reasons, but one which was not without management difficulties, especially during the season's early races. Further credit should go to the men from the Prancing Horse for being able to maintain concentration throughout the whole season, supporting Fernando Alonso in the best possible way to enable him to complete the best season of his career.

NEW DEVELOPMENTS

Banning exhaust blow straight into the diffusers' lateral channels with more precise restrictions on where to locate exhaust terminals stimulated the designers' imagination in an incredible manner and, for once, it wasn't Adrian Newey who pulled the rabbit out of the hat in 2012. A contribution to that situation was made by the Federation, which banned the original developments of the RB8 project which included – as with Lotus – extremely sophisticated brake air intakes that practically formed a sort of slide to carry the blow to the bottom of the rear tyres.

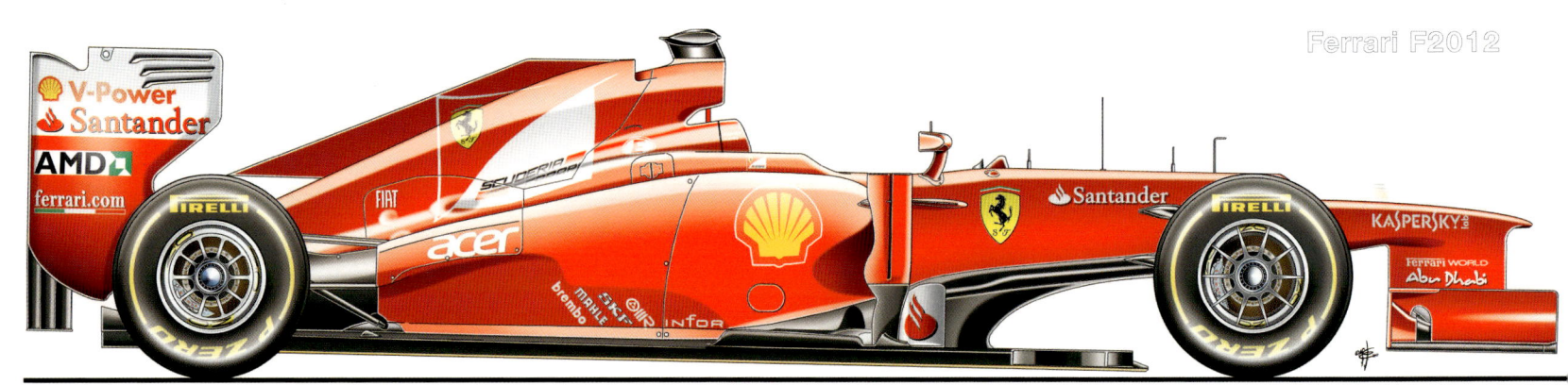

For once – and it was a pleasant surprise – the minor teams came up with the most interesting developments. Top of the class was Sauber, which revolutionized the shape of its sidepod ends, dispensing with the classic Coca Cola progression and bringing back the Ferrari F2008-type hole in the nose, although adapted to existing regulation restrictions. And then there was Williams, not just because of Maldonado's victory in the Grand Prix of Spain – their first since the 2004 Brazilian GP, won by Columbian Juan Pablo Montoya – but especially because the FW came out with many interesting, if not brand new, solutions. That was the case with their retention of the miniaturized gearbox and the new front brake air intakes, which were completely closed inside the channel between the intake itself and the chassis; a development that set a trend during the course of the season.

FERRARI'S RECOVERY
Having begun with a problematical project, Ferrari worked especially hard at the start of the season, its cars with almost one second's delay on the top performers.
Initially, the pull rod front suspension seemed to be the cause more than anything else, due to its increased difficulty of management. Development during the season was adversely affected by wind tunnel problems and the imperfect correlation between indoor simulation and essential on-track verification during Friday practice. The problem arose after an inability to immediately exploit planned updates, as happened with the front wing end plates that first appeared at Valencia but not raced until Hungary. Sometimes, as in Japan with the rear wing, a new development had to be completely set to one side, which never happened towards the end of the season, when work in the Toyota wind tunnel began to bear fruit. However, less effective was the shape of the sidepods' back ends and the original version of the exhaust exit, but after tests at Mugello just before the Spanish GP things improved. Often, qualifying performance was markedly inferior to that in the race. Yet the F2012 showed it was at home on almost all the tracks and in the various weather conditions; Alonso was able to win three Grands Prix.

STEPPED NOSE
It was the season of the unattractive stepped nose, an indispensible price that had to be paid in favour of driver safety in case of lateral blows between two cars. With the obligation of moving from 625 mm – the chassis's maximum allowed height – to 550 mm in a space of just 150 mm, it was obvious that the cars wouldn't be able to boast elegant shapes. All except McLaren and Marussia, that is, because their cars didn't exploit the maximum height limit in 2011, so the connection between the two heights became less evident. It is interesting to note that Sauber and Red Bull exploited the stepped part of the nose to introduce two new developments. That of the Swiss team had already been described above, with the blow above the step. Instead, Adrian Newey used the step in which to locate an opening which, as well as giving some aerodynamic advantages, conducted air to the electronic management systems in the front of the sidepods.

MERCEDES-BENZ' FIRST VICTORY
Mercedes-Benz had many expectations of the 2012 season, but the front F-Duct did not have the impact of some of Ross Brawn's other clever tricks, like the double diffusers of 2009 for instance. The blow into the front wing may have been useful in qualifying when the DRS could be freely used, given that this new element was associated in its activation with the DRS control, but it didn't contribute to preserving the tyres in races, despite the adoption of a sophisticated suspension layout first used in 2011. That layout meant better roll and pitch control, with a hydraulic connection between the two axles. Still, Mercedes scored its first victory in China with Nico Rosberg, who saved the honour of the Stuttgart company even if – yet again – the 2012 season can't be considered positive.

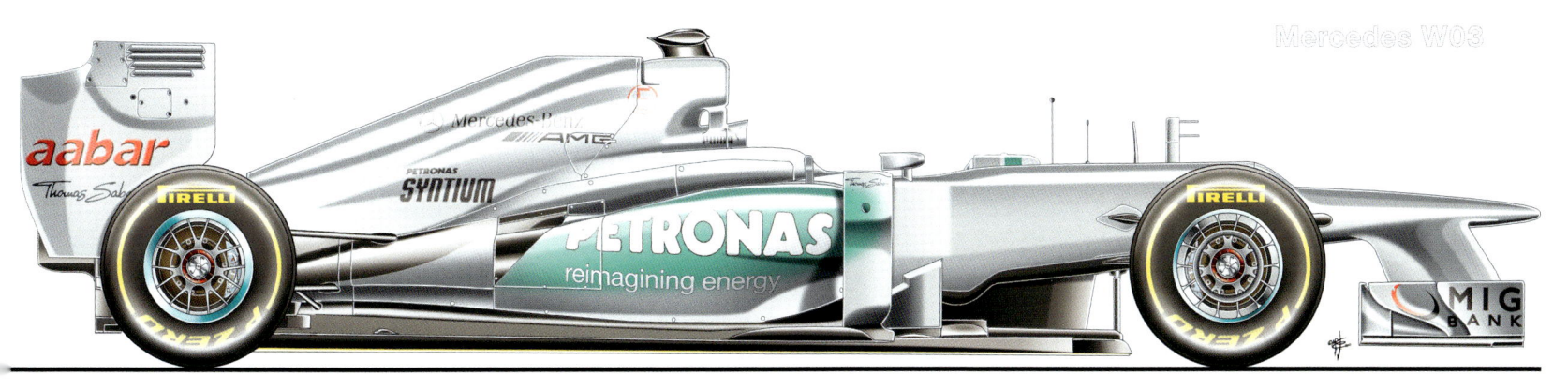

McLaren MP4-27

Mercedes W03

MINOR TEAMS
Despite direction by Mark Smith and the support of John Iley, Caterham were still unable to make that improvement in quality that would free them of the last row of the grid. They only succeeded in becoming the best of the three minor teams. The same thing goes for Marussia, which finally liberated themselves from their links with Wirth Research and collaborated with McLaren over the use of the British team's wind tunnel.

The RT adventure was completely negative, given that the team's budget wasn't anywhere close to sufficient to enter and stay in Formula 1; so its retirement at the end of the 2012 season can't have caused many regrets.

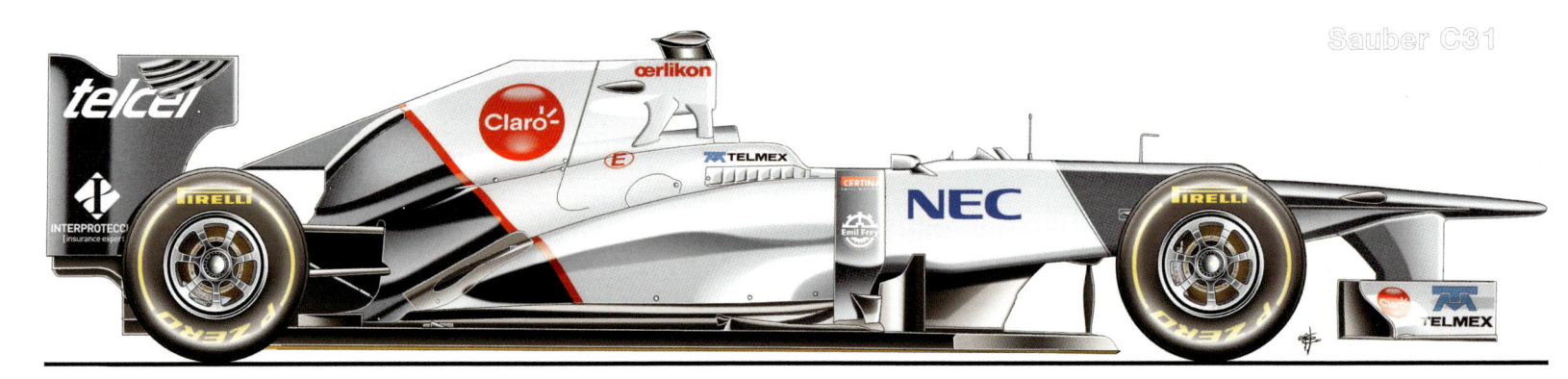

Lotus E20

Force India VJM05

Sauber C31

Toro Rosso STR7

The 2012 **SEASON**

The 2012 edition of the technical analysis has taken advantage of a contribution by Franco Nugnes for the engine chapter, from engineer Giancarlo Bruno on suspensions and tyres and engineer Kazuhito Kasai for the tyre chapter. And special thanks go to Mauro Piccoli of Brembo for the data he provided for the brakes analysis. The 2012 edition is enhanced with a new section devoted to the venting effects of the engines, written by Gary Anderson who, as well as being one of F1's most respected designers (Michael Schumacher debuted aboard his Jordan), has been the BBC's technical expert for years as well as co-author of the Autosport technical column together with Mark Hughes.

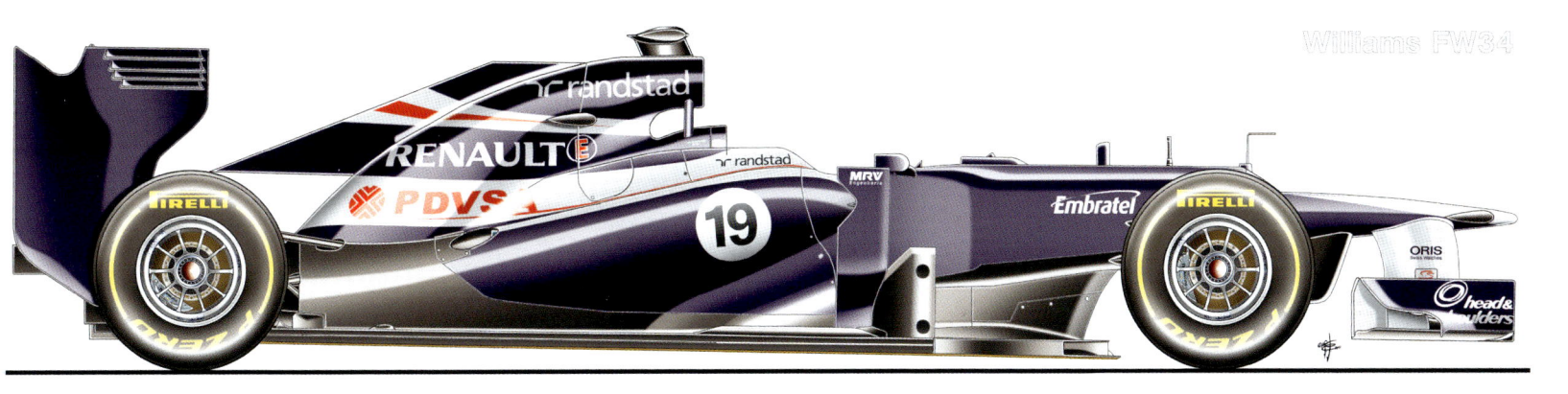

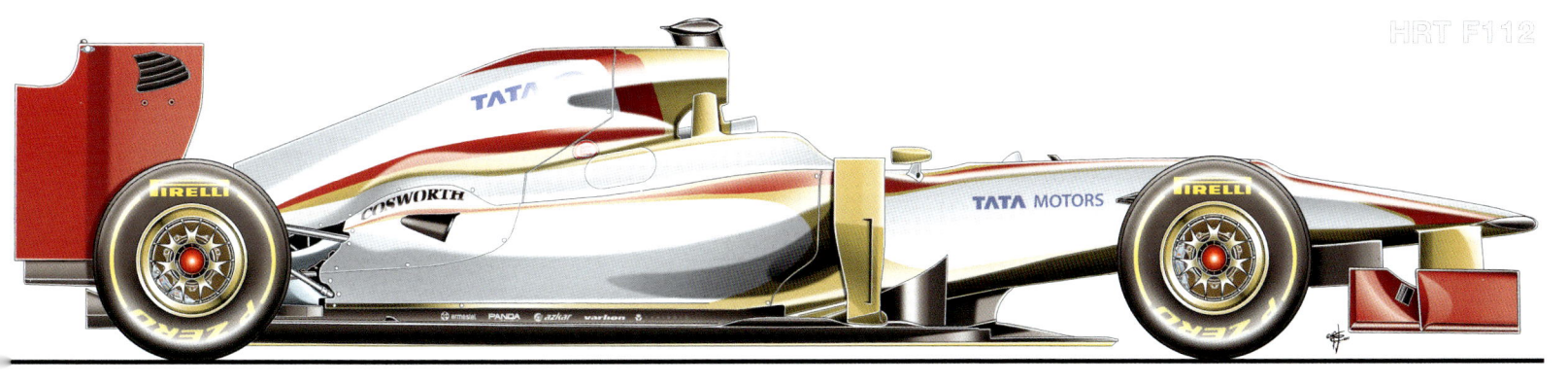

Williams FW34

Caterham CT01

Marussia MR02

HRT F112

The 2012 **SEASON**

Chassis HISTORY

The chassis graphics have, by now, assumed a historic interest in establishing which won most in the various races. With parc fermé coming into effect between qualifying and the races in 2008 and the abolition of the spare car, there are now only the two racecars in the pits plus a completely naked spare chassis, which is kept in a case for use in extreme necessity. Remember that even if an accident happens during the first few laps of practice in the morning, the teams are not allowed to assemble the monocoque for the afternoon session, but only for the following day or race, the latter if such a thing happened on the Saturday.

RED BULL
In 2011, Red Bull built six chassis, followed by Ferrari with five. The rest of the teams with only four. In 2012, the numbers dropped to five for Red Bull and Lotus. The remainder all built four chassis each.

WINNING CHASSIS
The 2012 season will be remembered like the one with the maximum number of different winners. Eight different drivers for 6 teams. Vettel and Webber for Red Bull, Alonso for Ferrari, Hamilton and Button for McLaren, Rosberg for Mercedes, Maldonado for Williams and Raikkonen for Lotus. The award for the most successful chassis of 2012 doesn't go as usual to Red Bull but to McLaren and its number 03 that won four GPs driven by Hamilton (3) and Button (1), followed by Red Bull chassis 01 driven by Vettel. Then follow three chassis: 295 Ferrari with Alonso, 02 Red Bull with Vettel and Webber and 04 McLaren with Hamilton. A single victory was achieved by 04 and 05 Red Bull with Vettel, 02 McLaren with Button, 03 Mercedes with Rosberg, 02 Williams with Maldonado and 05 Lotus with Raikkonen.

WHEELBASES
Like the 2010 and 2011 seasons, the longest car was the McLaren at 3,459 mm, followed in descending order by Mercedes (3440), Force India (3,411 mm), a team that uses the same engine and, in particular, the same gearbox. Then come Ferrari (3415), Sauber (3396,5), Williams (3358), Red Bull (3355 mm), Toro Rosso 3337 Lotus (3,318 mm). During the 2011 season Mercedes-Benz was far away the shortest, at just 3208 mm.

Chassis F2012	293	294	295	296
First run	07/02/2012	01/03/2012	16/03/2012	20/07/2012
Track	Jerez	Barcelona	Melbourne	Hockenheim
Km test	6.643,3	1.620	0	0
Km race	588,5	14.088,4	12.489,9	1.595,6

FERRARI • F2012 • N° 5-6

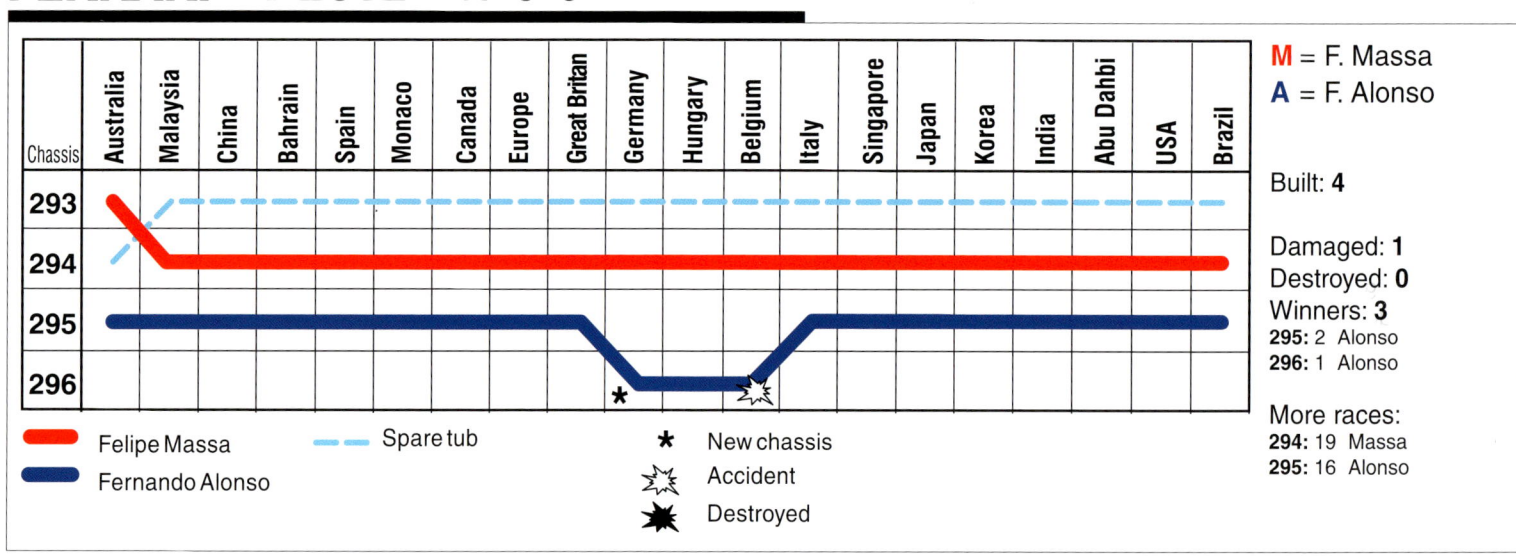

M = F. Massa
A = F. Alonso

Built: 4

Damaged: 1
Destroyed: 0
Winners: 3
295: 2 Alonso
296: 1 Alonso

More races:
294: 19 Massa
295: 16 Alonso

— Felipe Massa
— Fernando Alonso
- - - Spare tub
* New chassis
☼ Accident
✸ Destroyed

RED BULL • *RB8* • N° 1-2

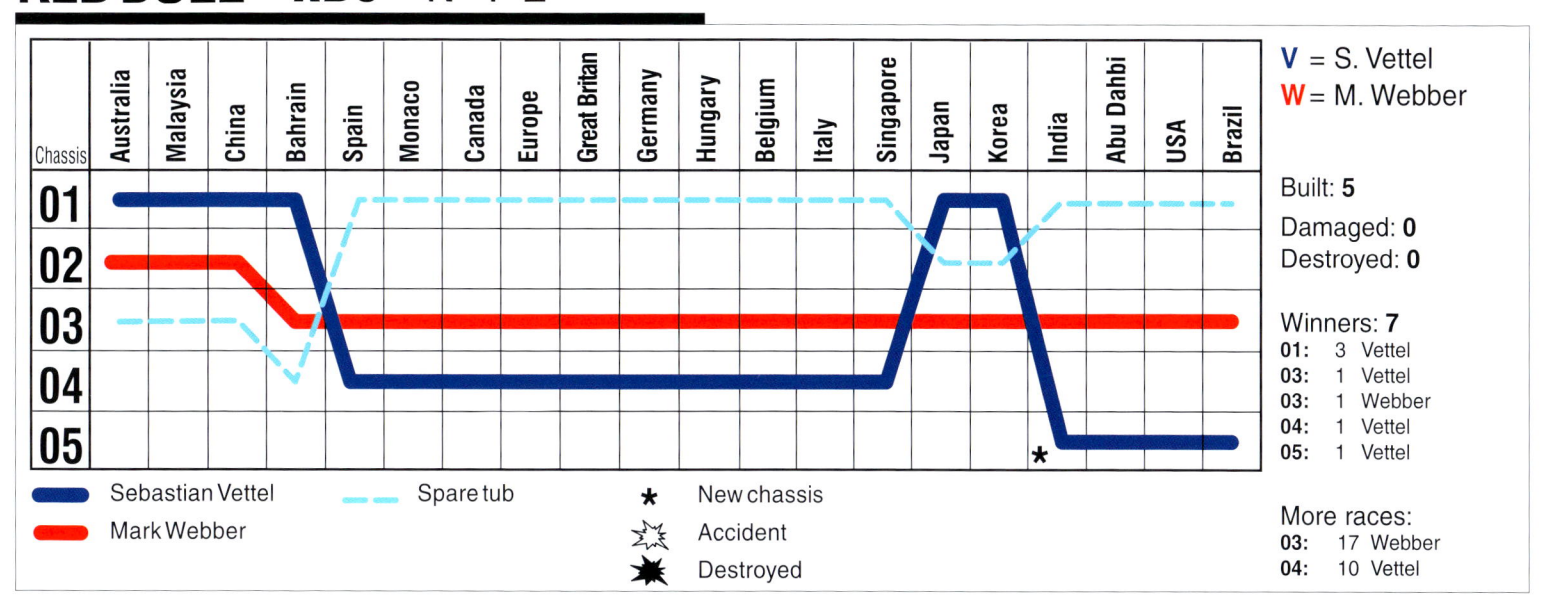

Chassis	Australia	Malaysia	China	Bahrain	Spain	Monaco	Canada	Europe	Great Britain	Germany	Hungary	Belgium	Italy	Singapore	Japan	Korea	India	Abu Dhabi	USA	Brazil
01																				
02																				
03																				
04																				
05															*					

— Sebastian Vettel   - - - Spare tub   * New chassis
— Mark Webber   ☼ Accident
                        ✸ Destroyed

V = S. Vettel
W = M. Webber

Built: **5**
Damaged: **0**
Destroyed: **0**

Winners: **7**
01: 3 Vettel
03: 1 Vettel
03: 1 Webber
04: 1 Vettel
05: 1 Vettel

More races:
03: 17 Webber
04: 10 Vettel

McLAREN • *MP4-27* • N° 3-4

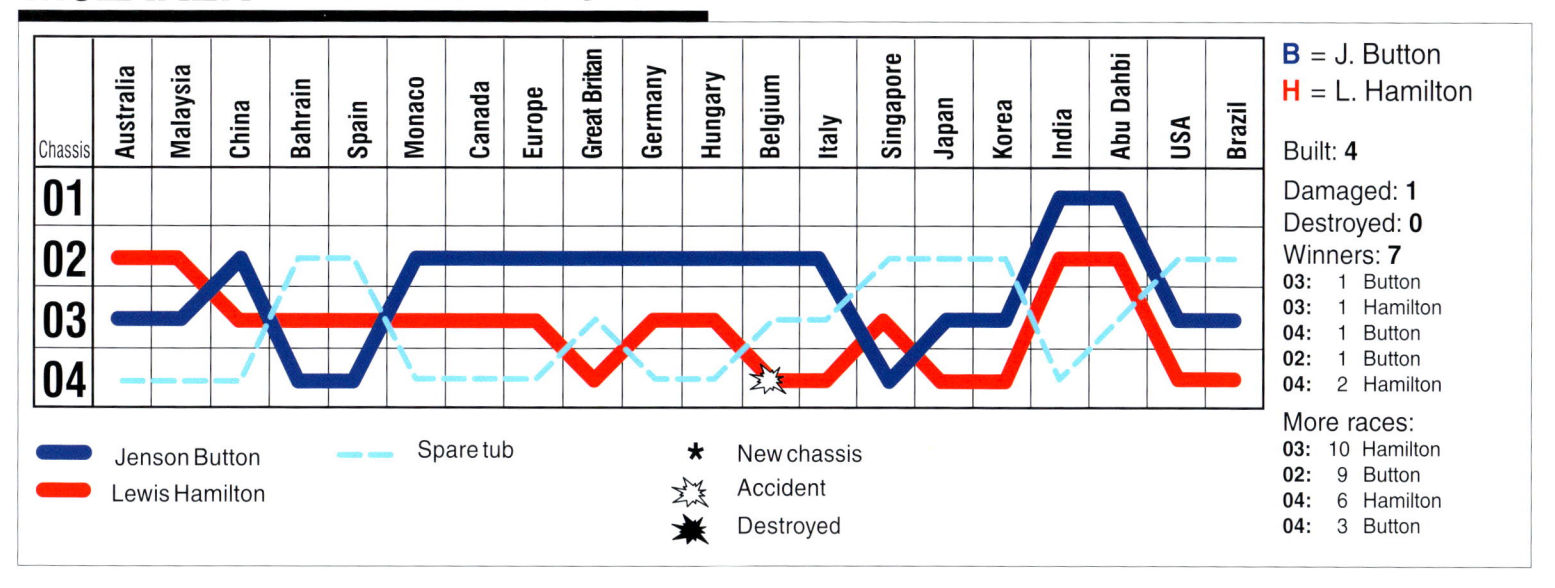

Chassis	Australia	Malaysia	China	Bahrain	Spain	Monaco	Canada	Europe	Great Britain	Germany	Hungary	Belgium	Italy	Singapore	Japan	Korea	India	Abu Dhabi	USA	Brazil
01																				
02																				
03																				
04												☼								

— Jenson Button   - - - Spare tub   * New chassis
— Lewis Hamilton   ☼ Accident
                        ✸ Destroyed

B = J. Button
H = L. Hamilton

Built: **4**
Damaged: **1**
Destroyed: **0**
Winners: **7**
03: 1 Button
03: 1 Hamilton
04: 1 Button
02: 1 Button
04: 2 Hamilton

More races:
03: 10 Hamilton
02: 9   Button
04: 6   Hamilton
04: 3   Button

The most reliable team was Red Bull, whose cars covered an incredible 96,2% of the total number of laps that comprised the 2012 world championship. Followed by Ferrari with 95,3%, Toro Rosso on 93,2%, Caterham at 93,0, F. India 92,7, Marussia 90,5, McLaren 90,1, Mercedes 87,9, KLotus 85,8, Williams 83,7, Sauber 82,6. As usual HRT last at 76,5.

	laps completed %	finishes	technical failures	accidents
Red Bull	2294 (96,2%)	35	3 alternator	2
Ferrari	2273 (95,3%)	37	1 suspensions	2
Toro Rosso	2223 (93,2%)	35	3 steering - undertrail - suspensions	0
Force India	2212 (92,7%)	35	3 suspensions - undertrail - brakes	2
Caterham	2190 (92,0%)	36	4 steering - suspensions - alternator - engine	0
Marussia	2158 (90,5%)	32	5 oil pressure - driveshaft - brakes - (2) engine	0
McLaren	2150 (90,1%)	30	5 (2) differential - gearbox - fuel pressure - fuel pump	5
Mercedes	2096 (87,9%)	29	6 wheel loose - (2) gearbox - DRS - fuel pump - stop gearbox	5
Lotus	2047 (85,8%)	32	2 alternator - wheel	6
Williams	1997 (83,7%)	28	6 engine - brakes - (2) suspensions - hydraulics - kers	6
Sauber	1969 (82,6%)	29	5 gearbox - differential - suspensions - hydraulics - undertrail	5
HRT	1825 (76,5%)	27	6 wheel loose - brakes - (2) steering - undertrail - throttle	5

Chassis **HISTORY**

Car TABLE

		1-2 RED BULL	5-6 FERRARI	3-4 McLAREN	9-10 RENAULT	7-8 MERCEDES
CAR		RB8	F2012	MP4-27	E20	MGP W03
	Designers	Adrian Newey Rob Marshall	Pat Fry Nikolas Tombazis Luca Marmorini	Jonatan Neale Paddy Lowe Neil Oatley	James Allison	Ross Brawn Bob Bell Aldo Costa
	Race engineers	Guillaume Rocquelin (1) Ciaron Pilbeam (2)	Andrea Stella (5) Rob Smedley (6)	Dave Robson (3) Andy Latham (4)	Mark Slade (9) Ayao Komastsu (10)	Peter Bonington (7) Tony Ross (8)
	Chief mechanic	Kenny Handkammer	Francesco Ugozzoni	Jonathan Brookes	Greg Baker	Mattew Deane
CHASSIS	Wheelbase	3355 mm*	3415 mm*	3459 mm*	3350 mm*	3440 mm*
	Front track	1440 mm*	1470 mm	1470 mm*	1450 mm	1470 mm
	Rear track	1410 mm*	1405 mm	1405 mm*	1420 mm	1405 mm
	Front suspension	2+1 dampers and torsion bars	Pull-rod 2+1 dampers and torsion bars	2+1 dampers and torsion bars	2+1 dampers and torsion bars	2+1 dampers and torsion bars
	Rear suspension	Pull-rod 2+1 dampers and torsion bars	Push-rod 2+1 dampers and torsion bars	Pull-rod 2+1 dampers and torsion bars	Pull-rod 2+1 dampers and torsion bars	Pull-rod 2+1 dampers and torsion bars
	Dampers	Multimatic	Sachs	McLaren	Penske	Sachs
	Brakes calipers	Brembo	Brembo	Akebono	A+P	Brembo
	Brakes discs	Brembo	Brembo CCR Carbon Industrie	Carbon Industrie Brembo	Hitco	Brembo
	Wheels	O.Z.	BBS	Enkey	AVUS	BBS
	Radiators	Marston	Secan	Calsonic - IMI	Marston	Secan
	Oil tank	middle position inside fuel tank	middle position inside fuel tank	middle position inside fuel tank	middle position inside fuel tank	middle position inside fuel tank
GEARBOX		Longitudinal carbon	Longitudinal carbon	Longitudinal carbon	Longitudinal titanium	Longitudinal carbon
	Gear selection	Semiautomatic 7 gears	Semiautomatic 7 gears	Semiautomatic 7 gears	Semiautomatic 7 gears	Semiautomatic 7 gears
	Clutch	A+P	Sachs	A+P	A+P	Sachs
	Pedals	2	2	2	2	2
ENGINE		Renault RS27-2011	Ferrari 056	Mercedes FO108Y	Renault RS27-2011	Mercedes FO108Y
	Total capacity	2400 cmc	2400 cmc	2400 cmc	2400 cmc	2400 cmc
	N° cylinders and V	8 - V90	8 - V90	8 - V90	8 - V90	8 - V90
	Electronics	Magneti Marelli	Magneti Marelli	McLaren el.sys.	Magneti Marelli	Mercedes
	Fuel	Elf	Shell	Mobil	Elf	Mobil
	Oil	Elf	Shell	Mobil	Elf	Mobil
	Dashboard	Red Bull	Magneti Marelli	McLaren	Renault F1	Mercedes

1 Ascanelli left the Team after British GP

14-15 SAUBER	11-12 FORCE INDIA	18-19 WILLIAMS	16-17 TORO ROSSO	20-21 CATERHAM	24-25 MARUSSIA	22-23 HRT
C31	WJM05	FW34	STR7	CT01	MR-01	FRT F112
Matt Morris	Adrew Green	Mike Coughlan	Giorgio Ascanelli[1] James Key	Mark Smith	Pat Symonds	Tom Cuquerella
Francesco Nenci (14) Marco Schüpbach (15)	G. Lambiase (11) Bradley Joyce (12)	Xevi Pujolar (18) Tom McCullogh (19)	Riccardo Adami (16) Andrea Landi (17)	J. P. Ramirez (20) Tim Wright (21)	Michael Harre (24) Paul Davison (25)	Angel Baena (22) Mark Hutchenson (23)
Urs Kuratle	Chris King Greg Borrill	Carl Garden	Rado Cardinali	Nick Smith	Kieron Marchant	Richard Pegram
3396 mm*	3411 mm*	3358 mm*	3337 mm*	3328 mm*	3318 mm*	3249 mm*
1460 mm	1480 mm	1480 mm	1440 mm	1470 mm	1440 mm	1425 mm
1400 mm	1410 mm	1420 mm	1410 mm	1405 mm	1410 mm	1411 mm
2+1 dampers and torsion bars	2+1 dampers and torsion bars	2+1 dampers and torsion bars	2+1 dampers and torsion bars	2+1 dampers and torsion bars	2+1 dampers and torsion bars	2+1 dampers and torsion bars
Push-rod 2+1 dampers and torsion bars	Pull-rod 2+1 dampers and torsion bars	Pull-rod 2+1 dampers and torsion bars	Pull-rod 2+1 dampers and torsion bars	Pull-rod 2+1 dampers and torsion bars	Push-rod 2+1 dampers and torsion bars	Push-rod 2+1 dampers and torsion bars
Sachs	Sachs	Williams	Koni	Sachs	Koni	Sachs
Brembo	A+P	A+P	Brembo	A+P	A+P	Brembo
Brembo	Hitco - Brembo	Carbon Industrie	Brembo	Hitco	Hitco	Brembo
O.Z.	BBS	O.Z.	O.Z.	BBS	BBS	O.Z.
Calsonic	Secan	IMI Marston	Marston	Secan	Marston	Secan
middle position inside fuel tank	middle position inside fuel tank	middle position inside fuel tank	middle position inside fuel tank	middle position inside fuel tank	middle position inside fuel tank	middle position inside fuel tank
Longitudinal titanium	McLaren longitudinal	Longitudinal titanium	Longitudinal carbon	Red Bull longitudinal	Marussia Xtrac	Xtrac longitudinal
Semiautomatic 7 gears	Semiautomatic 7 gears	Semiautomatic 7 gears	Semiautomatic 7 gears	Semiautomatic 7 gears	Semiautomatic 7 gears	Semiautomatic 7 gears
A+P	A+P	A+P	A+P	A+P	A+P	A+P
2	2	2	2	2	2	2
Ferrari 056	Mercedes FO108Y	Cosworth CA2011	Ferrari 056	Renault RS27-2011	Cosworth CA2012	Cosworth CA2012
2400 cmc	2400 cmc	2400 cmc	2400 cmc	2400 cmc	2400 cmc	2400 cmc
8 - V90	8 - V90	8 - V90	8 - V90	8 - V90	8 - V90	8 - V90
Magneti Marelli	McLaren el.sys.	-	Magneti Marelli	-	-	-
Shell	Mobil	Esso	Shell	Esso	BP	BP
Shell	Mobil	Esso	Shell	Esso	BP	BP
Magneti Marelli	P.I.	Williams	Toro Rosso	Williams	Williams	Williams

2012 REGULATIONS

The Federation only introduced two new regulations for the 2012 season: one banned exhaust blow into the diffusers and the other set a height limit for noses for safety reasons. The first severely influenced new car designs, because not only was the engine's hot air blow prohibited, limiting the electronic management of the power units, but important restrictions were placed on exhaust terminal positioning so as to drastically reduce their blow effect on the diffusers; a limitation that was brought forward to the GP of Great Britain, the only race won by Ferrari. In practice, the Federation banned the exhausts from the diffuser area and, therefore, from the rear axle, imposing a kind of "box" area in which they had to be contained. The limits of that "box" were dictated by articles 5.6 1-2-3 of the technical regulations. They had to be within an area between 500 mm and 1200 mm from the rear axle, raised between 250 mm and 600 mm from the reference plane (the lowest point of an F1 car, used as a reference for all height measurements) and between 200 mm and 500 mm from the car's centreline in a transversal sense. That effectively created a "container" 700 mm long, 300 mm wide and 350 mm high in which the exhausts had to be located. As can be seen from the top view comparison, the 2012 layout shows the exhausts a long way from the rear wheels and the extractor planes. As a result, they don't have a great influence on the car's lower aerodynamics as happened in 2011, when terminals blew low, just a few millimeters from the diffuser's lateral channels, increasing the downforce effect. To further limit the designers' imagination, the Federation also ruled that the terminal area of the exhausts – the last 100 mm – had to be completely straight and with a section obligatorily round, with an internal diameter of 75 mm. There was angle freedom of between 10° and 30° upwards in relation to the longitudinal axis, and of 10° to the transverse. It was no coincidence that, especially in private testing and the early races, we saw a considerable variety of interpretations of these requirements by the teams in an attempt to bring back engine blow in draught form more or less towards the upper or lower part of the rear wing group. As always happens when severe new limitations come into effect, the various teams' technical offices multiplied their efforts to get around this regulation, creating shapes that helped the flow of air to direct a good percentage of the blow so as to recover lost load. Exploiting the Coandă effect, new shapes were introduced in the terminal section of the sidepods, which acted as a sort of "slide" for the exhaust blow, redirecting it downwards, as described in the New Solutions chapter.

The second area of intervention concerned safety in the case of lateral collisions between cars. The crash test of the safety structure at the sides of the chassis was made more severe, with a test of upwards compression and, more evident, a brusque increase in the maximum permitted height of a cars' nose. The height limit of the front hoop of the chassis stayed at 625 mm from the reference plane as in 2011, but within just 150 mm it had to become 550 mm. Most of the teams complied with this rule by designing a steep step, all except McLaren and Marussia.

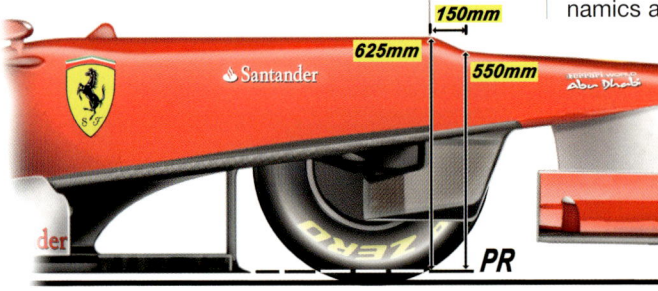

NOSE

To limit danger in case of a lateral collision between two cars, the Federation made the crash test more severe in the sidepod area, and especially required a height reduction in the front part of the car. The height of the chassis' first hoop stayed at 625 mm from the reference plane as in 2011, but in just 150 mm it had to drop to a height of 550 mm. That ushered in a kind of abrupt step high up on the nose, although it must be said that not all the cars exploited the maximum limit of 625 mm in 2011, when among teams that used a relatively low nose was McLaren. That's why theirs was the only one – together with that of Marussia – without a step at the start of the 2012 season. In the last design there is a comparison between the Ferrari and the McLaren from which it can be seen that the MP4/27 had a lower final chassis hoop compared to the regulation 625 mm, so the required move to a height of 550 mm for noses didn't require the use of a step.

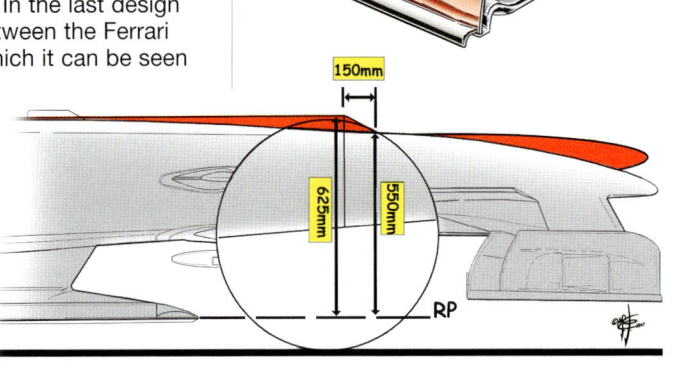

EXHAUST COMPARISON

The Federation brought out a highly detailed regulation, which is shown in a quick comparative illustration using the outline of the Ferrari F150 Italia. The two different exhaust positions are synthesized: the one that was widely used in 2011, with the low blow directed to the diffuser's lateral channels, and the new one imposed by the 2012 regulations with the exit a long way from the diffusers.

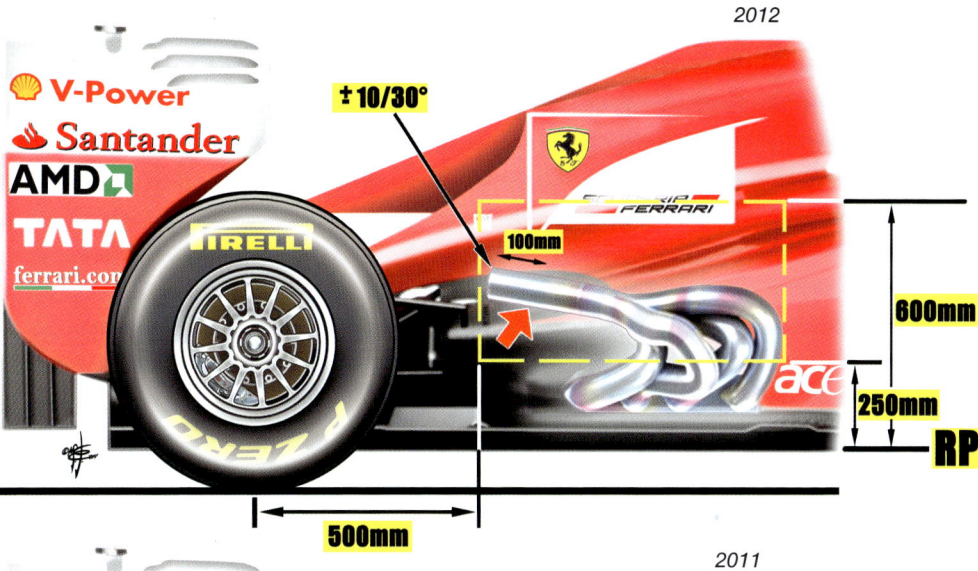

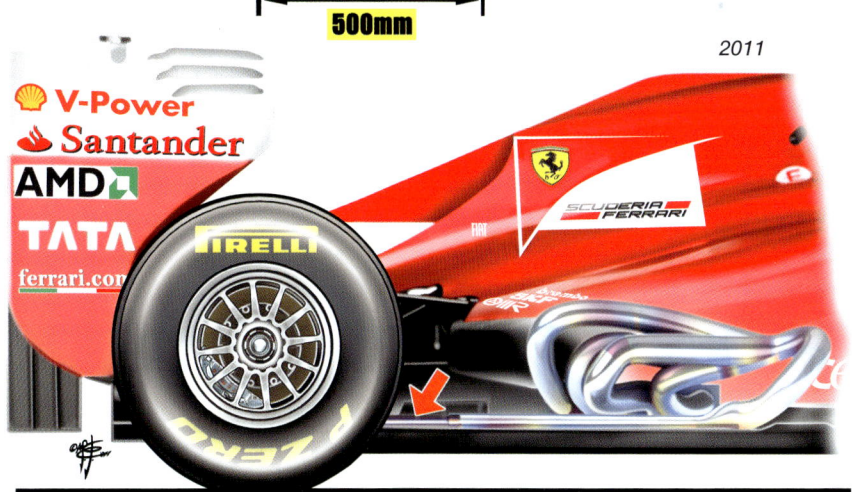

TOP VIEW

The top view comparison shows the 2011 (below) and the 2012 (above) systems in which the position of the exhaust terminals can easily be seen, having been physically moved further away from the diffuser area. In addition, the last 100 mm of the terminals had to be perfectly straight and placed far from the rear axle, with a determinate inclination for their terminal portion, so between 10° and 30° upwards in relation to the longitudinal axis, and 10° in relation to those which were transversal. The shape was also obligatory, as it had to have a 75 mm diameter round section.

SIDE VIEW COMPARISON

The Federation brought out severe limitations on the position of the exhausts for the 2012 season. They had to blow a long way from the rear wheels and therefore from the diffusers. They had to be between 500 mm and 1,200 mm from the back axle and in height terms had to be positioned between 250 mm and 600 mm from the reference plane, but also between 200 mm and 500 mm from the car's centreline in a transverse sense. That's how the 700 mm long, 300 mm wide and 350 mm high "box" was created to contain the exhausts.

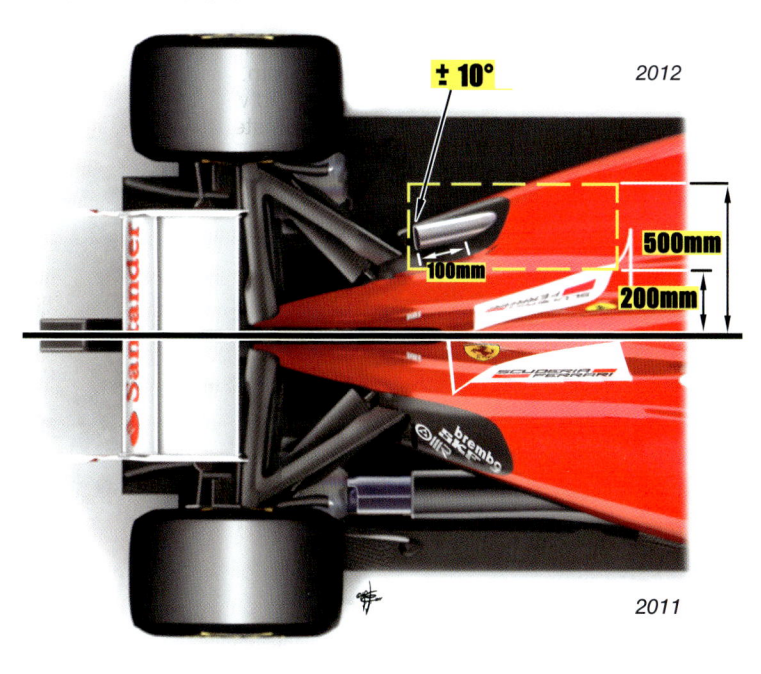

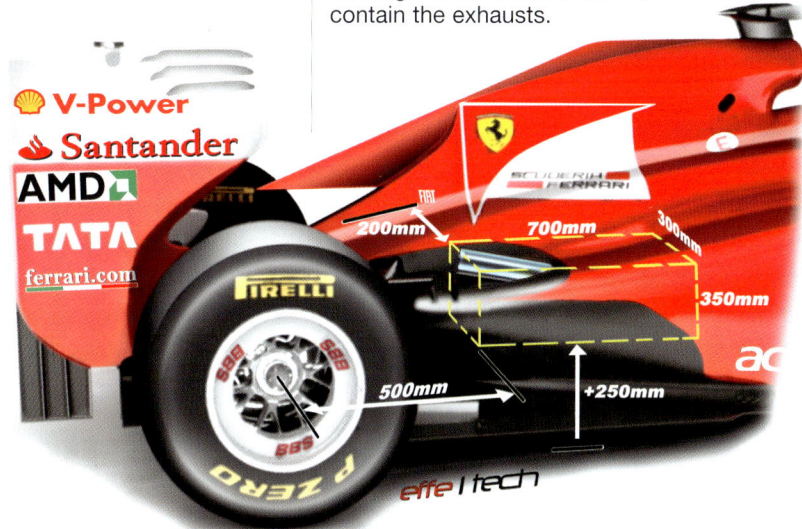

2012 REGULATIONS

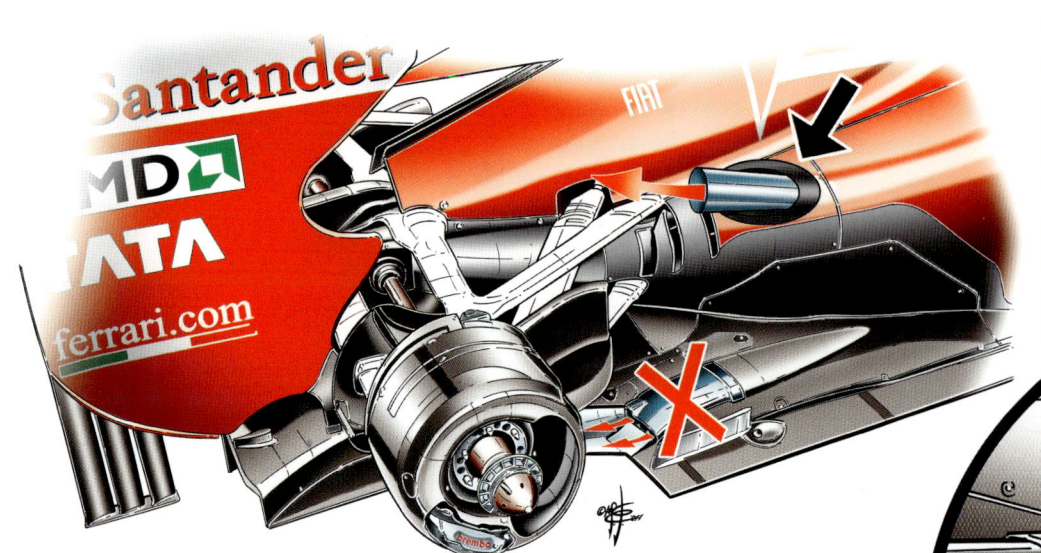

PROHIBITED SOLUTIONS
The Federation not only outlawed exhaust blow straight into the diffusers as shown in this illustration, it also imposed severe limitations on the shape of their terminal area.

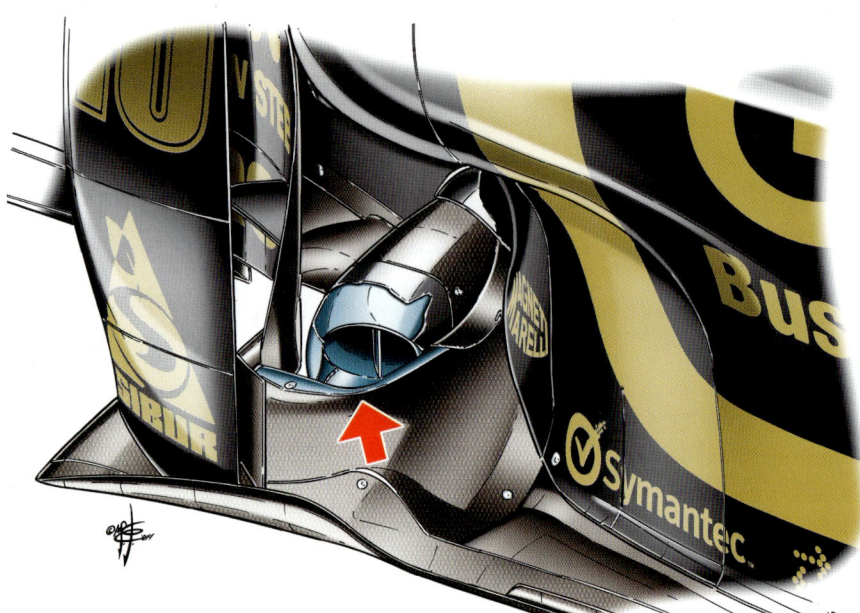

MERCEDES-BENZ
The sinuous progression of the car's rear end as on the 2010 Mercedes-Benz was banned. Regulations dictated that the final 100 mm had to be perfectly straight and with a freedom of angle of between 10° and 30° in relation to the longitudinal and just 10° to the transverse.

RENAULT
The front blow of the Renault was, obviously, banned even though the French constructor would certainly not have continued to use that technique which, unfortunately, turned out to be unsuccessful. As well as the location of the exhausts in a precise area, the Federation also prohibited the oval section in the terminals, which had to be round and with a maximum 75 mm diameter.

VIRGIN
The classic "salami slice" exhaust terminals were also banned, like those of Virgin during the closing part of the season. And the exhausts had to be raised in relation to those locations, returning to the "box" required by the Federation.

2012 REGULATIONS

Controversies 2012

This was a season without any disqualifications due to technical irregularities, but it was one that did take place in a climate of suspicion, often created, or at least blown up, by web sites in which the enthusiasm for technical matters sometimes translated into a witch hunt and scoop with the charge of presumed irregularities. In this analysis we shall, of course, limit ourselves to the controversies that were the object or clarification by the Federation, or at least had a matter for comparison. But we will leave the controversy over Red Bull's Renault engine mapping to the Engines chapter; it blew up during the GP of Germany and the subject of a retraction, no less, by the commissioners concerning the wording up of the technical regulation text. The first important clarification that was made in early January, way before the 2012 season had begun, following the publication of the Lotus front suspension design. It was no coincidence that this sophistication of the set-up corrector came from the technicians directed by James Allison, given that this team already had a hydraulic interconnection between the front and rear ends in the suspension layout as early as the 2011 season. This further update was tried out during the young drivers' test at Abu Dhabi and initially passed unobserved. A layout that was first judged regular, because it was not electronically controlled but was run by the driver pressure on the brake pedal. However, after requests for clarification from other teams, the Federation declared the system illegal, because it was considered a mobile aerodynamic device.

At the same time, it also halted the Red Bull and Lotus projects for sophisticated and complicated rear brake air intakes, created for the purpose of circumventing restrictions on the hot exhaust blow diffuser area.

The Mercedes-Benz front "F-Duct", perhaps the development most in conflict with the spirit of the regulation, was considered legal despite Lotus's official protest made at the GP of China. The argument put forward by James Allison, the Lotus technical director, was not accepted, nor was the fact that, at least in spirit, the development had gone against one of the basic aspects of the Formula 1 technical regulations.

The norm prohibits the alteration of a car's aerodynamics in movement and was stipulated way back in 1969 after the accidents that occurred at that year's Grand Prix of Spain; it has been at the basis of many disqualifications in the recent history of Formula 1. But it should be underlined that in recent years, the Federation did make in a number of amendments to improve the spectacle of the sport: in 2009 and 2010 it permitted the adjustment of the front flap, and from 2011 in came the ability to modify the incidence of the rear wing flap (the abbreviation is DRS). It is here that the astuteness of Ross Brawn, who is always able to exploit the loopholes in the regulations, came into play.

The flap's support was designed so that it came into operation with the movement of the control for the system that stalled the front wing. The nub of this question is all here and not in the system itself, which was legal even if completely passive, but in its activation by the driver as a secondary function of the DRS control. Yet article 3.15 cited in the Lotus protest is unequivocal because, as well as prohibiting any intervention by the driver on a car's aerodynamics apart from the activation of the DRS, it says, "besides the DRS, any system or procedure that uses or is suspected of using driver intervention to modify

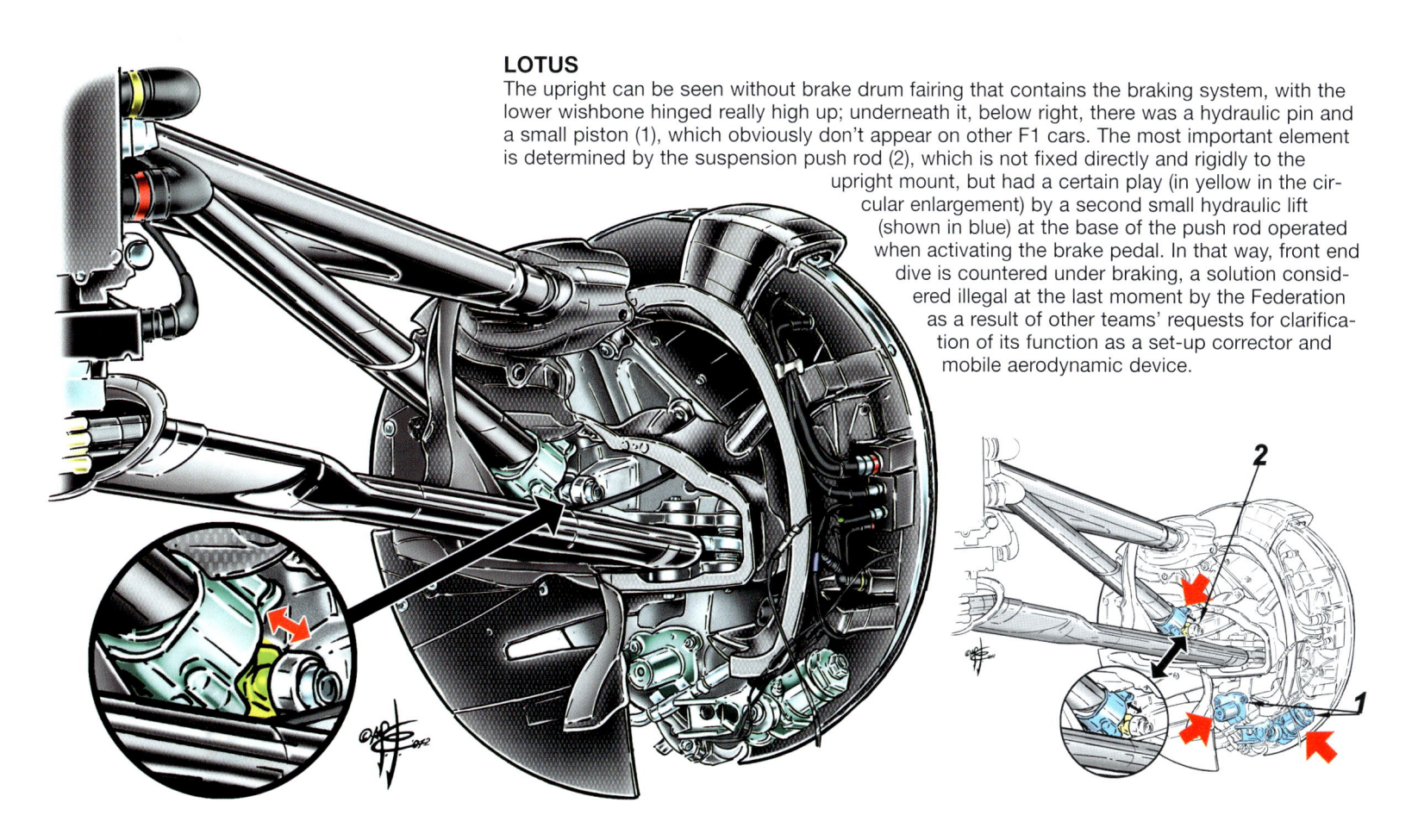

LOTUS
The upright can be seen without brake drum fairing that contains the braking system, with the lower wishbone hinged really high up; underneath it, below right, there was a hydraulic pin and a small piston (1), which obviously don't appear on other F1 cars. The most important element is determined by the suspension push rod (2), which is not fixed directly and rigidly to the upright mount, but had a certain play (in yellow in the circular enlargement) by a second small hydraulic lift (shown in blue) at the base of the push rod operated when activating the brake pedal. In that way, front end dive is countered under braking, a solution considered illegal at the last moment by the Federation as a result of other teams' requests for clarification of its function as a set-up corrector and mobile aerodynamic device.

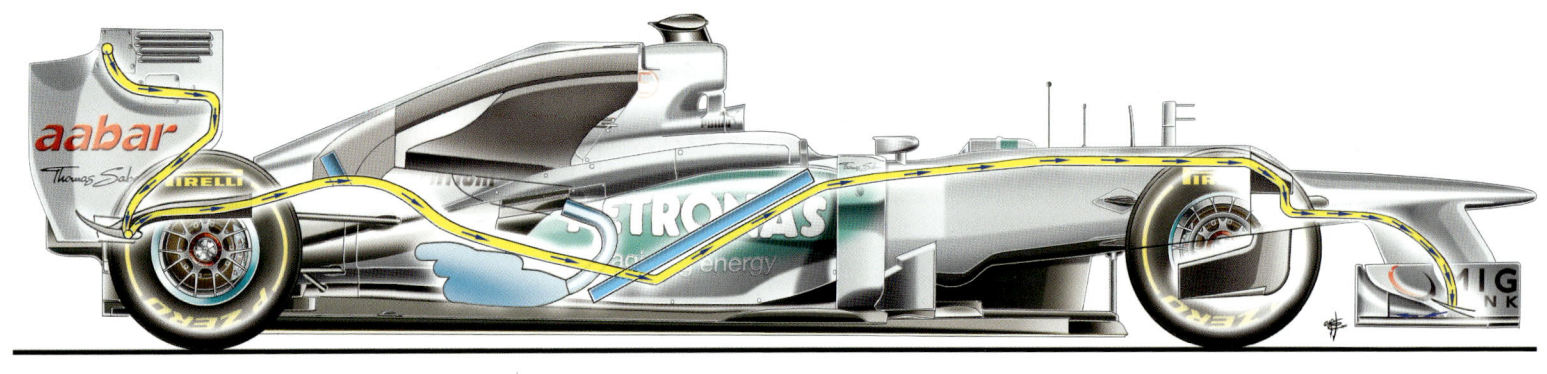

MERCEDES-BENZ F-DUCT

This illustration shows the complicated layout of the Mercedes-Benz front F-Duct.
The air entered the rear wing end plates when the DRS was activated by a visible hole, as shown in the detail circle. Using the same system devised in 2010 for the rear F-Duct, the air passed through the end plates, then the beam wing to run along the whole car with about a 3-4 centimeter diameter channeling that exits from the front area of the chassis (second circle), generally covered by a kind of plug. Lastly, it passes through the front wing support pillars, as in the passive system introduced at Suzuka in 2011 to then blow into the lower part of the flap.

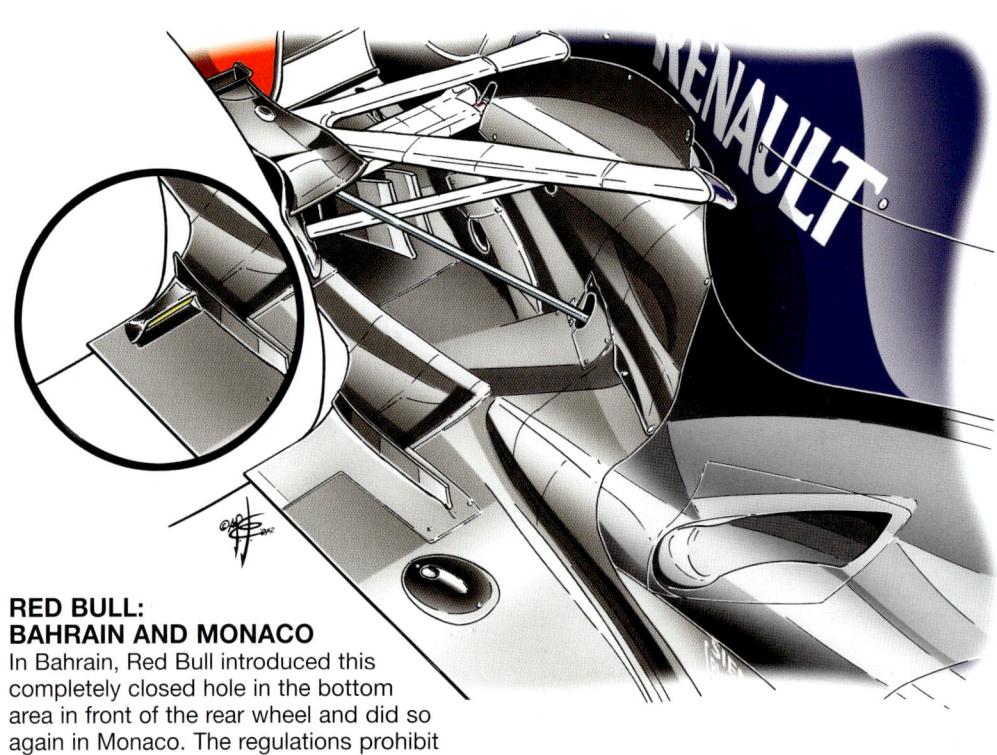

the aerodynamic characteristics of the car is prohibited". In every day logic, it would appear evident that the front F-Duct coming into function is linked hand in glove to the activation by the driver of the DRS and, therefore, the front F-Duct was operated by the driver; however, in F.1 the theory of the secondary function ruled the day.

Subsequent attempts to block or seek clarification by the Federation during the season involved Red Bull, always on the limit in exploiting every inference of the technical regulations. But in some cases, the Adrian Newey developments that were banned had successfully passed several scrutineering. They included, for example, the hub holes introduced from the start on the RB8, but not considered illegal until the GP of Canada, together with a call to respect the regulations concerning the "fully closed hole" at the bottom of the area in front of the rear wheels. That wasn't respected in the two previous races in Bahrain and Monaco.

And in Canada – even if it did only come to light in Budapest at the GP of Hungary – the case of the miniaturized tool to regulate the height from the ground of the RB8's third damper, which we believe remains the least clear episode of the entire season, given that the regulation (Art- 3.4.5.) prohibits any alteration to a car during parc fermé and prescribes, without a shadow of a doubt, the use of a clearly visible tool.

The final controversy was, in practice, a provocation by Red Bull to stimulate the Federation into clarifying the possible use of variable geometry for the brake drum ducts, perhaps exploiting metals with various expansion characteristics. In fact, McLaren successfully brought in the ability to vary the aperture of a gap in the brake drums, carried out by a mechanic during a pit stop, along the lines of normal front wing flap adjustment. But Red Bull put together a development that would be operated autonomously on the basis of G-force that acts in a longitudinal sense on the car. The attempt was ruled illegal by Charlie Whiting during a mini-press conference at the penultimate race in Austin, Texas.

RED BULL: BAHRAIN AND MONACO

In Bahrain, Red Bull introduced this completely closed hole in the bottom area in front of the rear wheel and did so again in Monaco. The regulations prohibit holes but permit apertures that have no closed perimeter, a legacy of the complicated reasoning of the 2009 season that sanctioned the legality of the double diffusers and which even culminated in the analysis of the terms in an English language dictionary. The circle on the right shows the legal interpretation of the same solution on the Sauber.
After the Monaco race, McLaren, Mercedes and Ferrari asked for clarification so that Red Bull was requested to comply with the regulation for the subsequent Canadian GP, which they did as shown in the large illustration, so without the hole that was, quite rightly, banned.

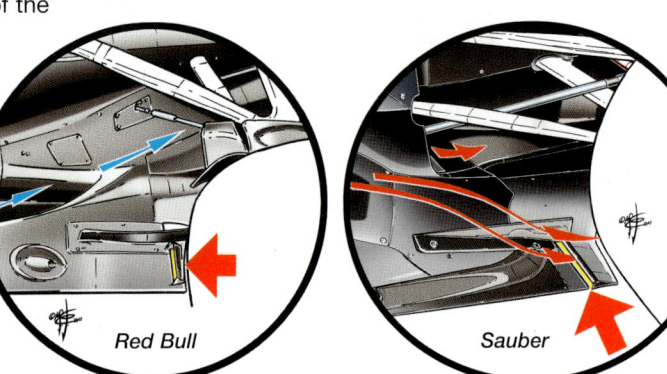

Controversies **2012**

BLOWN HUBS
One of Adrian Newey's new developments on the RB8 was blow into the front wheel hubs. A complicated system that also required special rims that allowed the passage of air through the central area. That way a partial hub cap effect was created, which directed the air flow from the front brakes into a precisely determined zone of the wheels themselves: after having passed scrutiny at the first six races, the technique was then deemed illegal because the blow effect took place through the rotating part of the hub, transforming it into a mobile aerodynamic device.

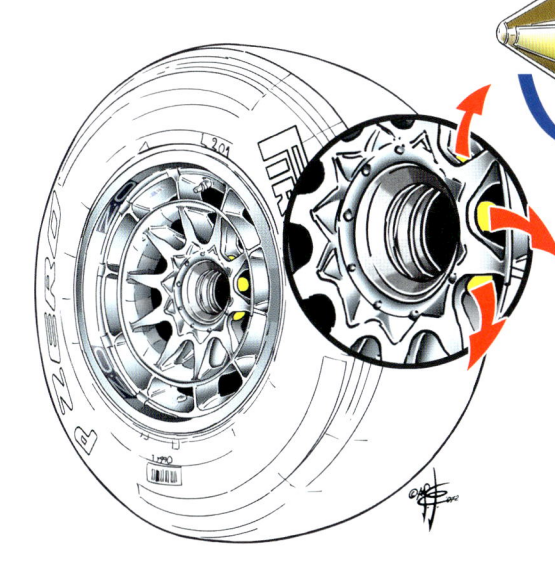

THIRD DAMPER
The accused was not so much the third transverse damper in the Red Bull's front suspension, with its cabling, shown here, that went to the electronic management systems as on all the others cars.
It was the miniaturized instrument made especially to maintain height from the ground by working on the damper's rim. The regulations said that that function had to be clearly visible, and the instrument had to be of such dimensions that it could easily be seen by the technical officers.

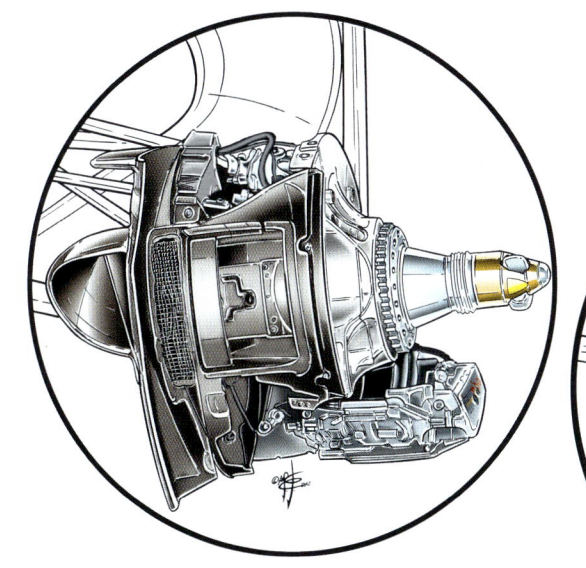

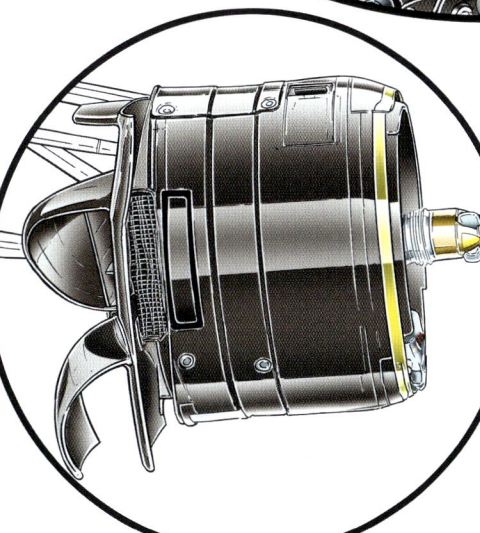

VARIABLE BRAKE DRUMS
Red Bull carried out highly secret tests from Friday practice at the GP of Italy on its front brake drum ducts, which had a small variable window. In practice, the system was extremely simple and light and was based on the longitudinal G forces exerted on the car to open the small channel under braking and close it under acceleration, a sort of stopper with longitudinal movement. Charlie Whiting later pointed out that the variable adjustment developed by McLaren, with activation by a mechanic during pit stops, was permitted.
In practice, it avails itself of the same principle, for which it was possible to vary the incidence of the front wing flap.

Controversies 2012

New DEVELOPMENTS

Only two new regulations came into effect for the 2012 season: one banned exhaust blow directly into the diffusers and the other limited the height of the nose, both amply described in the appropriate chapter. But despite such measures, the imagination of the designers ran wild and came up with new developments, even if some of them were revivals of those from the past. Like the one that occupied people's attention during the winter break and then actually appeared on the new Ferrari: a revival of the pull rod layout for the front suspension, rather like that which happened in 2009 with the same solution at the rear end of Adrian Newey's Red Bull. It was the only example of this method in 2012.

Another resurrection was the hole up high in the chassis. Banned by the Federation after Ferrari introduced it on the F2008, it crept in again, limited by current regulations.

At the time, it was one of the Ferrari world championship-winning weapons on Kimi Raikkonen's debut with the Rosse, and of the group directed by Aldo Costa.

It was the last new Ferrari development before the front suspension of the F2012. It was an intelligent technique, which enabled the team to improve the car's aerodynamics in the front area and it would have been spread to other teams the following season, if the Federation hadn't prohibited the passage of air between the upper and lower parts of the nose.

Both Sauber and Red Bull came out with vents in the noses of their cars. Sauber simply reproduced the system brought out as a major new development by Ferrari, but with the vent limited by the regulations.

Different from the way the vent worked in the stepped area of the nose dreamt up by Newey for the RB7. But the element that most significantly characterised the 2012 season was the extreme research carried out to recover as much exhaust blow effect into the diffusers as possible, despite the severe regulations imposed by the Federation.

There were so many different and complex methods in this area that they have had to be described in the Engines chapter.

But the one that set the trend and surprised everyone was certainly the shape of the terminal part of the Sauber's body, and the partial return of exhaust blow with a clever use of the Coanda effect. They were able to bring back exhaust blow to the foot of the wheel, due to the opportune shape of the body so that it fed the diffuser's lateral channels, even if in a less effective way than in 2011.

They worked on even more complex methods of the brake air intake air flow management, the aerodynamic function of which had become basic at both the rear and front ends of the cars. Especially noteworthy in this sector were the intakes at the rear end of the Mercedes-Benz and Williams and the fronts of the British car, which moved the cooling function from inside the pan to the outside in the small space between the pan itself and the tyre, notably improving aerodynamic efficiency in the channel between the wheel and the chassis.

A system that set a trend and was also used by Sauber, Lotus, Ferrari, Force India and Toro Rosso.

There were another two new developments in the brake air intake field: the ability to use the dissipation of heat to influence tyre temperatures by the mechanics during pit stops, introduced by McLaren; and the sophisticated creation of wheel hubs and rims of the RB7 project. The latter was banned by the Federation after six races, as you will see in the Controversies chapter.

The final development of note, but no less interesting, was the drive shaft fairing by Adrian Newey. Described from the RB8's first track test with the illustration here, this discovery only came into the public domain with the introduction of the "D" version of the car at the GP of Valencia, partly because, in theory, the regulations say the drive shafts may not be faired. Newey had ably got around that obstacle by designing the car's rear suspension in such a way that the rear arm of the lower wishbone and the toe-in links were not only at the same height as the drive shafts, but also fairly close to them.

In that way, exploiting the opportunity of fairing the suspension arms with a ratio of 3.5 between the chord and thickness, the drive shafts turned out to be inside the overall fairing. This, too, is a revival of what Newey himself did on Ayrton Senna's Williams FW16.

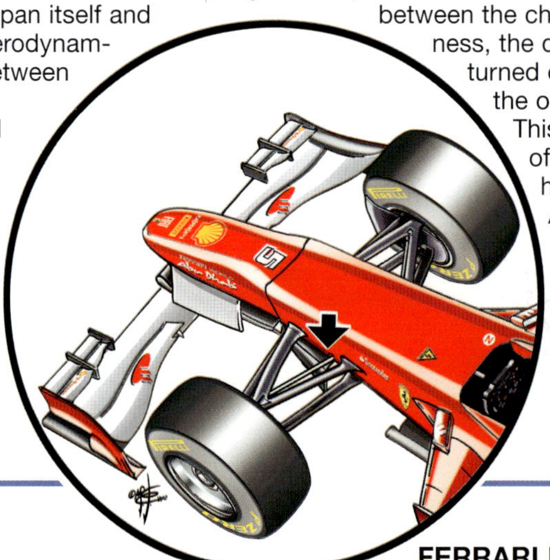

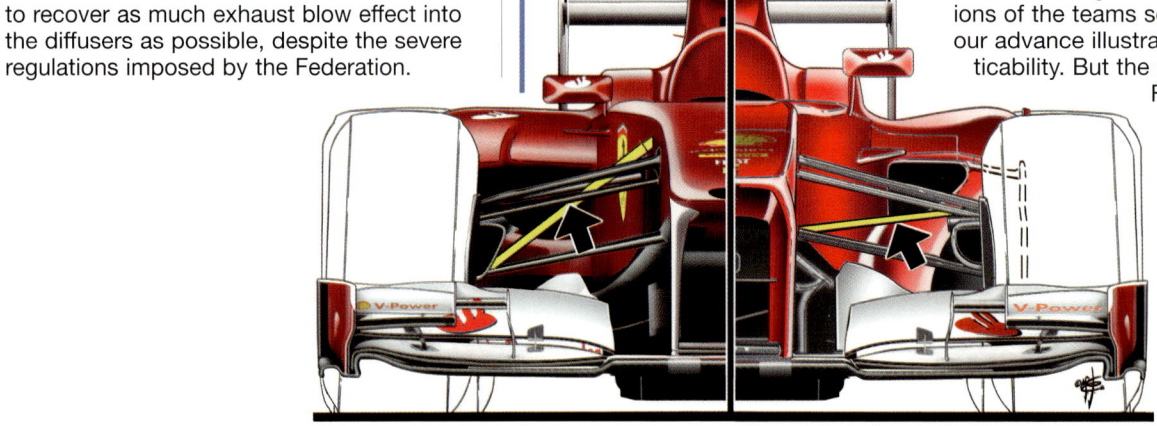

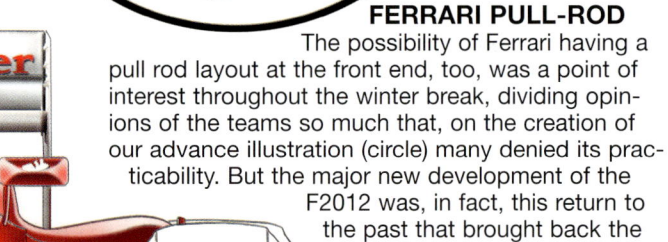

FERRARI PULL-ROD

The possibility of Ferrari having a pull rod layout at the front end, too, was a point of interest throughout the winter break, dividing opinions of the teams so much that, on the creation of our advance illustration (circle) many denied its practicability. But the major new development of the F2012 was, in fact, this return to the past that brought back the pull rod suspension layout, last used 11 years earlier by Minardi during the 2001 season.

Among other things, it was a car driven by a young Fernando Alonso, while Arrows went in the opposite direction that year and moved from pull rod to push rod.

Ferrari F2008

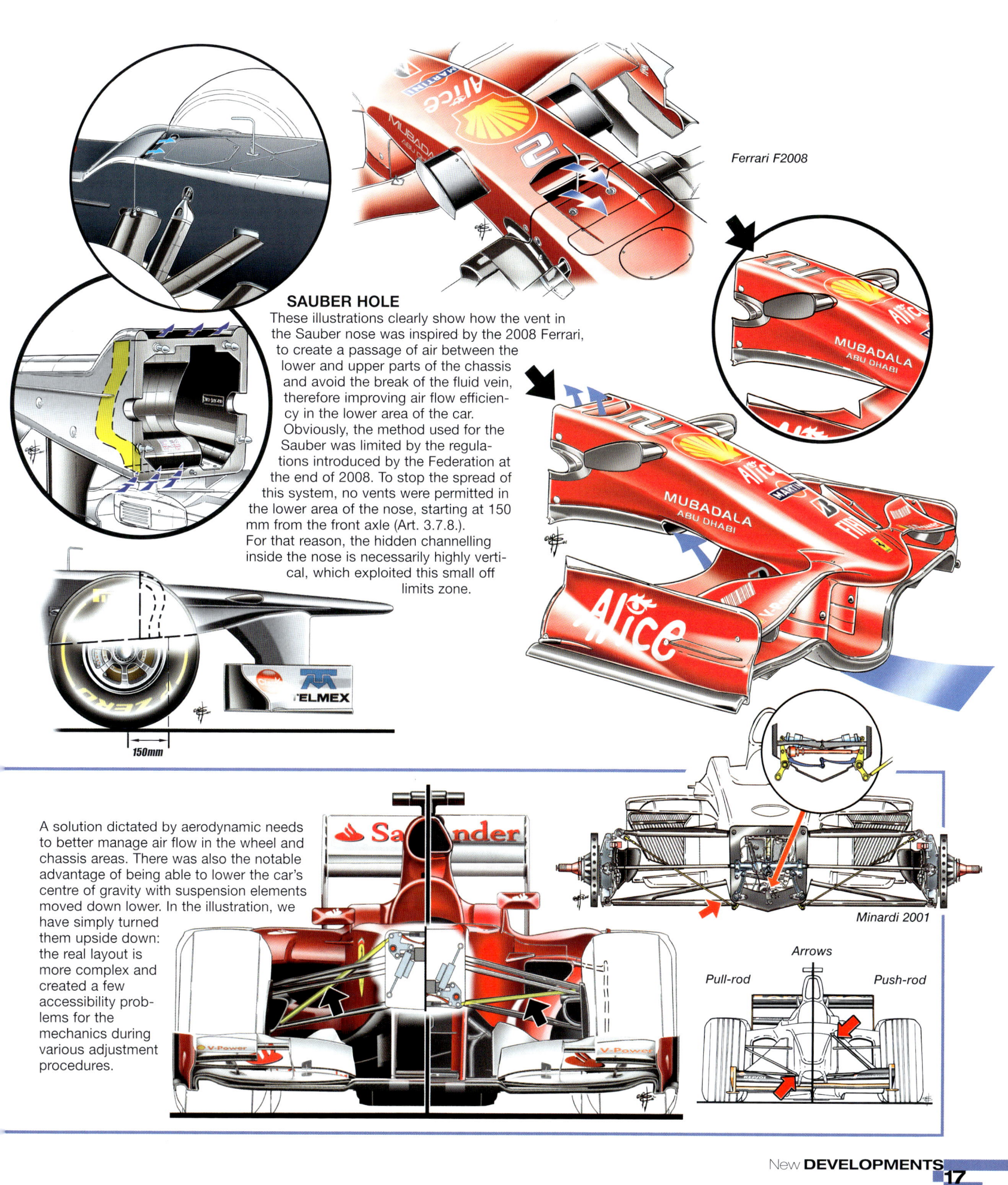

SAUBER HOLE

These illustrations clearly show how the vent in the Sauber nose was inspired by the 2008 Ferrari, to create a passage of air between the lower and upper parts of the chassis and avoid the break of the fluid vein, therefore improving air flow efficiency in the lower area of the car. Obviously, the method used for the Sauber was limited by the regulations introduced by the Federation at the end of 2008. To stop the spread of this system, no vents were permitted in the lower area of the nose, starting at 150 mm from the front axle (Art. 3.7.8.). For that reason, the hidden channelling inside the nose is necessarily highly vertical, which exploited this small off limits zone.

150mm

A solution dictated by aerodynamic needs to better manage air flow in the wheel and chassis areas. There was also the notable advantage of being able to lower the car's centre of gravity with suspension elements moved down lower. In the illustration, we have simply turned them upside down: the real layout is more complex and created a few accessibility problems for the mechanics during various adjustment procedures.

Minardi 2001

Arrows

Pull-rod   Push-rod

New **DEVELOPMENTS** 17

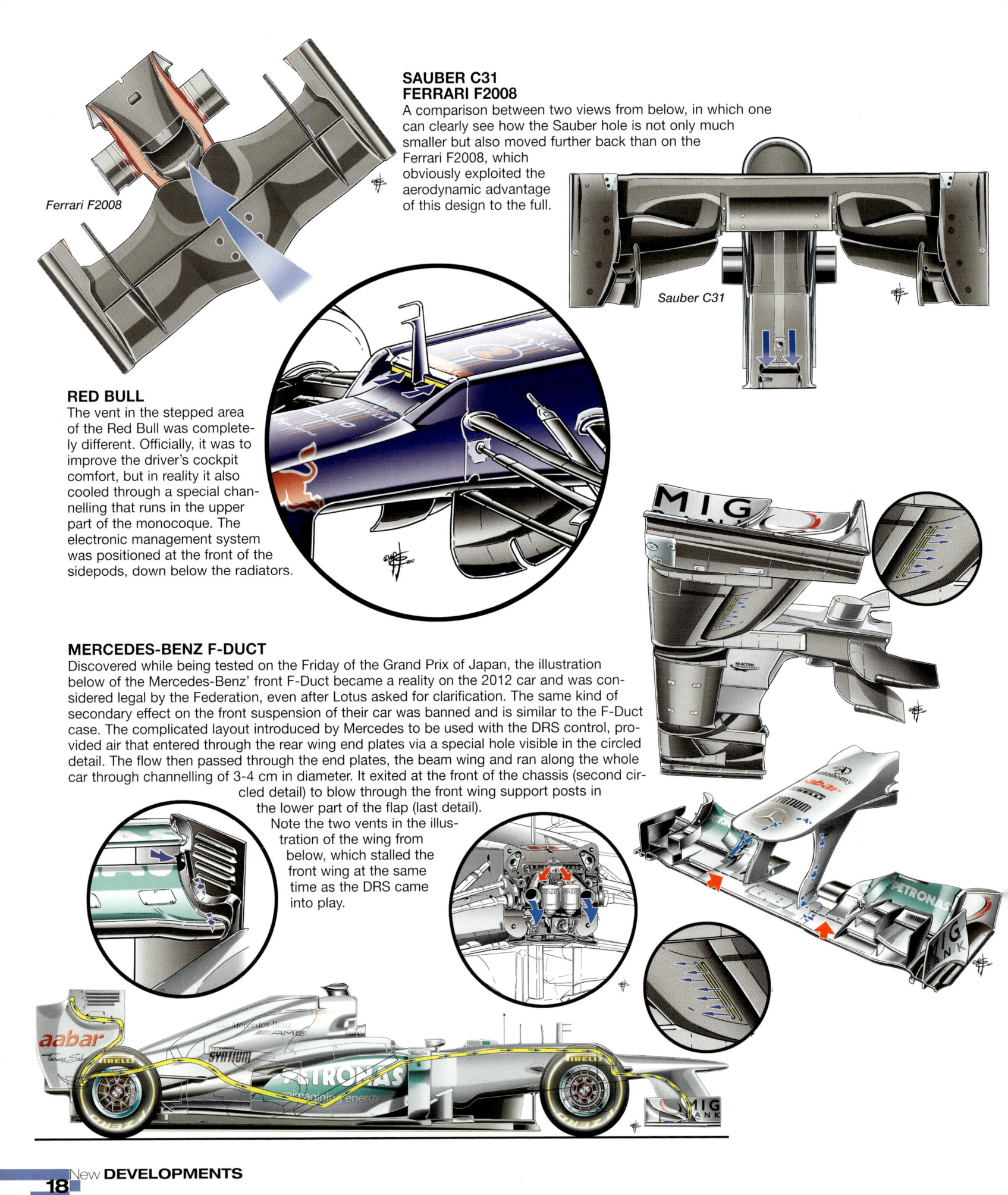

SAUBER C31 FERRARI F2008
A comparison between two views from below, in which one can clearly see how the Sauber hole is not only much smaller but also moved further back than on the Ferrari F2008, which obviously exploited the aerodynamic advantage of this design to the full.

Ferrari F2008

Sauber C31

RED BULL
The vent in the stepped area of the Red Bull was completely different. Officially, it was to improve the driver's cockpit comfort, but in reality it also cooled through a special channelling that runs in the upper part of the monocoque. The electronic management system was positioned at the front of the sidepods, down below the radiators.

MERCEDES-BENZ F-DUCT
Discovered while being tested on the Friday of the Grand Prix of Japan, the illustration below of the Mercedes-Benz' front F-Duct became a reality on the 2012 car and was considered legal by the Federation, even after Lotus asked for clarification. The same kind of secondary effect on the front suspension of their car was banned and is similar to the F-Duct case. The complicated layout introduced by Mercedes to be used with the DRS control, provided air that entered through the rear wing end plates via a special hole visible in the circled detail. The flow then passed through the end plates, the beam wing and ran along the whole car through channelling of 3-4 cm in diameter. It exited at the front of the chassis (second circled detail) to blow through the front wing support posts in the lower part of the flap (last detail). Note the two vents in the illustration of the wing from below, which stalled the front wing at the same time as the DRS came into play.

New **DEVELOPMENTS**

FW16

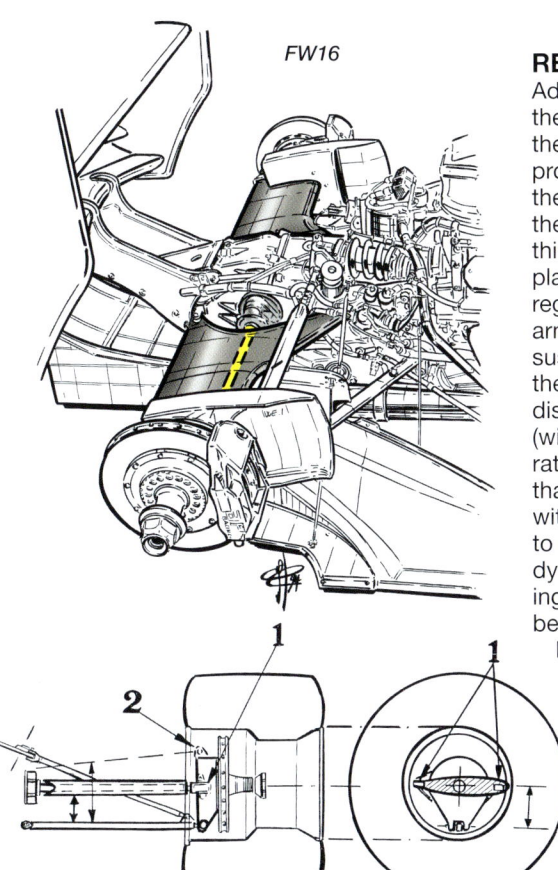

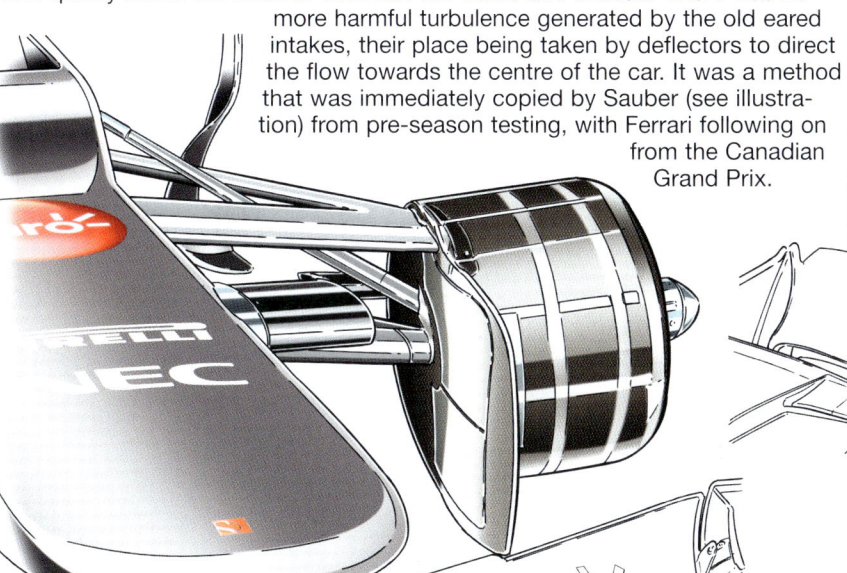

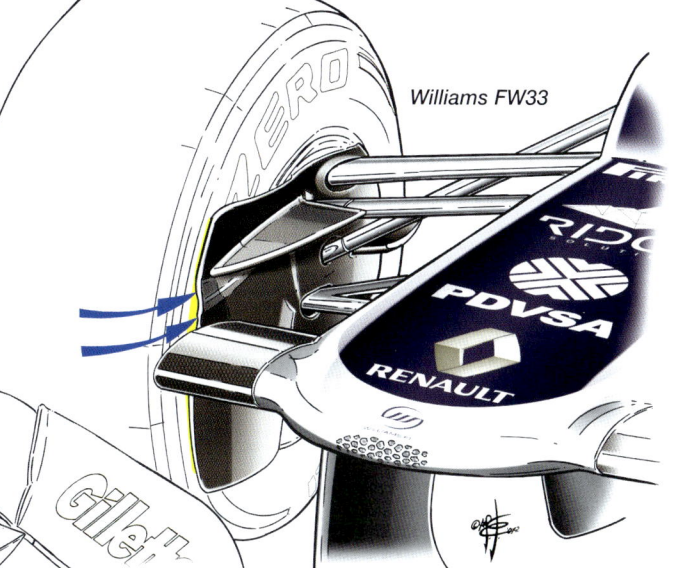

RED BULL

Adrian Newey brought back the faired drive shaft, which he introduced with little success on the 1994 Williams FW16. At that time, he had brought in a large wing plane that incorporated the upper wishbone and the drive shaft. It was a move that immediately caused structural problems when the car was tested and was banned by the Federation, limiting the ratio of the fairing of the suspension arms 3.5 cm wide between thickness and chord of the eventual plane. But Newey circumvented the regulation by positioning the lower arms and the toe-in link of the rear suspension at the same height as the drive shafts and at such a distance that the relative fairing (within the limits of the 3.5:1 ratio) formed a single plane that enclosed the drive shafts within it. All of this, of course, to produce substantial aerodynamic benefits in conveying the air flow towards the beam wing. Also note the brake air intakes with cascading winglets, their purpose to increase the rear end's downforce.

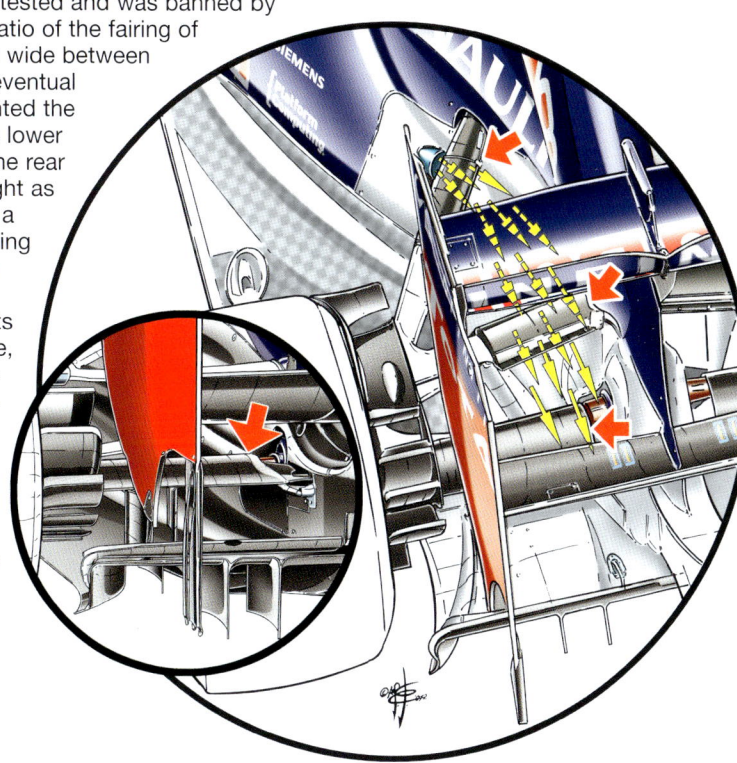

WILLIAMS-SAUBER

Williams must take the credit for having come up with brake air intakes without internal directional ears with the debut of their FW33. They took the air in the small space between the carbon fibre pan and the wheel, with obvious benefits in air flow quality inside the channel between the wheel and chassis. There was no more harmful turbulence generated by the old eared intakes, their place being taken by deflectors to direct the flow towards the centre of the car. It was a method that was immediately copied by Sauber (see illustration) from pre-season testing, with Ferrari following on from the Canadian Grand Prix.

Williams FW33

Sauber C31

New **DEVELOPMENTS**

REAR BRAKE AIR INTAKES
The Williams and Mercedes-Benz rear brake air intakes were really sophisticated and created a seal with the diffuser's lateral channels due to a vertical extension encompassed in the intake design on the Williams and a combination of intake and diffuser on the WR03. Extreme solutions permitted by the regulations which, of course, all had their influence on the cars' aerodynamics.

Williams

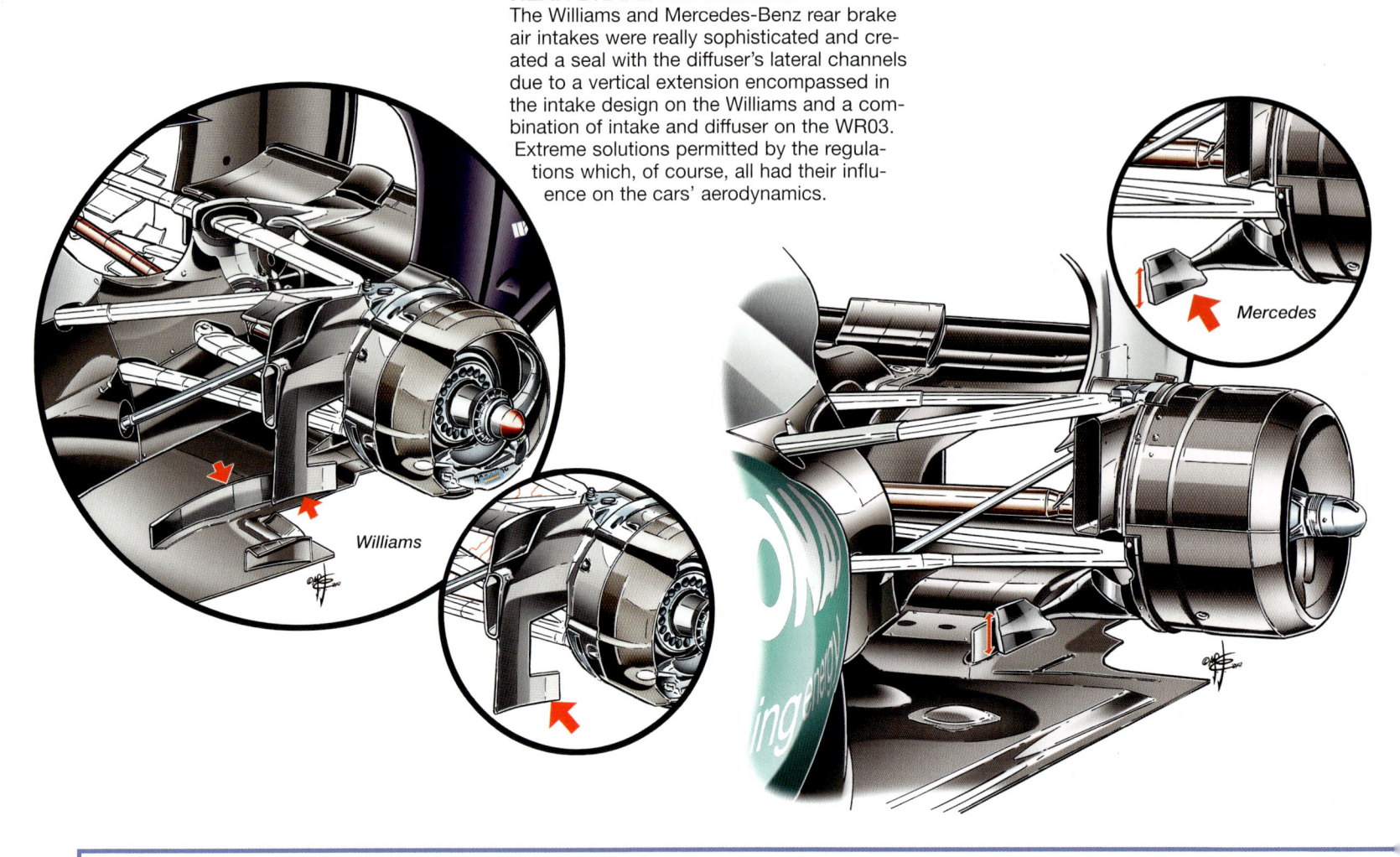

Mercedes

RED BULL
After using hot air blow through holes in the uprights for six races, Red Bull had to give it up because it was judged irregular by the Federation, after a request for clarification from McLaren. In the illustrations, we see the new air blow applied to the central part of the wheel's hub, which has the holes. And they correspond, as many of these are inside the rim for the purpose of channelling

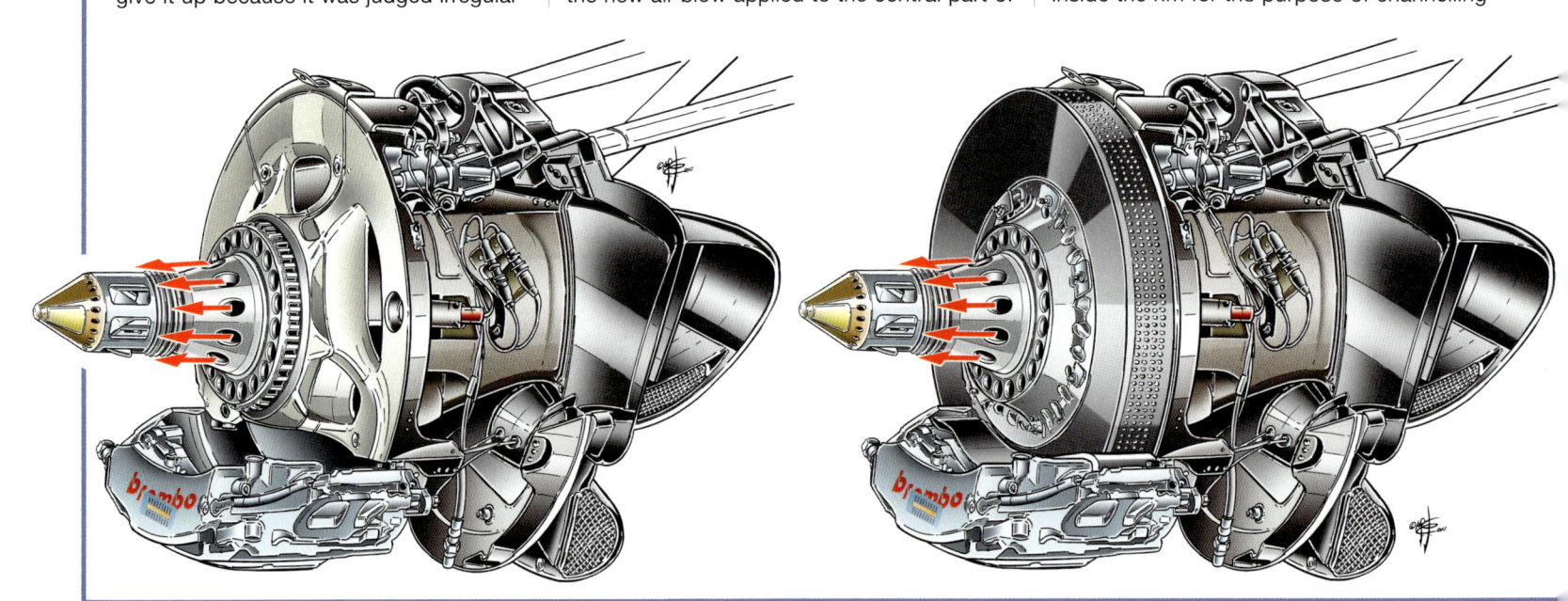

New DEVELOPMENTS
20

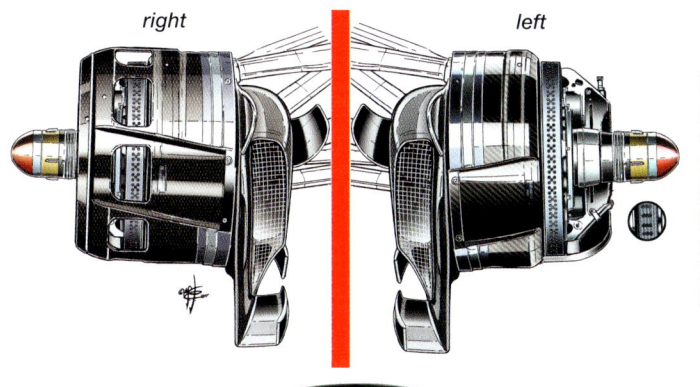

McLAREN
Since 2009, McLaren had experimented with the hot air blow of the discs conveyed towards the inside of the wheels to improve tyre temperature management. In 2011, they even tested asymmetrics at the front end, as described in the McLaren chapter. On the last MP4-27 they introduced the ability to vary the hot air flow inside the rims during tyre change pit stops. They had tried to convey the hot air to a precise point on the outside of the rear rim as early as 2001.
For that reason, the MP4-27's rims had additional holes through which to expel the hot air coming from brake drums.

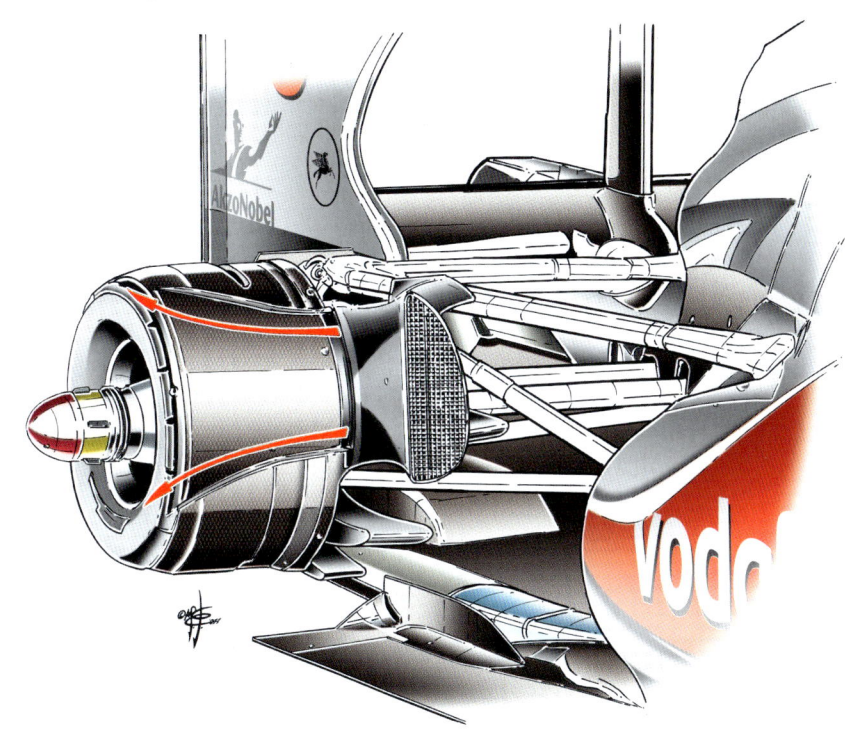

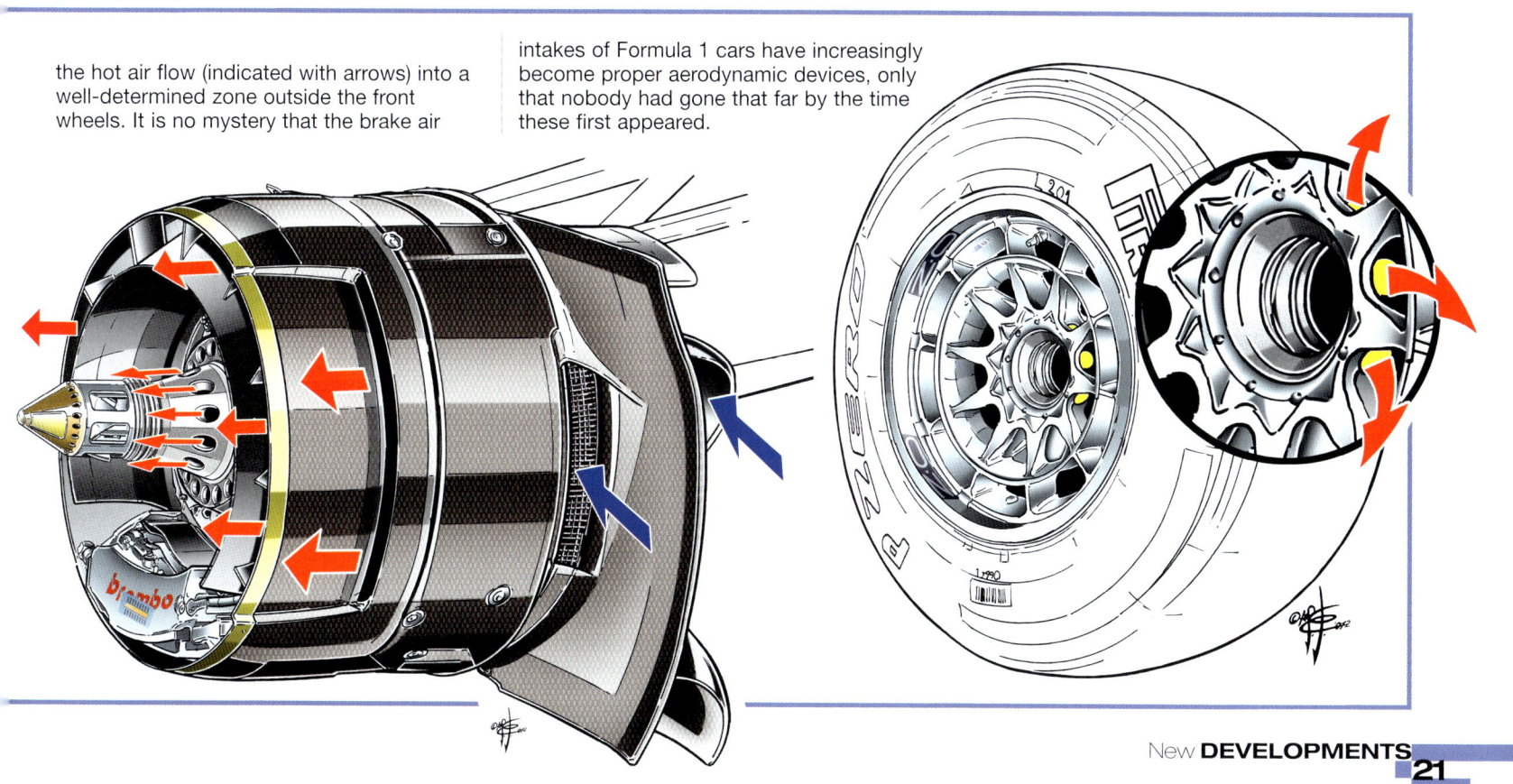

the hot air flow (indicated with arrows) into a well-determined zone outside the front wheels. It is no mystery that the brake air intakes of Formula 1 cars have increasingly become proper aerodynamic devices, only that nobody had gone that far by the time these first appeared.

New DEVELOPMENTS 21

VARIABLE GEOMETRY

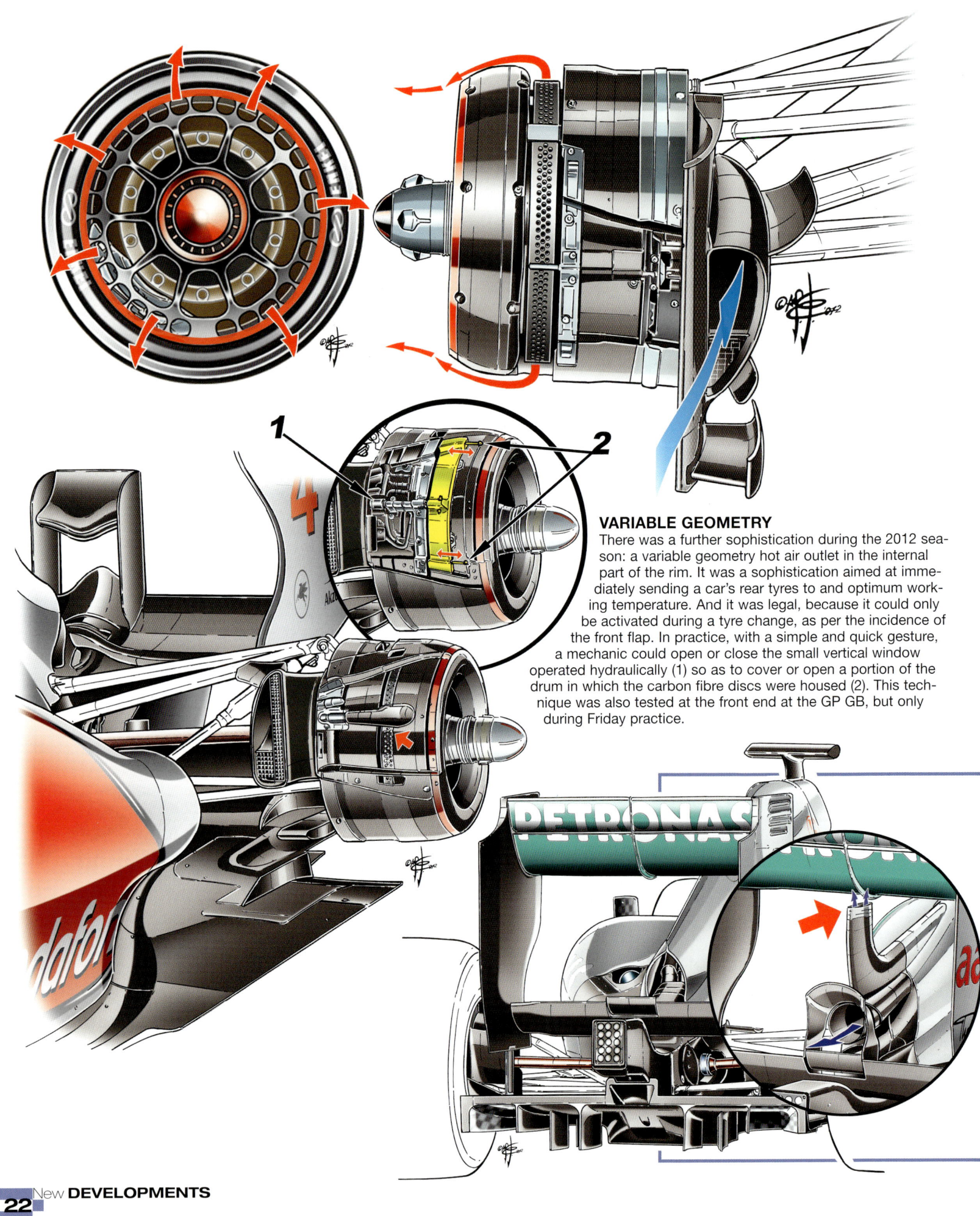

There was a further sophistication during the 2012 season: a variable geometry hot air outlet in the internal part of the rim. It was a sophistication aimed at immediately sending a car's rear tyres to and optimum working temperature. And it was legal, because it could only be activated during a tyre change, as per the incidence of the front flap. In practice, with a simple and quick gesture, a mechanic could open or close the small vertical window operated hydraulically (1) so as to cover or open a portion of the drum in which the carbon fibre discs were housed (2). This technique was also tested at the front end at the GP GB, but only during Friday practice.

New DEVELOPMENTS

RED BULL: DOUBLE DRS

Introduced by Red Bull from the Grand Prix of Singapore, it was very simple and immediately usable. This time, Adrian Newey had chosen simplicity and effectiveness by adopting the double DRS with a layout activated in synchronisation with the first DRS, without getting into in a laborious set-up as required by the passive control system selected by Lotus and Mercedes-Benz. The hole came to light hidden as it was by the raised fixing of the flap, the passage of air fed the inside of the end plates to then blow onto the trailing edge of the beam wing, reducing drag.
Red Bull competed in all of the last races of the season with this system.

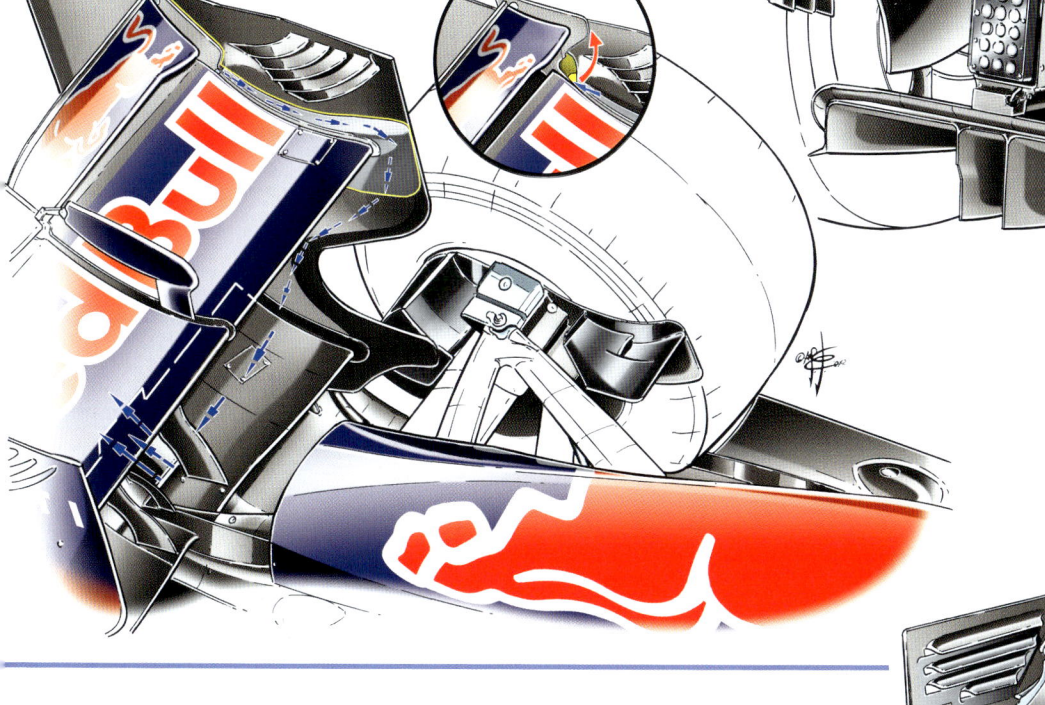

LOTUS - MERCEDES-BENZ

During the second half of the season, first Lotus and then Mercedes-Benz introduced a kind of passive double rear DRS with a particular F-Duct fed by two ears at the sides of the airbox. The air channelled into the engine cover could exit down low (red arrows) and brush the trailing edge of the beam wing, or be diverted upwards (blue arrows), through the principal plane. It could then exit at the sides of the end plates, reducing the negative vortices that form in that area. Lotus did so at the German GP and Mercedes from the Belgian, with a slightly different method. The blow wasn't linked inside the plane, but brushed the lower part of the plane itself, reducing the downforce effect. Neither team used this passive system in racing, but they did gather data to transfer to their respective 2013 projects.

New **DEVELOPMENTS** 23

Talking about COCKPITS

It was a season that rather confirmed the technology of 2011 – the return of Kers and the introduction of DRS – for all the teams, with at least a certain amount of research aimed at optimising and simplifying the driver's "office". The most significant new developments came from Ferrari, who introduced two additional rocker arms, two buttons and a further small paddle to the back of their steering wheel computer from the earliest tests. All, obviously, in an attempt to make the management of the various functions more immediate and intuitive to their drivers. At Ferrari, there were the new means of operating both Kers and the flap, which were moved to the rear of the wheel so that the drivers could work them with the middle finger instead of the thumb. All this so as not to move the thumb from holding the wheel. But even more important was the fact that the two Ferraristi further differentiated the use of their wheels during the season. Fernando Alonso preferred to drop the two upper paddles, partly because in the meantime the flap control was moved to the left foot area, while Felipe Massa was given an eighth paddle. And it is on the left foot flap control that we shall concentrate much of the analysis in this chapter. It is a facility that was also used by two other teams, Mercedes-Benz and McLaren.

The steering wheel computers of the two Ferrari drivers were more or less unchanged and they remained in the same position in relation to the driver's body.

Renault, which had followed Ferrari in increasing the number of their paddles at the rear of the wheel, dropped from eight to six from the first race.

McLaren, which had already eliminated one of its six paddles introduced back in 2009, made no change to the shape of its steering wheel. But it's worth pointing out that for the 2012 season Red Bull and Toro Rosso stayed loyal to the jet-type wheel and, therefore, they were the only two without an integrated display, but one positioned at the centre of the cockpit.

FERRARI WHEEL

Compared to the steering wheel computer of the F150 Italia, that of the F138 was more or less unchanged as far as both its shape and disposition of the various controls were concerned. The only differences were concentrated at the rear, as can be seen in the comparison on the right.

In the description of the various functions it is worth remembering that they may be modified in line with the circuits' characteristics and the needs of the driver, which can be different from each other.

1) The display was the same, given that the regulation was the same for all the cars. The Led readouts confirm the right moment to change gear as they lit up in sequence.
2) Lights confirmed that the Kers was working.
3) To engage the pit lane speed limiter.
4) The buttons at the rear of the wheel with which to activate the mobile flap on the rear of the wheel.
5) Kers recharger.
6) Adjusts Kers power.
7) Ensures higher engine revolutions.
8) Regulates engine torque.
9) Provides access to the selection of functions on the central lever.
10) Confirms the choice made on the lever.
11) Inserts various programmes for the wet.
12) Inserts various management programmes of set-up in relation to the tyres.
13) Engages the pre-selected adjustments during practice for the start.
14) Central "lever" that provide access to the different management programmes.
15) Burn-out, which permits wheel spin.
16) A button the purpose of which remained secret for the entire season.
17) Inserts the oil scavenger pump.
18) Gives access to the mineral salts drink.
19) Varies the fuel/air mix.
20) Radio.
21) Regulates the engine revs.
22) Regulates differential management.
23) Indicates the position on the back of the flap control.
24) Inserts neutral gear.
25) Permits the use of the flap.

24

F2012 — Kers — DRS

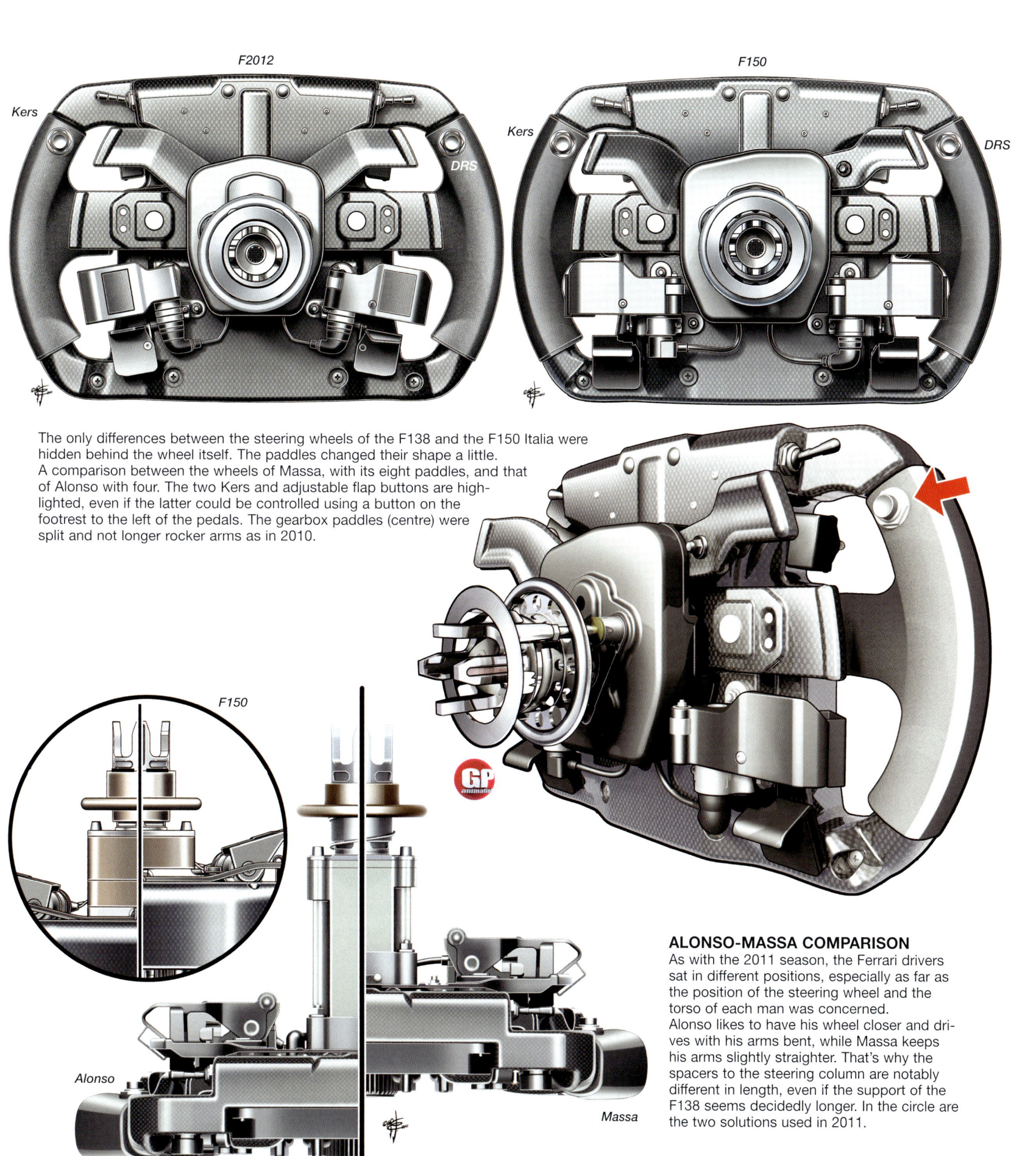

F150 — Kers — DRS

The only differences between the steering wheels of the F138 and the F150 Italia were hidden behind the wheel itself. The paddles changed their shape a little. A comparison between the wheels of Massa, with its eight paddles, and that of Alonso with four. The two Kers and adjustable flap buttons are highlighted, even if the latter could be controlled using a button on the footrest to the left of the pedals. The gearbox paddles (centre) were split and not longer rocker arms as in 2010.

F150

Alonso

Massa

ALONSO-MASSA COMPARISON

As with the 2011 season, the Ferrari drivers sat in different positions, especially as far as the position of the steering wheel and the torso of each man was concerned.
Alonso likes to have his wheel closer and drives with his arms bent, while Massa keeps his arms slightly straighter. That's why the spacers to the steering column are notably different in length, even if the support of the F138 seems decidedly longer. In the circle are the two solutions used in 2011.

Talking about **COCKPITS** 25

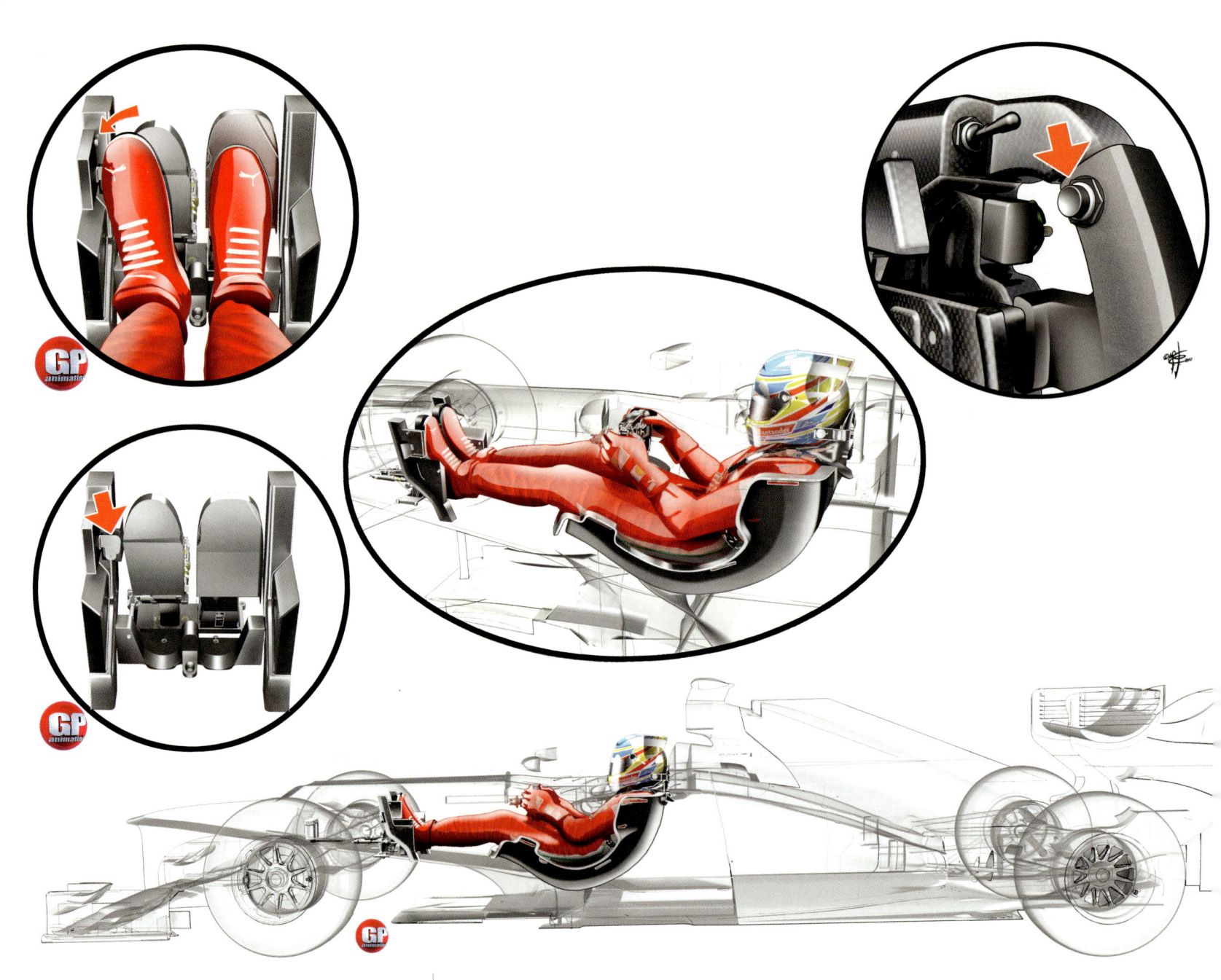

DRS AT THEIR FEET

As a preference, the Ferrari drivers control the DRS with a button located where the footrest is usually found (as well as the usual button at the back of the steering wheel, visible in detail upper right) by working it with the left foot. In this series of illustrations taken from an animation, you can easily see both the driving position inside the F138 and the detail of the system. It is more functional and safer because it allows better synchronisation of the moment in which the flap must return to the "load" position, it being determined obligatorily by the moving of the foot so that it can work the brake pedal. The small fraction that intervenes between the two moments helps the flap to return to its load position to guarantee maximum grip under braking.

PEDALS

Again in this detail taken from an animation, the Ferrari pedals seen from the brake pump side, supplied by Brembo; its electronic management of the division of the braking between the two axles. Remember that in F1 you can only vary braking between the two axles. The transverse effect is prohibited between one wheel and another, a rule that came into effect in 1994 after Williams tested this technique in the preceding season.

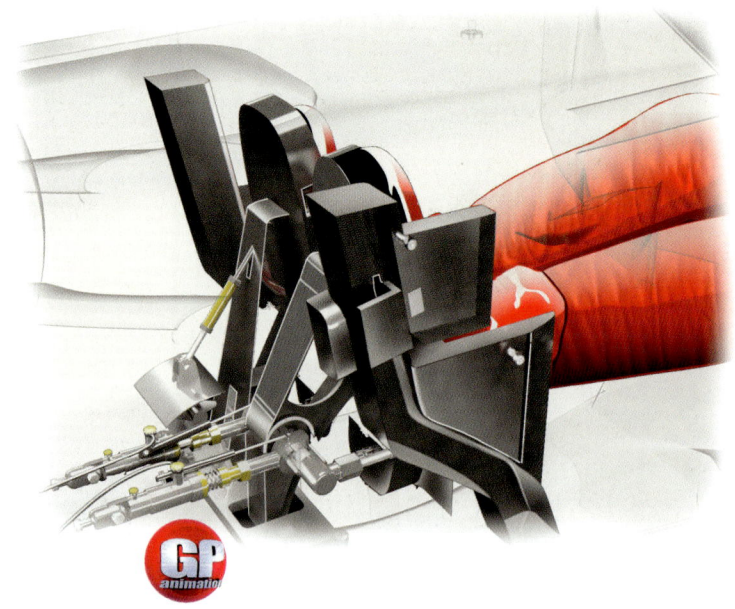

Talking about **COCKPITS**

MERCEDES-BENZ

The Mercedes-Benz wheel computer was similar to that of the Ferrari with six paddles at the rear, the high ones to manage the Kers with both hands. Note the DTRS button above left, but especially the one for neutral (red arrow) which, if pressed for a few seconds engaged reverse gear.

McLAREN

The steering wheel computer of the Mp4/27 was generally unchanged from the 2011 unit. After being the first to introduce six paddles to the rear of their wheel in 2009, they had eliminated one of them by 2011. They moved the flap control to the base of the footrest so that it could be operated by the left foot on a straight and better synchronise the switch during the braking phase, in which the adjustable flap has to return to its load position to avoid the locking the rear wheels.

RED BULL

The Red Bull wheels were practically the same as those of 2011 and 2010, despite the introduction of Kers and rear wing flap management. The two upper paddles work the Kers. In fact, Red Bull was the only team – together with its "cousin" Toro Rosso – without a display incorporated in the characteristic shape of the horizontal-X wheel.

RENAULT

After the seven paddles at the rear of the steering wheel computer of the Ferrari, Renault came back with eight controls (detail at the side) in 2011. The two small ones below, almost hidden by the others, were both used to operate the rear wing flap to ensure easy management with one of the driver's two hands, dependent on the position of the wheel at any given time. For the 2012 season, the paddles went back to being six, with the two above for the management of Kers.

Talking about **COCKPITS** 27

Talking about BRAKES and TYRES

The development of 2012 season braking systems had to take two major factors into account. The first concerned the introduction of the new Pirelli tyres, which didn't really have too much effect on the brakes all that much. In fact, even if the 2012 covers produced less yet more constant wear, the overall level of grip was unchanged.
But the second aspect, banning blown exhausts, modified both the division of the aerodynamic load on the two axles and Kers strategies, which severely conditioned balance under braking. And it was no coincidence that the balance had decidedly moved to the front wheels, obliging teams and brake system suppliers to take the diversification between the front and rear brakes into account as early as the design stage.
To support the changes in the division of the cars' new configurations, Brembo worked jointly with its clients by proposing systems that concerned both the hydraulic part – brake calipers – and friction material – discs and pads.
Most of the teams supplied by the Italian manufacturer decided to reduce the rear brake caliper hydraulics, using smaller size pistons, to align themselves with the minor requirement of rear axle torque and consequently reducing the weight of the braking system.
With regard to friction material, disc dimensions were changed. The external diameter went from the prescribed 278 mm – the maximum allowed by the regulations – to 270 mm, and the thickness 25 mm instead of the standard 28 mm.
Being unable to increase the front axle's discs width or diameter, fixed rigidly by the regulations, Brembo worked on ventilation geometry, reverting to concepts and developments already seen the previous year in an effort to permit an increase in the disposable power of the braking system. So we saw a reduction in the diameter of the ventilating holes but a drastic increase in their number, reaching over 1,000 apertures per disc.

BREMBO CER DISCS
On the harshest tracks, Red Bull and Ferrari used new Brembo brake discs with five aligned holes for a total of almost 1,000 around the whole circumference. The CER material from which they were made was also new, having taken the place of CCR so as to reduce wear at the end of a race from 4 to just 1 mm. An incredible development in materials research, which means the teams that used CER were not subjected to wear problems.

With the same objective, Brembo worked on the shape of the pads, lengthening them radially and increasing their area of contact with the disc. The result was a reduction in the disc/pad interface temperature and an increased limit in material fade.
The new pad geometry obviously required the modification of the caliper body, needed to ensure the friction material worked in the best possible way. The pistons were repositioned, with greater distance between them to optimize pressure distribution on the rear of the pad itself.

FERRARI
For Canada, the harshest on brakes, Ferrari followed Williams in the adoption of front brake air intakes without an internal inlet but with all of the air supply obtained from the space between the pan and the wheel. This space increases with the movement and tyres' lateral flexing on the track and with it so does the air input. The detail shows the thin intakes.

BRAKE CALLIPERS
The severe limits imposed by the Federation on braking systems – maximum six pistons, two pads and discs 28 mm thick – didn't leave much room for the calliper manufacturers, whose number one responsibility is to make units for the varying needs of their customers. The 2012 F1 cars were sub-divided like this as far as calliper suppliers were concerned:
BREMBO: Ferrari, Red Bull, Mercedes-Benz, Sauber, Toro Rosso, HRT.
A+P: Lotus, Williams, Force India, Caterham, Marussia.
AKEBONO: exclusively to McLaren.

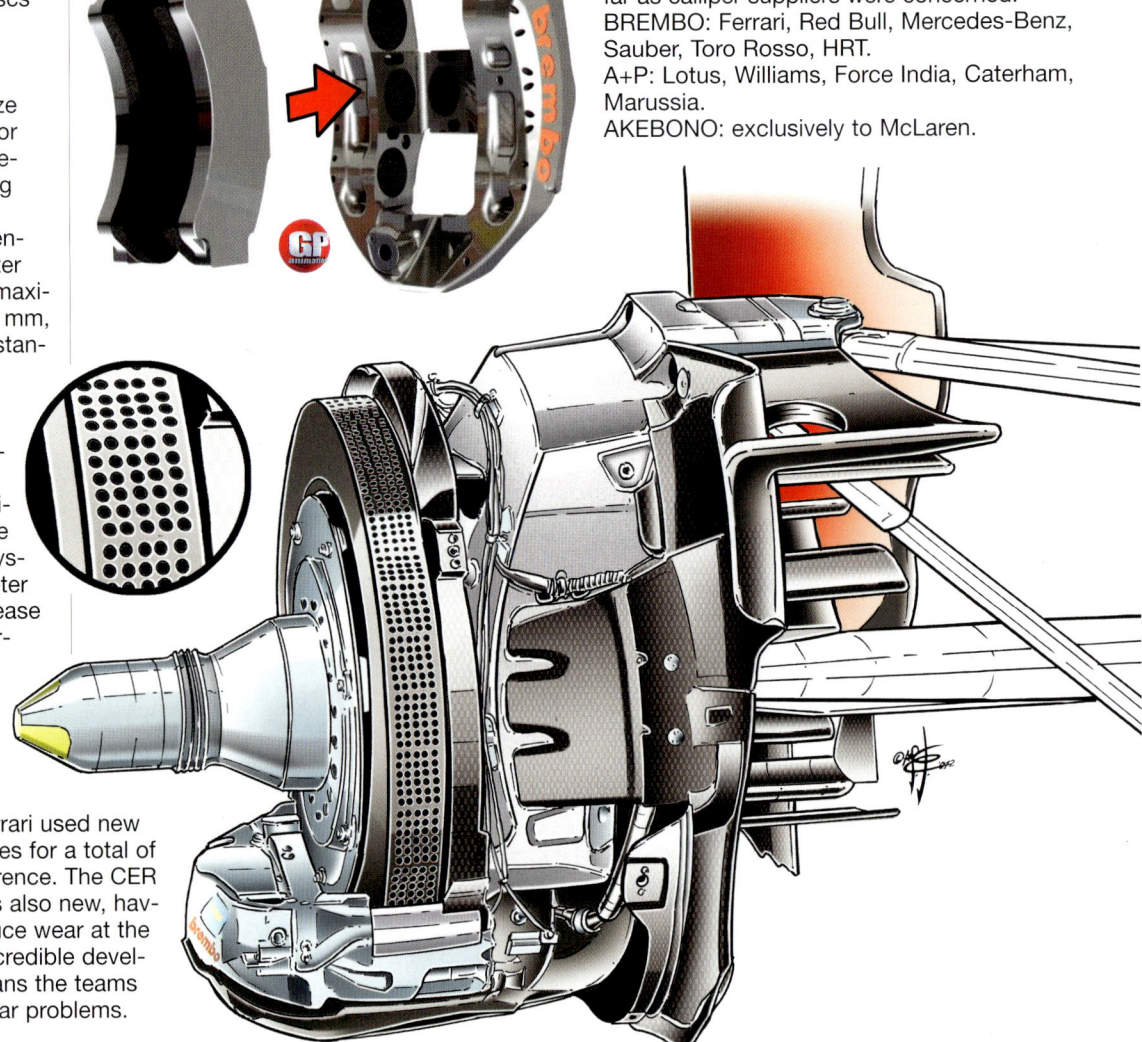

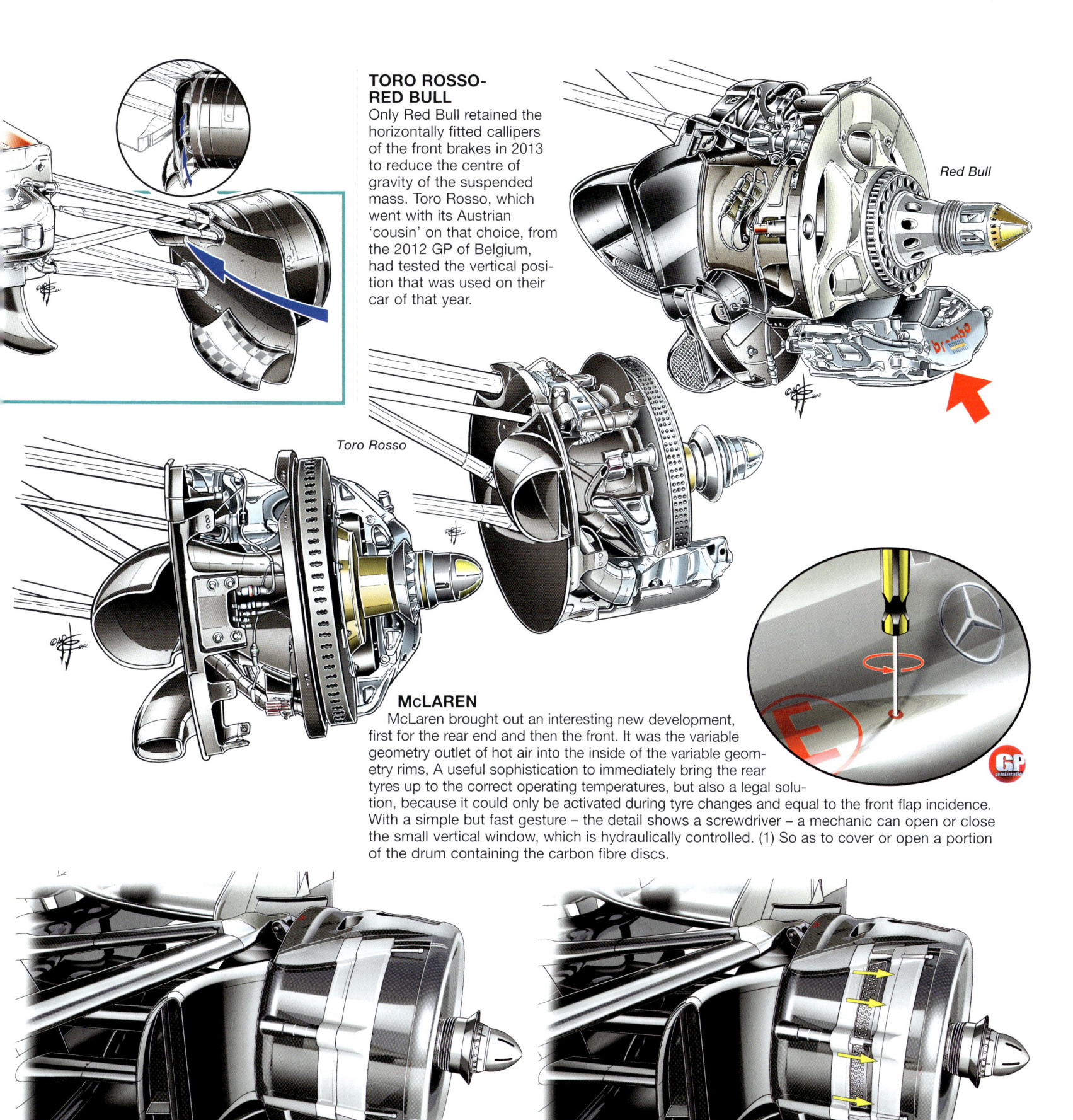

TORO ROSSO-RED BULL

Only Red Bull retained the horizontally fitted callipers of the front brakes in 2013 to reduce the centre of gravity of the suspended mass. Toro Rosso, which went with its Austrian 'cousin' on that choice, from the 2012 GP of Belgium, had tested the vertical position that was used on their car of that year.

Red Bull

Toro Rosso

McLAREN

McLaren brought out an interesting new development, first for the rear end and then the front. It was the variable geometry outlet of hot air into the inside of the variable geometry rims, A useful sophistication to immediately bring the rear tyres up to the correct operating temperatures, but also a legal solution, because it could only be activated during tyre changes and equal to the front flap incidence. With a simple but fast gesture – the detail shows a screwdriver – a mechanic can open or close the small vertical window, which is hydraulically controlled. (1) So as to cover or open a portion of the drum containing the carbon fibre discs.

Talking about **BRAKES** and **TYRES**

TYRES

Having overcome 2011, the "run-in" year that marked the return of Pirelli to Formula 1 after being absent for two decades, 2012 was their confirmation and a period of development of their technical decisions and constructional philosophy.

The Milanese technicians continued their commitment to improve the spectacle of Formula 1, promoting overtaking and the number of pit stops; they also carried out targeted modifications to their tyres during the season.

The exhaust blow regulation change, reduced in entity compared to that which was possible in 2011, produced a reduction in aerodynamic load at the rear of the cars and, therefore, moved the centre of pressure towards the front. The effect was a reduction in aerodynamic grip on the rear axle, which was compensated for with changes to the tyres' construction, tread compounds and the profile of the rears, which became squarer for a larger footprint with less rounded corners for better wear, especially on the shoulders.

A bigger footprint meant a more uniform pressure and temperature distribution, all of which produced more mechanical grip and also reduced blistering – the excessive heat build-up in just certain areas of the tyre.

That way, maximum performance of the tyre was achieved over a greater number of laps, while the overall wear rate remained unchanged as it was linked to the kind of tread compound.

The profile of the front tyres was also slightly changed, with a less rounded progression of the shoulder.

With the exception of the supersoft, the compounds were softened compared to those of the previous year with the objective of reducing time differences to less than a second a lap between one type and the next.

In fact, the medium compound of 2012 was almost the equivalent of the hard of 2011; in the same way, the soft was close to the 2011 medium and so on. The compound comparison table shows the decisions made by the Pirelli technicians compared to those of 2011.

The supersoft, the only unmodified compound, was used four times on the same tracks as in 2011. They were the circuits that were not especially critical in the demands they placed on the tyres, their abrasiveness or energy dissipation.

The soft used on all the 2011 tracks was used at 15 of the 20 2012 Grands Prix and only four times as the Prime tyre; the mediums were used 12 times instead of seven, seven of them as the Prime tyre.

And the hards were used nine times on those circuits where the lateral and vertical stress was especially severe, like Barcelona, Silverstone, Spa, Monza, Delhi and Suzuka. Analysing tyre use, we can deduce that, having been the compound softened, the decision was to increase the number of pit stops during the races to favour differentiated strategies and livelier GPs.

Excluding the Grands Prix of Malaysia and Brazil, events in which rain modified race strategies, it is interesting to note that in six races out of 18 – so one in three – the winner's strategy was to make one single pit stop.

In the remaining 12 races, the winner made two pit stops; only in Barcelona and Bahrain did the victors go for three. The choice of the most appropriate moment to change tyres pinpointed the winner of the race; that was the case, for example, with Maldonado's win at Barcelona, which was decided by a tyre change that was two laps earlier than Alonso's.

A different use of the compounds was the key to the British GP; Alonso, who started with Hards and then used a Soft–Soft sequence, was unable to close the gap between himself and Webber, who started with Softs and then had two sets of Hards fitted.

P: prime **O**: option (super soft - soft - medium - hard)   **In**: intermediate **W**: wet

Talking about **BRAKES** *and* **TYRES**

The grooved tyres were unchanged, except that their name became Cinturato and the sidewall colour went from blue to green. But the extreme wets adopted the blue sidewall colour in place of 2011's orange and were profoundly modified, especially the rears. They were given a different profile to improve water ejection and reduce aquaplaning potential. In 2012, they were able to expel over 60 litres of water per second at 300 kph, almost six times more than the tyres of a high performance road car.

To help modify their 2012 tyres, Pirelli also developed a data collation system during testing and the races that enabled their technicians to monitor the use, performance, wear and evolution of every tyre while in action on the track. The information, as well as that in a server at Pirelli's Izmit, Turkey, factory where the tyres are built and classified, was correlated with the set-up of the car and other data gathered by telemetry by the F1 teams to produce a complete "story" of every single tyre.

While the tyre regulations were unchanged, the number of sets available during a race weekend – 11 sets of slicks and seven of wets – had to be delivered to the teams before the start of the first practice; a set of the harder compound had to be returned before the start of the second practice. One set of harder compound (Prime) and one of softer compound (option) had to be returned before the beginning of the third practice.

The other sets of all compounds had to be given back at the end of the third practice, so that the teams would have six sets available to them, three of each compound, for qualifying and the race.

Eng. Giancarlo Bruno

This illustration shows a section of a Pirelli tyre with its various components:
1) The bead that goes inside the rim to stop the tyre detaching from the wheel.
2) The carcass, the structural part of the tyre, which absorbs the forces that interact between the tyre and the asphalt.
3-4-5) The belt pack, comprising small multiples of synthetic material (nylon, polyester) that augment the tyre's resistance.
6) The tread with various synthetic rubber compounds, which change dependent on the demands of the track and asphalt.

Talking about **BRAKES** and **TYRES**

ENGINES 2012

The 2012 season was the penultimate in which 90° V8 2.4-litre engines were used, as they will soon make way for a V6 turbo hybrid unit. Four constructors supplied the 12 teams with their engines.
They were Renault for Red Bull Racing, Lotus, Williams and Caterham; Ferrari for themselves, Sauber and Toro Rosso; Mercedes-Benz for themselves, McLaren and Force India; and Cosworth for Marussia and HRT. Each driver was permitted a maximum of eight power units per season, so that a total of 176 engines were used for the championship. Statistically, the most effective unit was the Renault RS27 2012, which amassed nine victories, nine pole positions and 11 fastest laps in the year's 20 races.

All credit to Viry-Châtillon, which won its third consecutive drivers' world championship with Sebastian Vettel and the constructors' title with Red Bull Racing and also having won at least once with three of its four teams (Red Bull 7, Lotus 1 and Williams 1).
Mercedes-Benz scored seven wins with their FO108Z, six with McLaren and one by its own team. But the Ferrari 056 K10 only won with its own team by taking three victories, two pole positions and recording two fastest laps, while Cosworth played a marginal role with its CA2012, an old concept engine that never once finished in the points with either Marussia or HRT, the Cinderellas of the circus.

With regulations mainly static due to the desire to contain costs, there were two variations of the rules that affected the engine specialists: the FIA tried to stop the exacerbation of exhausts blowing into the rear diffusers, which were so prominent in 2011, saying that they should no longer have any influence on the aerodynamic behaviour of the car. In addition, the International Federation established that the lay-out and control parameters on the MES (McLaren Electronic System) electronic management method, which was previously regulated by a simple technical directive, were an integral part of the technical regulations.
The rule came about to punish those who wanted to design a form of mapping that included the reuse of exhaust blow when the engine was in deceleration. Two norms which, as we shall see, were ably circumvented by the teams' technicians.

Article 5.8.1. of the F1 technical regulations imposed an extremely precise position for the exhausts in a car. In 2011, they were moved to the bottom of the car to maximise the blow effect and play an aerodynamic role; in fact, the best systems were worth up to a second a lap. For 2012, they had to be at a certain height from the reference plane and contained in a sort of "virtual box" measuring 700 mm long, 300 mm wide and 350 mm high. The last 100 mm of the terminals had to be straight, the circular section with an internal diameter no more than 75 mm.
Adding an angulation of its axis of +/- 10° in relation to the car's centerline if seen from above, and between 10° and 30° laterally. Charlie Whiting, FIA's technical boss, thought he had "caged" the designers, but that wasn't the case: Sergio Perez of Sauber took second place in the GP of Malaysia by exploiting the Coandă effect, as a result of which the Swiss aerodynamicists were able

COANDA EFFECT
This is the tendency of a jet of fluid to follow the contours of a nearby surface. In the case of an F1 car, it is a flow of hot air from the exhaust terminals that follows the determined shape of the body which, due to the regulation, had to have a specific upwards inclination of between 10° and 30°.

SAUBER
The first surprise came from Sauber, which revolutionised the shape of their car's terminal area, abolishing the Coca-Cola bottle form and bringing in a descendent terminal zone, exploiting the Coandă effect on the exhausts.

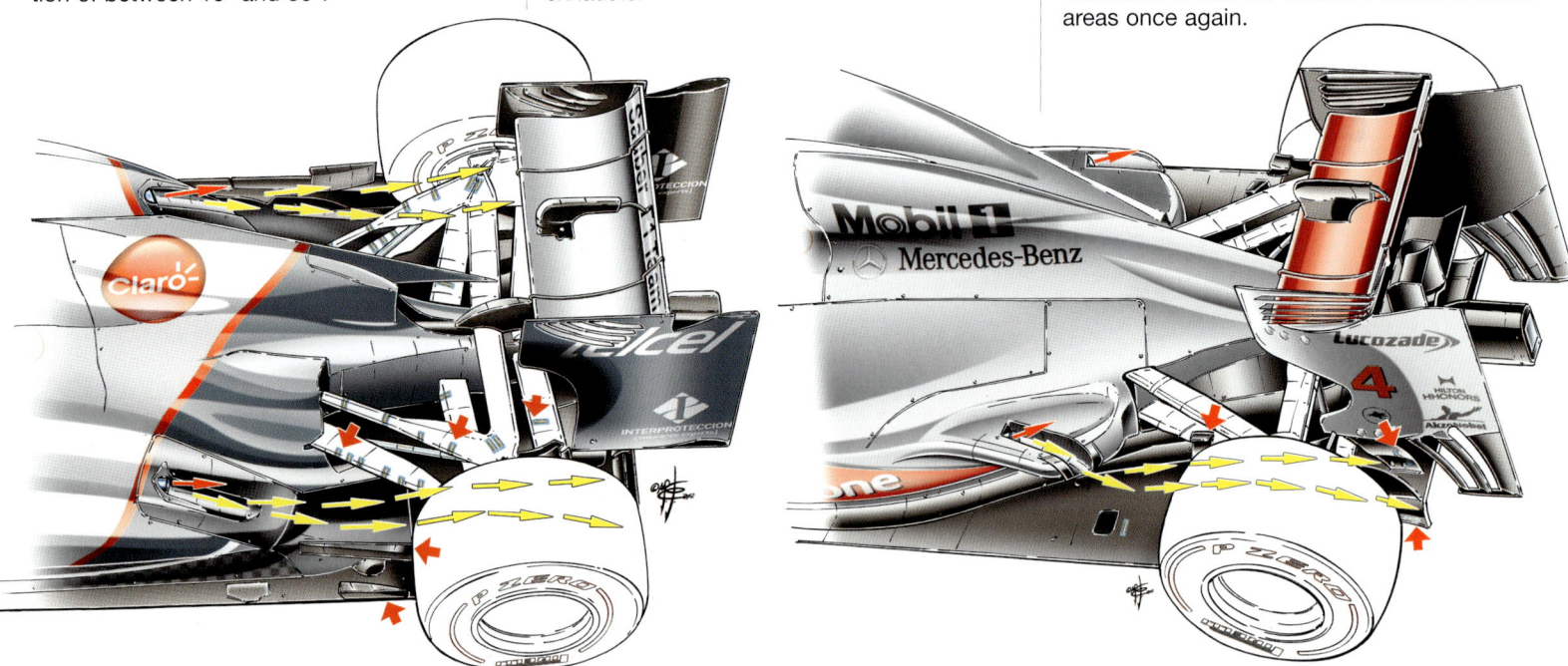

McLAREN
It was the technique introduced by McLaren at the start of the season that made most converts. Note that the flow, indicated in yellow, doesn't follow the trajectory of the exhausts shown with the red arrow, but descends to lick the diffusers' lateral channel areas once again.

to take the precious red hot exhaust gas blow up to where it was able to generate a "thermal mini-skirt", essential to increasing aerodynamic load at the rear end.

The Coandă effect is the tendency of a jet of fluid to follow the contours of a nearby surface. While McLaren and Ferrari tried to "tune" the flow of gas between the rear tyre and the wing's end plate, some like Adrian Newey, designer of the RB 8, gave the end of the belly a ramp, which permitted maximum exploitation of the Coandă effect and led to the hot blow licking the bottom of the car. After the FIA constraints, the technicians thought they wouldn't be able to recover more than 30% of the exhaust blow, but they did well to go beyond that, turning this phenomenon into the key element in the development of the cars. Jo Bauer, the federal technical delegate, placed the two Red Bull Racing cars under examination at the GP of Germany: the result was that the maximum torque generated by the Renault engine at medium revolutions was clearly below to that recorded at other events, due to a special mapping of the electronic management system. According to the FIA, article 5.5.3. of the technical regulations was not respected, which says the engine must be able to increase the torque value with the increase in revolutions at medium rpm of use, as a result of which that particular mapping was banned.

I should add that it's not easy for the FIA to check that situation, because while the engines are always the same – in 2008, there was a freezing of the regulations that prohibited the development of internal components, although it is possible to move accessories like the pumps and modify the chassis mounts – fuels and lubricants change, so in reality performance is improved.

At just about every Grand Prix there were different exhaust solutions to optimise the cars for use on specific circuits.
The Ferrari 2012, in particular, seemed to be in difficulty during the first part of the season and the problems weren't resolved until the only test session, at Mugello.
The trouble was linked to the exhaust blow but once solved, the team made a prodigious climb back up the championship table that enabled Fernando Alonso to fight for the title until the last GP.
So it is interesting to discover that, in the face of having to use eight engines a season per driver, the constructors were forced to produce around 100 units. Why?
Mainly to test them for reliability on the bench, but also for the development of new ideas – like the exhausts – that have to be determined in a series of long runs.

We reached a point at which the aerodynamicists worked side-by-side with the engine specialists to decide on the various terminals. With the introduction of blown gas, the engines lost about 30 hp: over the last three years they clawed back 5 hp per season with more extreme developments. The terminal diameters reached 640 mm, but in 2012 they were no larger than 500 mm. To "tune" an engine, which is similar to a pipe organ, it is necessary to study the play of waves.
The intake ducts must be in tune with the revolutions and the exhausts.
The "resonator", first launched by Ferrari at the 2011 GP of Belgium, is a closed added tube fitted forward of the four per cylinder bank, especially designed to compensate for the greater length of the terminals.
In 2011, exhaust blow was responsible for a noticeable increase in fuel consumption, but in 2012 it was contained at 4%.
The commitment of the constructions in keeping the reliability of the V8 high was enormous. The life of an engine is estimated at 2,500 km or about three GPs, plus the various Friday practice sessions.
To develop a modification, a long run on the test bench is not enough, so they run two or three.

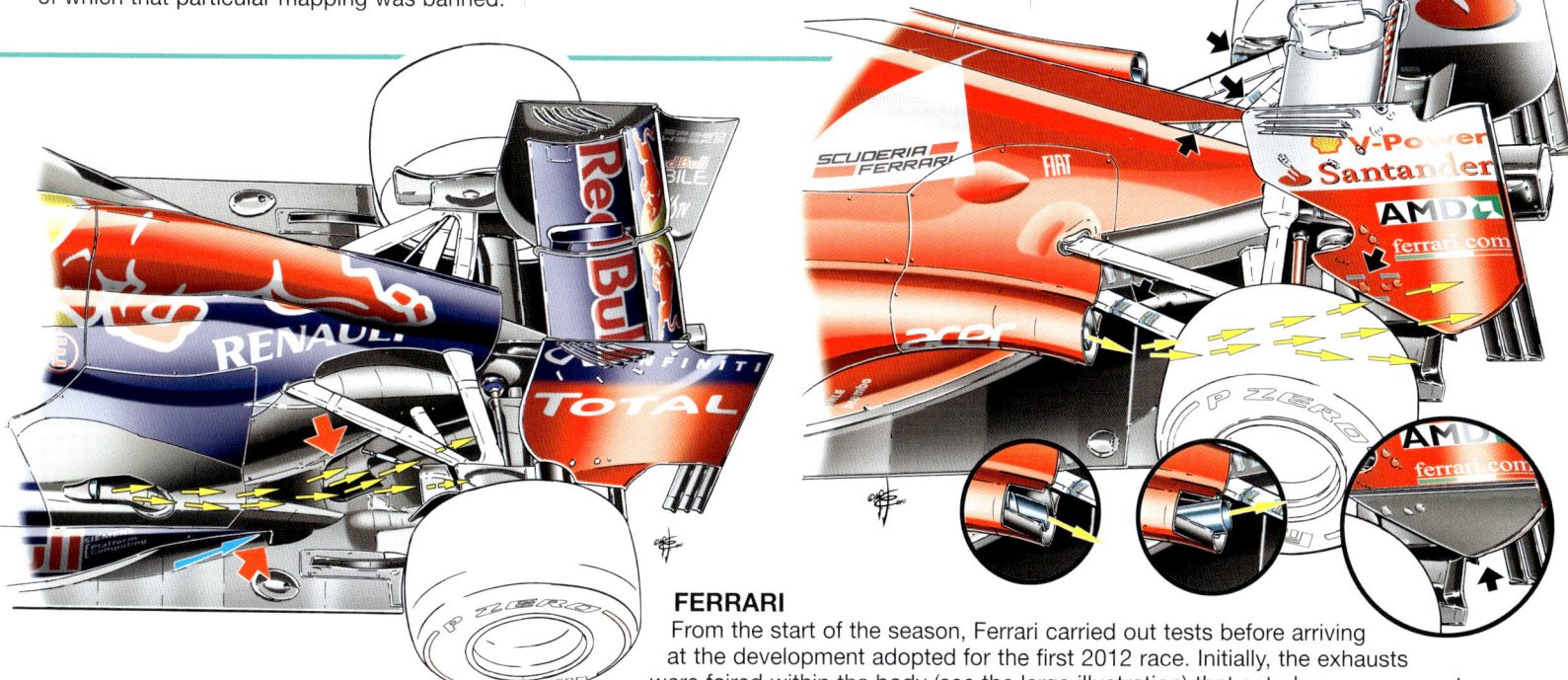

RED BULL
For the RB8, Adrian Newey hit on a Sauber-type solution that was, obviously, extreme. He brought in a second air flow channel into the lower area of the car. It was a technique that required laborious setting up before it became perfectly integrated with the rear aerodynamics.

FERRARI
From the start of the season, Ferrari carried out tests before arriving at the development adopted for the first 2012 race. Initially, the exhausts were faired within the body (see the large illustration) that acted as a conveyor to direct the hot air flow towards the low area and lick the internal part of the rear wheels. A modification was made from the first laps, in which the upper part of the body was cut as it "cooked" due to the high temperature (first detail to the left). And in the first practice session longer, inwardly inclined terminals were tested. They seemed to have given positive indications (centre circle, low). In the latest test at Barcelona one appeared that was even more similar to those of the blow towards the central part of the Red Bull, with a further cut to the body and the relocation of the terminals, which were more inward inclined (large circle above), mostly repeating the solution selected for the Red Bull's debut.

ENGINES 2012

At Maranello and Viry-Châtillon they use tests with "mean" cycles, so that they simulate Monza, the most probative track for a V8. Reliability is also assured by what the people of the racing department call the test lots: there are components like gaskets, which are produced in large quantities.
And even if the supplier certifies the conformity of each item, samples are checked at the test bench. Ferrari has a couple of dynamic cells plus three stationary ones that they also use for engine tests and others to verify lots.
So there are engines running every day, which can be for Scuderia Ferrari, Toro Rosso or Sauber; that work never ends.

It's interesting to note that Ferrari also carries out test drives of 056s coming to the end of their lives, as with running-in before the approval: the units are not certified after only one long run. Before they are installed in a car they are disassembled once again, verified piece-by-piece, reassembled and then put back on the test bench. The technicians have all the data on every engine, which is why it becomes important to discover what breaks and why after a unit runs for the distance of three GPs.

This now standard procedure meant that Ferrari engines didn't break down at all in 2012, while Renault "lost" six and Mercedes-Benz two. A drop in fuel pressure was behind the M-B failures (Schumacher at Monaco, Hamilton in Abu Dhabi), while it was the alternators that knocked out the French power units – once on Romain Grosjean's Lotus and three times on the Vettel and Webber Red Bulls.

Dietrich Mateschitz, the Red Bull owner, took the matter up with Magneti Marelli – in 2012 – only the RS27 supplied to Milton Keynes had MES alternators – accusing the Italian manufacturer, but only later did it emerged that the electrical component had not been modified and the problem still happened for other reasons. According to Rob White, chief technician of Renault F1, at certain times Red Bull asked for more current than the Marelli system could provide: the tension that was generated related to the function of the rotation speed. When one produces an electrical balance, one must take account of the variations and the peaks: at low revs there isn't much electricity, but the amount increases at high revolutions, so it must be made to operate within that curve. But if it goes beyond the specifications, overheating occurs and the tolerance goes, for which reason an alternator suddenly breaks.

The feeling is that the RB8 goes into overload during the exhaust blow stage, "piloting" the ignition and injection of the Renault engine in a more extreme manner compared to others to keep the butterflies open. To all of that we must also add the aggravation of the vibration profile, which was greater than that of the other teams supplied by Renault. In fact, Red Bull Racing went to the limiter on long straights using a seventh gear that was shorter so that their cars could reach top speed before their competitors.
As can be expected, notwithstanding the ban on developing the inside of engines, the technicians still tried to increase performance. There were those who tried to use aromatics (prohibited in the petrol) in lubrication.

One solution that would presuppose high consumption, while the actual orientation was to take on as little oil as possible, using a liquid that reduces friction in favour of efficiency. Various matrices were tried during the season, but only the ones that gave a precise guarantee of reliability were developed.
The tendency was not to push the temperature of the lubricant: it is no longer thinkable that there are the 140 degrees of oil entering, the limit of the water being fixed by regulation at 125°C. As the engine is an exchanger, the temperature of the two liquids has to increase in parallel to obtain appreciable results.
So attention was concentrated on the reduction of friction. For example, Ferrari took great care of the containment of degradation in the second and third race. Luca Marmorini's engineers sought performance stability: in recent years, engines have lost 15 hp after a Grand Prix and about 30 hp in the next one. There were no performance increases in pure power in 2012, but degradation was reduced between one race and another, which yielded a perceptible recovery of horse power.

KERS
Significant development work took place on Kers during the 2012 season. Its use was optional but advised by the FIA, and it was adopted by 10 of the 12 Formula 1 teams, the exceptions being Marussia and HRT. Caterham, who moved on to Renault engines, installed the French company's system as it had a rear end designed by Red Bull.

"RESONATOR"
The so-called resonator, a sort of closed chimney applied in a precise area of the exhausts, was widely used during the 2012 season. Re-launched by Ferrari at the 2011 GP of Belgium, it was adopted by almost all the big teams. The illustration shows the Red Bull version, with the detail of the "chimney" used by Ferrari the previous season. It is really an added tube which is closed, fitted to the bottom of the four cylinder banks, especially designed to compensate for the longer terminals. To "tune" the engine, which are akin to a "pipe organ", it is necessary to study a play of waves. The intake ducts have to be in tune with the revolutions of the engine and the exhausts.

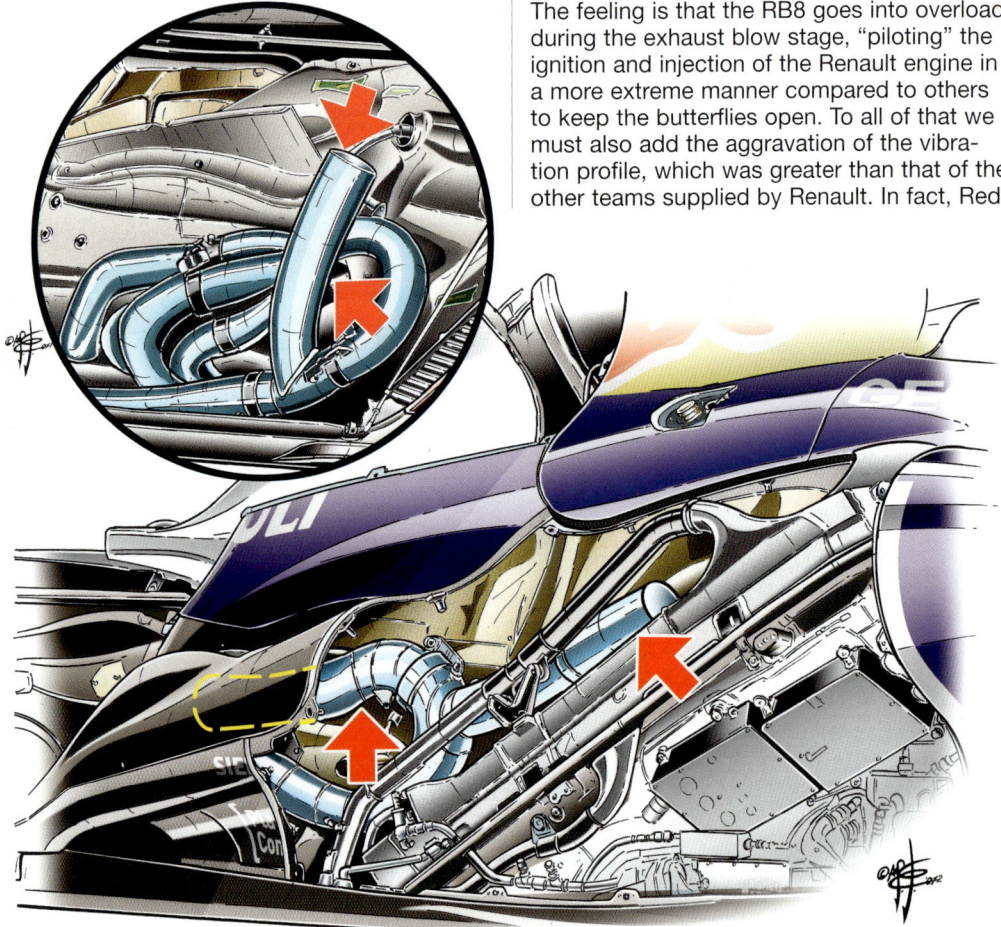

Kers is a system for the recovery of kinetic energy during braking – the accelerator must have been released and the driver has to exert at least a 2 bars of pressure on the brake pedal – and that transforms into electric energy of 400 Kj for each lap, which can be used as extra power by the thermal engine of 60 Kw or about 80 hp for a maximum of 6.6 seconds per lap. Charging the system and the management of the power boost is the task of the driver, who presses a button on his steering wheel-computer.

KERS RED BULL

During the 2012 season, Adrian Newey was obstinately true to the installation of Kers and its accessories on the RB8, despite numerous reliability problems. The batteries were split, miniaturised and placed in an area useful for weight distribution and the cars aerodynamics. Logistically, though, they were a major penalty. In practice, he placed the two packs in one of the hottest points of the car, behind the exhausts. To improve cooling, there was a complicated channelling system (blue arrow) inside the chassis and the engine cover.

The system was supplied to customer teams for €1 million, while each constructor had a €5 million expenditure limit for research. Compared to 2011, when there was quite a drop in Kers weight from 35 kg for the complete system to a little over 20, the system was optimised, but without any revolutions. Renault slightly modified the layout in the car; Magneti Marelli lightened the engine-generator by about 5 kg by also using parts made of carbon fibre.
The battery suppliers were able to progress their miniaturisation work, saving another kilo. At Viry-Châtillon, they studied a more radical evolution of the system that took up less space in the car, but it wasn't implemented so as to maintain the car's level of performance.

Research was aimed at improving the management of the system's energy with greater efficiency, and that was done on two fronts. By dissipating less energy so that it required less cooling, and bettering the system's recharging process so that it could be used on all the championship's tracks without problem.

In 2009, the year Kers was introduced, the system was only used for 30% of a lap, with one part on charge and then supplying 6.6 seconds worth of extra power. So there were long moments during which the system was "switched off". The time percentage changed in 2012 with an evolution that ensured the system worked at 100%. The way the charging phase was managed was changed, and the power was distributed in more discharge actions sub-divided over the lap after studies that were carried out in the simulation stage.

Kers became more efficient because it dissipated less heat: in 2009 the motor-generator was replaced at every GP, but in 2011 it was used for five or six races. Now, an MGUK unit has achieved a life of over 7,000 km, meaning the entire season can be covered using just three units. And the life span of the lithium ion batteries has increased, each now being used for three of four GPs. The other positive effect of increased efficiency was the reduction of the radian mass for cooling a system that prefers refrigeration – the ideal temperature is 70°C, considerably less than that of the thermal engine's water of up to 125°C.

Ferrari are proud of the fact that they didn't have to replace Kers parts in parc fermé in 2012, except on one occasion for precautionary reasons: no work on the Rosse and none on their clients' cars, something of which other engine designers were unable to boast, given that the FIA publishes a list of the parts replaced at every GP: energy recovery doesn't have the obligations of the V8. Not only has the lifespan of this material increased, the cost has been reduced by 20% against that of 2009. A major drop, if one considers drivers with 056 engines never had to give up a power boost, not for a single lap.
On circuits like Monte Carlo and Silverstone, which have very few violent deceleration areas, the energy recharge was always a problem. But with the latest systems, even that problem has been brilliantly overcome. However, the Kers influence on lap times varies considerably, depending on the characteristics of the track concerned.
At Monza, for example, it can be worth 0.4 second, but at Montreal, another circuit of heavy braking and violent acceleration, it is worth 0.3 sec. In Canada, telemetry also revealed an 8 kph increase in top speed and, as a result of the recovered energy, cars made six metres at the start (the system is only activated at over 100 kph).
There again, the Kers effect is noticeably reduced at Monte Carlo, where it can be most useful at the start.

So for circuits like the Principality, the technicians developed a specific unit able to produce a power output of only 40 Kilojoules, but with a smaller battery pack and, more importantly, one that was lighter.
There was talk of a significant weight saving of 2-3 kilos, which means more performance to an F1 car over a whole lap.
Unlike the other teams that housed their Kers system in a kind of "suitcase" between the chassis and the engine under the fuel tank, Red Bull Racing placed their batteries on the left side of the Renault power unit and in the gearbox. This to the advantage of a more favourable distribution of the mass, but they could have used a more effective "mini-Kers".

In the electronic management energy recovery system there are two processors: one controls the electric motor and is run by the constructor, while the programmes of the second are written by the teams' engineers, who vary the codes in line with the needs of the individual tracks and their different strategies. The drivers never complained again about the negative effect Kers was able to generate in deceleration – the system only recharges under braking – given that it varies in line with its ability or inability to accumulate energy, so a deceleration could be different from the previous lap, causing a driver reference crisis.

The regulations permit two boosts per lap – before the finish line and after the start – to attempt to overtake, but the teams preferred to subdivide the Kers use strategy into small packages of brief duration.
Activation usually took place exiting a corner as soon as the necessary grip came on stream to avoid wheel spin.
Red Bull Racing pushed this concept on their RB8, often choosing to install a short seventh gear so that the torque came in earlier and the car made top speed before the opposition, at the cost of covering the last section of the straight on the engine rev limiter at 18,000 rpm. Even if Sebastian Vettel's and Mark Webber's top speed in a trap was clearly below that of the competition – as much as 10 kph – the lap time comparison was in their favour.

Franco Nugnes

ENGINES 2012
35

VENTING EFFECTS

FERRARI
Ferrari's initial exhaust package seem to forget the basis principles of the aerodynamic requirements of a current Formula One car, they compromised the coke bottle are to much and I doing so lost a lot of potential downforce.

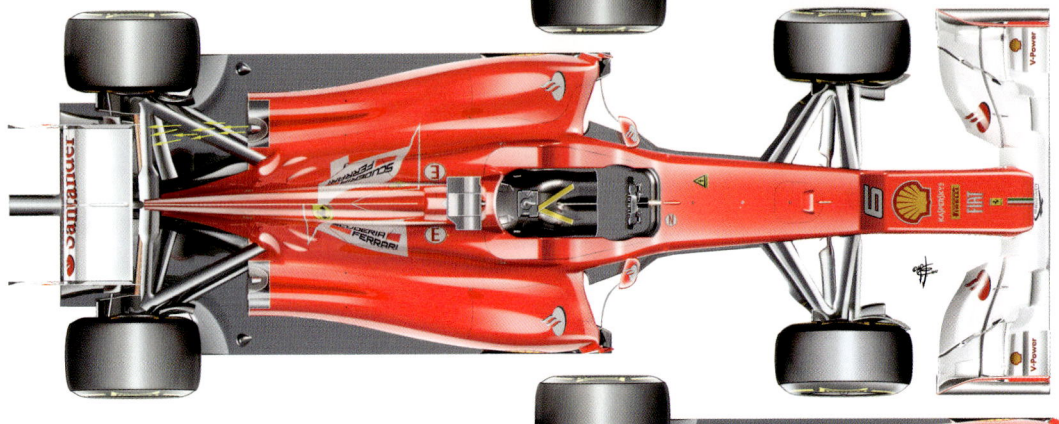

Step two again focused on the exhaust positioning and outlet to make the most of the exhaust blown diffuser principles but again the coke bottle area was neglected.

Step three moved the exhaust outlet forward and improved the coke bottle airflow together they were a reasonable compromise to the initial concept.

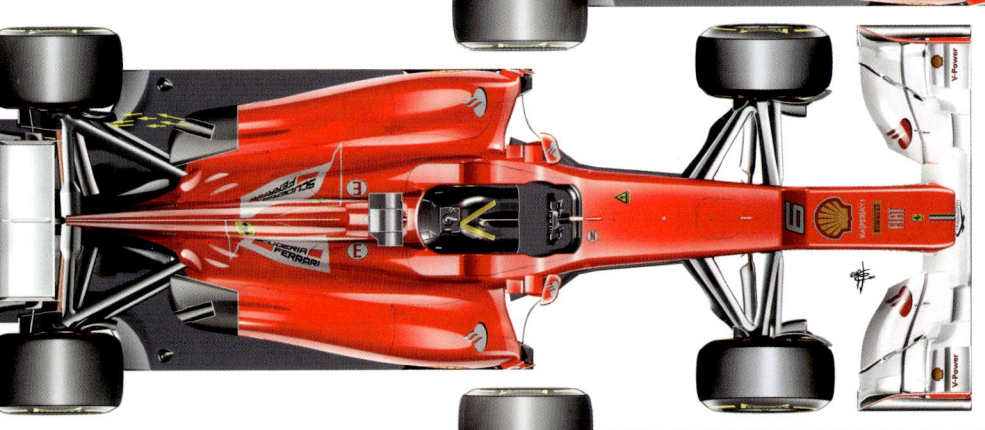

Step four brought the exhaust outlets nearer to the area of the diffuser that sees an improvement from the increased exhaust gas velocity but through all these developments they never really got on top of an initially poor concept.

RED BULL
Initially Red Bull followed the intention of the regulations; this allowed them to understand the development direction the rest of the car required before introducing a revised package.

ENGINES 2012

Step two was a revised coke bottle with a long top surface and the exhaust outlet located on the outer corner of the body work. They were actually the first team to create a surface to attempt to optimise the Coandă effect; this then took the exhaust gasses to the area of rear brake duct that creates more rear downforce directly on the rear tyre.

Step three saw further development of this concept especially in the coke bottle underside duct that feeds air into the central part of the rear diffuser, the exhaust outlet is also further rearwards.

Step four was again focused on better airflow to the central section of the underflow and exhaust pipe outlet detail revised to direct the high speed exhaust gasses more directly to the inner side of the rear brake duct.

LOTUS

Lotus read the regulations as intended and went for a simple exhaust out location, blowing the high speed exhaust gases in this area increases the mass airflow velocity under the rear wing and improves overall downforce of this component.

Step two was to locate the exhausts further out blowing the high speed gases at the inside of the rear wheels, if this can be done correctly it will give more downforce when the driver presses the accelerator and requires more rear grip to help the traction.

ENGINES 2012 **37**

McLAREN

McLaren were the first team to introduce what was called the "Coandă exhaust outlet" this came from a Romanian aircraft designed that discovered that if you blew high speed exhaust gases over a surface that was working at a low pressure the high speed gases would attach itself to that surface and they could be directed onto another part of the airplane, unfortunately his plane was made from fabric and it caught fire and destroyed itself.

The McLaren system in reality was nothing like this as it blew the high speed gases across a gap to make the wing sections that are mounted on the inner surface of the brake ducts work more efficiently, this in turn increased the rear downforce when the accelerator was open.

Step two was to realign the exhaust outlet, initially it pointed outwards at the rear tyre inner shoulder, realigning this reduced the temperature in the rear tyre inner shoulder.

Step three was again realignment and a revised coke bottle detail, the further forward the exhaust outlet the more outward it needs to point because the high speed exhaust gasses get washed inboard by the mass airflow coming around the coke bottle.

MERCEDES-BENZ

Mercedes like Lotus started the season with the exhausts pipe outlet very far forward this meant that they give a very small overall benefit when the accelerator was open but they also did very little harm when the accelerator was closed so really in a very benign location.

ENGINES 2012

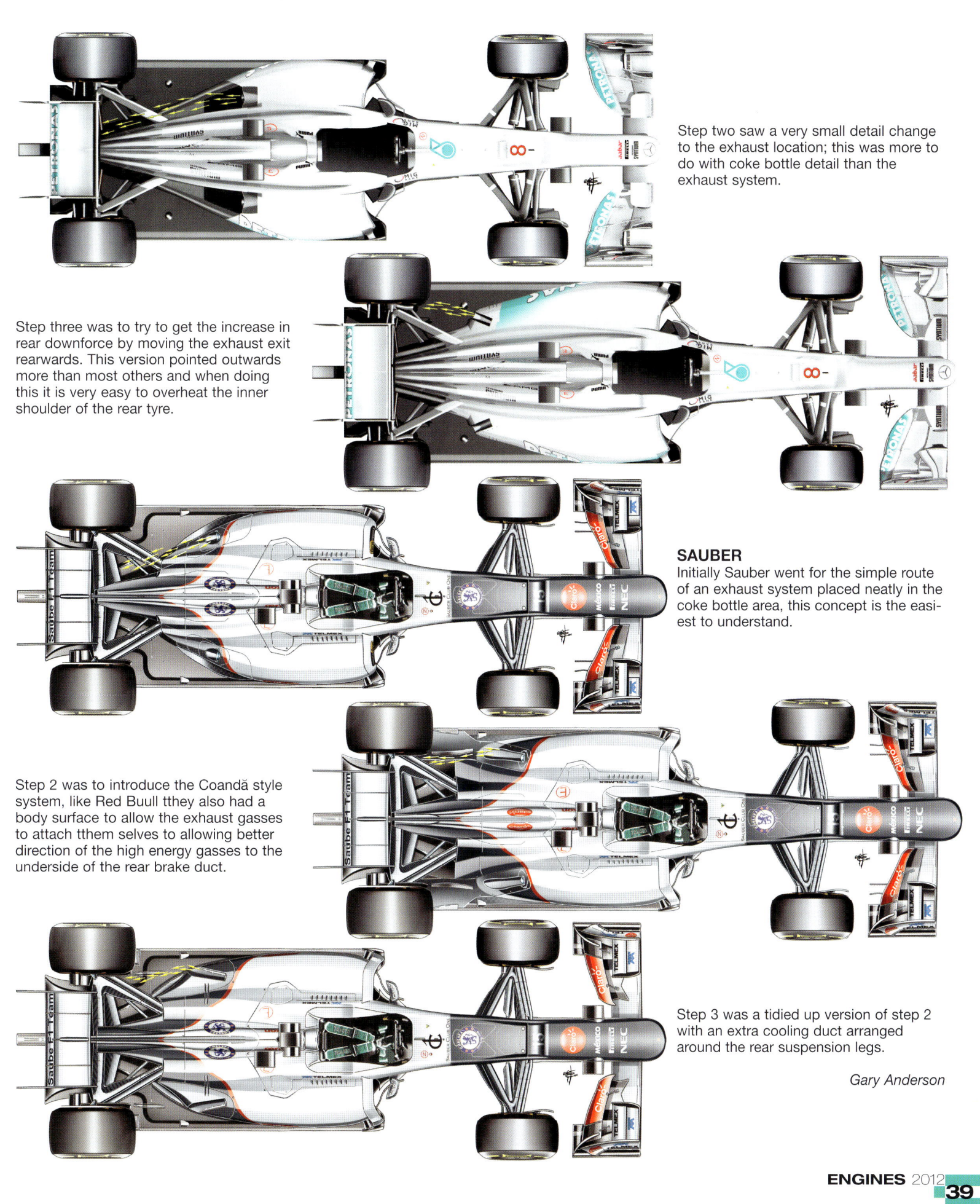

Step two saw a very small detail change to the exhaust location; this was more to do with coke bottle detail than the exhaust system.

Step three was to try to get the increase in rear downforce by moving the exhaust exit rearwards. This version pointed outwards more than most others and when doing this it is very easy to overheat the inner shoulder of the rear tyre.

SAUBER

Initially Sauber went for the simple route of an exhaust system placed neatly in the coke bottle area, this concept is the easiest to understand.

Step 2 was to introduce the Coandă style system, like Red Buull tthey also had a body surface to allow the exhaust gasses to attach tthem selves to allowing better direction of the high energy gasses to the underside of the rear brake duct.

Step 3 was a tidied up version of step 2 with an extra cooling duct arranged around the rear suspension legs.

Gary Anderson

ENGINES 2012

Talking about SUSPENSIONS

The various teams' technicians designed the suspensions of the 2012 cars in relation to indications that emerged during the previous season on the characteristics and performance of their Pirelli tyres.
Given the objective of creating more interesting and lively Grands Prix – an objective achieved with tyres of reduced endurance capability – suspensions did not have to be especially aggressive on the covers to safeguard their yield during races, but they did have anyway to ensure grip during qualifying.
Naturally, the aerodynamic efficiency of the car remains the element that conditioned the technical choice on suspension typology and geometry, but during the season more than one team intervened with corrections – some of them substantial – which confirmed that adequate geometries for the tyres produce better performance in both qualifying and racing.
The most significant new development was, without doubt, Ferrari's front suspension, the only one with pull rod.
The reason for this choice was the chance to lower the suspension elements in the lower area of the monocoque; so rocker arm, torsion and roll bars plus dampers, with the appreciable benefits in terms of a reduction in the car's centre of gravity and the moment of polar inertia.

This suspension geometry enabled the team to move the chassis mounts' arms higher and the connection between the pull rods and rocker arms near the lower area of the chassis.
But the main reason was the need to improve air flow that hits the front part of the car; with this arm layout, it was possible to notably raise the lower plane of the monocoque and, therefore, influence the aerodynamic flow directed towards the keel, radiator air intakes and sidepods.
From the structural point of view, this technique imposed greater stress on the upper wishbone and the mounts to the chassis, which had to be suitably reinforced.
In addition, the ratio of the suspension changes considerably: at equal wheel movement, the rotation of the rocker arm was much reduced compared to that which happens using the push-rod.
That is why it was necessary to recalculate the flexibility of the elastic elements and damper settings to obtain equal ground stiffness.
With push-rods, the technicians moved the steering box even further upwards, but they retained the anti-roll bar control layout, which was practically composed of two blades connected to the rocker arms via a splined plane that acted on the torsion bars.

The uniqueness was in the connection mechanism, comprising a roller linked to the torsion bar that runs inside a curved guide, connected through the blade to the bar on the other side.
When the car tends to roll, being the rotation of the rockers discordant, the two extremes pushed one against the other and create a reaction force that opposes the roll; in the vertical movement phases, the roll slides to the inside of the guide without transmitting stress to the suspension.
Modifying the length of the arc in which the roller runs, they also obtained the bump stop of the suspension's vertical movement.
Having pointed out the benefits and the different adjustments of the set-up with pull rod solution, it should be said that the disposition of the various components was not the happiest, forcing the mechanics to make long and uncomfortable efforts when substituting or adjusting the various suspension elements.
With regard to front suspensions, all the other teams were loyal to the push-rod system, confirming and refining the constructional philosophy and geometry of the previous season.
McLaren modified the position of its steering box, which was moved higher. Meanwhile, at Lotus it was the anti-roll bar – the kind operated by tie rods connected to the rocker arm

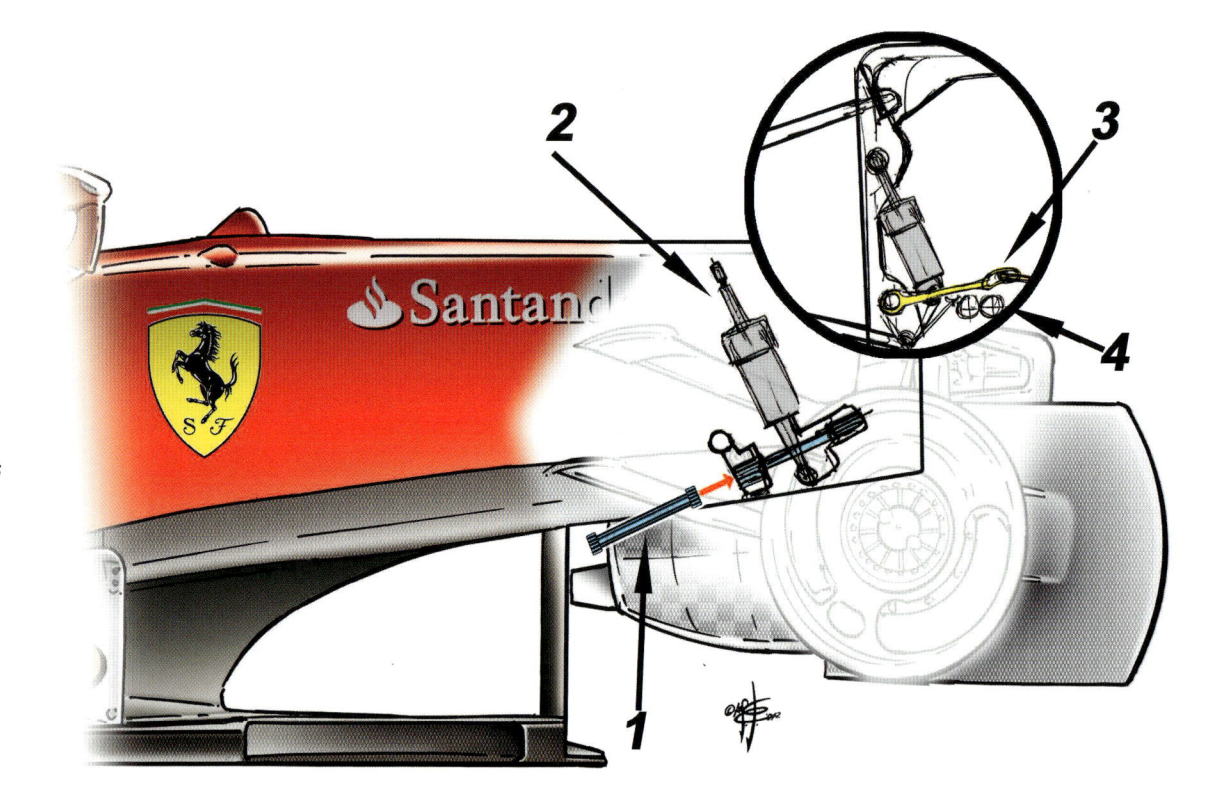

This rapid drawing shows the layout of the Ferrari front suspension.
1) torsion bar,
2) inclined damper,
3) anti-roll bar,
4) brake pump

– that found its housing outside the chassis but in a higher position, aligned with the front upper arm mount.

The steering box, as always outside the chassis and housed in a cavity, was no longer aligned with the lower arm, but raised.

The rear suspension layout universally adopted was pull rod, clearly inspired by Red Bull, which further developed and modified the position of a number of elements.

The lower wishbone remained at the height of the wheel centre, but the drive shafts, toe-in link and rear arm were closed in one single shell with clear aerodynamic ambitions.

The drive shafts' rotation generates an upward push – even if modest – so, closing it together with other suspension elements in a profile suitably shaped, the possibility of aerodynamic disturbance is reduced in a zone which is extremely critical, like that near the diffuser.

The technicians also worked on the geometry in the GP of Valencia, moving the mounting point on the upper wishbone's upright, which had its effect on the camber change and the height of the rear suspension's roll centre.

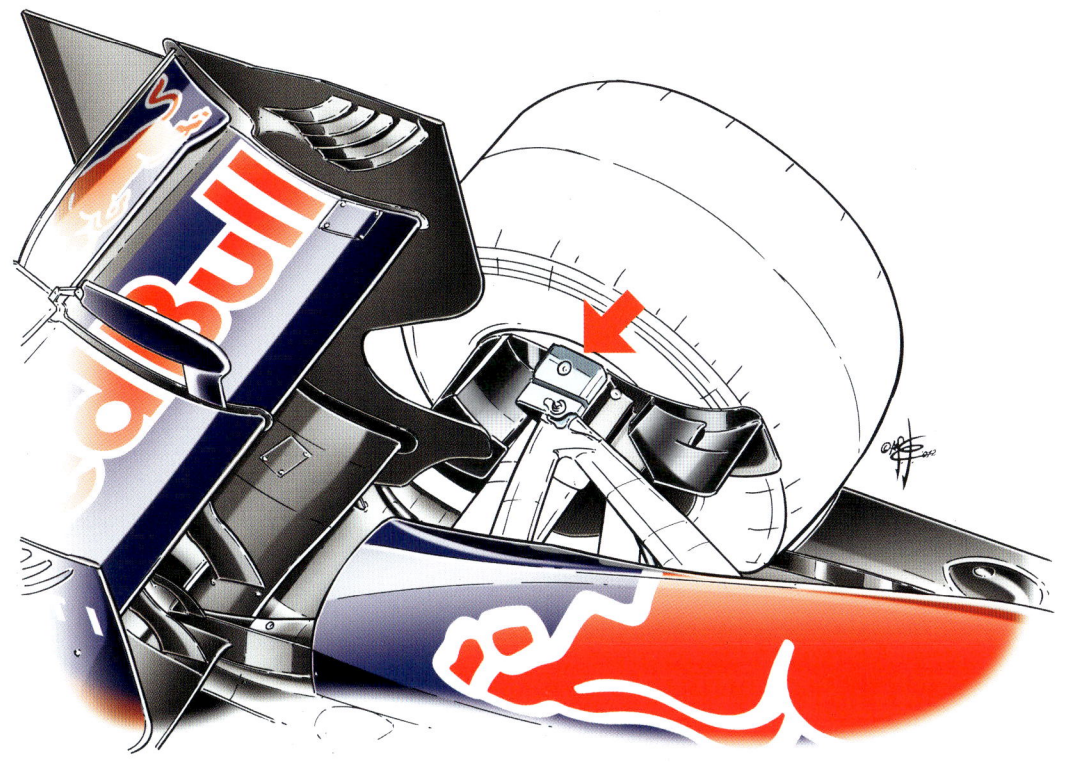

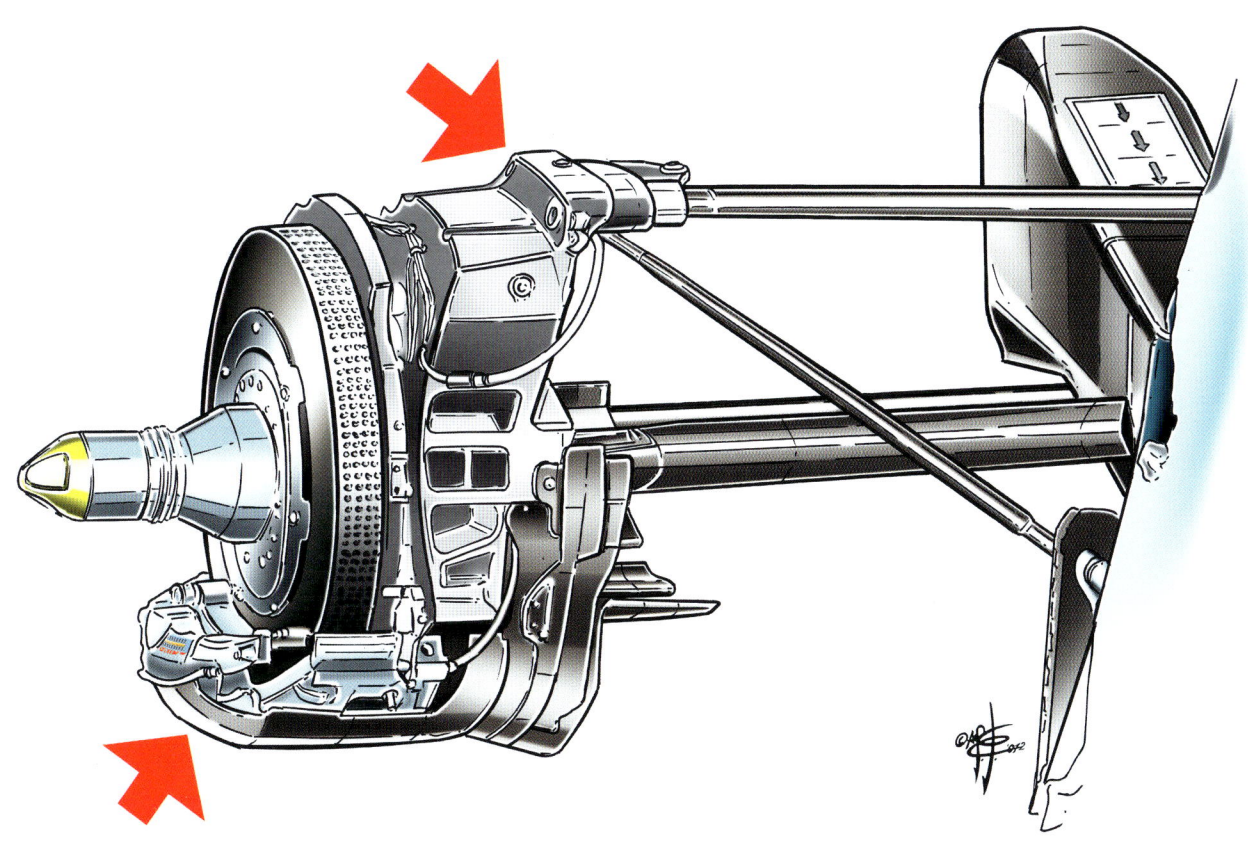

Talking about **SUSPENSIONS** **41**

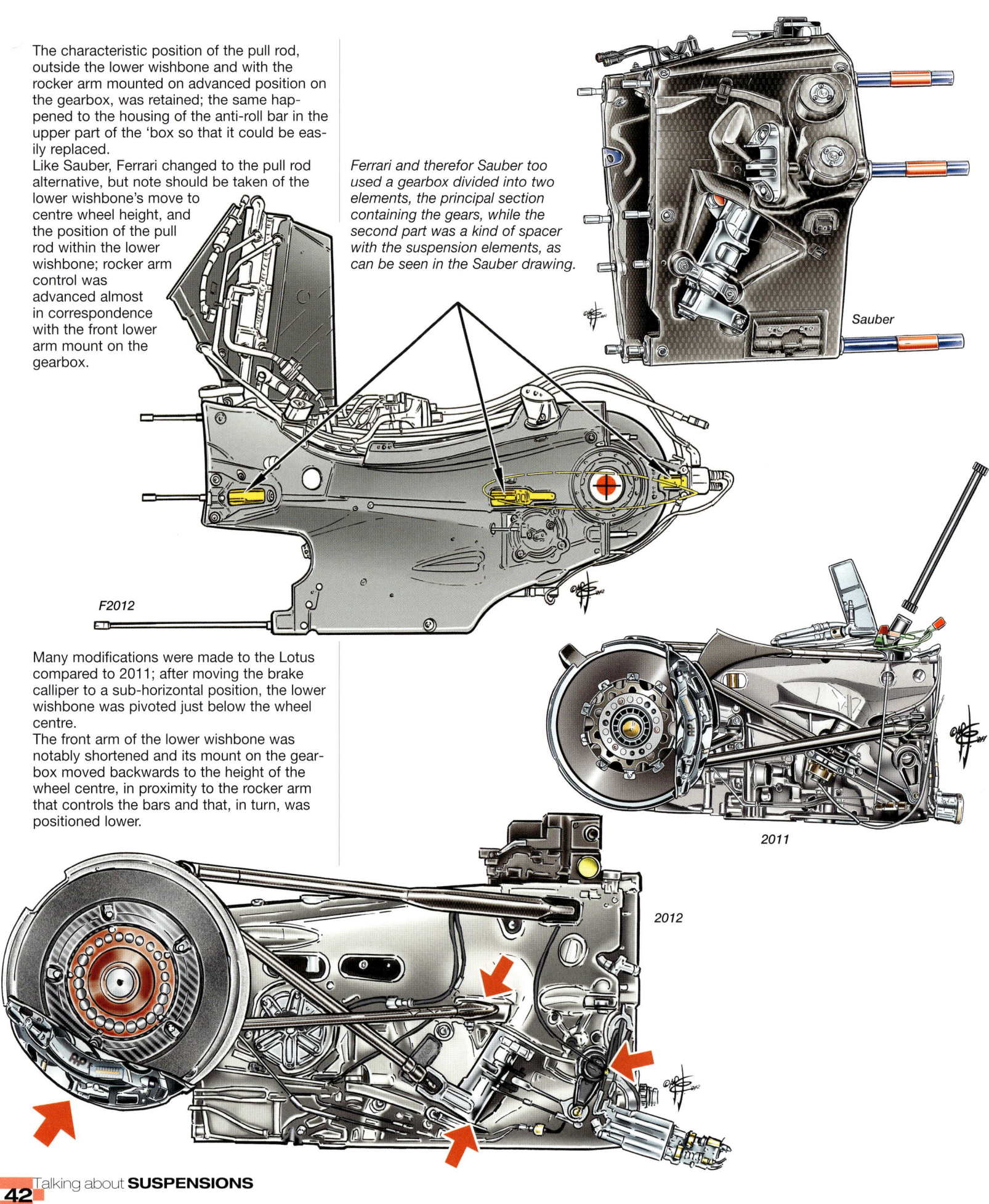

The characteristic position of the pull rod, outside the lower wishbone and with the rocker arm mounted on advanced position on the gearbox, was retained; the same happened to the housing of the anti-roll bar in the upper part of the 'box so that it could be easily replaced.
Like Sauber, Ferrari changed to the pull rod alternative, but note should be taken of the lower wishbone's move to centre wheel height, and the position of the pull rod within the lower wishbone; rocker arm control was advanced almost in correspondence with the front lower arm mount on the gearbox.

Ferrari and therefor Sauber too used a gearbox divided into two elements, the principal section containing the gears, while the second part was a kind of spacer with the suspension elements, as can be seen in the Sauber drawing.

Sauber

F2012

Many modifications were made to the Lotus compared to 2011; after moving the brake calliper to a sub-horizontal position, the lower wishbone was pivoted just below the wheel centre.
The front arm of the lower wishbone was notably shortened and its mount on the gearbox moved backwards to the height of the wheel centre, in proximity to the rocker arm that controls the bars and that, in turn, was positioned lower.

2011

2012

Talking about **SUSPENSIONS**

42

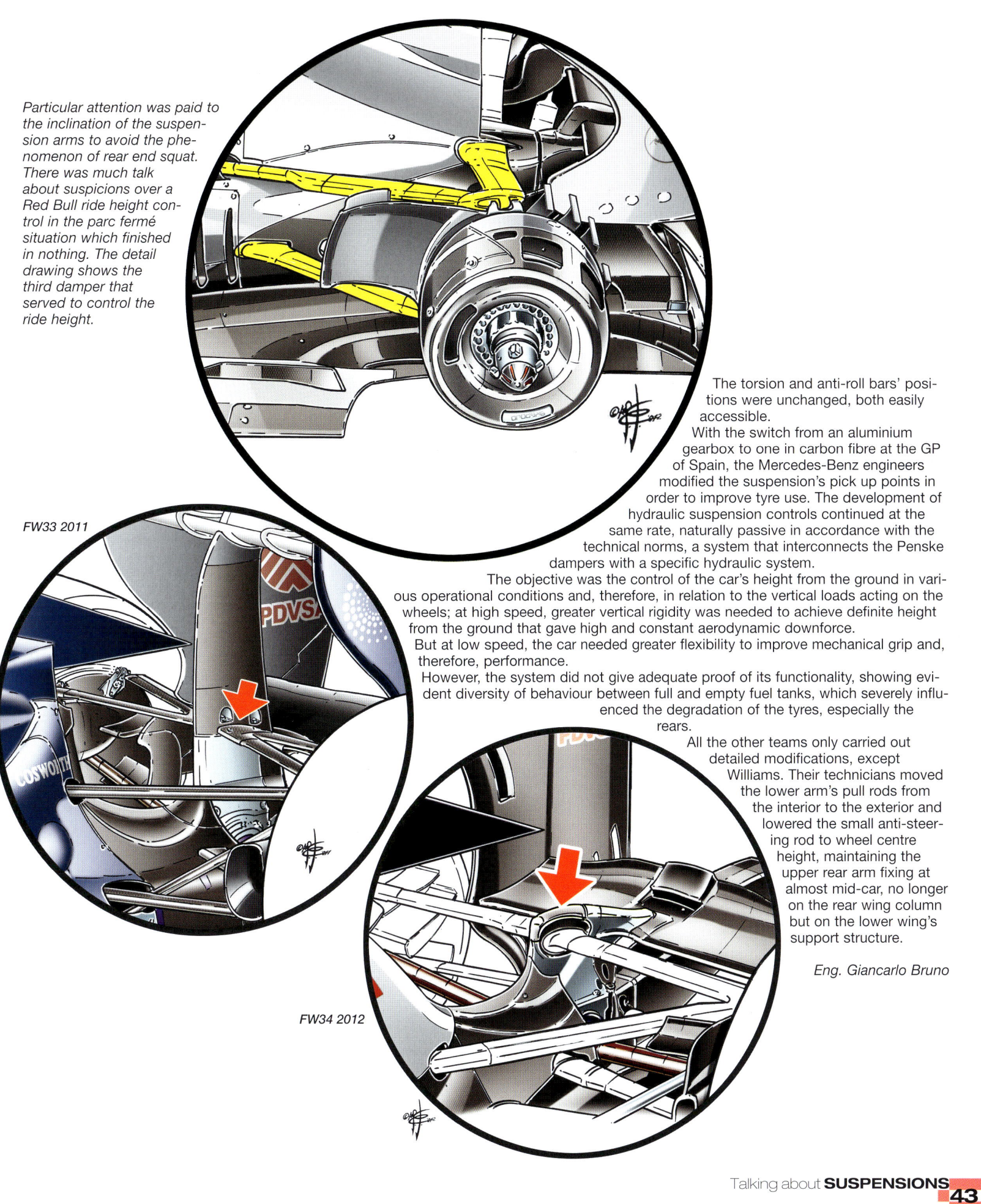

Particular attention was paid to the inclination of the suspension arms to avoid the phenomenon of rear end squat. There was much talk about suspicions over a Red Bull ride height control in the parc fermé situation which finished in nothing. The detail drawing shows the third damper that served to control the ride height.

FW33 2011

The torsion and anti-roll bars' positions were unchanged, both easily accessible.

With the switch from an aluminium gearbox to one in carbon fibre at the GP of Spain, the Mercedes-Benz engineers modified the suspension's pick up points in order to improve tyre use. The development of hydraulic suspension controls continued at the same rate, naturally passive in accordance with the technical norms, a system that interconnects the Penske dampers with a specific hydraulic system.

The objective was the control of the car's height from the ground in various operational conditions and, therefore, in relation to the vertical loads acting on the wheels; at high speed, greater vertical rigidity was needed to achieve definite height from the ground that gave high and constant aerodynamic downforce.

But at low speed, the car needed greater flexibility to improve mechanical grip and, therefore, performance.

However, the system did not give adequate proof of its functionality, showing evident diversity of behaviour between full and empty fuel tanks, which severely influenced the degradation of the tyres, especially the rears.

All the other teams only carried out detailed modifications, except Williams. Their technicians moved the lower arm's pull rods from the interior to the exterior and lowered the small anti-steering rod to wheel centre height, maintaining the upper rear arm fixing at almost mid-car, no longer on the rear wing column but on the lower wing's support structure.

Eng. Giancarlo Bruno

FW34 2012

Talking about **SUSPENSIONS** **43**

RED BULL

CONSTRUCTORS' CLASSIFICATION			
	2011	2012	
Position	1°	1°	=
Points	650	450	-200▼

Winning both 2012 championships shouldn't lead us to drawing the wrong conclusions. Red Bull didn't dominate the season with the RB9 as they did with its predecessor in 2011, even if it was the year's best car. It struggled more than once.
In this case, the statistics paint a precise picture of the situation: just consider that in 2011 the RB8 won 12 Grands Prix – Sebastian Vettel 11 of them – while in 2012 they "only" won seven, five by Vettel.
The difference in pole positions was even more marked: no fewer than 18 in 2011 against "just" eight in 2012 (six to Vettel).
The RB9 was also conceived using the 2009 car as a basis, as was the case with the RB8.
Two fundamental aspects influenced the yield of the RB9: the abolition of hot blow with additional limitations on the position of the exhausts to limit aerodynamic advantages for the diffusers, and the greater severity of scrutineering on the flexibility of the front wing.
Two areas that were Red Bull's strong points in 2011.
So it was logical that the penalisation would be deeply felt in relation to the competition, which had only achieved a lesser level of global efficiency.
In addition, Adrian Newey based the RB9 project on an astute interpretation of FIA's limitations on the positioning of the exhausts in relation to the rear axle. In practice, he circumvented the obstacle of the need for greater distance between the exhausts exits and the diffusers by designing sophisticated brake air intakes, which once again involved blow in the low area inside the rear wheels.
That technique, which was similar to Lotus's, was rejected by the Federation, which forced Newey to redesign the whole rear end of the car.
From that came the experimental phase, which saw Red Bull field very different exhaust exits during the early part of the season, even to the point of there being two different, completely opposed configurations in their garage at the GP of China. Vettel's RB9 had the exhaust position seen during testing, which ensured less downforce but greater stability; Webber had the latest version first used in Malaysia.
Black balling the "extreme" exhaust system on the RB9 didn't diminish the level of interest in the car, which embodied three new developments from its debut: the vent near the step

Red Bull RB7
2011

Red Bull RB8
Launch

Red Bull RB8
Melbourne

Red Bull RB8
Valencia

Red Bull RB8
Austin

RED BULL

(baptised the letterbox), the wide wing plane in the rear suspension that faired the driveshafts for the first time in recent years and the hot air blow towards the outside of the wheel through holes in the hub.

The first, which was most evident, was masked as an air conveyor in the cockpit, but it could channel air to cool the part of the electronic management system down low at the start of the sidepods through ducts in the upper part of the chassis.

The second, despite the fact that its presence was indicated by the author when the car was first unveiled, still went by unobserved until the GP of Valencia, when a new rear suspension was introduced and attention was concentrated on that area.

The fact is that, taking the regulation literally, the driveshaft fairing should have been prohibited, but Newey had the rear suspension designed in such a way that the lower wishbone and the toe-in arm were at the same level, near the driveshaft.

So the summation of the two elements' fairing – remember that its chord may be 3.5 times the thickness of the arm – naturally included the driveshafts. In practice, Newey brought back his original idea that he had applied to the Williams FW16 in 1994.

As far as the third development was concerned, despite the fact that it was fitted to the car from the first race and there for everyone to see as it was designed for the second GP of the season, its presence wasn't considered illegal until the seventh GP in Canada. An irreproachable decision in full respect of the regulation, seeing that, all in all, when the hubs rotated, this blow became a mobile aerodynamic device to all effects and purposes. But surprisingly, it wasn't outlawed during the project presentation period or even at the first race of the season, but after passing scrutineering no fewer than six times. On the brakes front, the RB9 was the only car with its front callipers fitted horizontally, down low in relation to the hub. Red Bull also used Brembo brake discs of slightly reduced diameter (as discussed in the Brakes chapter) to improve the hot air blow effect in connection with the car's aerodynamics. Immediately after the first pre-championship test session, Newey attempted to make up lost ground due to the rejection of his original project by renewing the whole RB9 rear end and achieving as a result sidepods that descended without the classic Coca-Cola bottle profile introduced by Sauber.

That was the form in which the RB9 competed in the first Grands Prix of the season.

In that way, too, Newey was still able to bring in something new, a sort of double bottom/blow in the lower part of the exhaust exit zone, which didn't work right away (hence Vettel's choice in China). But later, after continuous evolution (the most determinate in Valencia), it became one of the strong points of the RB9's set-up. The development of the car during the 2012 season took place in four fundamental stages: Bahrain (closed low blow); Spain (low blow reopened, but modified); Valencia and Singapore with the last two being a major, important evolutionary steps, which are worth closer examination.

The new version of the RB9 was fielded at Valencia, with all the elements of its rear suspension substantially modified and completely renewed sidepods.

Lastly, in Singapore a new nose was introduced with a pouch in the lower area and with greater flexibility – but within the limits of the regulations.

Most significantly of all, though, was the introduction of double DRS with a very simple and effective technique that notably improved the car's top speed, especially in qualifying where there is free use of the system.

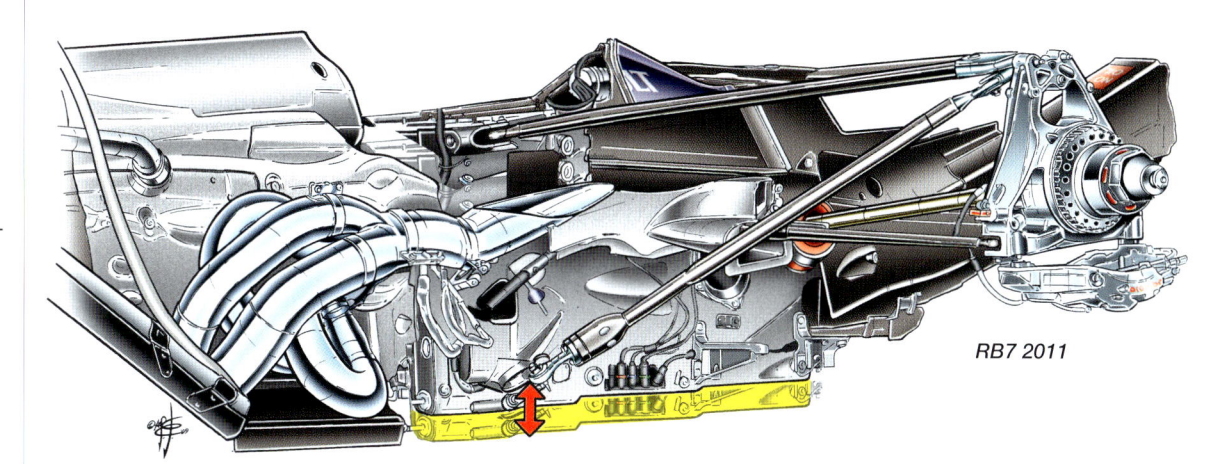

RB7 2011

GEARBOX AND KERS

The Red Bull gearbox has been completely revised each season in accordance with the demands of the aerodynamic configuration. With the dual diffuser the transmission was tall and narrow and had a kind of step in the lower section so as to create broad extractor channels either side. With the RB8 instead, the designers returned to a configuration similar to that of the 2009 car, with a wider but significantly shallower gearbox to privilege the flow of air towards the rear wing. Newey retained the configuration of the Kers elements. The electric motor (1) was fitted to the front of the engine, while the split batteries (2) in the exhaust area remained. This configuration continued to suffer from reliability issues despite a network of cooling ducts (3). Highlighted at (4) is the rocker of the pull-rod system with an external damper (6), while the anti-roll bar was easily removed from the side (5). Note the alignment between the lower suspension arms (7) and the half-shafts.

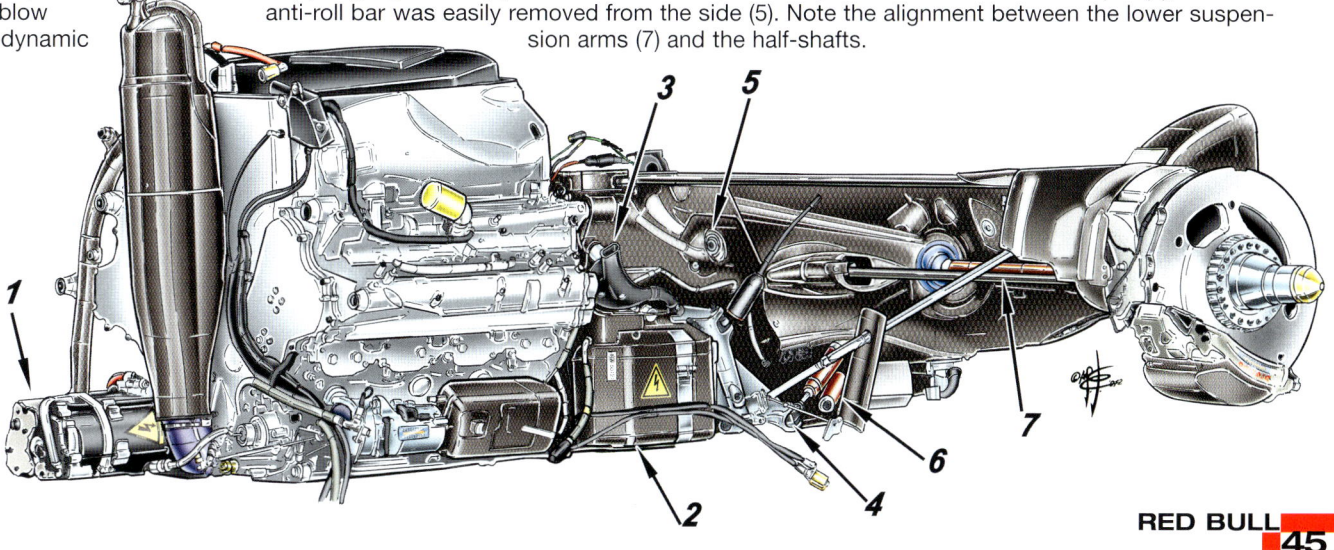

RED BULL 45

STEPPED NOSE

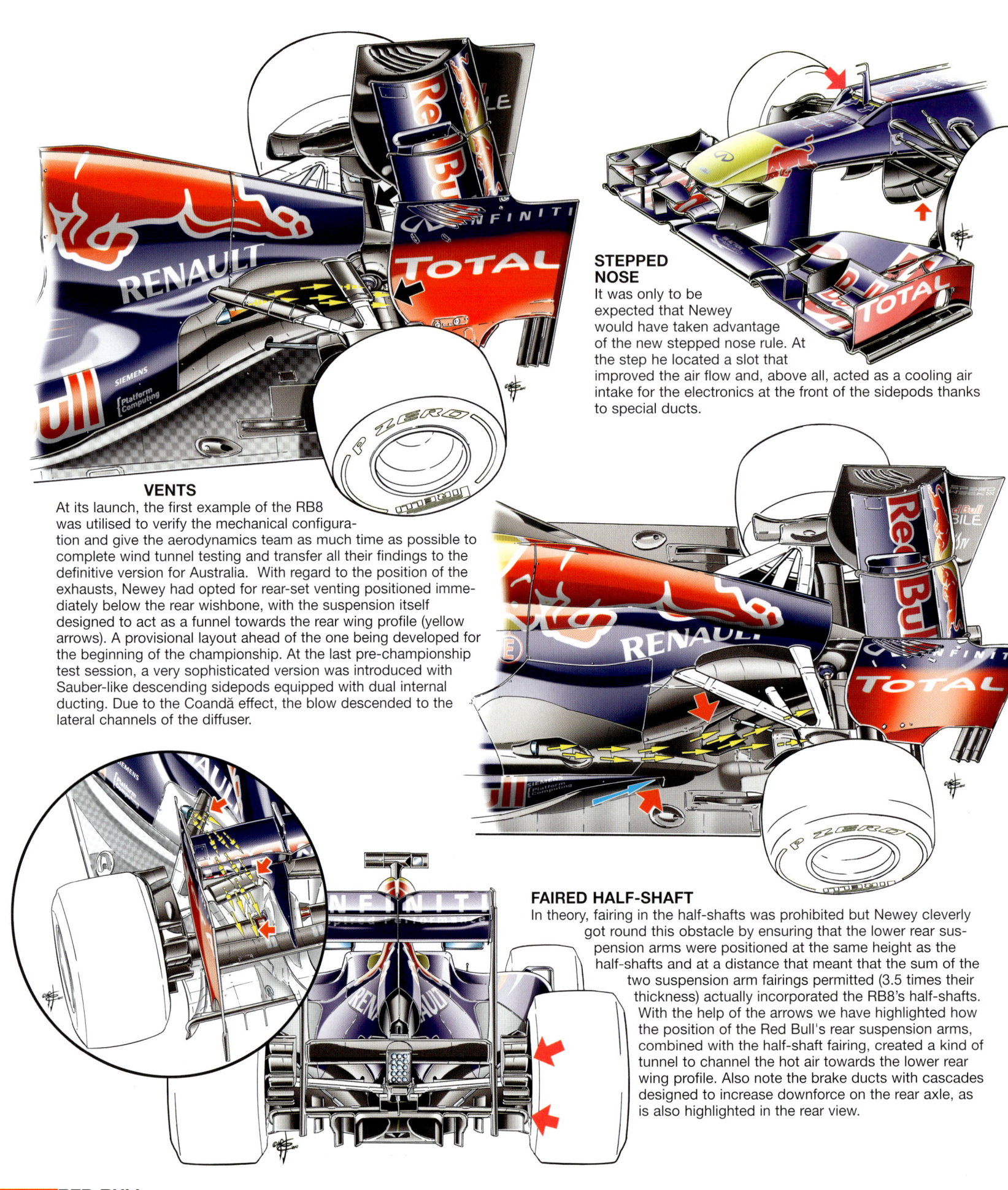

It was only to be expected that Newey would have taken advantage of the new stepped nose rule. At the step he located a slot that improved the air flow and, above all, acted as a cooling air intake for the electronics at the front of the sidepods thanks to special ducts.

VENTS

At its launch, the first example of the RB8 was utilised to verify the mechanical configuration and give the aerodynamics team as much time as possible to complete wind tunnel testing and transfer all their findings to the definitive version for Australia. With regard to the position of the exhausts, Newey had opted for rear-set venting positioned immediately below the rear wishbone, with the suspension itself designed to act as a funnel towards the rear wing profile (yellow arrows). A provisional layout ahead of the one being developed for the beginning of the championship. At the last pre-championship test session, a very sophisticated version was introduced with Sauber-like descending sidepods equipped with dual internal ducting. Due to the Coandă effect, the blow descended to the lateral channels of the diffuser.

FAIRED HALF-SHAFT

In theory, fairing in the half-shafts was prohibited but Newey cleverly got round this obstacle by ensuring that the lower rear suspension arms were positioned at the same height as the half-shafts and at a distance that meant that the sum of the two suspension arm fairings permitted (3.5 times their thickness) actually incorporated the RB8's half-shafts. With the help of the arrows we have highlighted how the position of the Red Bull's rear suspension arms, combined with the half-shaft fairing, created a kind of tunnel to channel the hot air towards the lower rear wing profile. Also note the brake ducts with cascades designed to increase downforce on the rear axle, as is also highlighted in the rear view.

RED BULL

MELBOURNE

Despite the B version introduced in the last test session at Barcelona, for Melbourne Red Bull introduced modifications to both the exhaust area, visibly closer to that of the McLaren, and the area in front of the wheels, with two different configurations being introduced. The one in the large drawing is the one used on the Friday, with a large horizontal slot in the bottom and a vane on the leading edge to direct part of the flow to the lower zone of the lateral channels. This configuration was replaced on the Saturday with a closed concave zone, again equipped with vertical vanes to manage the flows.

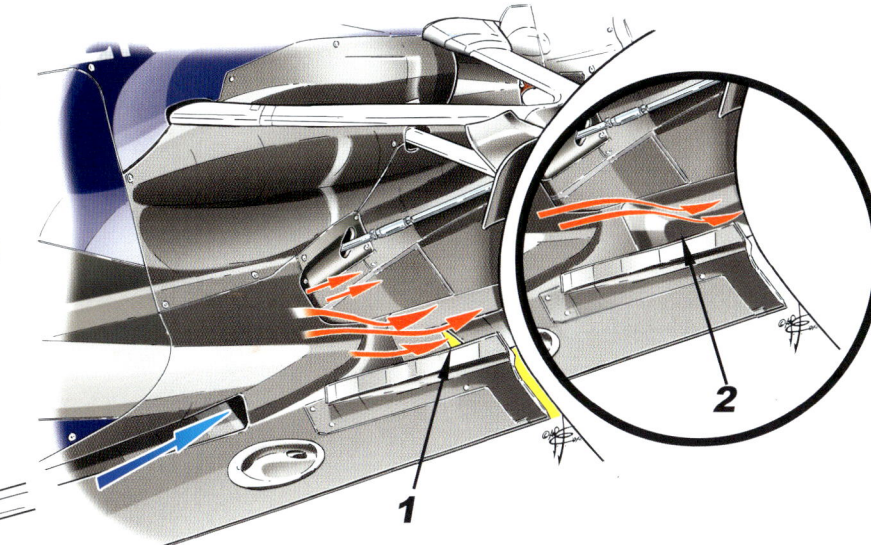

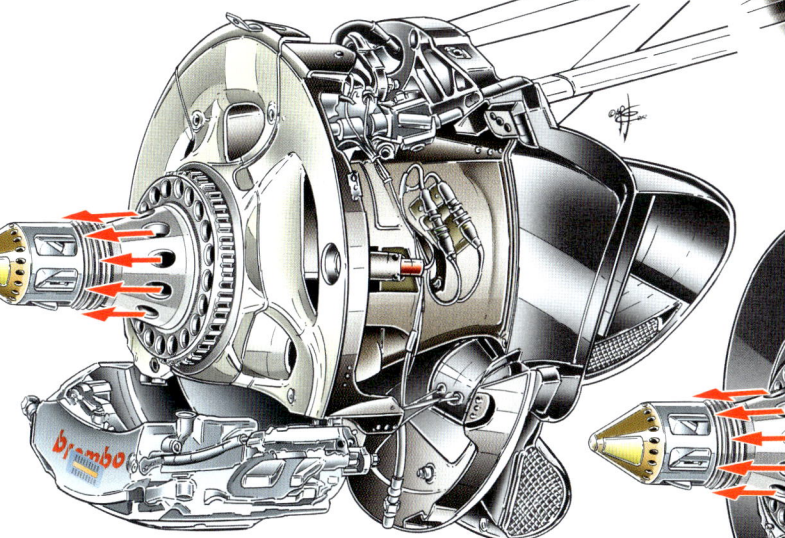

WHEEL VENTING

One of Adrian Newey's "tricks" on his RB8 was banned by the federation (being considered a mobile aerodynamic device) after having been used in no less than six races. This feature was a new air venting applied to the central part of the wheel hub that presented previously unseen holes that corresponded to others in the wheel rim designed to channel the flow of hot air (indicated by the arrows) to a well-defined area outside the front wheels.

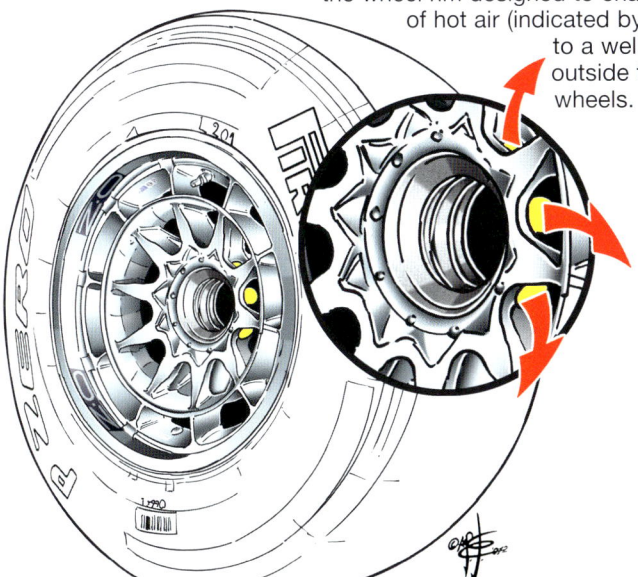

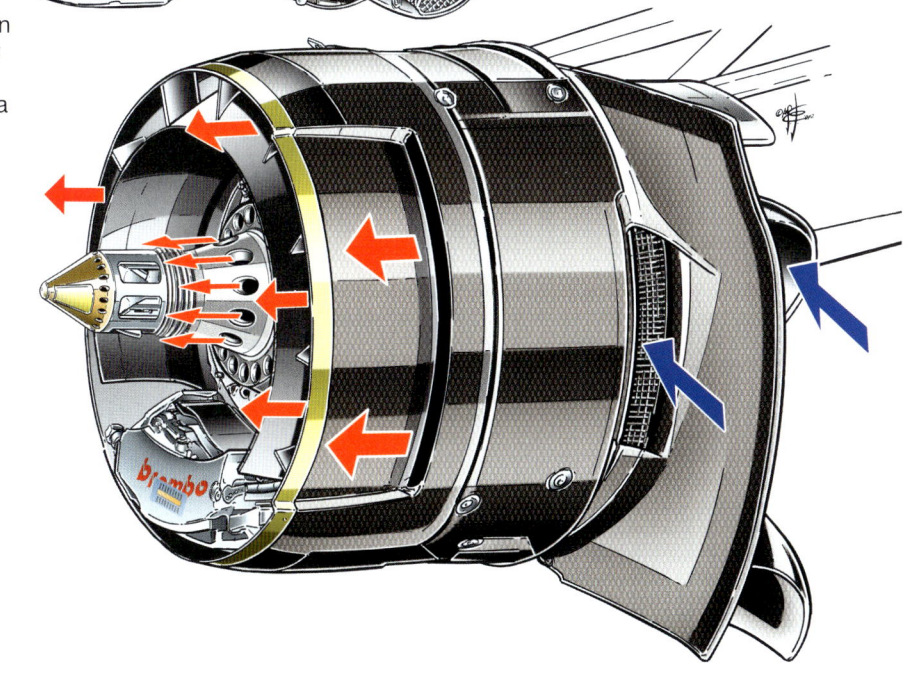

RED BULL

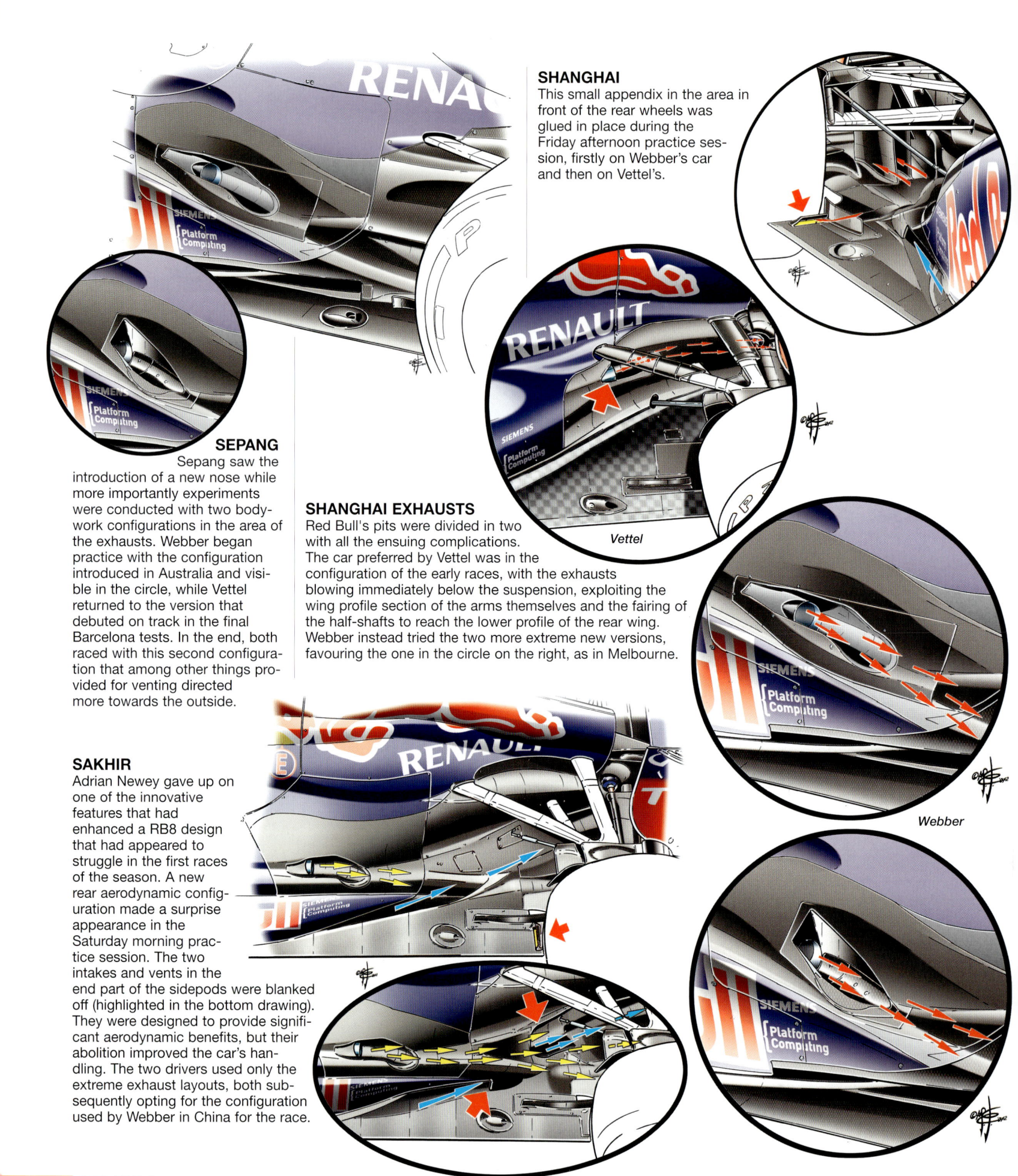

SHANGHAI
This small appendix in the area in front of the rear wheels was glued in place during the Friday afternoon practice session, firstly on Webber's car and then on Vettel's.

SEPANG
Sepang saw the introduction of a new nose while more importantly experiments were conducted with two bodywork configurations in the area of the exhausts. Webber began practice with the configuration introduced in Australia and visible in the circle, while Vettel returned to the version that debuted on track in the final Barcelona tests. In the end, both raced with this second configuration that among other things provided for venting directed more towards the outside.

SHANGHAI EXHAUSTS
Red Bull's pits were divided in two with all the ensuing complications. The car preferred by Vettel was in the configuration of the early races, with the exhausts blowing immediately below the suspension, exploiting the wing profile section of the arms themselves and the fairing of the half-shafts to reach the lower profile of the rear wing. Webber instead tried the two more extreme new versions, favouring the one in the circle on the right, as in Melbourne.

Vettel

Webber

SAKHIR
Adrian Newey gave up on one of the innovative features that had enhanced a RB8 design that had appeared to struggle in the first races of the season. A new rear aerodynamic configuration made a surprise appearance in the Saturday morning practice session. The two intakes and vents in the end part of the sidepods were blanked off (highlighted in the bottom drawing). They were designed to provide significant aerodynamic benefits, but their abolition improved the car's handling. The two drivers used only the extreme exhaust layouts, both subsequently opting for the configuration used by Webber in China for the race.

RED BULL
48

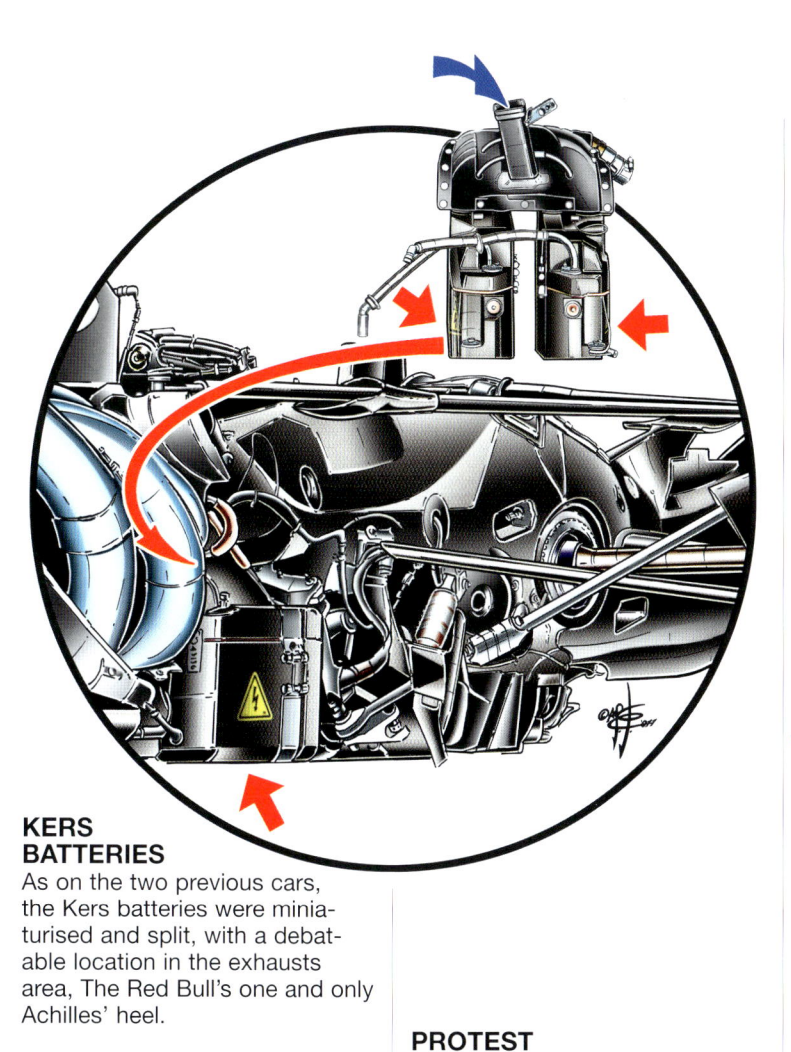

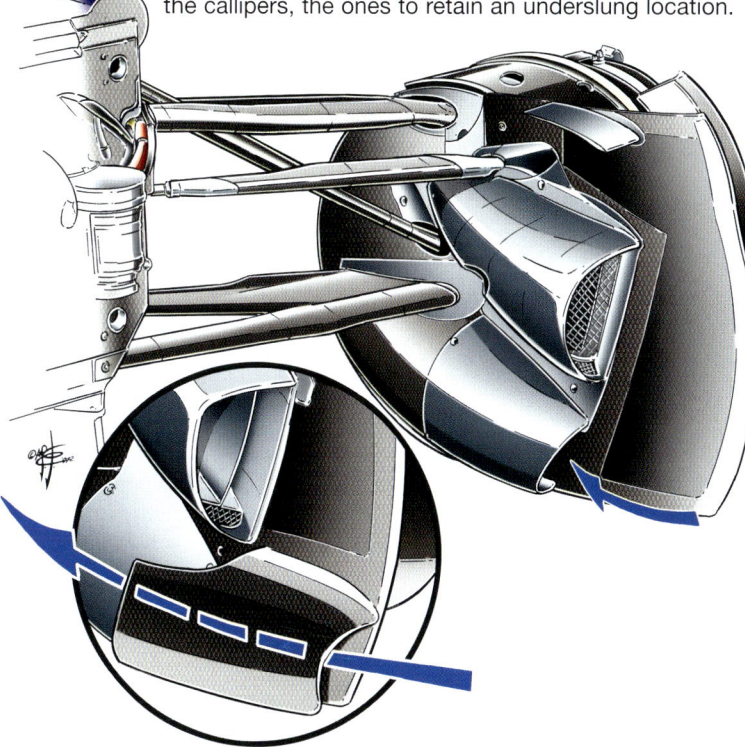

KERS BATTERIES

As on the two previous cars, the Kers batteries were miniaturised and split, with a debatable location in the exhausts area, The Red Bull's one and only Achilles' heel.

MONACO

In order to improve brake cooling, the low mounted vane (in the circle), which also had aerodynamic functions, was replaced by a second trumpet intake designed to improve cooling of the callipers, the ones to retain an underslung location.

PROTEST

Following the race in Monaco, Red Bull was urged to modify the area in front of the rear wheels before the next GP in Canada. The regulations in fact stated that there could be apertures but not circumscribed holes, while the perimeter of the hole on the RB8 was closed, without the presenting the required interruption of at least 1 mm.

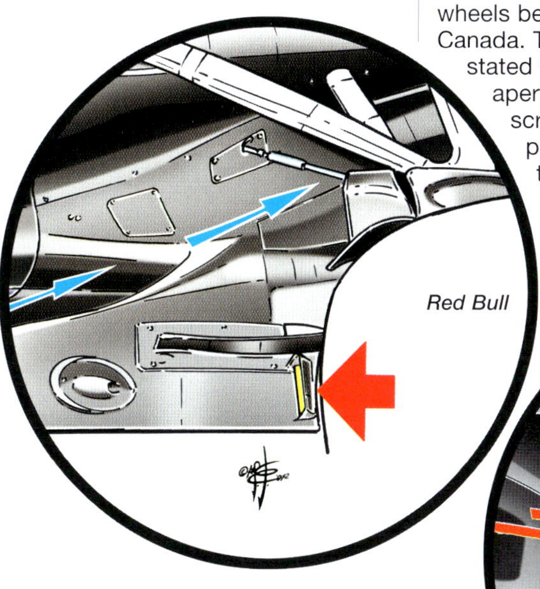

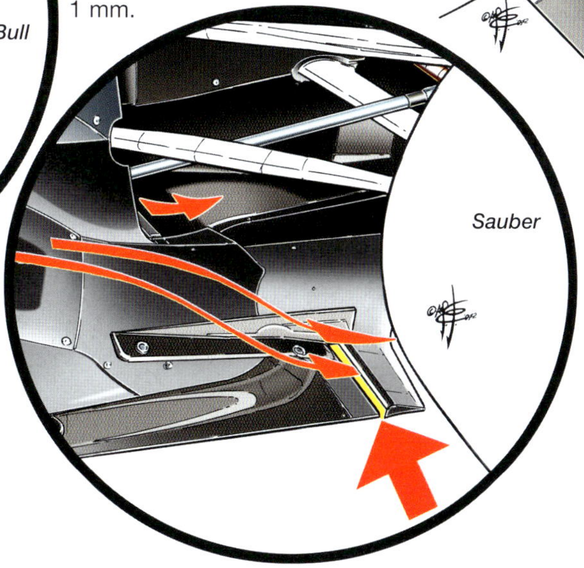

Red Bull

Sauber

MONTREAL

A new stepped bottom for the Red Bulls, without the hole contested at Monaco that lacked the slot interrupting the closed perimeter. The design of the extractor profile was virtually unchanged.

RED BULL 49

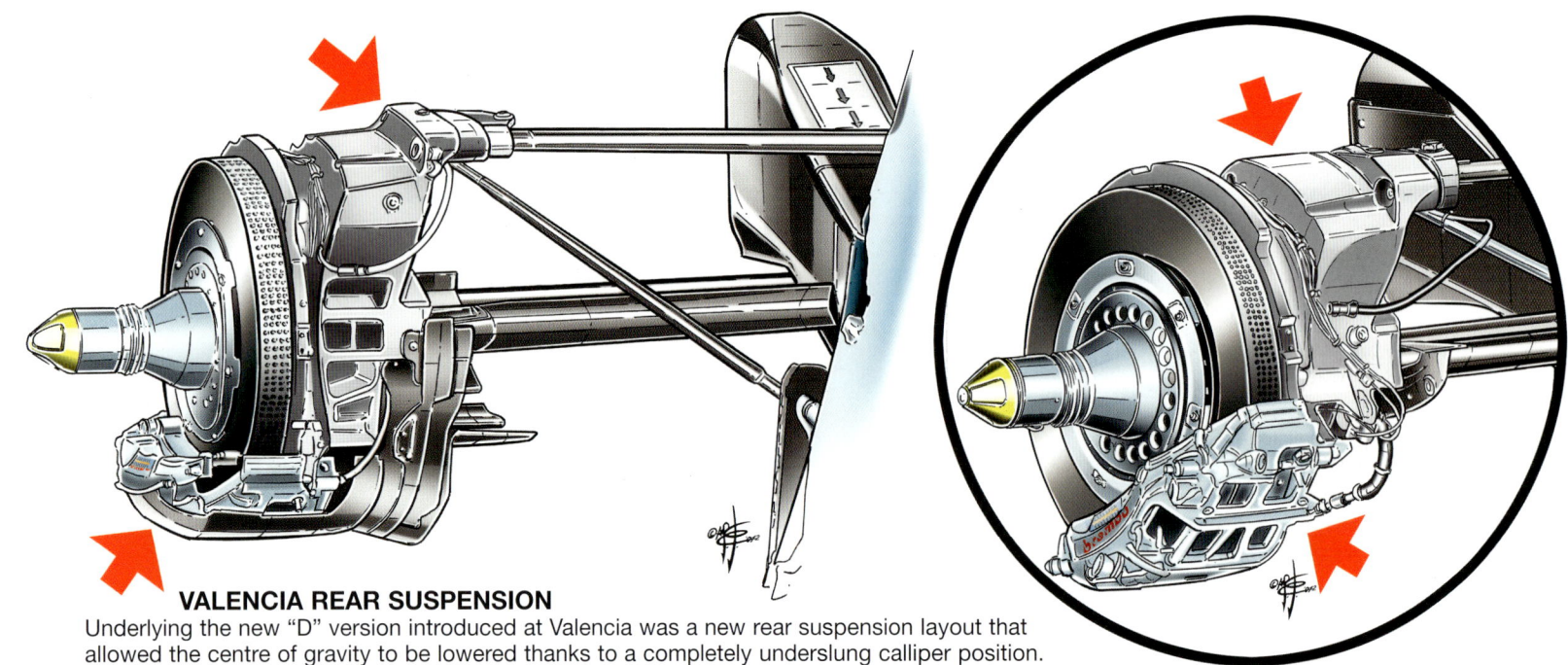

VALENCIA REAR SUSPENSION

Underlying the new "D" version introduced at Valencia was a new rear suspension layout that allowed the centre of gravity to be lowered thanks to a completely underslung calliper position. The hub carrier was of course new, with a raised upper wishbone mount with respect to the base version and therefore presenting new suspension geometries. This was designed to better conserve the rear tyres and provide for more extreme aerodynamics. Note how the lower wishbone and half-shaft are on the same level and are faired with a large wing profile, as seen in the rear view drawing.

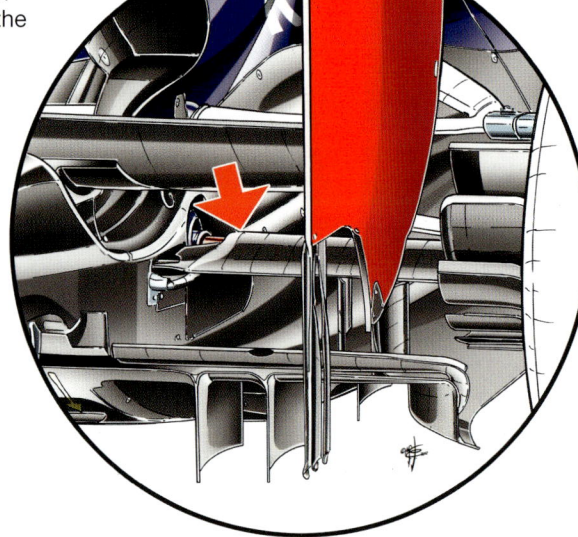

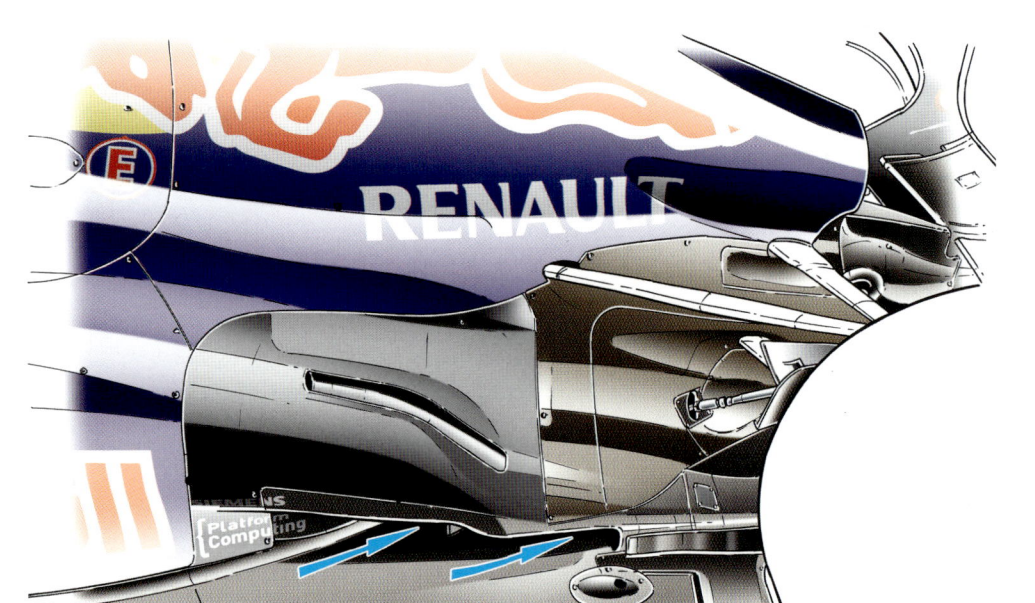

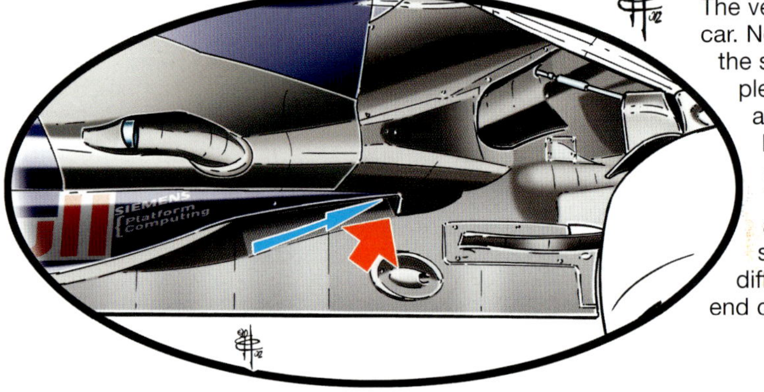

VALENCIA SIDEPODS

The version of the RB8 presented at Valencia was practically a new car. Newey reintroduced the venting that passed inside the end part of the sidepod in an even more sophisticated layout and with completely redesigned aerodynamics. In this configuration there is also a certain similarity to the forms of the "original" Sauber with the bodywork widening rather than narrowing Coke-bottle fashion and almost reaching the level of the raised plane.
The intake mouth of the internal channel was notably enlarged and then split into two separate channels: the first exited via the starter hole and the second vented around the central area of the diffuser. The hot air venting was also different being almost at the end of the gearbox rather than in the area in front of the half-shaft.

RED BULL

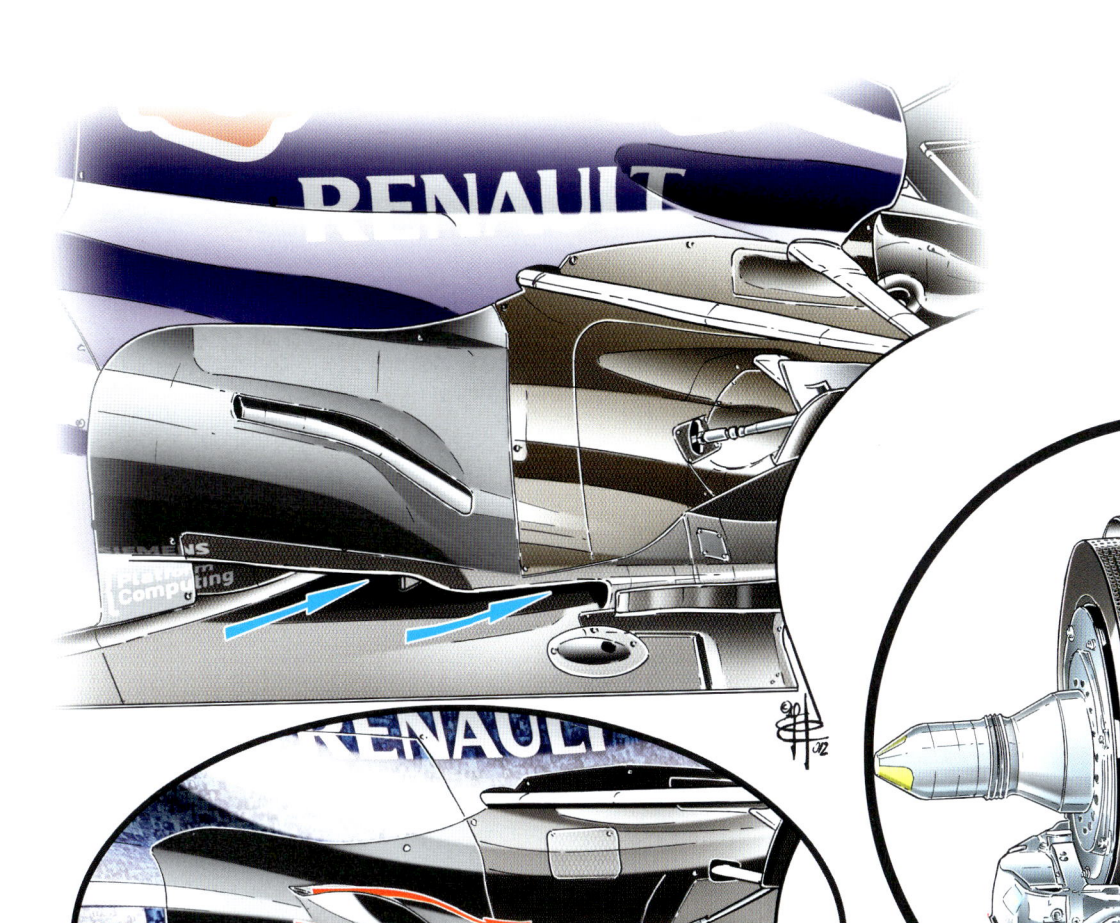

SINGAPORE

Red Bull and Ferrari used the new Brembo brake discs with no less than five aligned holes for a total of around 1,000 in the whole circumference. The CER material that replaced the earlier CCR was also new and permitted end of race wear to be reduced from 4 mm to just 1 mm.
An extremely important detail on what is considered to be the season's toughest circuit for the braking systems.

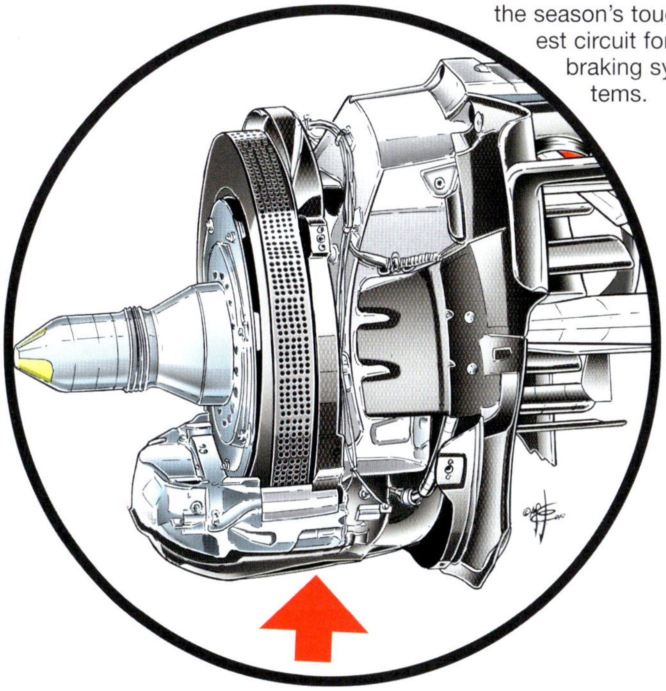

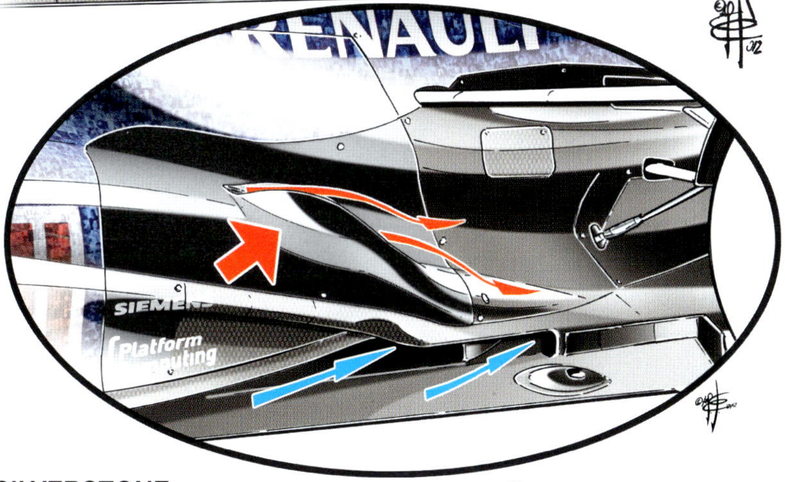

SILVERSTONE

Following the revolution introduced at Valencia, there was a minor correction in the form of a kind of hump in the area of the exhaust vents that improved the extraction of the hot air in terms of both the exhausts and the Coandă effect. Notable efforts were made to install the mechanical organs under the skin of the new sidepods that were lower and more cut-away with respect to the version used through to Canada.

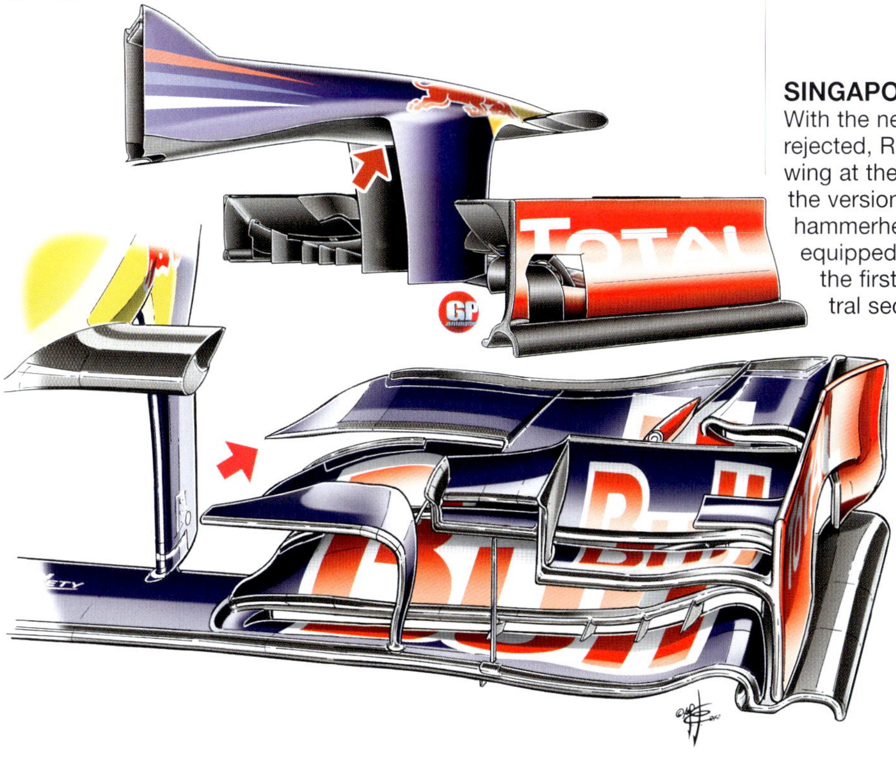

SINGAPORE

With the new longer nose being rejected, Red Bull adopted a new wing at the last minute based on the version of the nose with the hammerhead TV cameras (1) but equipped with new flaps, for the first time split in the central section, following the lead set some time earlier by Lotus. The rear view reveals the slight Lotus-style "marsupial" introduced on the new nose.

RED BULL

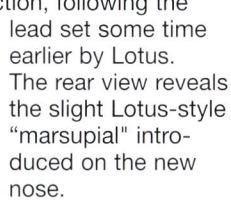

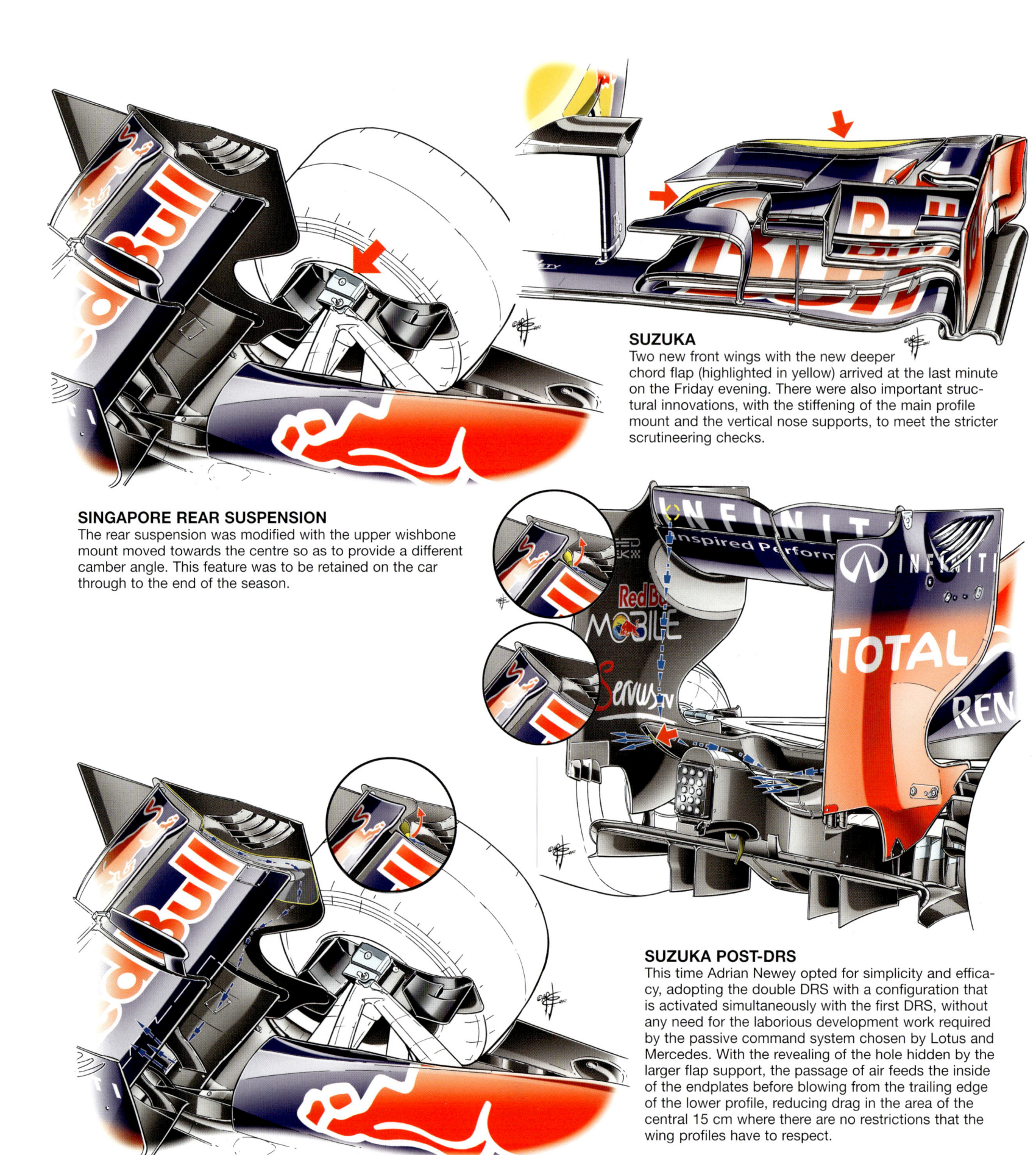

SUZUKA

Two new front wings with the new deeper chord flap (highlighted in yellow) arrived at the last minute on the Friday evening. There were also important structural innovations, with the stiffening of the main profile mount and the vertical nose supports, to meet the stricter scrutineering checks.

SINGAPORE REAR SUSPENSION

The rear suspension was modified with the upper wishbone mount moved towards the centre so as to provide a different camber angle. This feature was to be retained on the car through to the end of the season.

SUZUKA POST-DRS

This time Adrian Newey opted for simplicity and efficacy, adopting the double DRS with a configuration that is activated simultaneously with the first DRS, without any need for the laborious development work required by the passive command system chosen by Lotus and Mercedes. With the revealing of the hole hidden by the larger flap support, the passage of air feeds the inside of the endplates before blowing from the trailing edge of the lower profile, reducing drag in the area of the central 15 cm where there are no restrictions that the wing profiles have to respect.

RED BULL

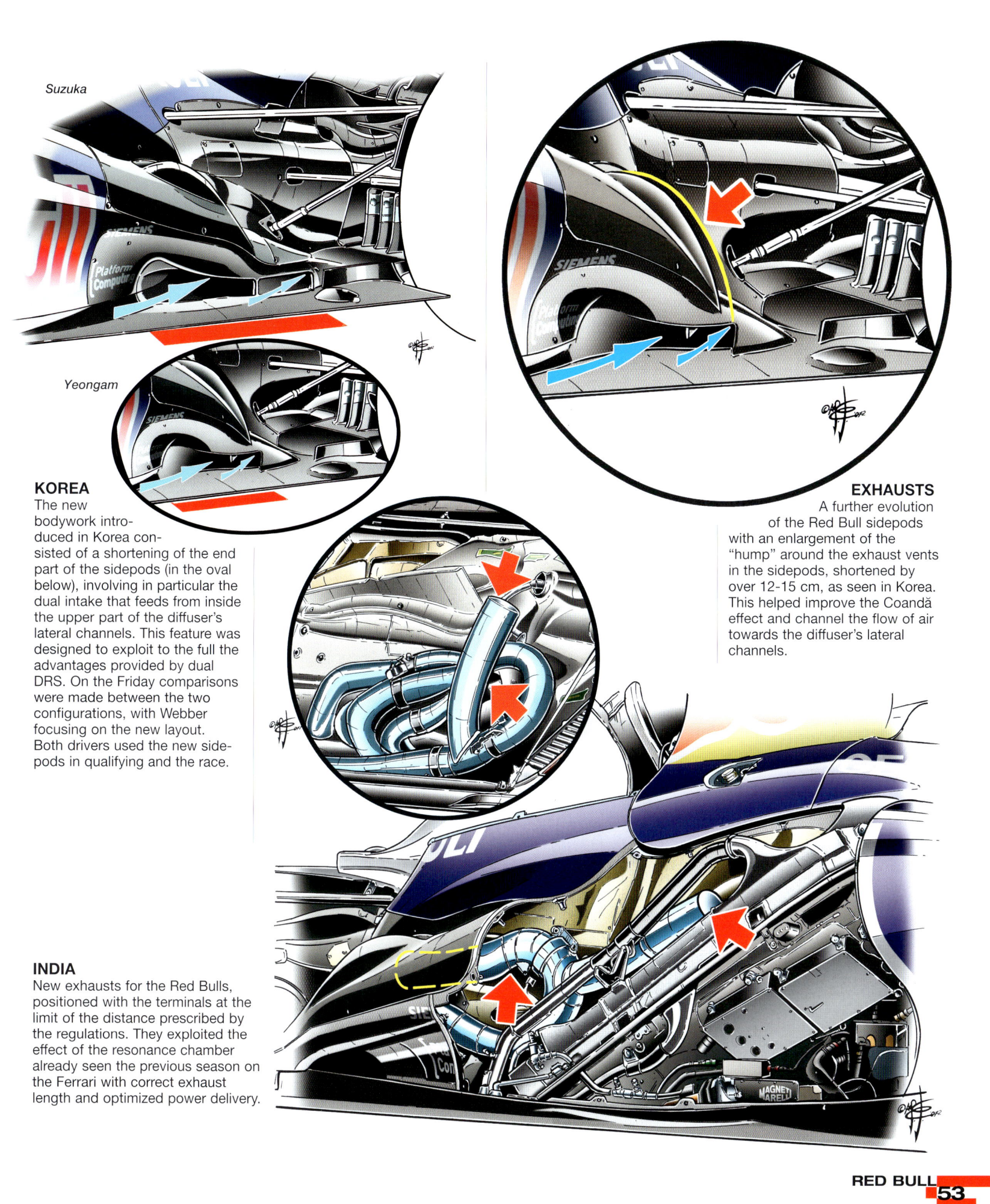

Suzuka

Yeongam

KOREA
The new bodywork introduced in Korea consisted of a shortening of the end part of the sidepods (in the oval below), involving in particular the dual intake that feeds from inside the upper part of the diffuser's lateral channels. This feature was designed to exploit to the full the advantages provided by dual DRS. On the Friday comparisons were made between the two configurations, with Webber focusing on the new layout. Both drivers used the new sidepods in qualifying and the race.

EXHAUSTS
A further evolution of the Red Bull sidepods with an enlargement of the "hump" around the exhaust vents in the sidepods, shortened by over 12-15 cm, as seen in Korea. This helped improve the Coandă effect and channel the flow of air towards the diffuser's lateral channels.

INDIA
New exhausts for the Red Bulls, positioned with the terminals at the limit of the distance prescribed by the regulations. They exploited the effect of the resonance chamber already seen the previous season on the Ferrari with correct exhaust length and optimized power delivery.

RED BULL 53

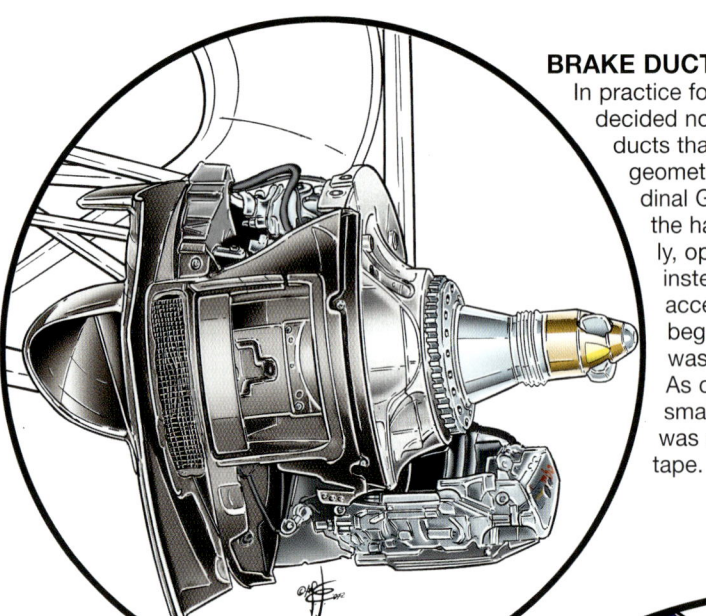

BRAKE DUCTS VARIABLE GEOMETRY

In practice for the GP of India, Red Bull decided not to use these new brake ducts that permitted variable geometry regulated by longitudinal G forces. Under braking, the hatch depressed slightly, opening a slot that instead closed under acceleration. Testing began at Monza and was completed in Korea. As can be seen in the small photo, the detail was carefully masked with tape.

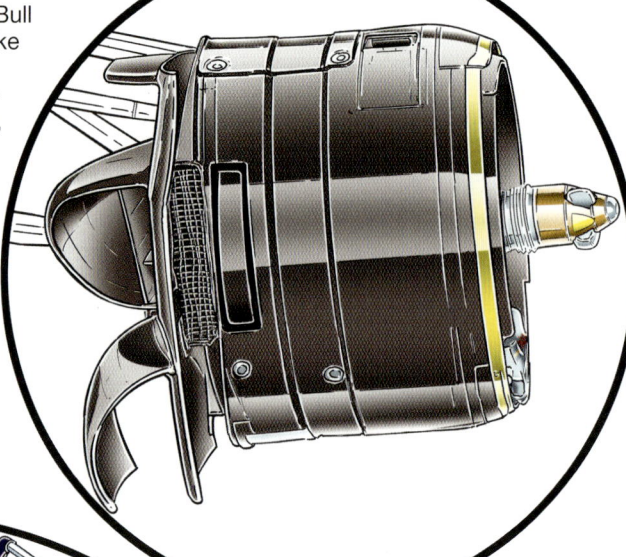

AUSTIN

An all-new rear wing: different slots at the top, different endplate widths to enhance the dual DRS and, above all, significant modifications to the lower part with a curvilinear configuration and a Ferrari-style multiplication of the fringes that reversed the previous trend which had seen them all but disappear.

3RD DAMPER

The third transverse damper fitted to the Red Bulls' front suspension might not have been a novelty but it was at the centre of dispute over this link which is actually the cabling to the CPU, as on all the other cars. Red Bull used the electronically controlled system only during unofficial practice to speed up development of the car.

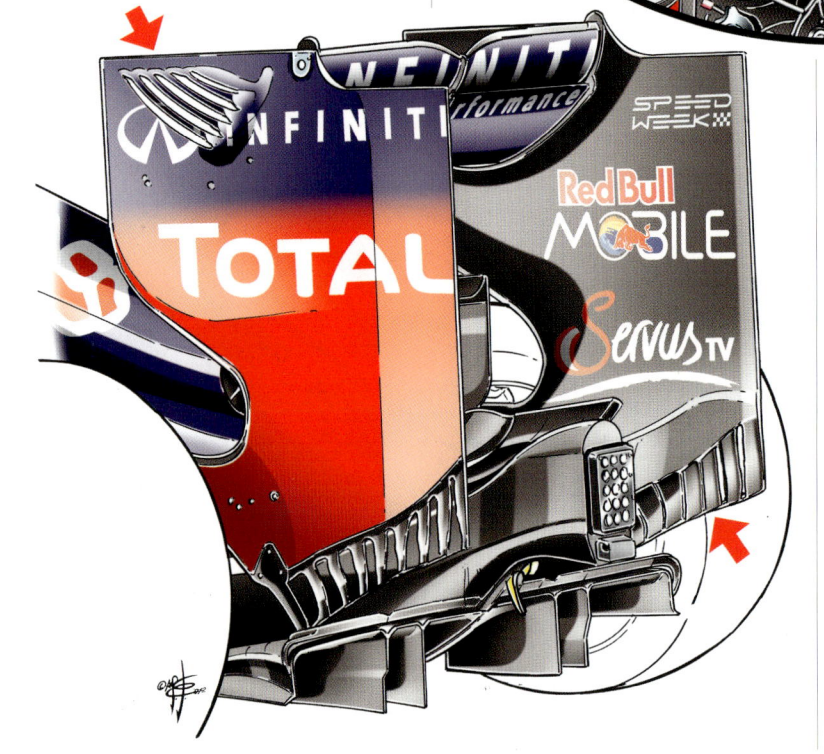

SAO PAOLO

Red Bull went into the last race in unchanged form with respect to the Austin configuration, with the front wing equipped with 3 vents in the second profile combined with the rear wing with the long fringes in the lower part of the endplates.

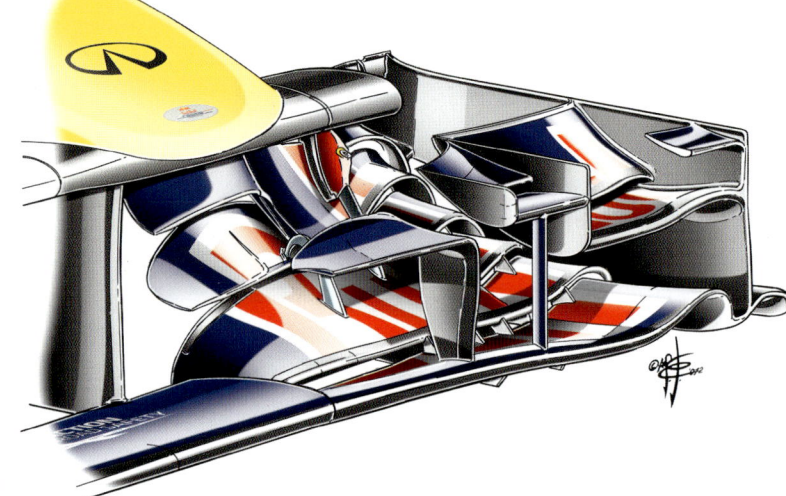

RED BULL

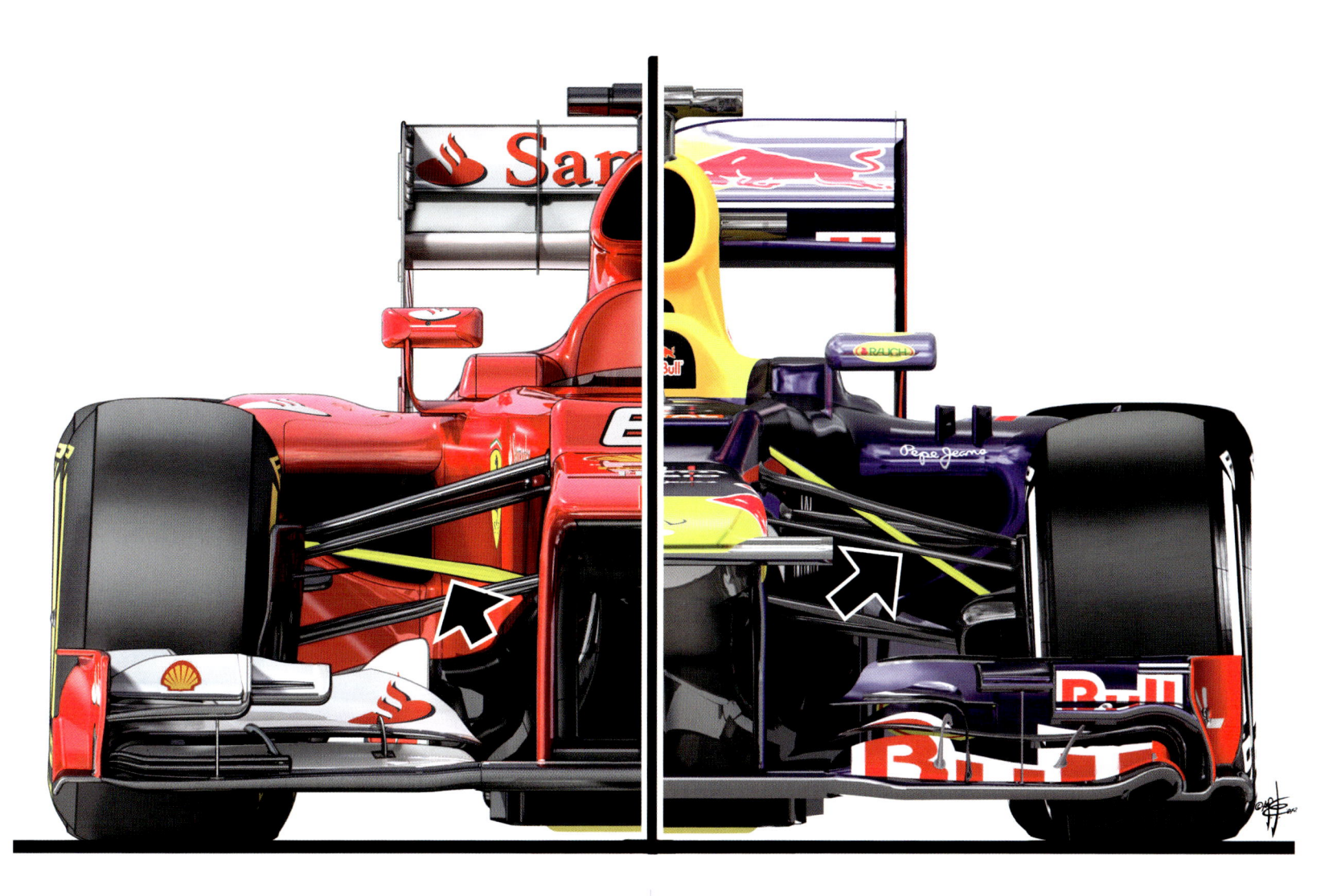

RED BULL – FERRARI COMPARISON
The two rivals compared: in the front view, highlighted in yellow, the main difference is represented by the Ferrari's pull-rod front suspension layout and the different philosophies behind the profiles in the front wing/endplates assemblies. The nose of the F2012 I more square-cut and higher and lacks the hammerhead TV cameras fitted to the RB8.
The view from above shows the shorter and square-cut nose of the F2012; the greatest differences are concentrated in the end part of the sidepods and in the exhaust blows, with the Red Bull's unusual dual internal duct (highlighted by the blue arrow).

FERRARI

CONSTRUCTORS' CLASSIFICATION			
	2011	2012	
Position	3°	2°	+1 ▲
Points	375	400	+25 ▲

Ferrari was able to battle for the world title right through to the last race of the 2012 season, despite an uphill beginning to the year with an F2012 lagging behind the opposition.
Their ability to fight is all credit to Fernando Alonso, who drove perhaps the finest season of his career, as well as to the group directed by Pat Fry, who continued the battle despite adversity. On the other hand, a running-in season was predictable, with a new working methodology imposed by the ex-McLaren technician. In part because the F2012 was a starting point compared to previous cars, its project based on extreme developments like the revival of front end pull-rod suspension for the first time in 11 years.
That layout was last seen in 2001 on a Minardi designed by Gabriele Tredozi, which was also driven by a young Fernando Alonso. It was one totally dictated by the aerodynamic need to have the best air flow quality in the zone above the front wing. There was also the opportunity of lowering the front end mass, but such high noses forced an "extreme" angle of the pull rods, the dimensions of which were notably increased for the occasion. All of this, together with the mechanics' greater operational difficulty, created a few more problems during the early part of the season.
At the car's presentation, the greatest impact was made by the shape of the nose, which was obviously stepped with the chassis on the 625 mm height limit, while on the F150 it was slightly lower but decidedly short and flush with the overhang of the wing. The shape of the car was squarer and reminded observers of the famous "duck" – the 639 by John Barnard.
The F2012's sidepods had an intake that was raised to the maximum, with the lower part was so concave that it left an ample flat area at the level of the stepped bottom. The 'pods contained vertically installed radiators, which were criticized due to a presumed aerodynamic blockage, but they remained unchanged for the whole season. To reduce bulk, the gearbox and Kers radiator was behind the engine and cooled by a second air intake, like the previous year's McLaren.
And for the first time, Ferrari adopted two long tie rods that connected the engine-gearbox group to the chassis to stiffen the rear end, clearly a Renault school technique.
The rear end was much tapered due to the reduced dimensions of the gearbox, helped by the union with the pull-rod suspension applied by Ferrari for the first time to the rear of the car as well as the front. In the original version, the exhausts "shot" air towards the rear wheels and they were modified a number of times before settling on a solution that was fairly similar to the McLaren in the May test at Mugello. They were transferred to the car from the GP of Spain.
Barcelona was the most important evolution step of the season and was followed by further refinements at the subsequent Canadian GP. For the 2013 season, Ferrari carried on with their continual development strategy, rather than grouping together specific large evolutionary pack-

Ferrari F150 Italia
2011

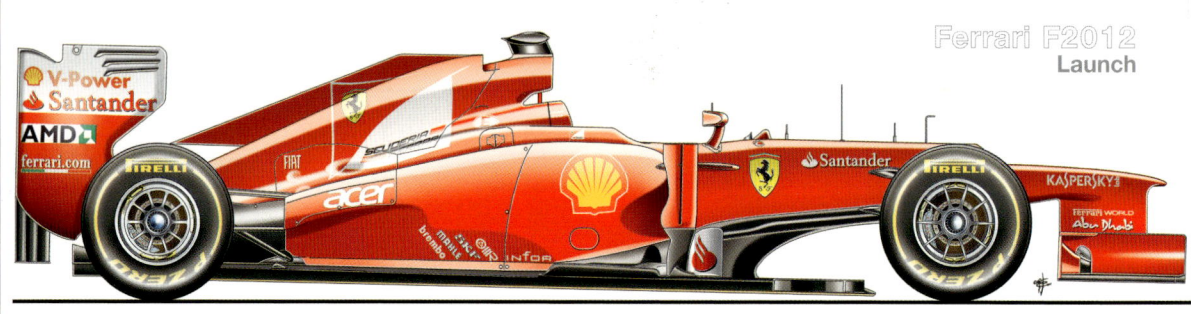

Ferrari F2012
Launch

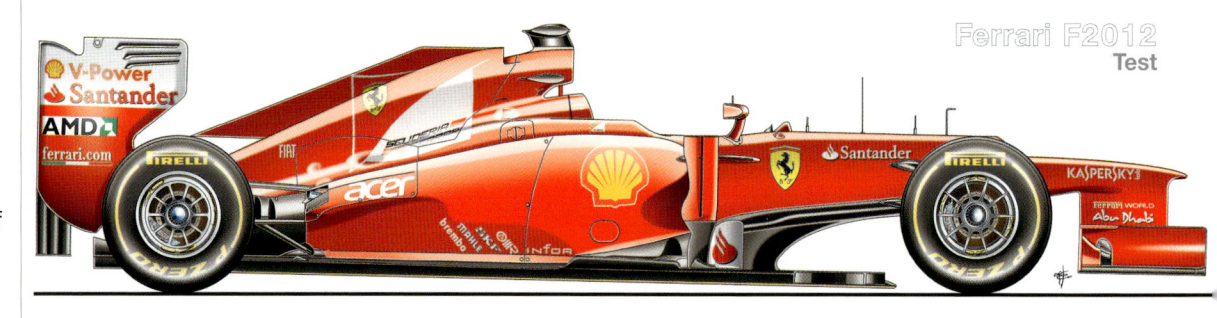

Ferrari F2012
Test

Ferrari F2012
Melbourne

56

Ferrari F2012
Valencia

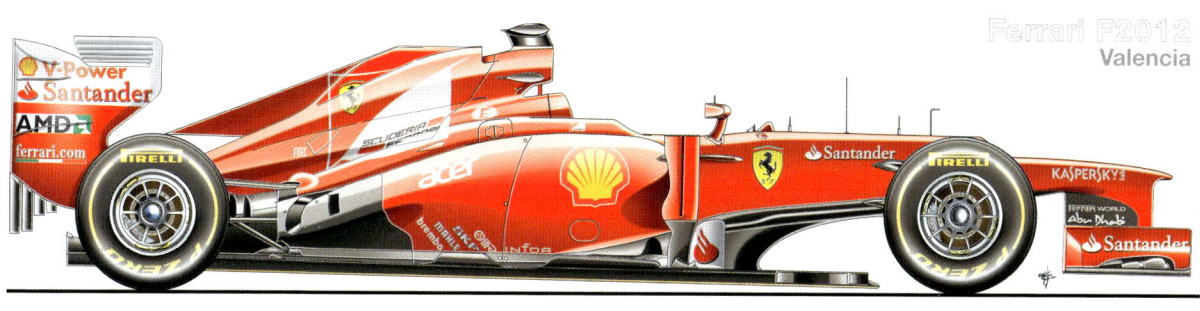

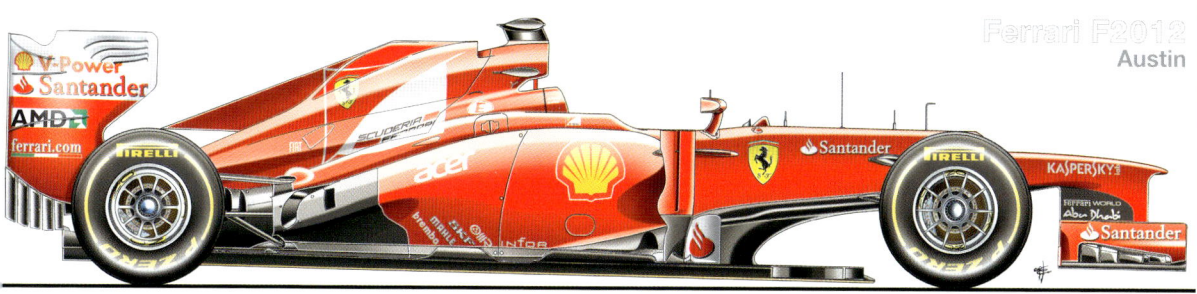

Ferrari F2012
Austin

ages in certain races.
But often, new developments were not introduced right away and in some cases were completely dismissed.
A problem associated with the difficulty of having a good correlation between wind tunnel studies, CFD simulations and track verification. Factors linked to problems in the Maranello wind tunnel and the lateness with which Ferrari used CFD analyses, because during the era of private testing they were able to check out experimental elements on their own Fiorano track.
The decision to use the Toyota wind tunnel started to bear fruit during the second half of the season. Unlike Lotus, Mercedes-Benz and Red Bull, Ferrari intentionally neglected research to use the double DRS to concentrate on optimizing means developed to meet the car's needs at the various circuits.
Having said that, at least 15 different versions of the front wing were produced, six families of rear wings – of which three never raced – 18 diffusers and about 10 versions of their brake air intakes – especially at the rear – and refinements to the position of the exhausts after the final updates in Spain and Canada.

FRONT COMPARISON

In this front comparison, one can see how Ferrari decided to raise the forepart of the car to the maximum to be able to exploit the lower zone for the conveyance of air towards the belly of the car and its diffuser.
1) The nose is higher than that of the F150, with the support pillars even more convergent (2) in the rear. 3) The television cameras have been exploited to better direct the air flow. 4) The major new aspect of the F2012 was the return of pull rod suspension at the front for the first time in 11 years to keep weight down.
5) The sidepods were tapered to the full in the area under the airbox and were very narrow down low to create a large step that fed the air flow towards the rear.
6) The sidepod inlets were placed higher and were smaller than those of the F150.
7) The deformable structures were transformed into aerodynamic elements, integrated into the initial part of the 'pods and linked to the turning vanes (partially dotted line).
8) Fin to straighten the air flow in that zone.
9) As on the McLaren, the sidepods were higher externally than in the area near the chassis, again to channel air to the rear.
10) The chassis was higher than that of the F150 and exploited the maximum permitted limit of 625 mm.
11) The engine air intake was triangular and smaller but it had an additional inlet, like the previous year's McLaren, to cool the hydraulics radiator.

FERRARI

STEPPED NOSE

The square nose of the F2012 was like that of the previous year's car, which earned it the nickname Donald Duck – as happened with John Barnard's legendary 1989 639. The nose fully exploited the height permitted by the regulations, so it had a large stepped area. The most interesting aspect was its much reduced section (shown in yellow) with the lower part slightly convex to ensure a substantial quantity of air was directed to the central zone and the diffuser.

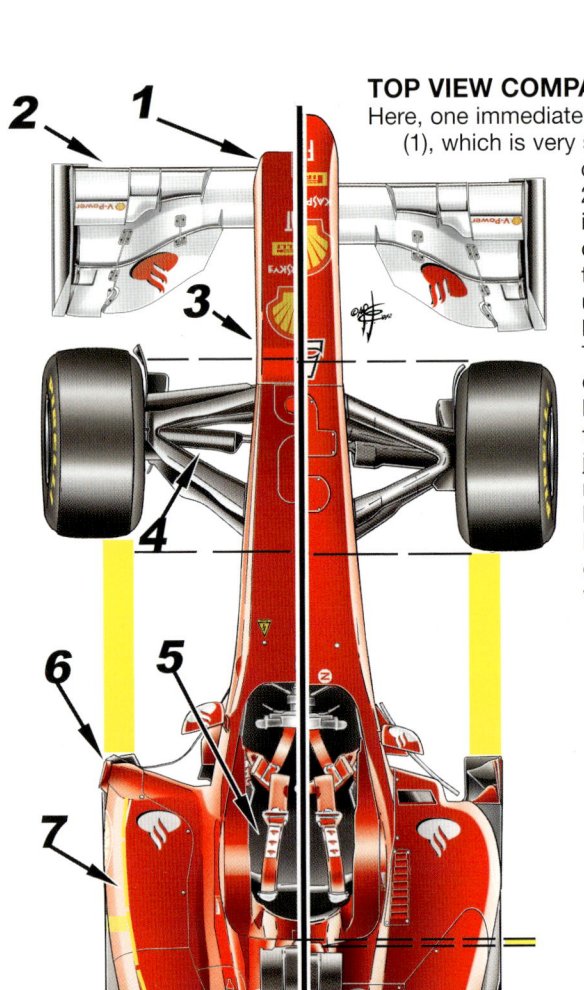

TOP VIEW COMPARISON

Here, one immediately notes the different shape of the nose (1), which is very square and flat, as well as shorter compared to that of the F150.
2) As with the rear wing, the front unit is the one seen during the last few races of 2011. 3) Ferrari opted for a high chassis on the 625 mm limit, with a large step. 4) The car's most unusual aspect was its front suspension with the pull rod layout, and an angulation of the arm that required substantially larger dimensions. The lengthening of the wheelbase with a different inclination of the front wishbones was the other major new development. That way, the harmful turbulence generated by the tyres was banished from the initial area of the sidepods. 5) At the specific request of Fernando Alonso, the driver sat in a more vertical position. 6) The deformable structures extended to the point of joining up with the vertical turning vanes. 7) The lower part of the sidepods was extremely narrow and formed an ample channel through which to feed the rear area. 8) The exhausts were hidden by this fairing and blew towards the lower part of the rear wing. 9) The gearbox and link suspension were new, the latter's arms heavily inclined forwards. 10) The rear end was extremely narrow and all the hot air from the sidepods was dissipated in that central area, which ended with a circular outlet.

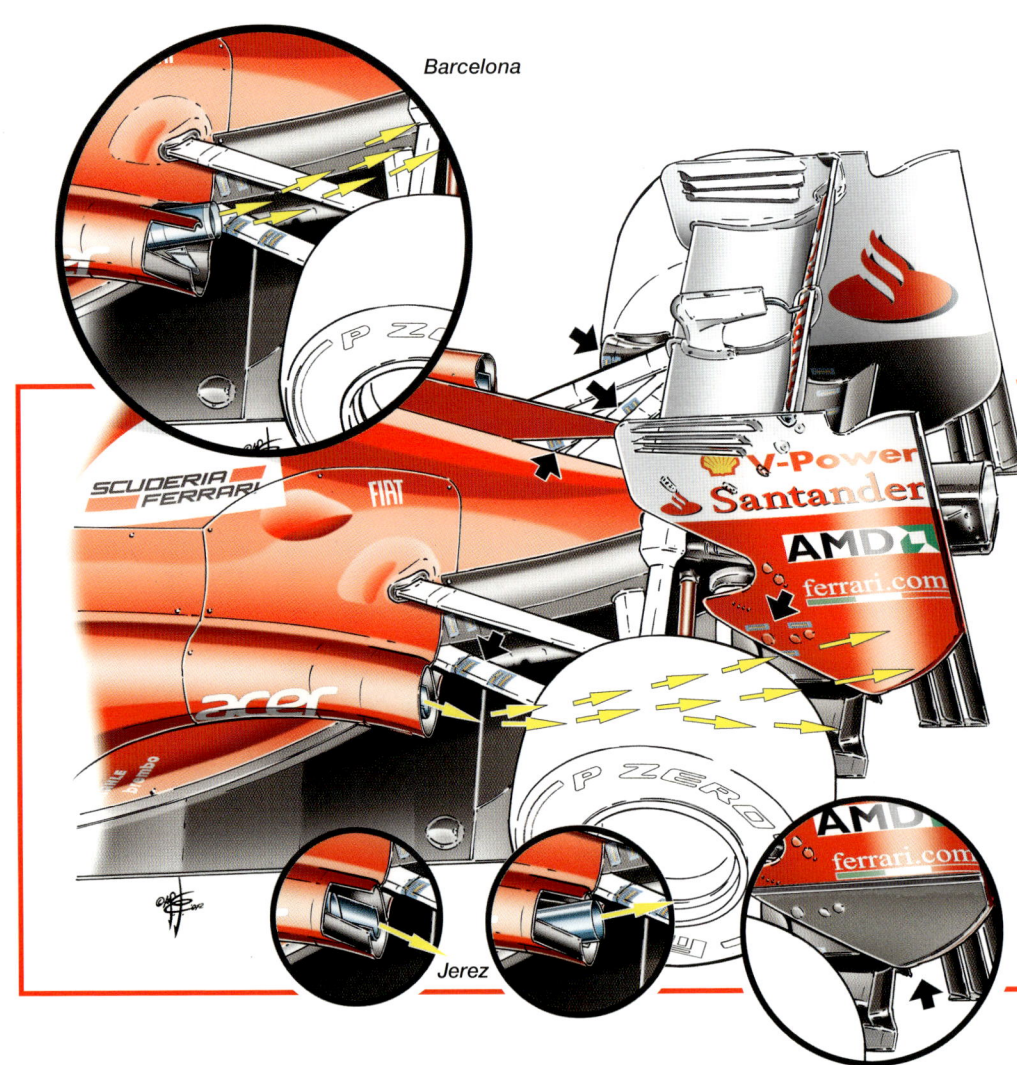

Barcelona

Jerez

F2012   F150

FERRARI

CHASSIS

The naked chassis of the Ferrari with an almost horizontal suspension tie rod (in yellow). The torsion bars no longer passed by the front part, where there were only the fixing holes of the nose; instead, they were set obliquely into the lower part of the chassis, in the suspension rockers (see the yellow dotted line). The brake air intake was derived from the last version of the previous season's car, with hot air outlets on the exterior.

RADIATORS

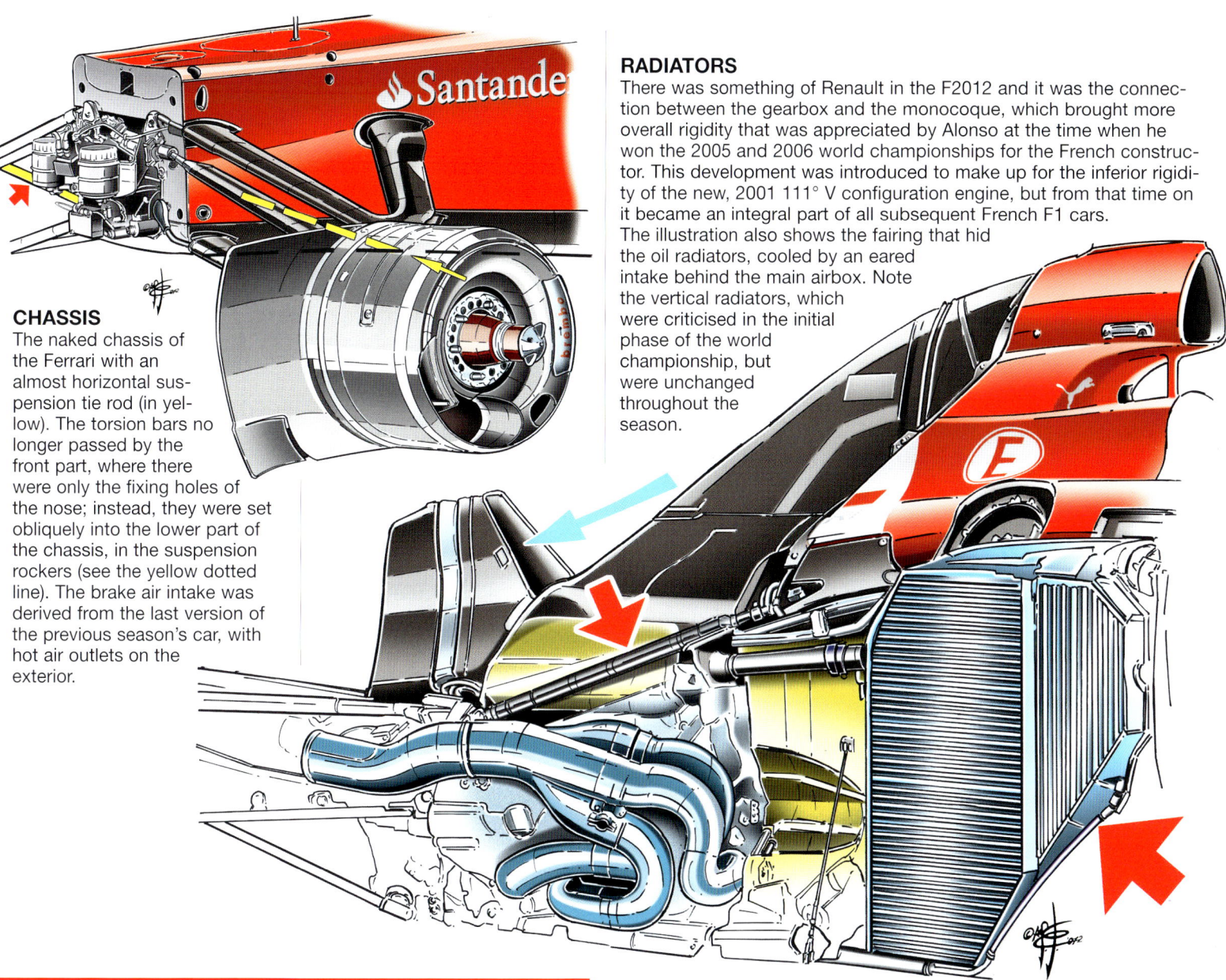

There was something of Renault in the F2012 and it was the connection between the gearbox and the monocoque, which brought more overall rigidity that was appreciated by Alonso at the time when he won the 2005 and 2006 world championships for the French constructor. This development was introduced to make up for the inferior rigidity of the new, 2001 111° V configuration engine, but from that time on it became an integral part of all subsequent French F1 cars. The illustration also shows the fairing that hid the oil radiators, cooled by an eared intake behind the main airbox. Note the vertical radiators, which were criticised in the initial phase of the world championship, but were unchanged throughout the season.

EXHAUST EVOLUTION

Ferrari introduced a continuous evolution of exhaust systems at each of the pre-season private test sessions in Spain.
Initially, they were faired inside the body (see the large illustration) that acted as a conveyor to direct the hot air flow towards the lower area and brush the internal part of the rear wheels.
It was a system adopted by McLaren and was revealed by the position of the thermo tapes and the protection applied at Jerez to the lower part of the wing's end plates (see circle below, right). But a modification was made during the early laps by cutting the upper part of the body, which "cooked" due to the high temperature (first detail on the left). And in the first test session, longer more inward inclined terminals were tried and it seemed they gave good results (circle below, centre). At Barcelona, we also saw a system that was even closer to the one that blew to the centre of the Red Bull, with further body cuts and the movement of the terminals more to the inside (large circle above), which repeated a larger part of the solution chosen for the Red Bull's debut.

SEPANG

Alonso tested a new nose on the Friday, after which both drivers eventually raced with it. This was the one that appeared at the last Barcelona test session, but was not used in Melbourne. It differed for its new end plates, which were unlike its predecessors in almost all details, especially the multiple vents. The main plane was also new and had two blowholes instead of one. The initial portion of the plane's chord seemed much reduced.

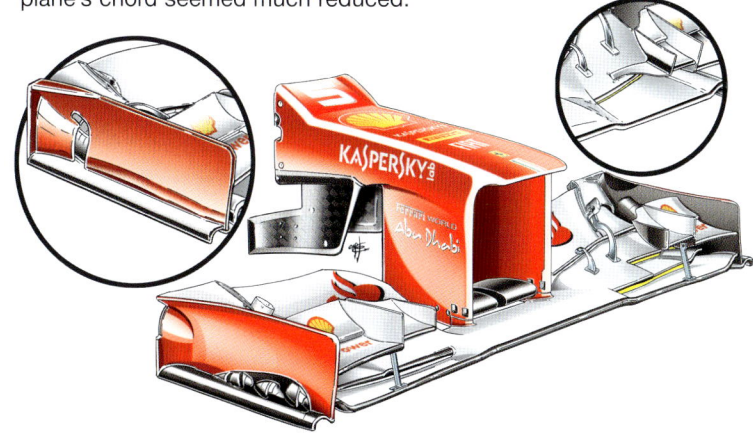

FERRARI

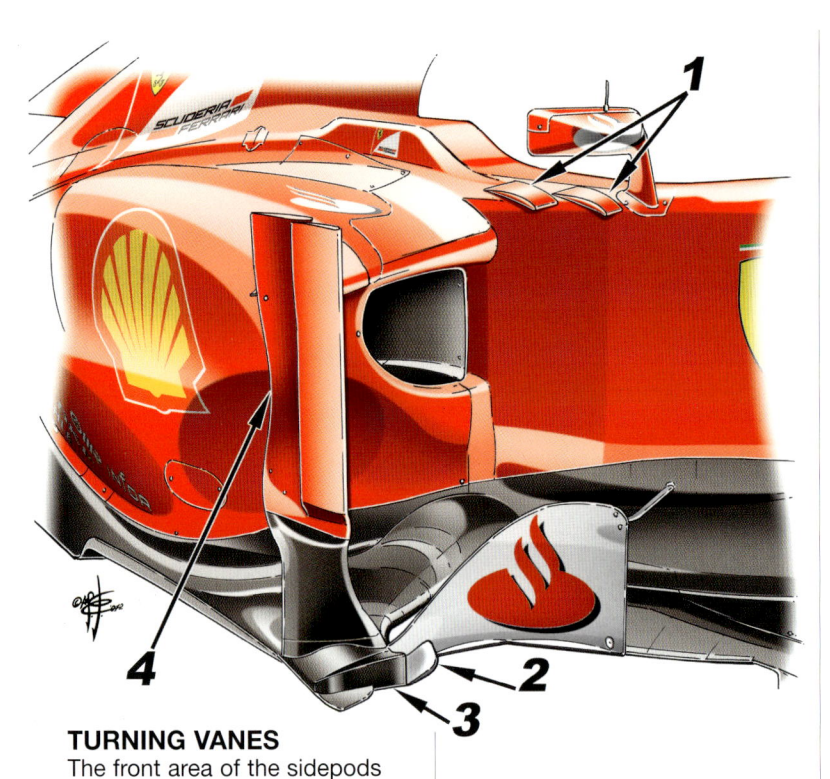

TURNING VANES
The front area of the sidepods was given a series of mini-aerodynamic devices; the one up high (1) was to limit the effect of raising in that area and the lower ones (2-3) were to better direct the air flow towards the car's rear. The vertical deflectors were also slightly modified (4).

SAKHIR
A comparison between the new wing (the old unit is in the insert) which had a different link (1) of the raised flap end plates to improve plane efficiency and reduce negative vortices in that area. The part of the flap close to the end plate (2) was also different and permitted better air flow towards the wheels' exterior.

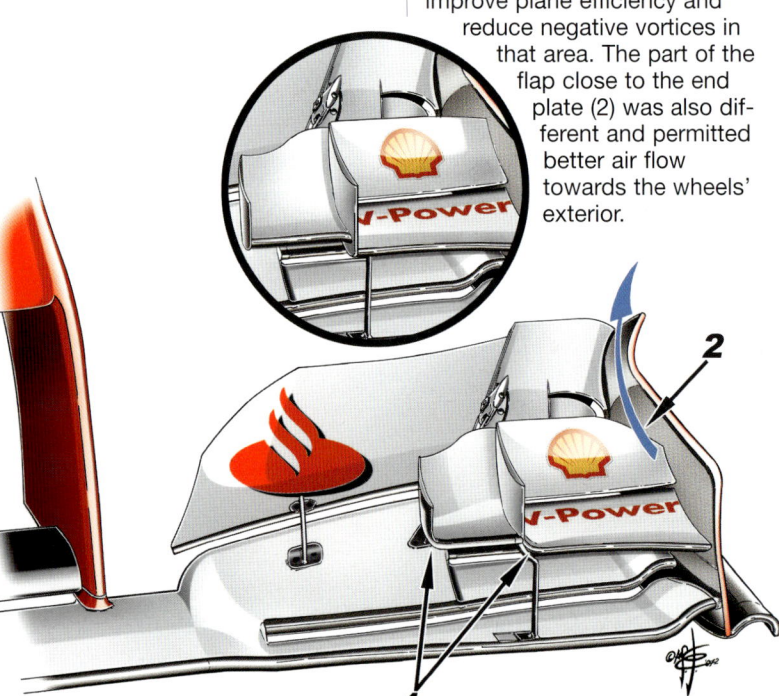

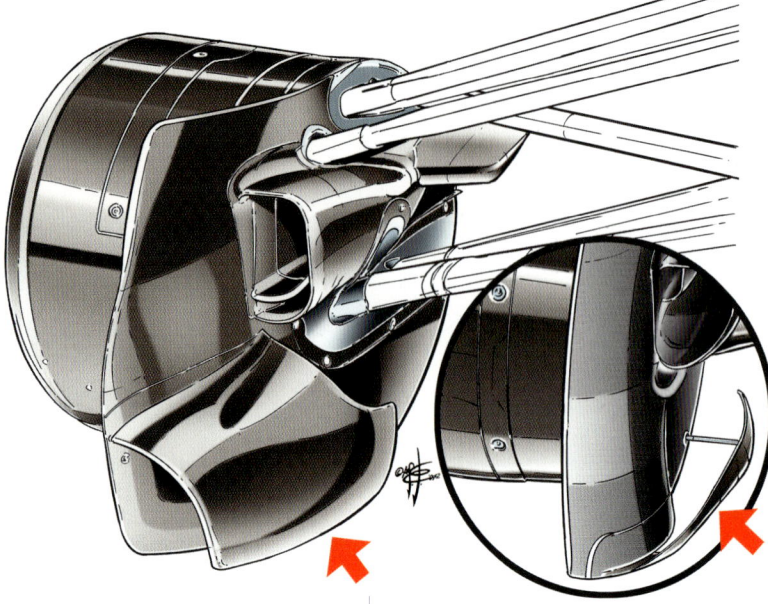

BRAKE AIR INTAKES
Ferrari kept the aerodynamic package introduced in China, which also included this new brake air intake, inspired by those that had been used by the opposition for some time, with a large, rounded turning vane. That had replaced the long, thin units in the lower part of the intake to better direct air around the wheels.

MINI-PLANE
Ferrari also joined the group of cars that had a mini-plane 15 cm wide between the two principal units of the beam wing.
This development energised the air flow in that area, improving extraction from the diffuser and, therefore, negative lift.

FERRARI

DIFFUSER

To complete the Ferrari package seen at Mugello, a new diffuser was fitted in Barcelona, which had curved links (1) between the middle vanes and the upper part of the unit to reduce turbulence in that area. Those end plates didn't have L-shaped cuts but round ones (2) to improve efficiency. The small flap (3) was also modified in its upper zone and that increased the area of the diffuser's channels.
The vertical "fringes" in the lower area of the end plates were also new.

BARCELONA: BEAM WING

A new beam wing made its debut at Mugello. It had McLaren-style end plates and various horizontal cuts in the upper area (the old one is in the insert above) plus an undulating lower plane (left). In Spain, it also had the raised mini-flap from its predecessor (in the insert with the straight plane) which was on the old version used in Bahrain to increase downforce.

Sepang

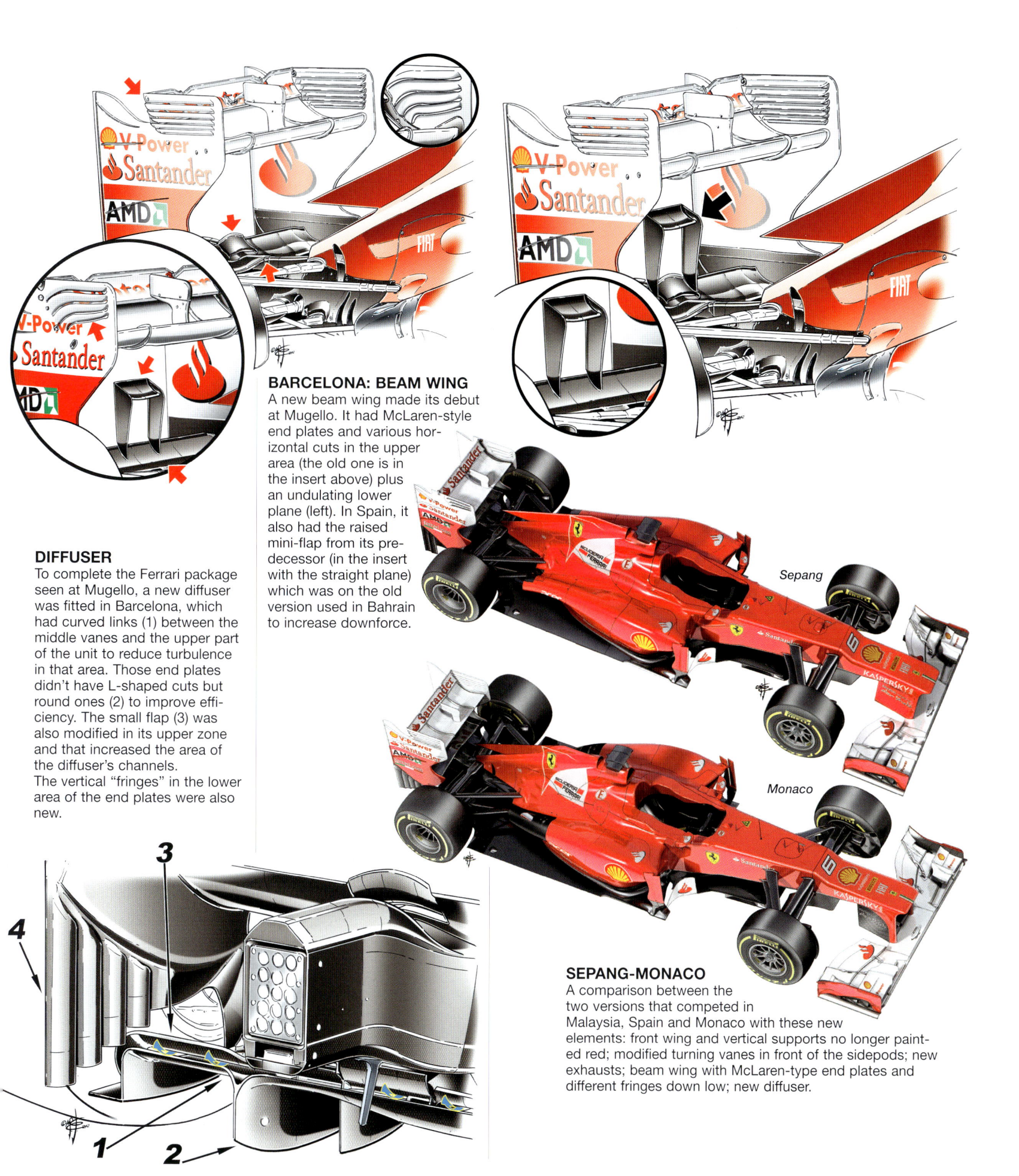

Monaco

SEPANG-MONACO

A comparison between the two versions that competed in Malaysia, Spain and Monaco with these new elements: front wing and vertical supports no longer painted red; modified turning vanes in front of the sidepods; new exhausts; beam wing with McLaren-type end plates and different fringes down low; new diffuser.

FERRARI 61

MONACO

Alonso and Massa raced with different front turning vanes. The Brazilian used those positioned below the chassis as on the Red Bull (see oval). The Spaniard had the usual units under the nose. There were new brake air intakes with modified Red Bull-style turning vanes and a greater amount of air in the eared intake. Fairing was applied in the area of the brake cylinders to save them from bumps in case of a nose replacement, as with the Mercedes-Benz.

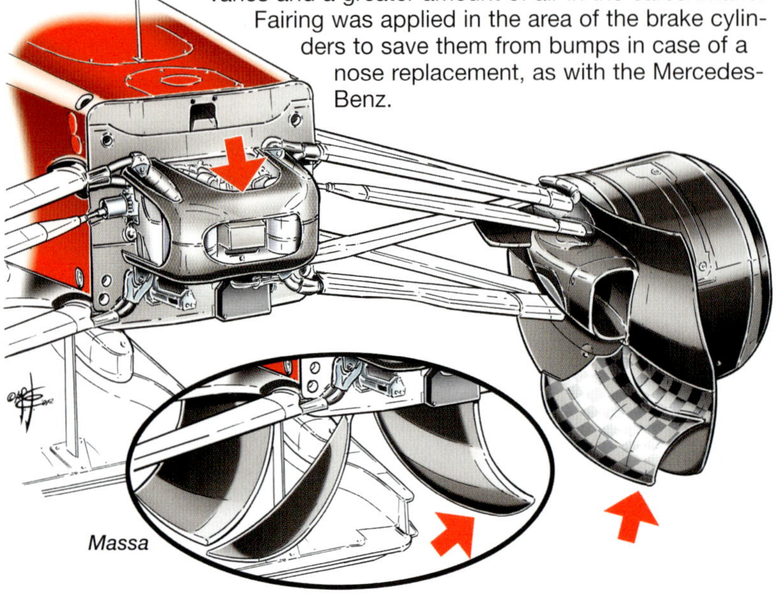

Massa

BRAKE AIR INTAKES

For the circuits hardest on the brakes, Ferrari followed Williams and adopted an audacious brake air intake without an entry inlet in the internal part, but all the input of air gathered in the space between the pan and the wheel. Note that with the movement and flexing of the tyres on the track, this space increases and with it the quantity of available air. The detail shows the entry intakes, while below is the method introduced by Williams from the moment the FW34 was presented.

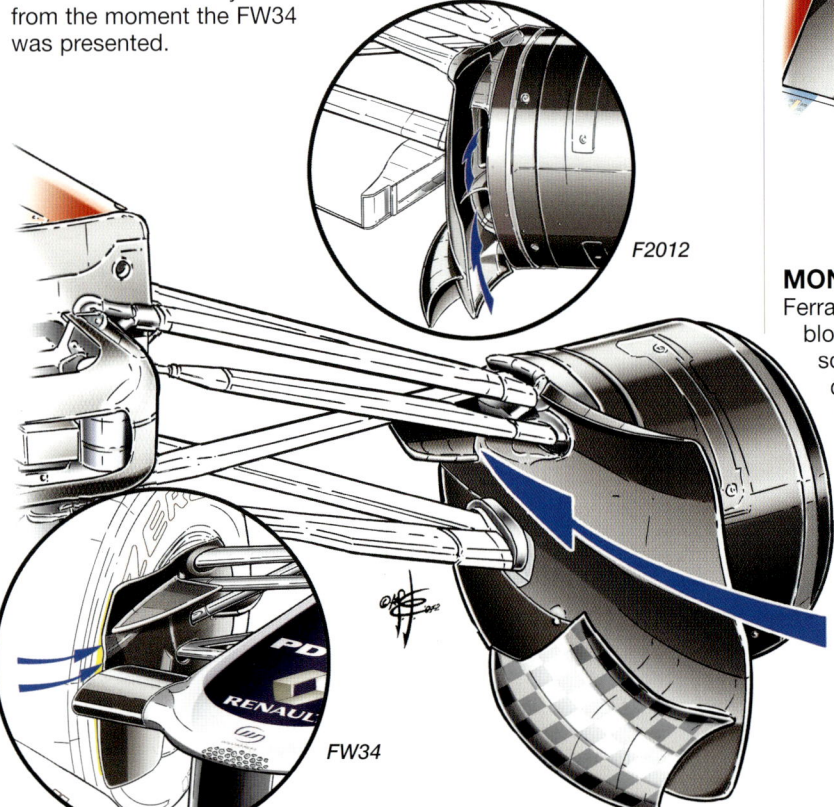

F2012

FW34

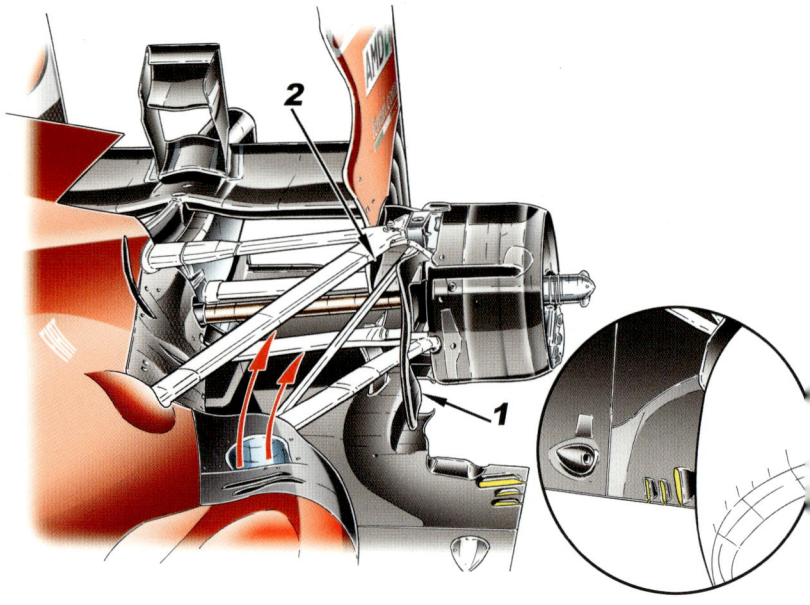

MONTREAL

Ferrari went back to the original low blow into the rear wheel foot. It did so by unifying itself with the group of cars that took up the solution first used at the start of the season by McLaren, obviously with a similar design on the Sauber since the Mugello test.
In the comparison, one can easily see that the blow of the old system was mainly internal. Note the new Williams-type brake air intakes (1) with a long, vertical seal. One of the many winglets applied to the intakes to create downforce can also be seen. And two longitudinal finlets were added at Montreal, to better direct the air flow to the inside of the rear wheels.

FERRARI
62

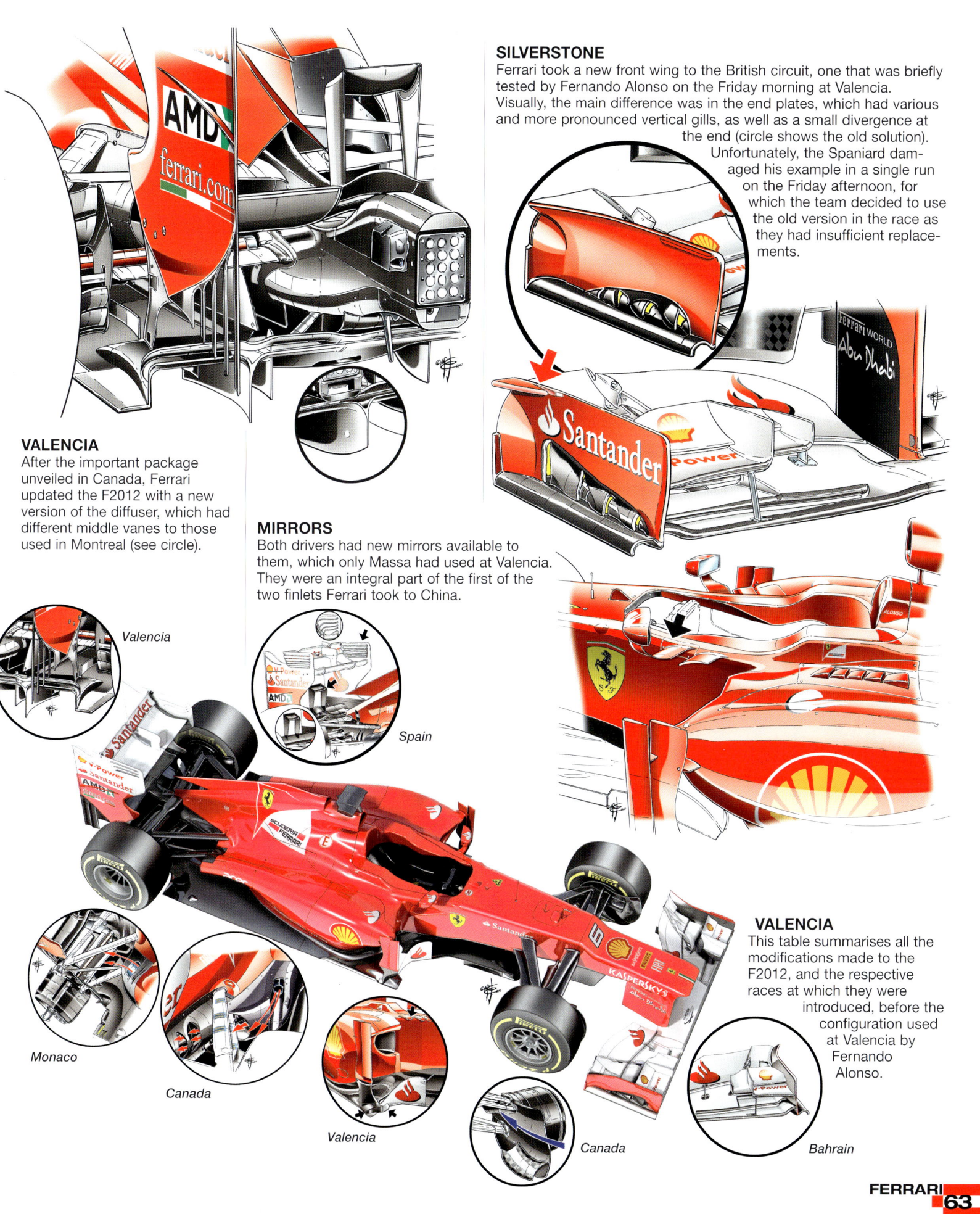

SILVERSTONE
Ferrari took a new front wing to the British circuit, one that was briefly tested by Fernando Alonso on the Friday morning at Valencia. Visually, the main difference was in the end plates, which had various and more pronounced vertical gills, as well as a small divergence at the end (circle shows the old solution). Unfortunately, the Spaniard damaged his example in a single run on the Friday afternoon, for which the team decided to use the old version in the race as they had insufficient replacements.

VALENCIA
After the important package unveiled in Canada, Ferrari updated the F2012 with a new version of the diffuser, which had different middle vanes to those used in Montreal (see circle).

MIRRORS
Both drivers had new mirrors available to them, which only Massa had used at Valencia. They were an integral part of the first of the two finlets Ferrari took to China.

Valencia

Spain

Monaco

Canada

Valencia

Canada

Bahrain

VALENCIA
This table summarises all the modifications made to the F2012, and the respective races at which they were introduced, before the configuration used at Valencia by Fernando Alonso.

FERRARI

Shangai

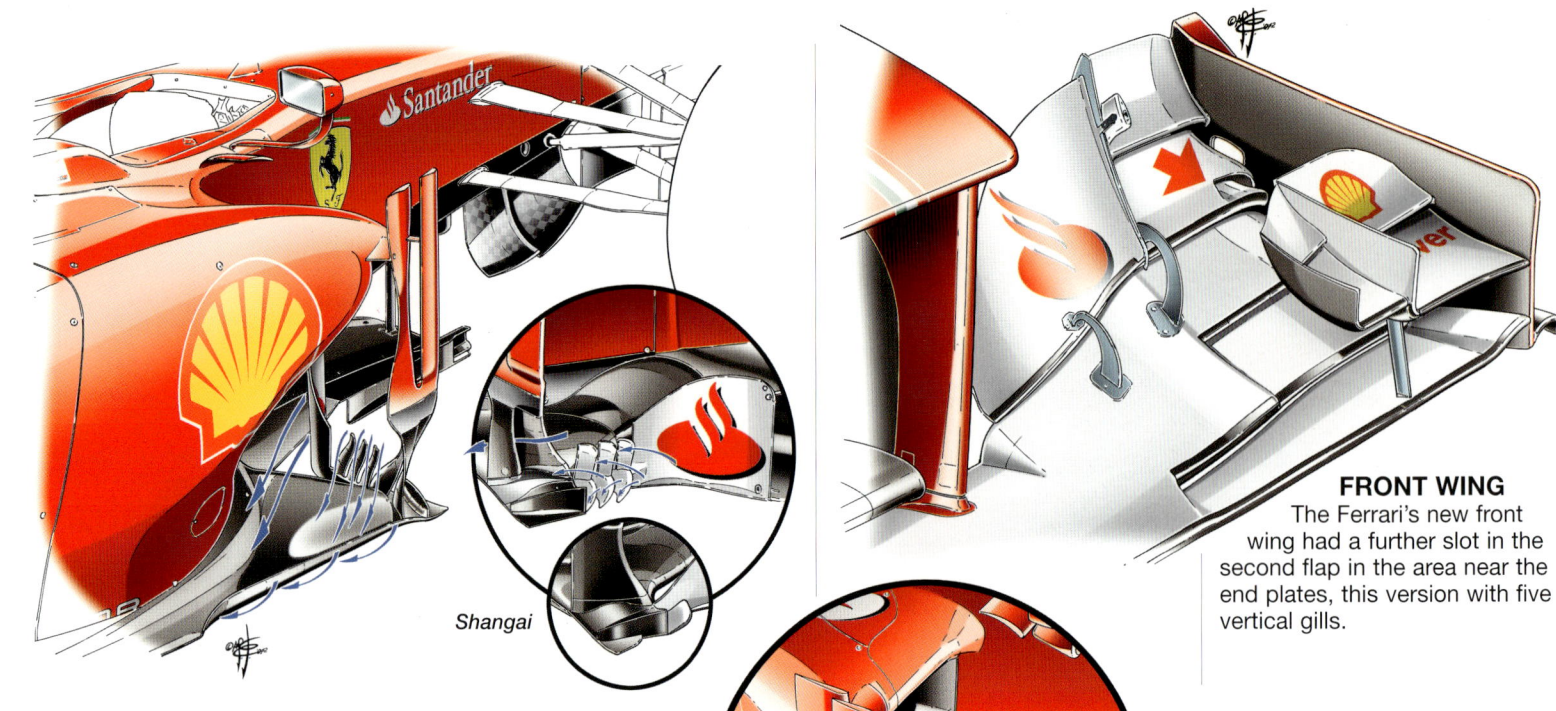

HOCKENHEIM
Another version of the barge boards in front of the sidepods. A single "tooth" was introduced in China in the lower area (see small circle) to which another two elements were added in Spain. Three twisted finlets were added to that zone in Germany to channel air towards the rear of the car. Note the blow in the low part of the barge boards, which made their debut at Silverstone.

FRONT WING
The Ferrari's new front wing had a further slot in the second flap in the area near the end plates, this version with five vertical gills.

TURNING VANES
On the Saturday morning at Budapest, Alonso tested another version of turning vane in front of the sidepods, with which he later raced.
They no longer had vertical finlets in the upper area, but a second mini vertical end plate in the zone of the three "teeth" down low. Massa used the version that first appeared in Germany.

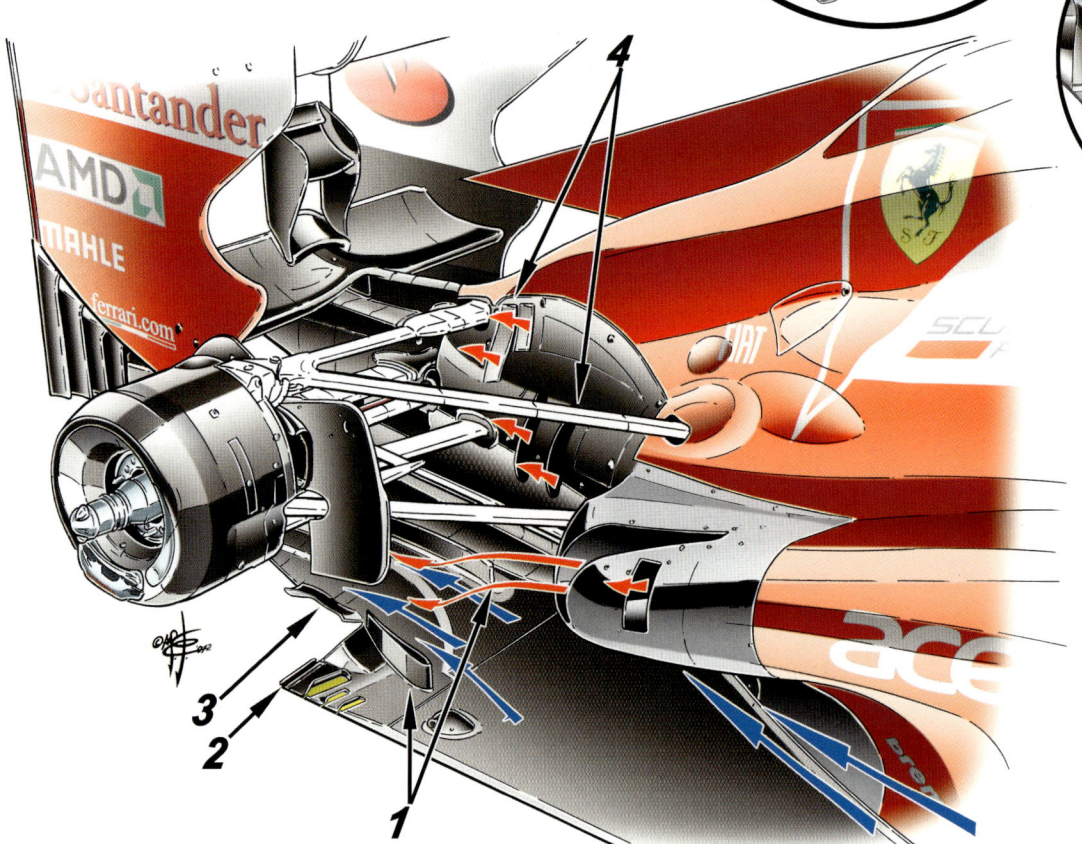

BUDAPEST
All the modifications in the diffuser area that were made for the last races of the season. With the introduction of the McLaren-type exhausts in Canada came, the double mini-fins (1) to convey air towards the diffuser's lateral channels with twisted borders (3). Three gills (2) remained with an additional small Gurney flap to strengthen the diffuser's downforce effect. Hungary's humid heat meant the team also retained the "shark's gills" (4) on the new engine cover that came out at Silverstone.

FERRARI
64

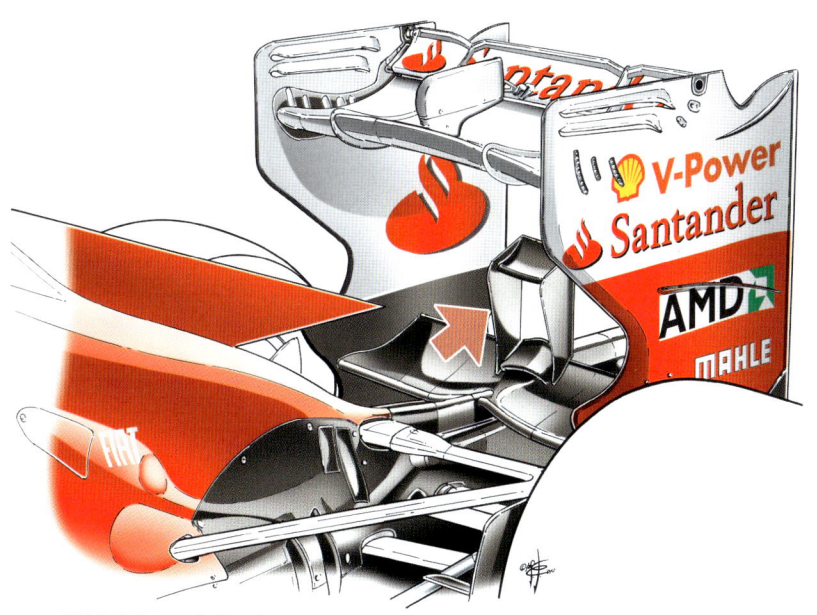

SPA-FRANCORCHAMPS
There was a new rear wing for the fast Belgian track. Note the end plates with just two gills up high and the new main plane. A mini-plane 15 cm wide was added to the beam wing.

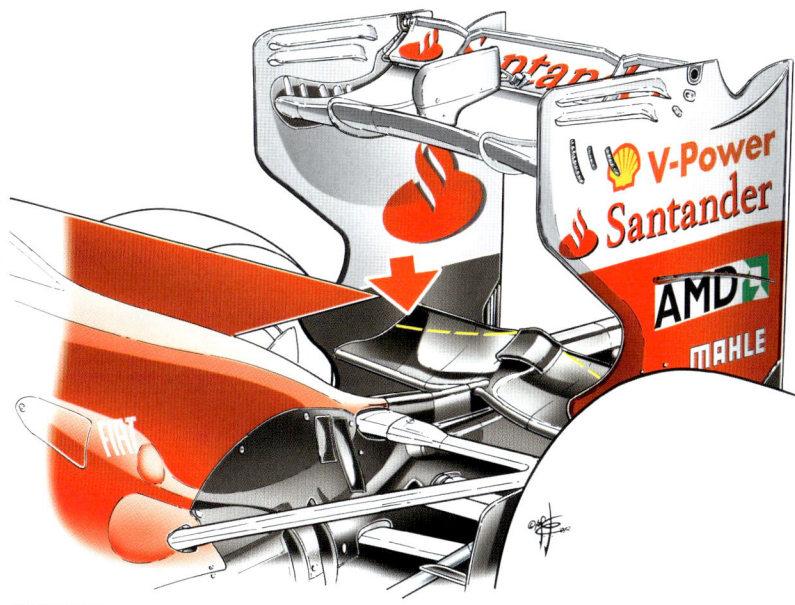

SPA-FRANCORCHAMPS: FRONT WING
The new front wing clearly designed for fast circuits like Spa and Monza. 1) The most significant difference was the abolition of the raised flaps. Examining the unit carefully, the divergences were to be found more or less in all the wing's sectors: different end plates without the last hole (2) and the triangular finlets (3) at the end. There were new planes with the mount (4) of the plate more curved upwards, which was retained in the subsequent planes. The latter with its four principal blow holes reduced to three, but with a different position of the mini-slot (5) in the last flap. 6) The incidence adjustment control was modified and, lastly, the chord of the second flap was reduced.

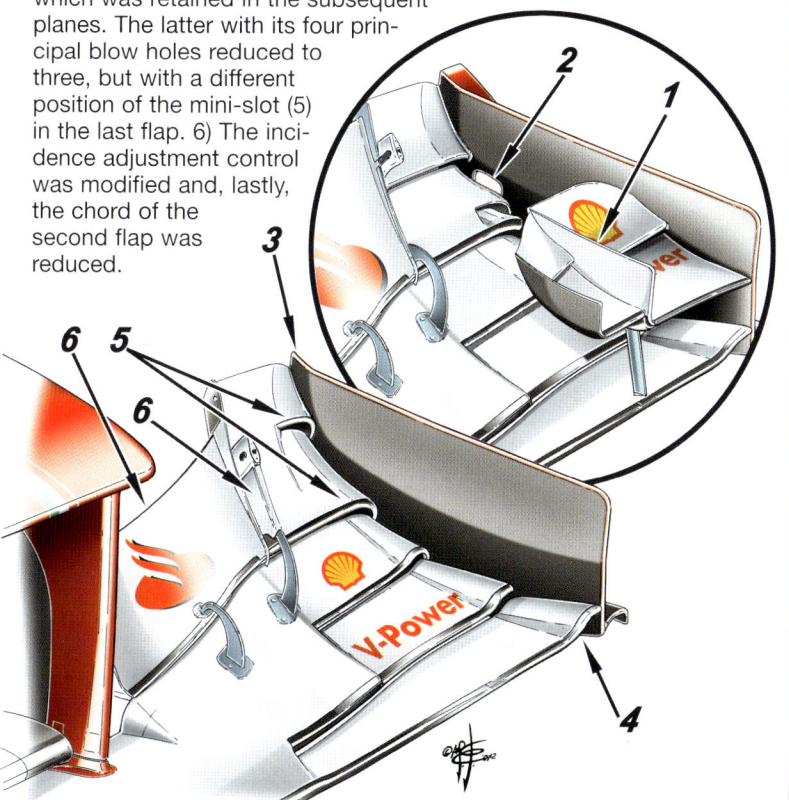

MONZA
Ferrari used the Belgian wing again, but with its main plane discharging differently in combination with two different types of lower plane at the height of the safety structure. Massa had the straight low plane combined with the upper part that produced slightly less downforce, while Alonso used the delta type with more load on the upper part.

DIFFUSER FLAP
At Spa, Ferrari debuted a different rear wing plane at the level of the gearbox; or rather, the two drivers raced with two different solutions: Massa had the straight plane and Alonso (2) the delta (dotted line). It was an alternative that only Ferrari had: the doubling of the mini-flap in the diffuser's (1) trailing edge was to create a component with a more inclined ramp and, therefore, more downforce.

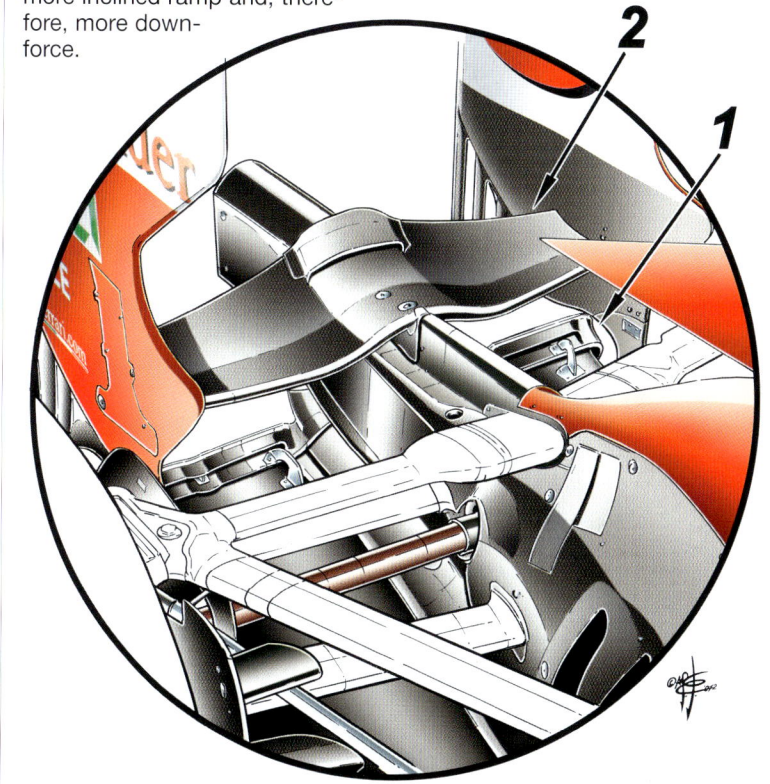

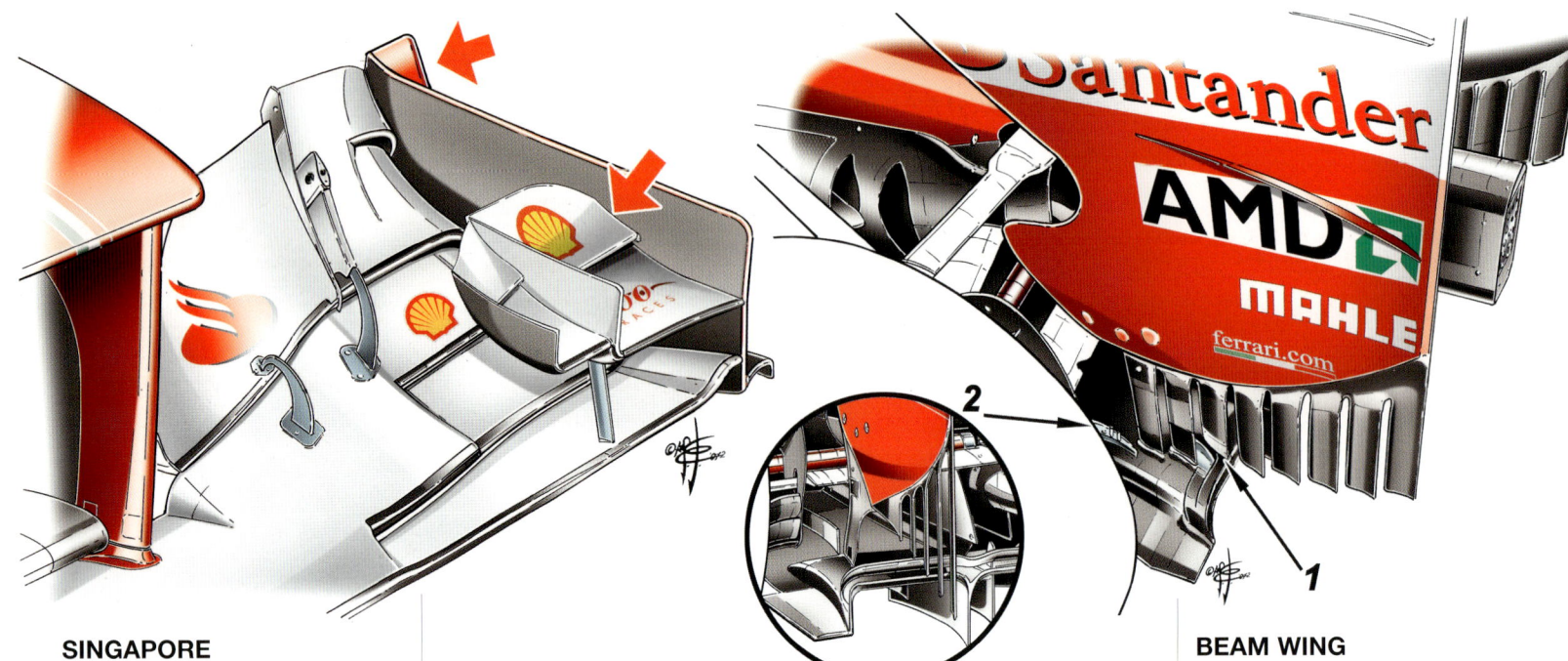

SINGAPORE
This was the official debut of the new front wing tested at Magny Cours. Raised flaps were added to the plane group that first appeared in Belgium. The end plates were also new and terminated with a small triangular fin.

SUZUKA
No fewer than three wings were tested by the two drivers at Suzuka, after which both used the oldest version, dropping the one tested by Alonso at Singapore and used by Massa (see oval) and a new version tested by Alonso. The latter was not only different in the shape of its vertical fringe, which was cut down low with a rounded upwards progression, but it had especially important new designs in the upper part of the end plates: in the trailing edge between the main plane and the flap there was a new step and the horizontal gills that had a different progression at the rear.

BEAM WING
On the Friday, only Alonso tested the new high load beam wing, which differed from the one used in Hungary in all its elements: principal plane, flaps and end plates. The illustration shows the fringe detail in the lower area of the end plates that had increased in number from five to eight (1), with the first fixed right on the lateral channels of the diffuser. In reality, there was another support (2) that was not used. In the circle is the version that was raced by both drivers.

BRAKE AIR INTAKES
There were micro-developments on the Ferrari, with new brake air intakes that were somewhat revised in just about all their aerodynamic devices and, as always, without cooling inlets inside the barge boards. The most evident detail was the addition of a further triangular fin up high, very similar to that which had been used for some time by Williams.

FERRARI

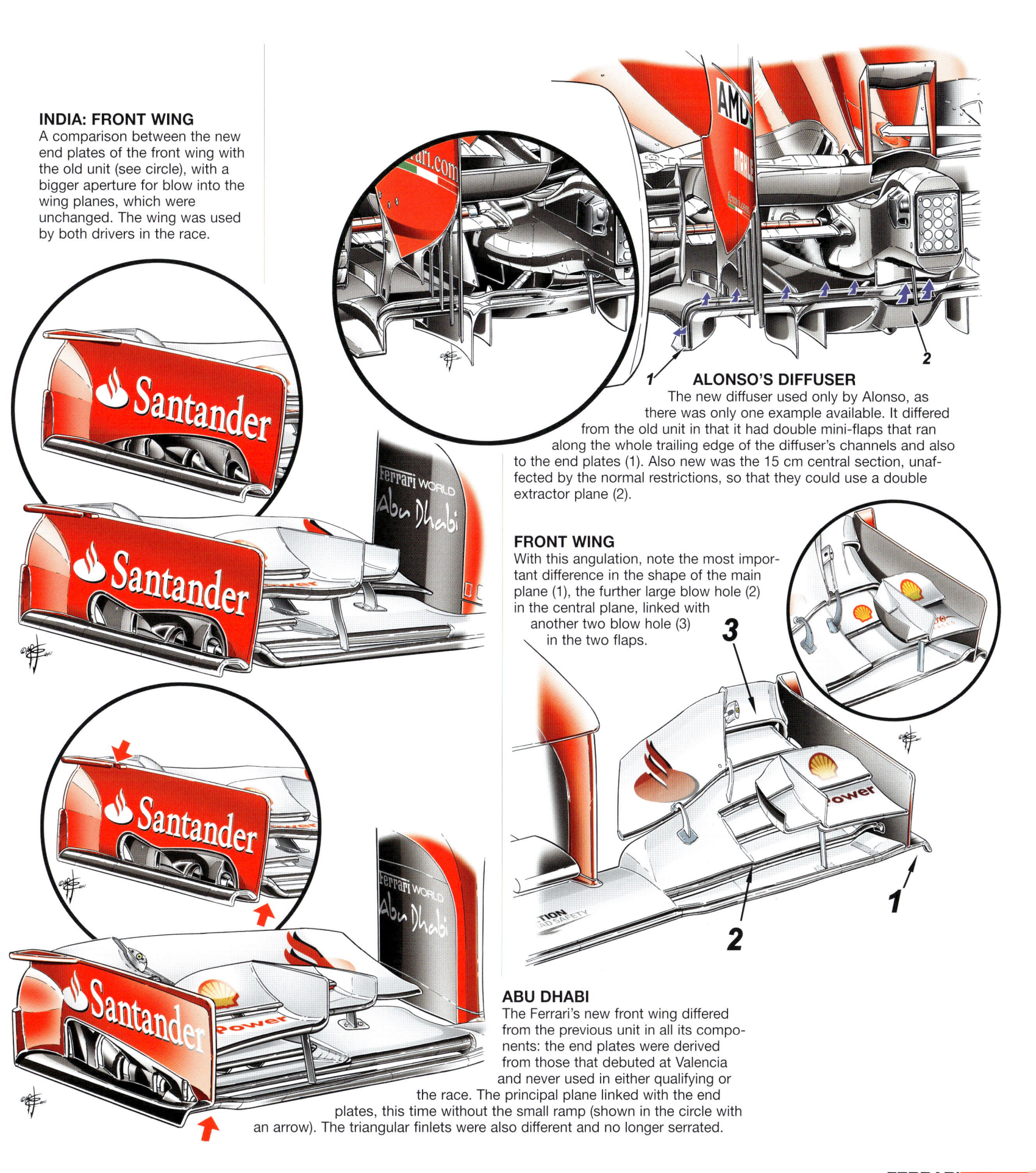

INDIA: FRONT WING
A comparison between the new end plates of the front wing with the old unit (see circle), with a bigger aperture for blow into the wing planes, which were unchanged. The wing was used by both drivers in the race.

ALONSO'S DIFFUSER
The new diffuser used only by Alonso, as there was only one example available. It differed from the old unit in that it had double mini-flaps that ran along the whole trailing edge of the diffuser's channels and also to the end plates (1). Also new was the 15 cm central section, unaffected by the normal restrictions, so that they could use a double extractor plane (2).

FRONT WING
With this angulation, note the most important difference in the shape of the main plane (1), the further large blow hole (2) in the central plane, linked with another two blow hole (3) in the two flaps.

ABU DHABI
The Ferrari's new front wing differed from the previous unit in all its components: the end plates were derived from those that debuted at Valencia and never used in either qualifying or the race. The principal plane linked with the end plates, this time without the small ramp (shown in the circle with an arrow). The triangular finlets were also different and no longer serrated.

FERRARI 67

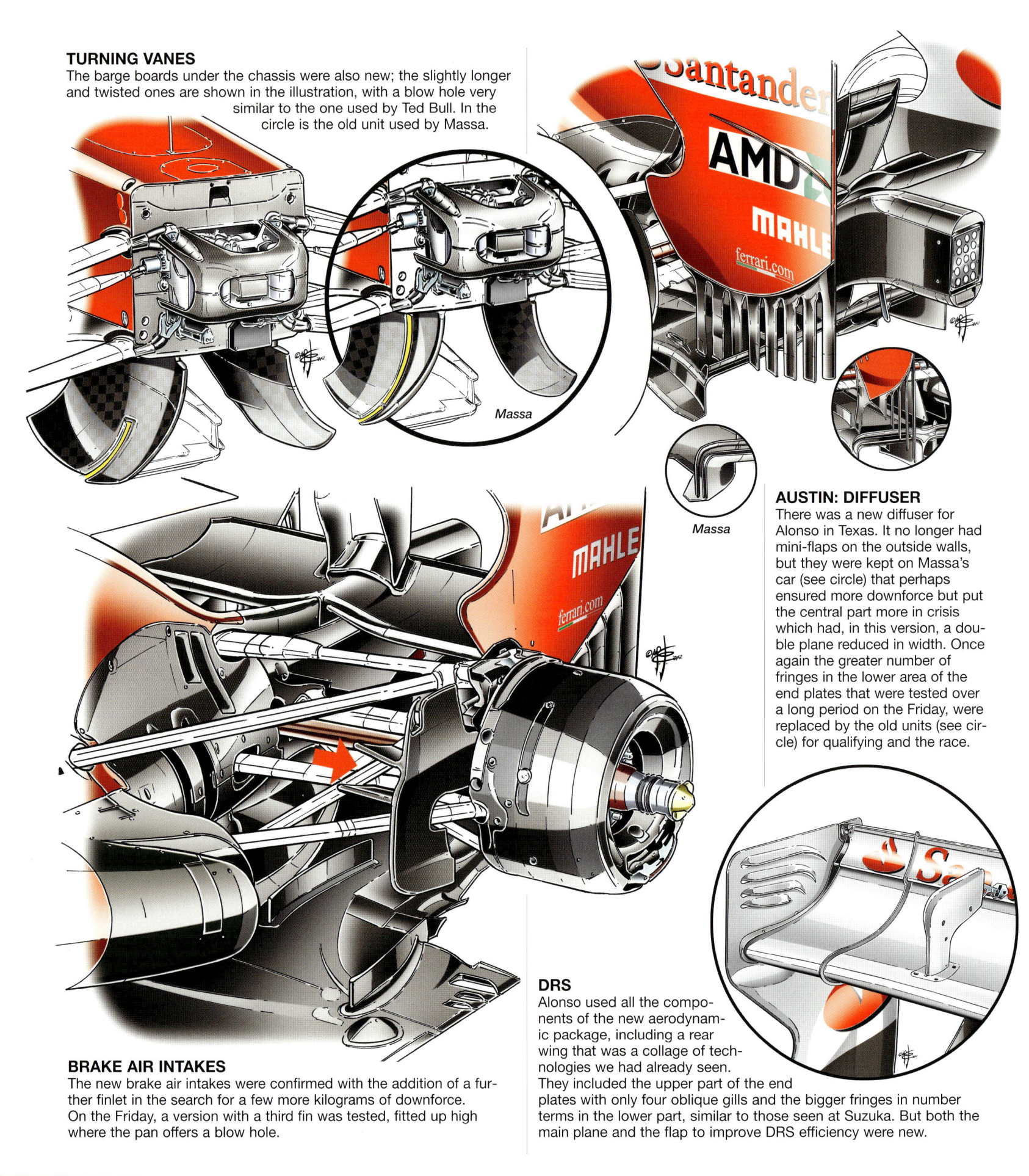

TURNING VANES
The barge boards under the chassis were also new; the slightly longer and twisted ones are shown in the illustration, with a blow hole very similar to the one used by Ted Bull. In the circle is the old unit used by Massa.

Massa

AUSTIN: DIFFUSER
There was a new diffuser for Alonso in Texas. It no longer had mini-flaps on the outside walls, but they were kept on Massa's car (see circle) that perhaps ensured more downforce but put the central part more in crisis which had, in this version, a double plane reduced in width. Once again the greater number of fringes in the lower area of the end plates that were tested over a long period on the Friday, were replaced by the old units (see circle) for qualifying and the race.

Massa

BRAKE AIR INTAKES
The new brake air intakes were confirmed with the addition of a further finlet in the search for a few more kilograms of downforce. On the Friday, a version with a third fin was tested, fitted up high where the pan offers a blow hole.

DRS
Alonso used all the components of the new aerodynamic package, including a rear wing that was a collage of technologies we had already seen. They included the upper part of the end plates with only four oblique gills and the bigger fringes in number terms in the lower part, similar to those seen at Suzuka. But both the main plane and the flap to improve DRS efficiency were new.

FERRARI
68

FRINGES

For the race, Ferrari retained the long series of fringes first seen in Singapore. They had always been put to one side in favour of the versions with fewer elements, as was the case at Austin.

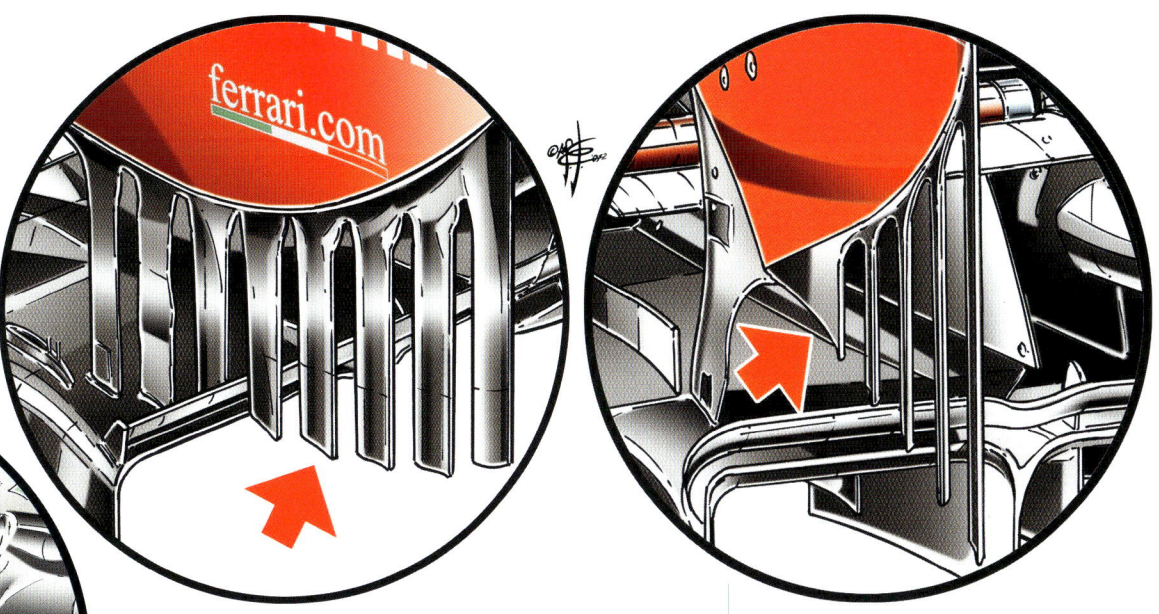

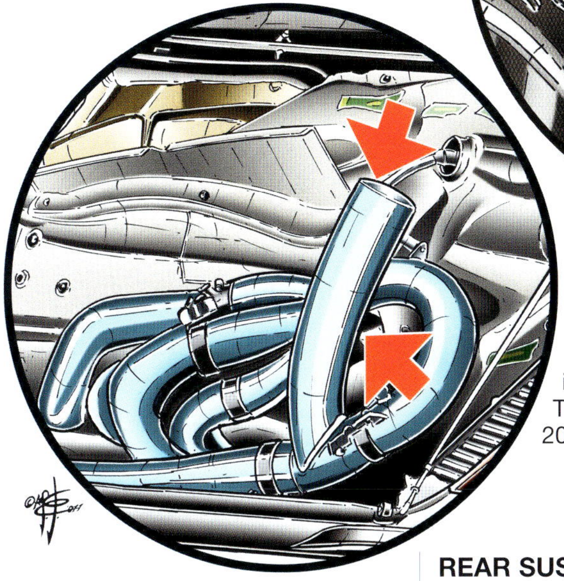

COMPENSATORY RESONATOR

Ferrari retained a sort of closed chimney they brought out at the 2011 Belgian GP, which was useful in compensating energy loads created by the post combustion effect. The technique was also adopted by many other teams in 2012.

REAR SUSPENSION

For the first time Ferrari adopted pull-rod suspension layouts both at the front and the rear. The old rear end had been the only car to retain a strut layout that brought all the suspension elements together in the upper part of the gearbox casing. The strut and the pull-rod of the two layouts are highlighted in yellow. Note how the pull-rod has a significantly smaller section and lower weight than the strut.

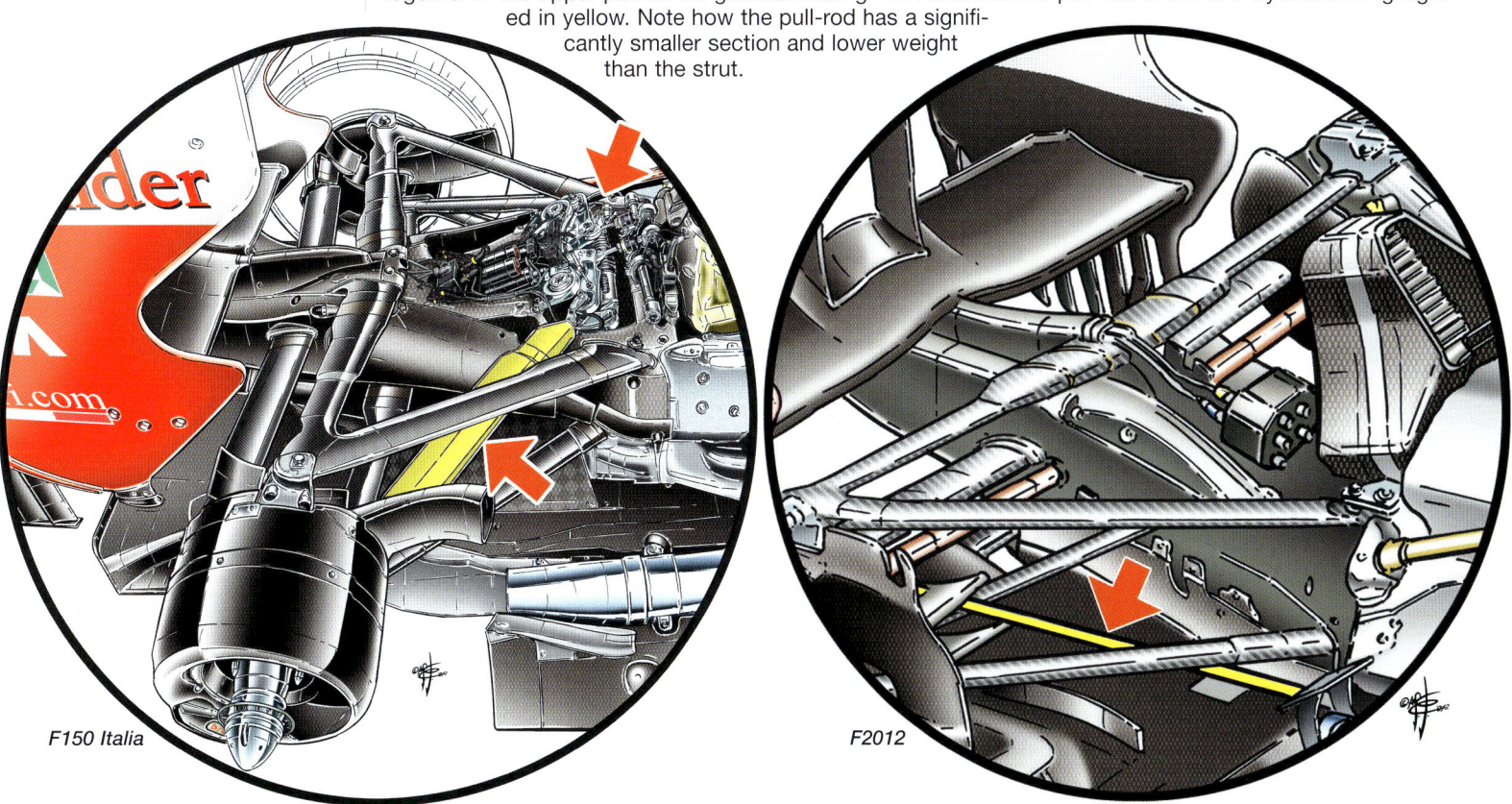

F150 Italia

F2012

FERRARI 69

GEARBOX

Comparison between the two gearboxes: that of the F150 assembled, complete with suspension and brakes and that of the F2012 stripped so as to reveal the unusual construction in two elements, with the suspension attached to a kind of spacer, illustrated in the chapter on the Sauber which used Ferrari engine and the same transmission.

F150 Italia

F2012

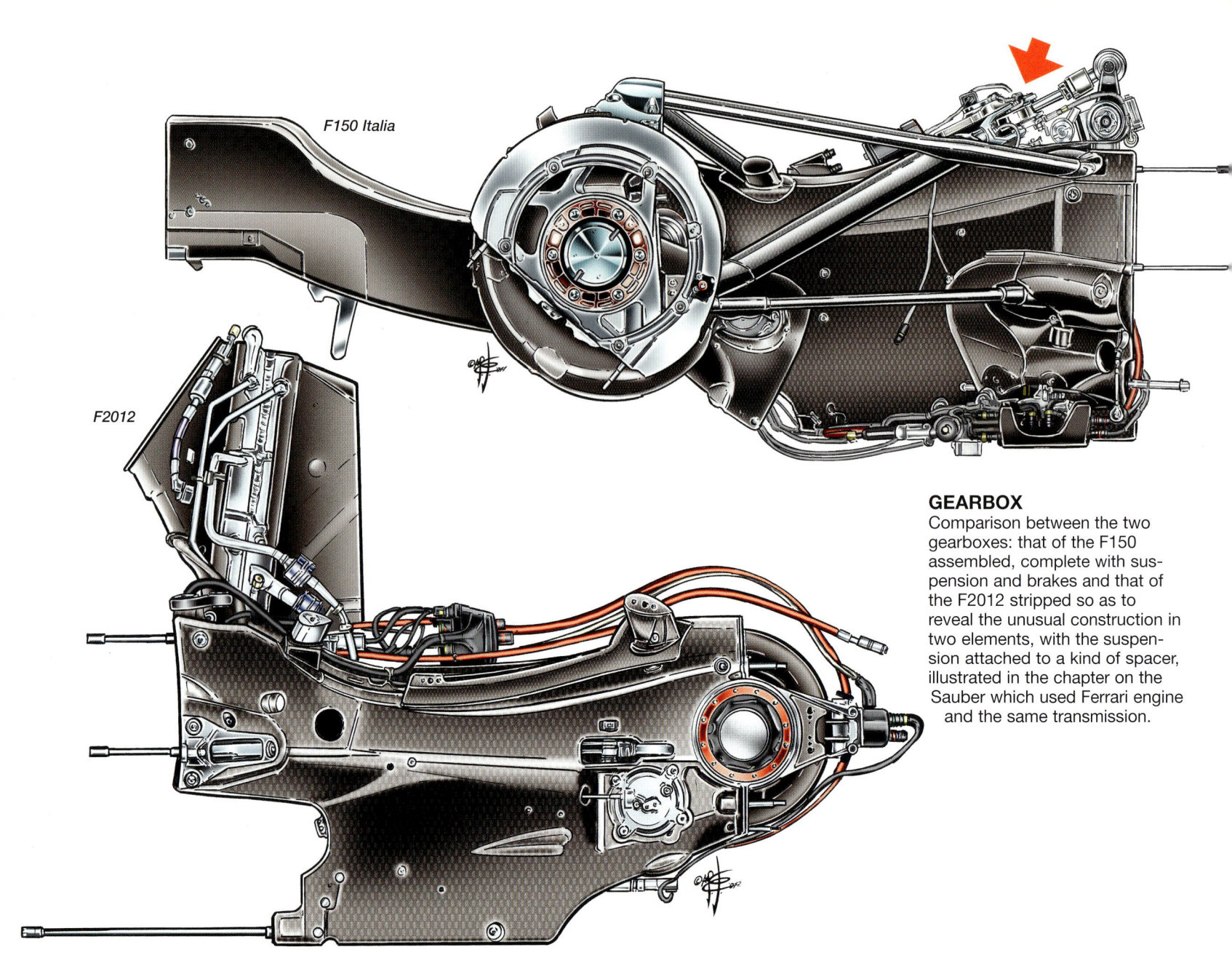

SIDE VIEWS

Despite the family feeling deriving from the chassis configuration (1), under the "skin" the two cars were very different. 2) The sidepods on both cars have fairly high mouths. the radiators that were almost always inclined (3) were now completely vertical and set in a fan formation. 4) The exhausts were very different and the stiffening arm between gearbox and chassis was a Ferrari first (deriving from the Renault school). 5) On the F150 the exhaust terminals were very long and blew in the area of the diffusers, on the F2012 their position was instead precisely established by the regulations. 6) The pull-rod rear suspension of

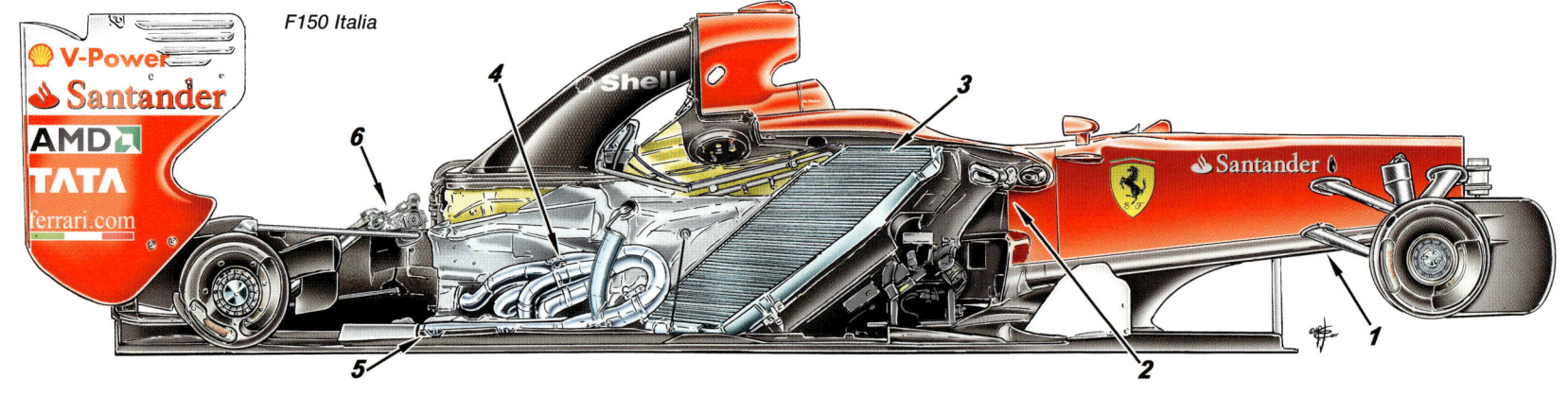

F150 Italia

FERRARI
70

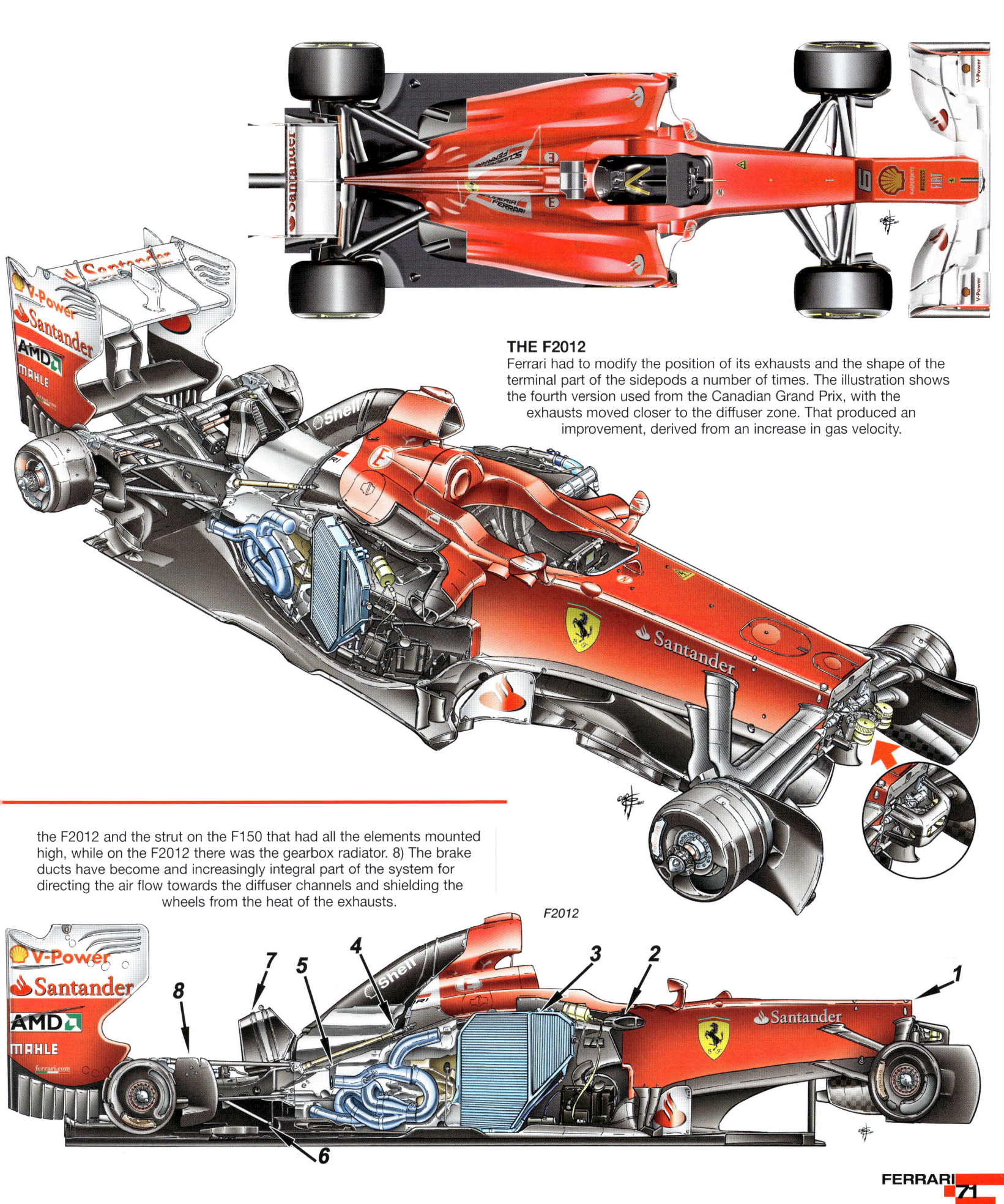

THE F2012
Ferrari had to modify the position of its exhausts and the shape of the terminal part of the sidepods a number of times. The illustration shows the fourth version used from the Canadian Grand Prix, with the exhausts moved closer to the diffuser zone. That produced an improvement, derived from an increase in gas velocity.

the F2012 and the strut on the F150 that had all the elements mounted high, while on the F2012 there was the gearbox radiator. 8) The brake ducts have become and increasingly integral part of the system for directing the air flow towards the diffuser channels and shielding the wheels from the heat of the exhausts.

F2012

FERRARI 71

McLAREN

CONSTRUCTORS' CLASSIFICATION			
	2011	2012	
Position	2°	3°	-1 ▼
Points	497	378	-119 ▼

A half full glass or a half empty one? McLaren's 2012 season can be judged either way.
It could be considered positive for them having built a more competitive car for almost the whole championship, and especially for having immediately created the best interpretation of the new aerodynamic limitations of the exhausts exit.
On the other hand, it could be considered negative, because the MP4-27 turned out to be most unreliable of the top teams cars, so much so that it was overtaken in the constructors' world championship by Ferrari, which also began the season with a less competitive F2012. At least three victories were lost due to gearbox and fuel pump issues, to which should be added pit stop problems during the first part of the season.
The 2012 McLaren was, once again, the longest car on the grid in wheelbase terms.
As far as the height of the chassis was concerned, the maximum 625 mm was not exploited, so that the car was the only one among the top teams that didn't need to use a step to drop down to the 550 mm required by the regulations. The only other team that took that direction was Marussia.
The main difference compared with the 2011 MP4-26 was in the sidepods, which were no longer L-shaped, concave in the centre or higher at the sides; they were of a more classical shape, with the air intakes high and horizontal like those of the 2011 car. The lower step was notably so, to generate a good flow of air towards the rear. McLaren should be credited with having immediately got the shape of the terminal part of the sidepods right to fully exploit the exhaust blow effect, despite the severe limitations imposed by the Federation. "Here, we were helped by the fact that, when we introduced exhaust blow in 2010, a problem came up associated with the Coanda effect.

McLaren MP4-26 2011

McLaren MP4-27 Launch

McLaren MP4-27 Melbourne

McLaren MP4-27 Barcelona

McLaren MP4-27 Hockenheim

So in determining the body shape around the exhaust exit, we took that experience into account", said Paddy Lowe with much simplicity.
The fact is the shape of the McLaren sidepods and exhaust exit set a trend in 2012, inspiring

the evolution of this sector for most teams.
But on the MP4-27 the solution of the beginning of the season stayed more or less the same, despite extremely intense development of the car in all its other sectors. The most evident concerned the nose. At the car's launch and initial tests, the MP4-27 had a nose much like that of the 2012 car, complete with a horizontal splitter in the lower area. However, that was dropped in favour of two "traditional" turning vanes as early as the pre-tests to then take the decision to develop a new nose for the Spanish Grand Prix; a high version, despite the height of the lower chassis compared to that of the competition. It stayed the same for the rest of the season. McLaren should also be credited with having opened up the road to further sophistication of the variable thermal dissipation brake air intakes (see the New Developments chapter).
The opportunity of varying the outlet inside the rims first began at the Chinese GP, but only at the rear end, and then at the front in Britain. It should be clarified that this variation could only be made during pit stops by the mechanics using screwdrivers, as with the adjustment of the front wing flaps.
McLaren's last major evolution appeared at the German GP. The car's entire aerodynamics were renewed from immediately after the front axle; if one considers that a completely new nose came in at the GP of Spain, there was little left of the original design. The sidepods became even more tapered at the front and rear and, above all, were considerably lower.
Other work was carried out on the new engine cover and lower aerodynamics; the rear wing end plates and brake air intakes were also modified.
Even more important were the less hidden modifications, seeing that the more tapered sidepods required a different radiator installation and exhaust manifold, redesigned so they could fit into the 'pods' more restricted space. The suspension geometry was also revised.
McLaren, according to Paddy Lowe's own admission, purposely ignored the development of a double DRS, preferring to concentrate on other aspects that led to an incredibly superior technique in mid-season.
But it was a potential that was, unfortunately, frustrated in the main by the lack of mechanical reliability suffered by the MP4-27 during the summer.

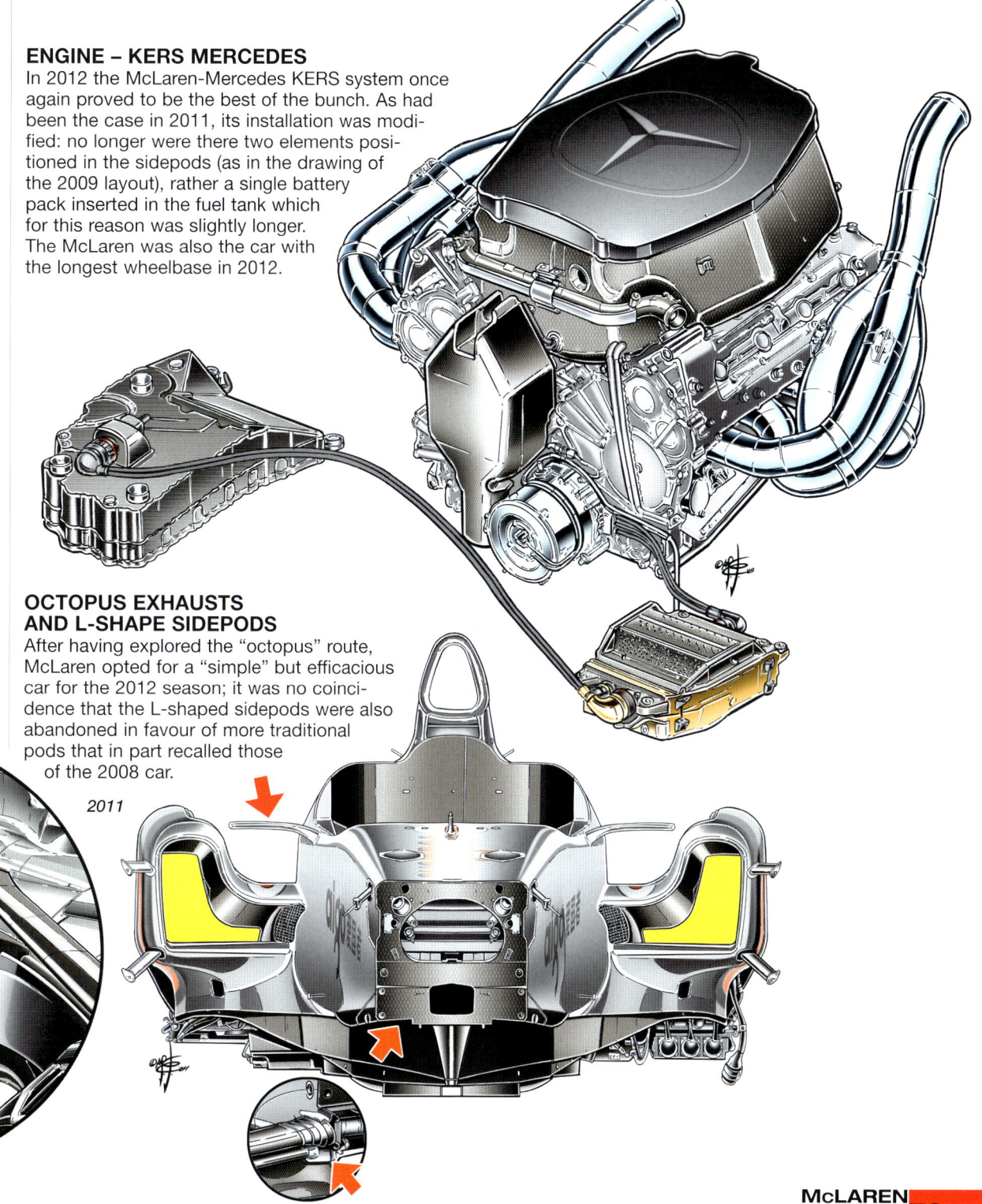

ENGINE – KERS MERCEDES
In 2012 the McLaren-Mercedes KERS system once again proved to be the best of the bunch. As had been the case in 2011, its installation was modified: no longer were there two elements positioned in the sidepods (as in the drawing of the 2009 layout), rather a single battery pack inserted in the fuel tank which for this reason was slightly longer. The McLaren was also the car with the longest wheelbase in 2012.

OCTOPUS EXHAUSTS AND L-SHAPE SIDEPODS
After having explored the "octopus" route, McLaren opted for a "simple" but efficacious car for the 2012 season; it was no coincidence that the L-shaped sidepods were also abandoned in favour of more traditional pods that in part recalled those of the 2008 car.

2011

McLAREN 73

2008

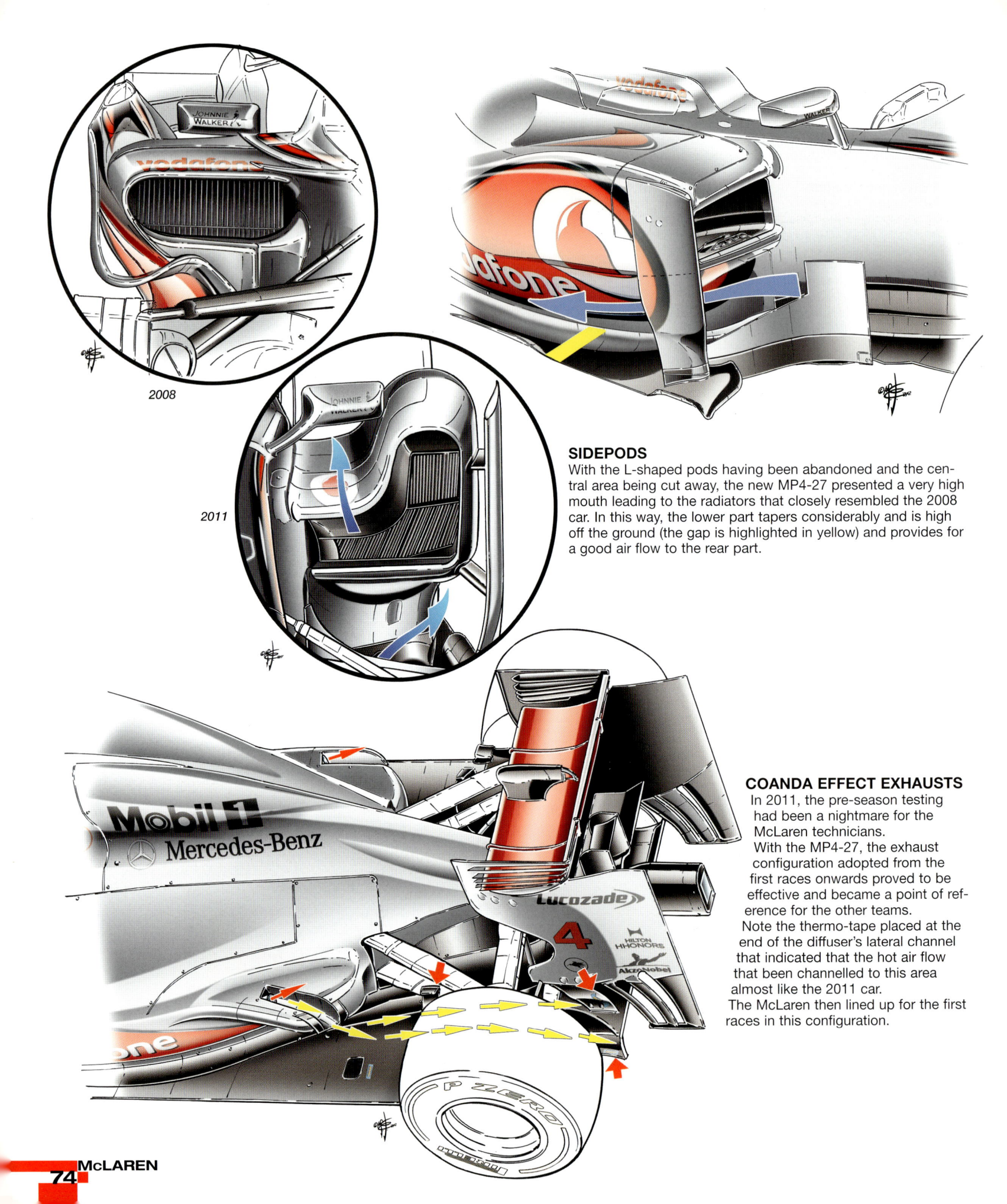

2011

SIDEPODS
With the L-shaped pods having been abandoned and the central area being cut away, the new MP4-27 presented a very high mouth leading to the radiators that closely resembled the 2008 car. In this way, the lower part tapers considerably and is high off the ground (the gap is highlighted in yellow) and provides for a good air flow to the rear part.

COANDA EFFECT EXHAUSTS
In 2011, the pre-season testing had been a nightmare for the McLaren technicians.
With the MP4-27, the exhaust configuration adopted from the first races onwards proved to be effective and became a point of reference for the other teams.
Note the thermo-tape placed at the end of the diffuser's lateral channel that indicated that the hot air flow that been channelled to this area almost like the 2011 car.
The McLaren then lined up for the first races in this configuration.

McLAREN

SHANGHAI

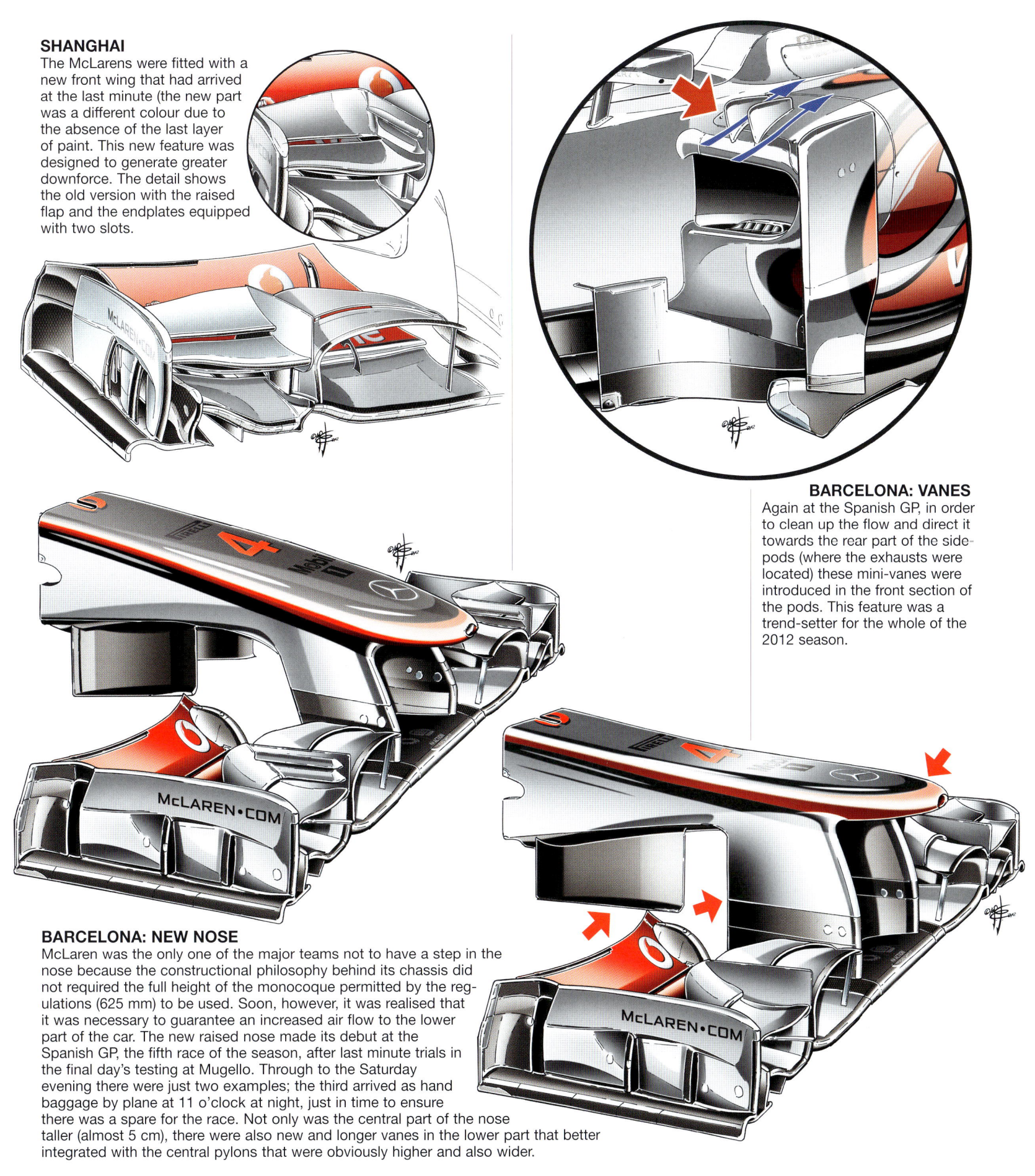

The McLarens were fitted with a new front wing that had arrived at the last minute (the new part was a different colour due to the absence of the last layer of paint. This new feature was designed to generate greater downforce. The detail shows the old version with the raised flap and the endplates equipped with two slots.

BARCELONA: VANES

Again at the Spanish GP, in order to clean up the flow and direct it towards the rear part of the sidepods (where the exhausts were located) these mini-vanes were introduced in the front section of the pods. This feature was a trend-setter for the whole of the 2012 season.

BARCELONA: NEW NOSE

McLaren was the only one of the major teams not to have a step in the nose because the constructional philosophy behind its chassis did not required the full height of the monocoque permitted by the regulations (625 mm) to be used. Soon, however, it was realised that it was necessary to guarantee an increased air flow to the lower part of the car. The new raised nose made its debut at the Spanish GP, the fifth race of the season, after last minute trials in the final day's testing at Mugello. Through to the Saturday evening there were just two examples; the third arrived as hand baggage by plane at 11 o'clock at night, just in time to ensure there was a spare for the race. Not only was the central part of the nose taller (almost 5 cm), there were also new and longer vanes in the lower part that better integrated with the central pylons that were obviously higher and also wider.

McLAREN

right | left

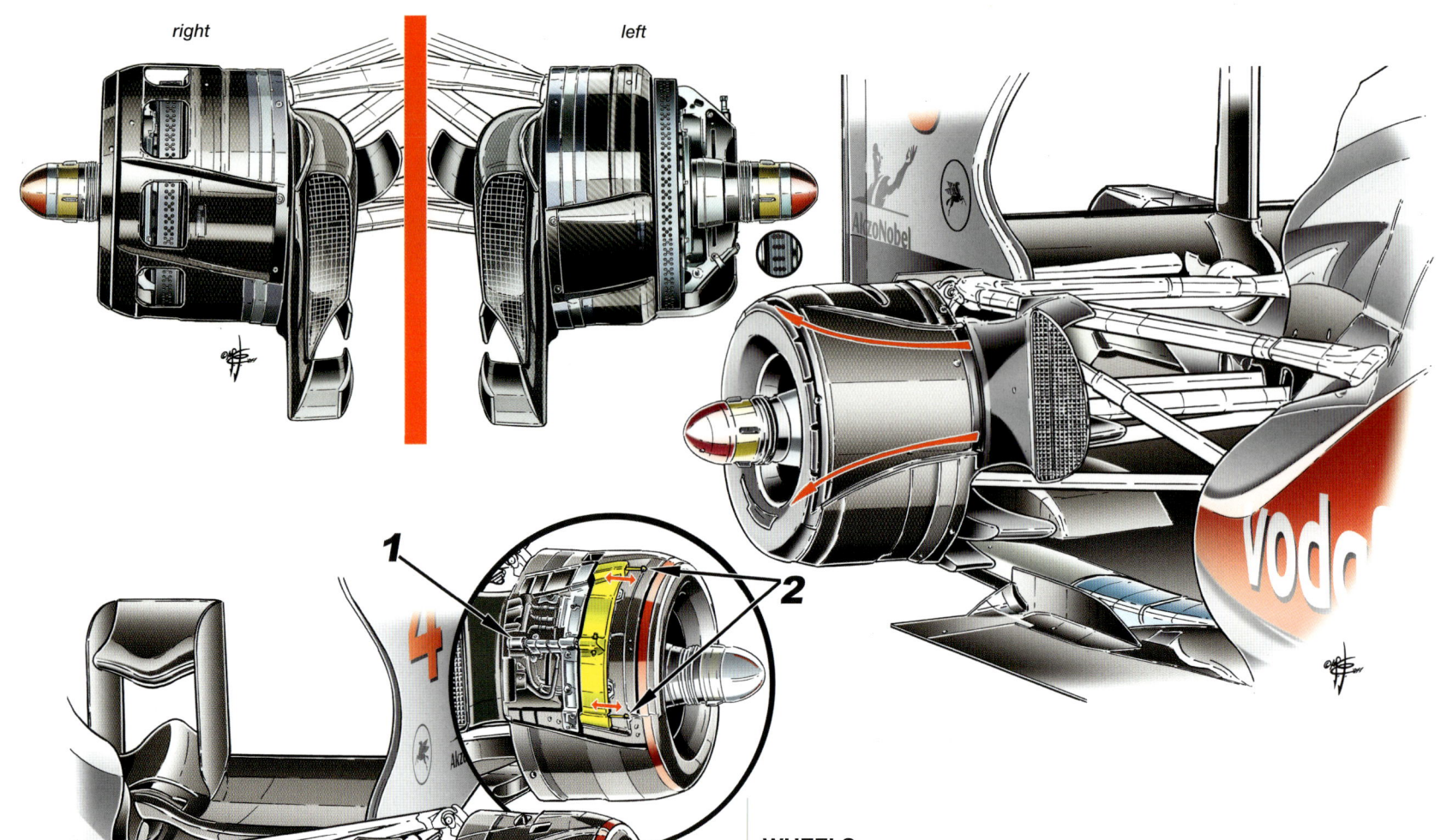

WHEELS
The wheels of the MP4-27 were designed to exploit this new feature, with new small radial apertures (indicated by the arrow) capable of appropriately directing the hot air flow from the brake ducts.

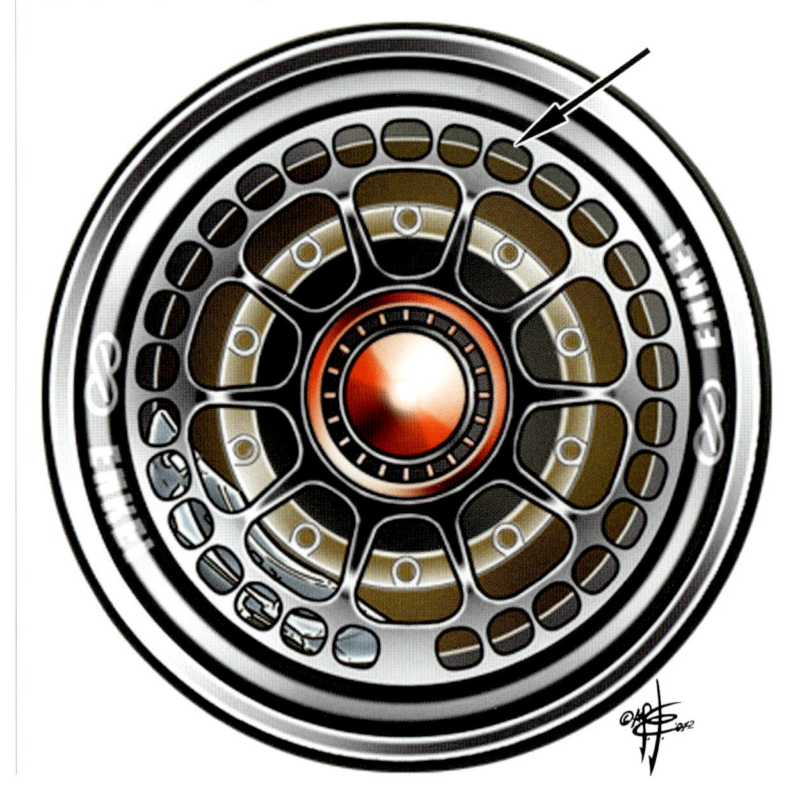

BRAKE DUCTS
McLaren had the honour of having introduced a significant refinement to the braking system, tested from the start of the season. In theory, in this specific area since 20112 McLaren had distinguished itself with asymmetric front brake ducts and rear ducts designed to exploit fully the aerodynamic effect of the hot air blow. In practice, on the MP4-27s during the pit stops, the evacuation of air from the multi-piece shrouds could be varied. The aperture of a vertical "window" could also be modified to allow the heat from the discs to disperse towards the tyres, thus influencing their running temperature.
The basic drawing shows the disc with the open shroud, while the detail reveals the mechanism controlling the opening with:
1) the hydraulic piston controlling the movement of the flange (in yellow) inside the shroud; 2) the stop controlling the movement.

McLAREN

VALENCIA

McLaren continued to experiment with the new rear suspension introduced in Canada on Hamilton's car only and tested on the Saturday at Valencia by Button too. It had a different mount for the front arm of the upper wishbone allowing the anti-dive characteristics to be modified.

SILVERSTONE: FRONT WING

The new front wing differed with respect to the old one with two flaps (1) divided into two sections widthwise. The external one remained fixed and served to better direct the flow in the area of the wheels, while the internal one was adjustable (2) and allowed the incidence of the two flaps to be modified without significantly interfering with the flows that affected the rest of the car.

old

new

SILVERSTONE: FRONT BRAKE DUCTS

McLaren tried the adjustable front ducts allowing heat to be expelled from the central section, as had been the case with the rear ducts from the Spanish GP. Here too, there was a hydraulic piston that served to open and close the slot covering the discs. Thanks in part to the shape of the shrouds, the heat is expelled towards the outside, in the area where McLaren had introduced new holes in the wheel rims.

McLAREN

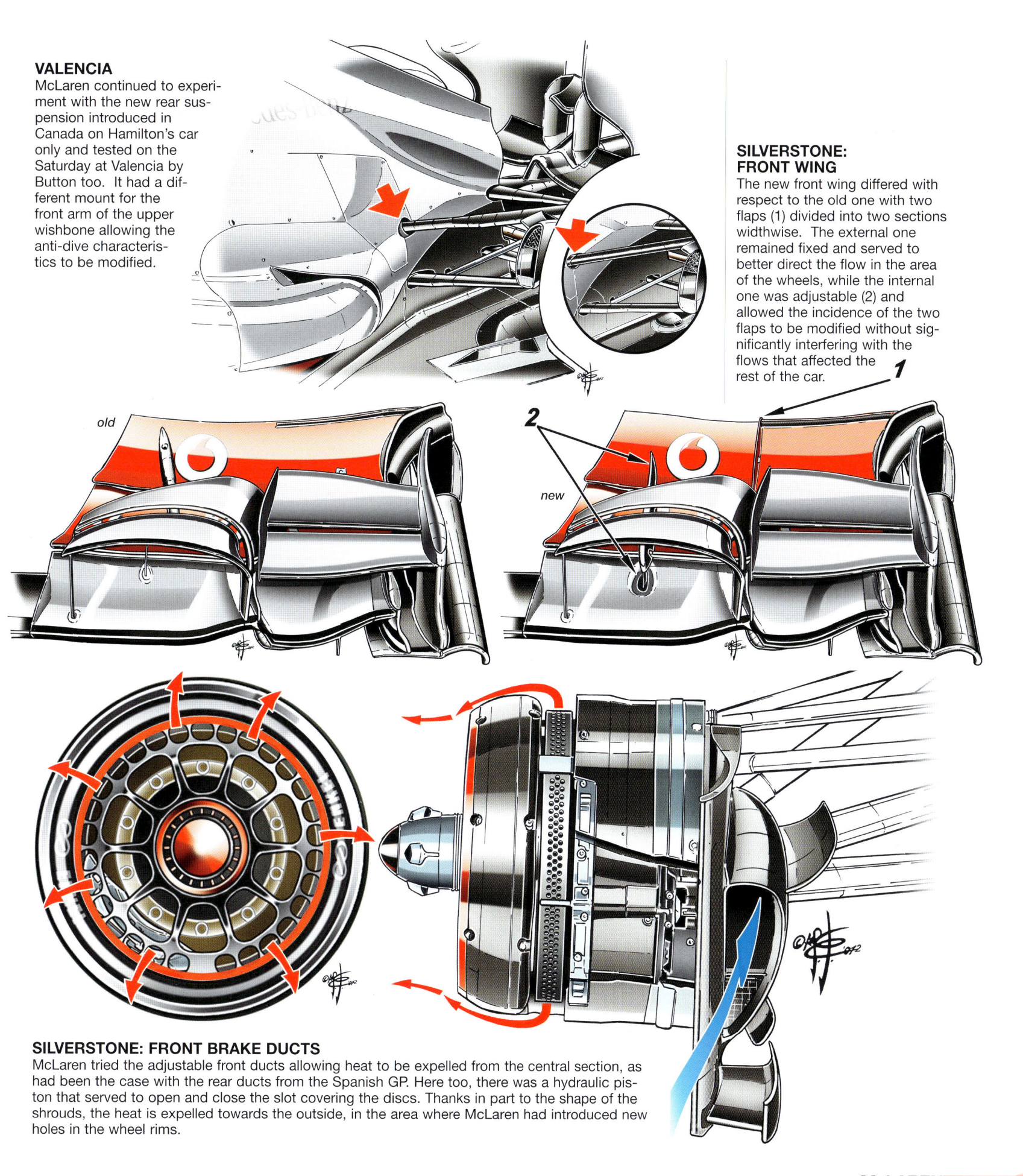

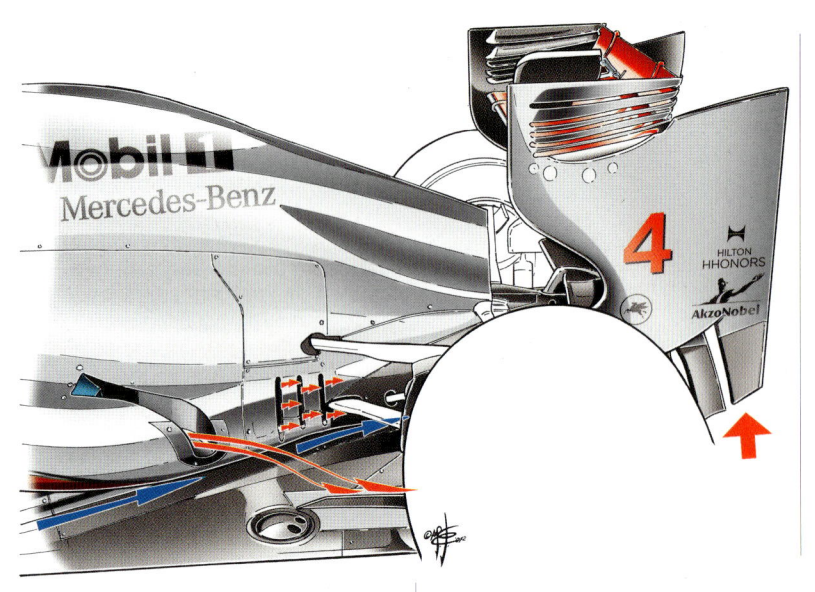

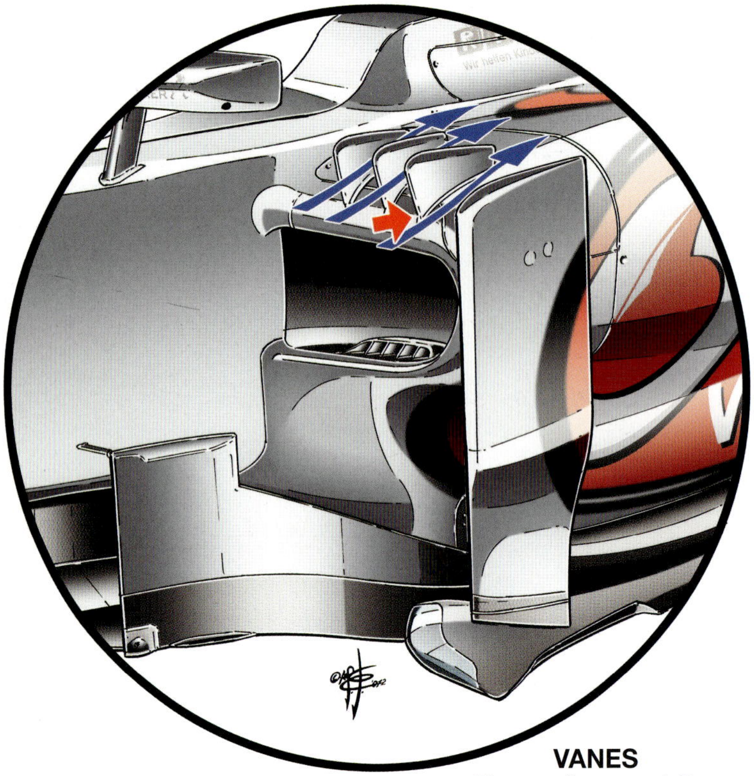

HOCKENHEIM: SIDEPODS

The car McLaren presented at the German GP may be considered as a "B" version with very low sidepods that were cutaway in the lower section to better guarantee the Coanda effect with the exhausts blowing at the base of the rear wheels.
Note the gill-like slots designed to expel the hot air. There were also new diffuser lateral channels and vertical appendages in the lower part of the endplates.

BUDAPEST

The major evolution of the MP4-27 introduced in Germany was completed in Hungary with a new diffuser characterised by rounded edges and the presence of min-flaps like on almost all the other cars.
The fringes in the lower part of the endplates were also modified, becoming shorter, especially the last one. The drawing of the sidepods clearly shows how McLaren tried to create the same effect of the dual channel feeding the air flow towards the diffuser, with the bodywork descending in a fairly accentuated manner in the exhaust blow area.
The rear brake ducts were also new, with the apertures being adjustable to increase the running temperatures of the tyres.

VANES

The small vanes at the start of the sidepods, introduced at the Spanish GP, now totalled three with the addition of a new element. The aim was as ever to direct the flow to the rear part of the sidepods.

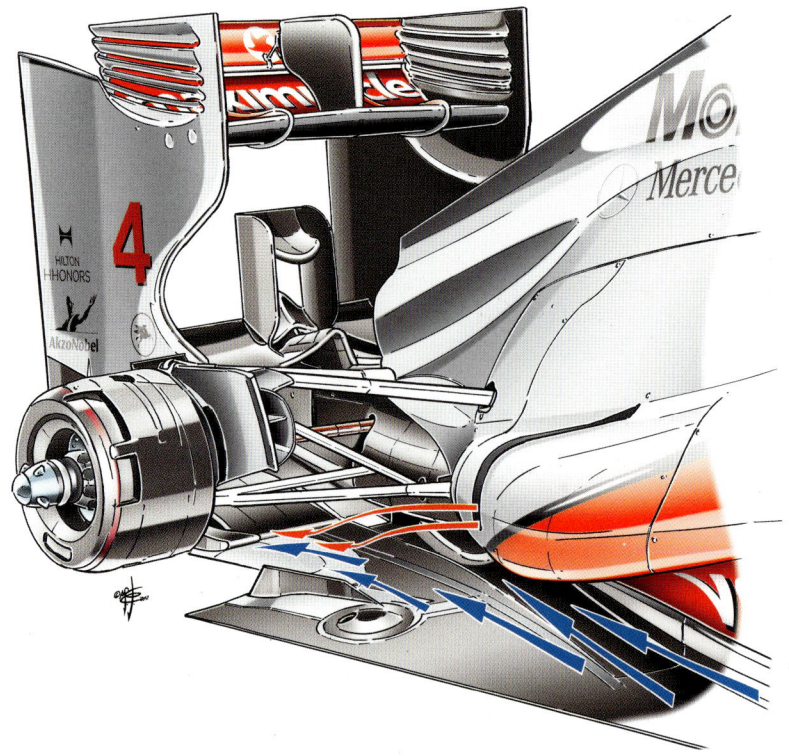

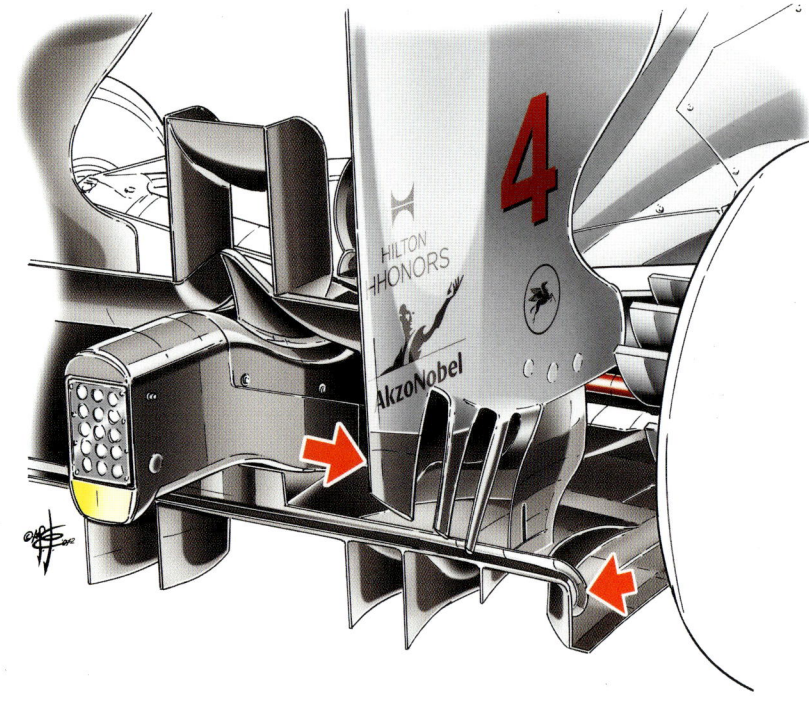

McLAREN
78

Button

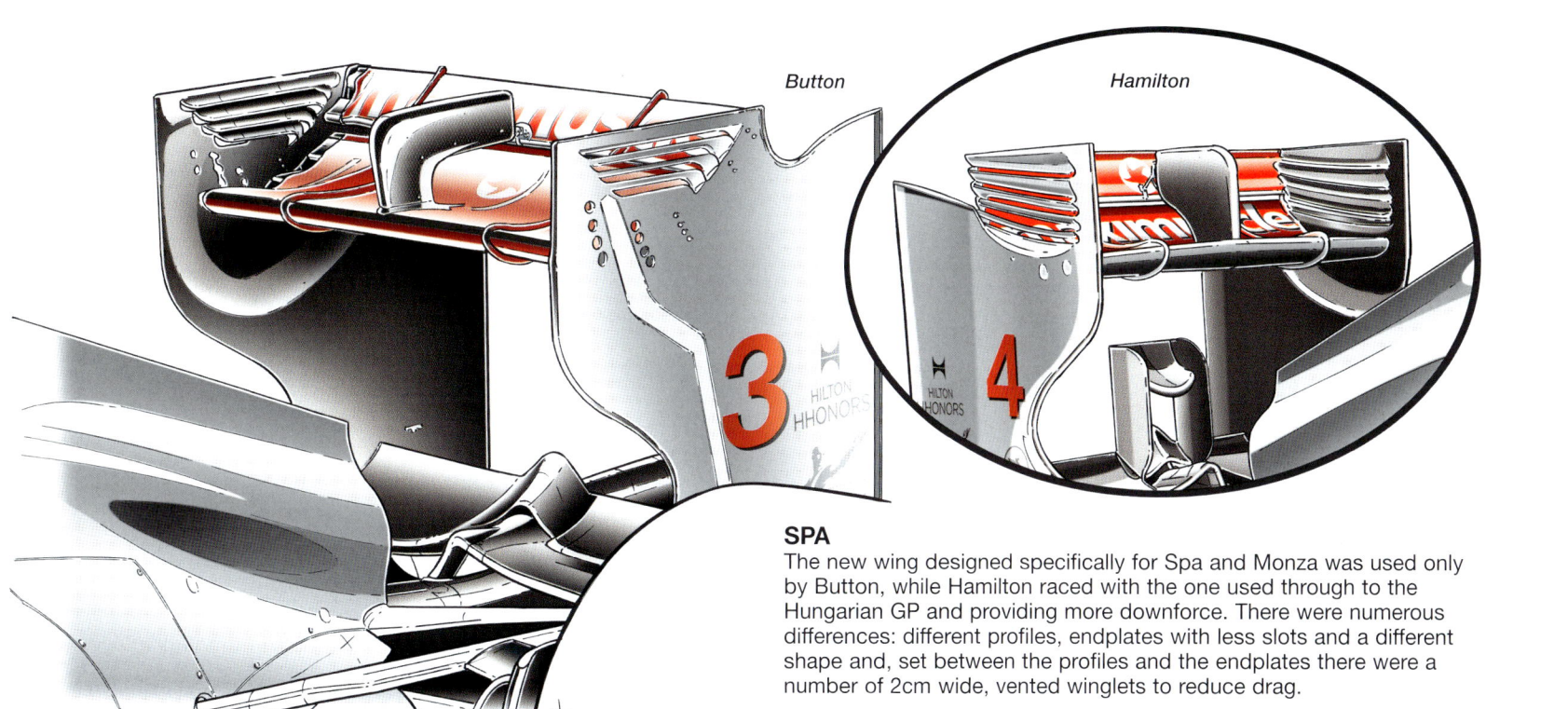

Hamilton

SPA
The new wing designed specifically for Spa and Monza was used only by Button, while Hamilton raced with the one used through to the Hungarian GP and providing more downforce. There were numerous differences: different profiles, endplates with less slots and a different shape and, set between the profiles and the endplates there were a number of 2cm wide, vented winglets to reduce drag.

SPA VANES
Unexpectedly, McLaren again modified the aerodynamic appendages above the front of the sidepods. The vertical fins of which three had been fitted at the German GP (the copied by almost all teams) were eliminated. In their place came a large overturned L-shaped profile that took to the extreme the feature introduced some time earlier by Sauber.

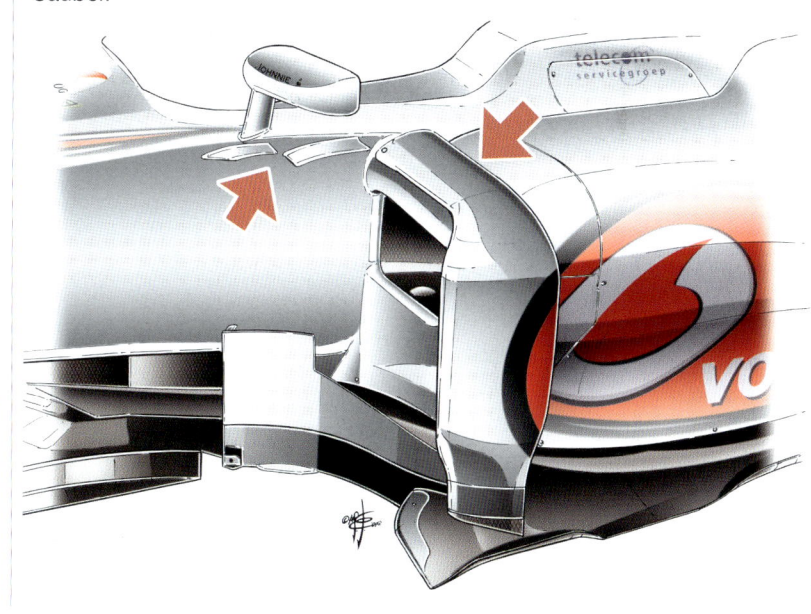

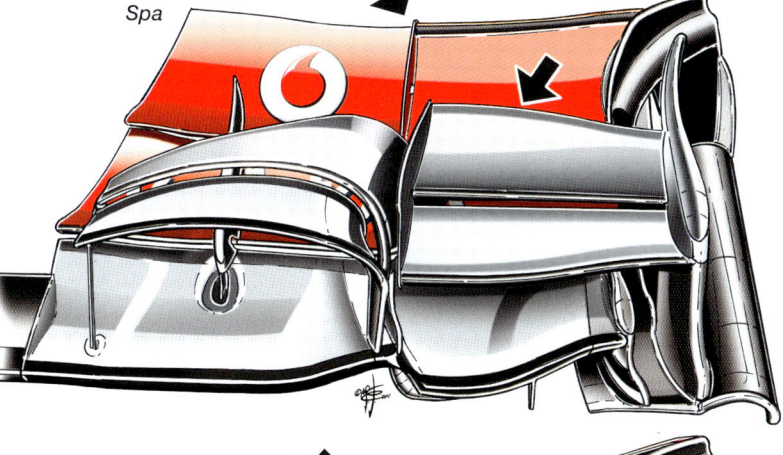

Spa

Monza

MONZA: FRONT WING
At Monza, McLaren introduced a new front wing that was in effect the Valencia wing without the second flap divided into two, introduced at Silverstone (above). In its place was a full-width flap with a reduced chord. The raised flaps attached to the endplates have been removed, thus revealing the shape of the second vertical plate that follows the line of the wing profiles.

McLAREN

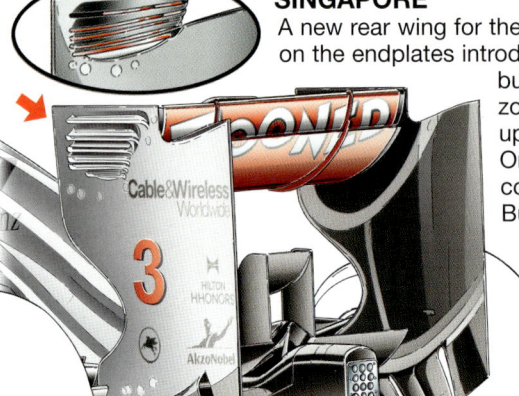

SINGAPORE

A new rear wing for the McLarens, based on the endplates introduced in Belgium but with more horizontal slots in the upper part.
On the Friday it was compared with the Budapest version (in the oval with the endplate divided into two sections) and then chosen for the race by both drivers.

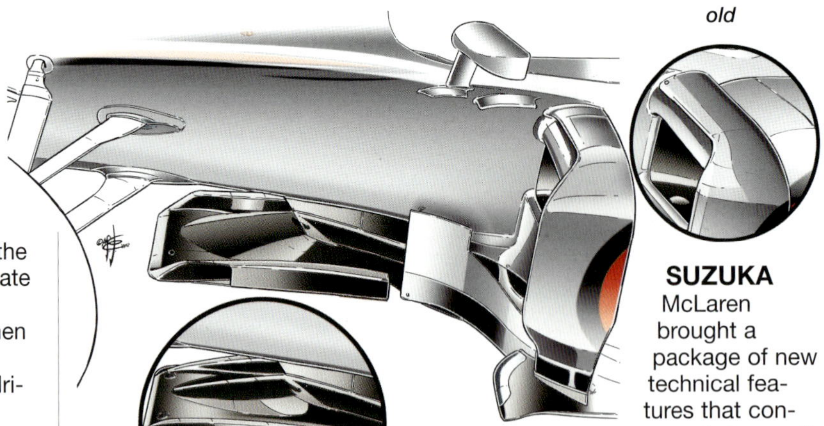

ABU DHABI

New rear brake ducts with shrouds featuring partial apertures (one to the outside and two in the central section). Hamilton used the French C.I. discs, while Button used Brembos.

AUSTIN

McLaren introduced a new front wing that differed significantly with respect to the one used almost throughout the season. All its components were different from the main plane with a more rounded "step" (1) midway along its length. The curved dual flap (2) present on the MP4 from the Singapore GP in 2010 was eliminated in favour of a single Lotus-style vertical fin (2). The profile then joined the endplate with a very rounded section and a more conspicuous vent between the various profiles thanks in part to the elimination of the second min-endplate (4) linked to the external one. The final section (5) of the endplate was rounded to improve flow management in the area ahead of the front wheels.

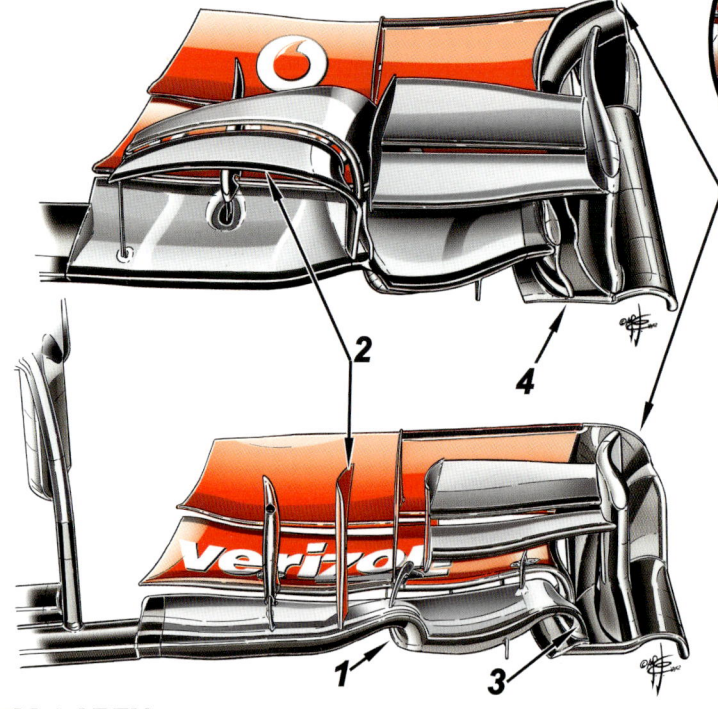

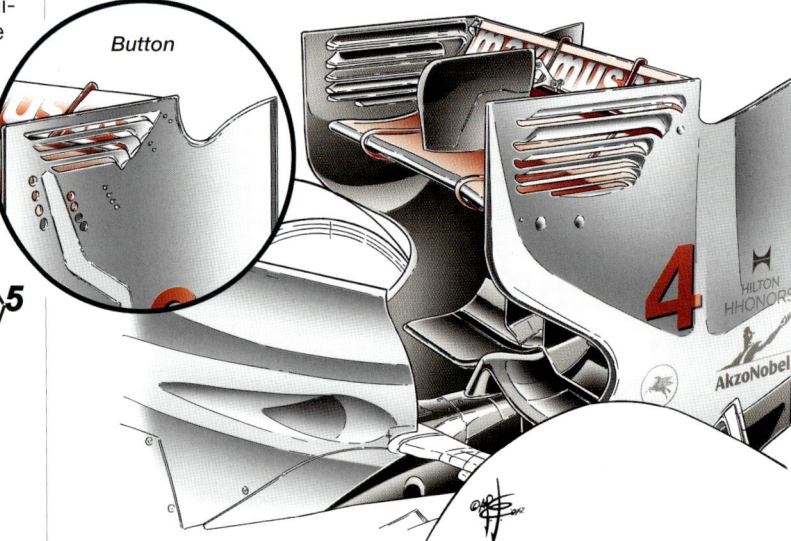

SUZUKA

McLaren brought a package of new technical features that concerned above all the central part of the car. The was a new T-Tray, the semi-flat section below the chassis, that became more angular, with a more accentuated initial ramp and a lateral vent as on many other cars (in the circle the old version). There were also new overturn L-shaped profiles at the start of the sidepods. The drawing reveal the new more raised version of the sidepod skin, with a slightly modified shape as can be seen from the comparison with the old version in the circle.

SAO PAOLO

At the last race of the season, the two McLarens went into Friday practice with two different aerodynamic packages, but only so as to evaluate the behaviour of the 2012 Pirelli tyres; on the Saturday Button, like Hamilton, used the higher downforce wing.

McLAREN

LOTUS

CONSTRUCTORS' CLASSIFICATION			
	2011	2012	
Position	5°	4°	+1▲
Points	73	303	+230▲

Topped by Kimi Raikkonen's victory in the Grand Prix of Abu Dhabi, 2012 was Lotus's best season since it was Renault and won both world championships in 2006 with Fernando Alonso.

The E20 was often the fastest car in race set-up and scored seven podium finishes, but it was penalised by being less competitive in qualifying.

Without that impediment, it would have been able to win at least in Bahrain, due to its ability to preserve its tyres throughout the whole race and the soft set-up of the suspension, its pitch and roll controlled by a hydraulic interconnection between the two axles, which had no negative effect on its aerodynamics.

That was a development the team first used in 2011, one that could have become even more effective if the set-up control for the front end had not been outlawed before the start of the championship (see the Controversies chapter), it having been tried by young drivers at Abu Dhabi.

As far as the E20 was concerned, James Allison set his cap at creating a reliable and cost-effective car without risking a second flop, after the over-bold adventure of exhaust blow at the front of the sidepods.

The E20 took on the shape and aerodynamics of the previous model, and it was no coincidence that it was the most traditional car of all the 2012 competitors.

Stung by the lack of success of the 2011 car, the Lotus technicians didn't completely exploit the Coandă effect, opting for a position of the exhausts that directed air flow towards the diffusers' lateral channels.

After considerable work in the wind tunnel and with CFD simulations, they went for a version of the exhausts that privileged the generation of power and its maximum exploitation, partially renouncing the blow effect that would have caused the loss of over 15 hp at top speed.

Even so, the Coandă effect solution was never completely abandoned; it made its debut during the season's finale – before that it was only on Raikkonen's car in Korea – when the advantages of that technique were more significant than those achieved earlier in the year.

So the E20 improved considerably in slow corners and especially its performance in qualifying, which enabled the Finn to start from the second row and lay the foundations for the team's only win of the season at Abu Dhabi.

The only negative side to that new development was a slightly higher degree of rear tyre wear during races.

But substantial development work was carried out throughout the season, mainly concentrated on the first part, producing continuous refinements to the front aerodynamics, so the nose, front wing, end plates and brake air intakes.

The nose was given a sort of trend-setting pouch from the Hungarian GP, while the passive double DRS made a brief appearance during practice for the GP of Germany. In reality, it resurrected the exact concepts and mechanisms of the 2010 F-Duct, obviously without the driver having to operate it.

The development was only used on an experimental basis during Friday practice, given that setting it up was difficult to be able to exploit further stalling of the rear wing safely and positively.

The experiment continued throughout the final part of the season, mainly with a view to its introduction in 2013.

Mercedes-Benz also followed the French team's example from the Belgian Grand Prix, but without ever using the double DRS in either qualifying or racing.

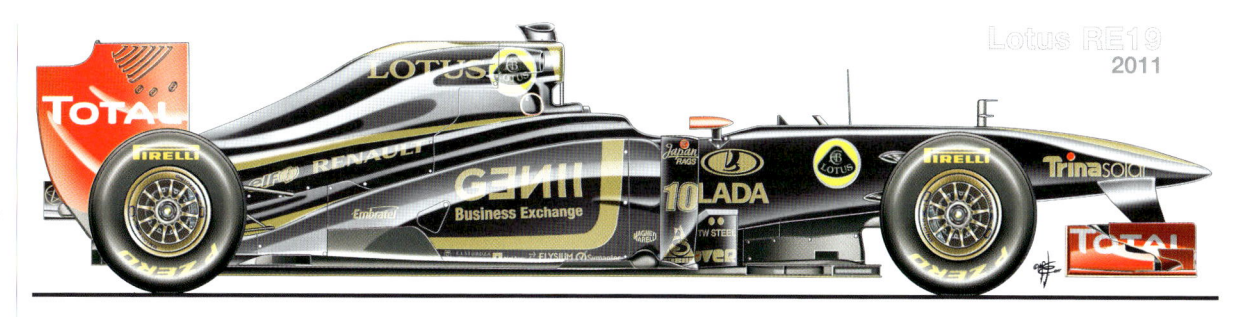

Lotus RE19 2011

Lotus E20

Lotus E20 Yeongam

81

RIDE HEIGHT ADJUSTER

The season began early for Lotus with the FIA giving the thumbs down to a feature presented in the test sessions following Abu Dhabi. This was a kind of wholly passive ride height adjuster with the car in movement, without the intervention of the driver. A feature that was explained in the "Controversies" chapter. The detail drawing shows: the hub carrier with the lower wishbone pivoting very high and, below it, to the bottom right, a hydraulic cylinder and a piston (1) which obviously do not appear on the other F1 cars. The most important element was the suspension strut (2) which was not attached directly to the mount on the hub carrier but had a certain degree of "play" (in yellow in the circular enlargement), thanks to a second small hydraulic jack highlighted in blue at the base of the strut. A clever feature that was rightly banned by the federation before the season got underway.

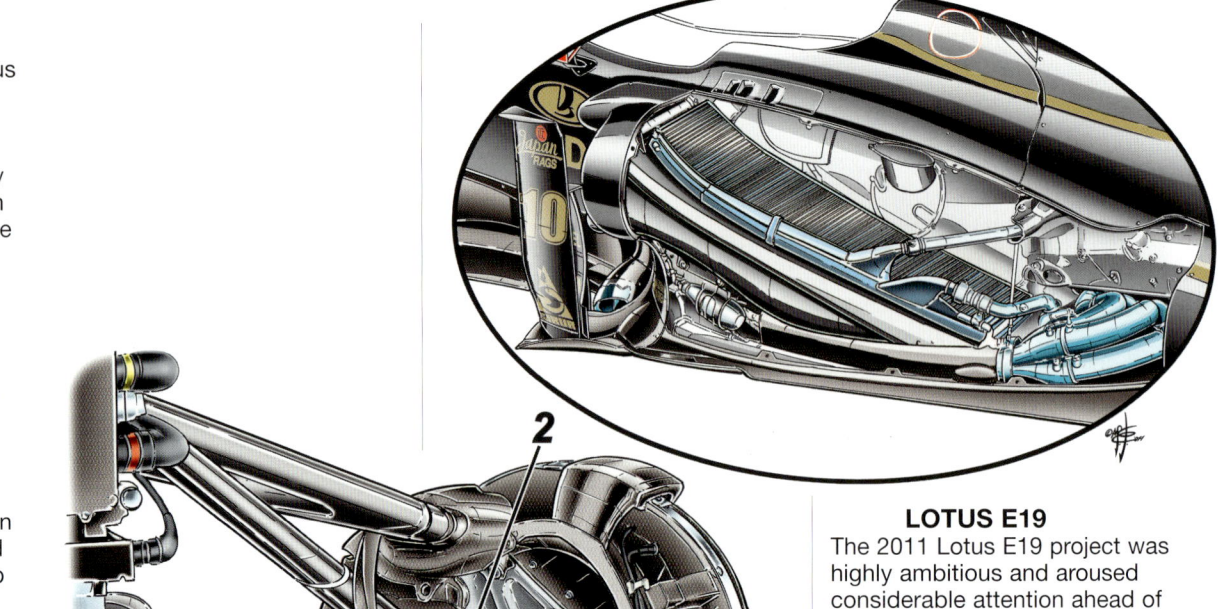

LOTUS E19

The 2011 Lotus E19 project was highly ambitious and aroused considerable attention ahead of the championship. It was designed to create downforce little influenced by variations in height from the ground and very close to the car's centre of gravity; instead it soon proved to be a flop.

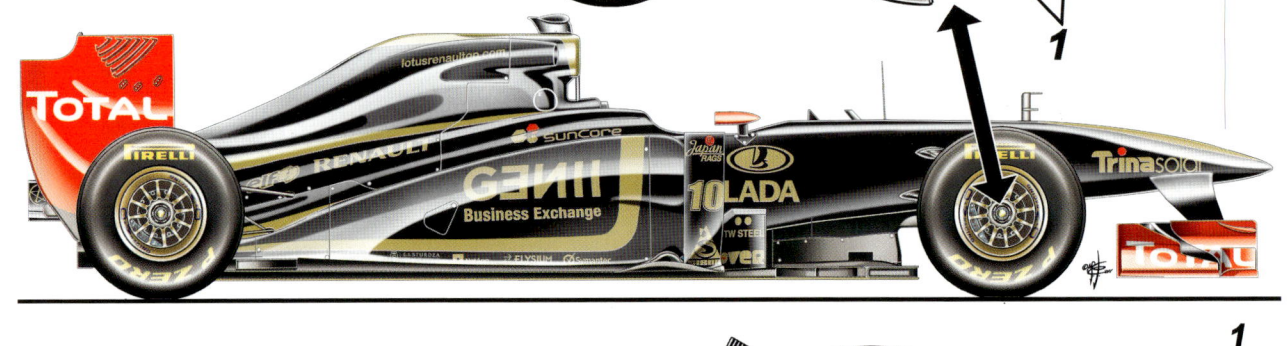

REAR SUSPENSION

Many modifications were made to the Lotus compared to 2011; after moving the brake caliper to a sub-horizontal position, the lower wishbone was pivoted just below the wheel centre.

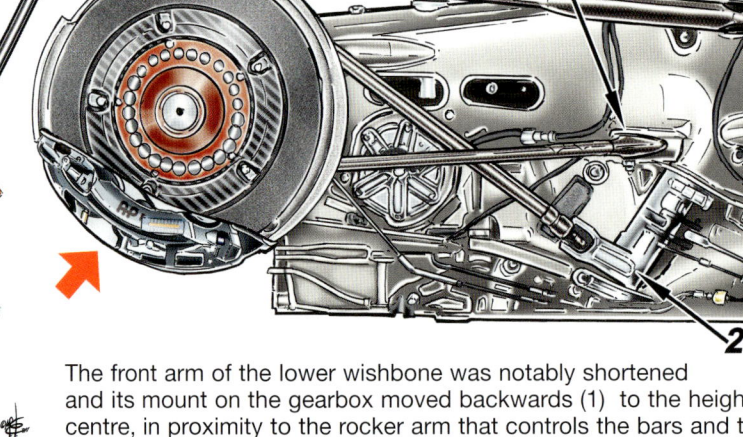

The front arm of the lower wishbone was notably shortened and its mount on the gearbox moved backwards (1) to the height of the wheel centre, in proximity to the rocker arm that controls the bars and that, in turn, was positioned lower (2). The torsion and anti-roll bars' positions (3) were unchanged, both easily

LOTUS

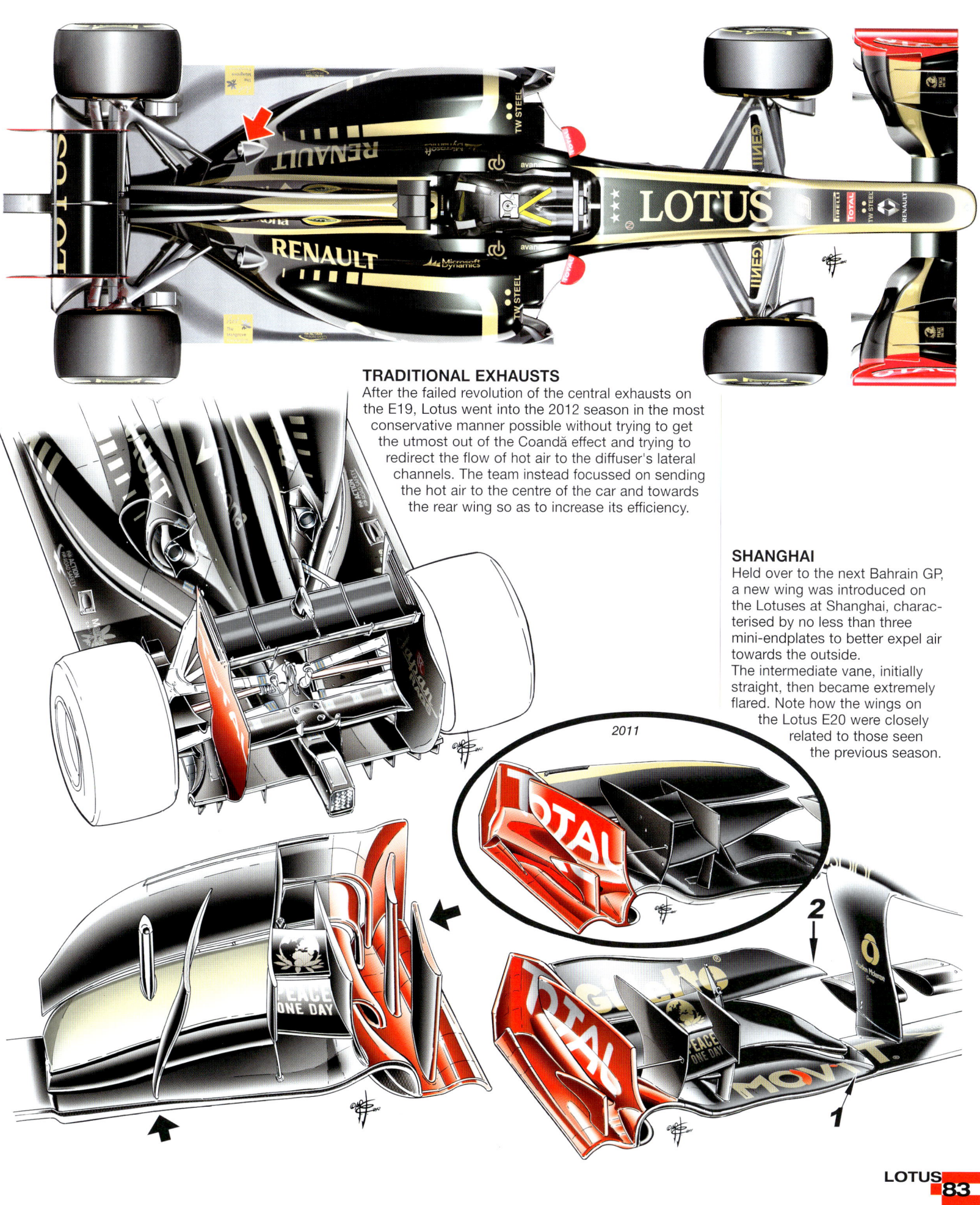

TRADITIONAL EXHAUSTS
After the failed revolution of the central exhausts on the E19, Lotus went into the 2012 season in the most conservative manner possible without trying to get the utmost out of the Coandă effect and trying to redirect the flow of hot air to the diffuser's lateral channels. The team instead focussed on sending the hot air to the centre of the car and towards the rear wing so as to increase its efficiency.

SHANGHAI
Held over to the next Bahrain GP, a new wing was introduced on the Lotuses at Shanghai, characterised by no less than three mini-endplates to better expel air towards the outside.
The intermediate vane, initially straight, then became extremely flared. Note how the wings on the Lotus E20 were closely related to those seen the previous season.

2011

LOTUS 83

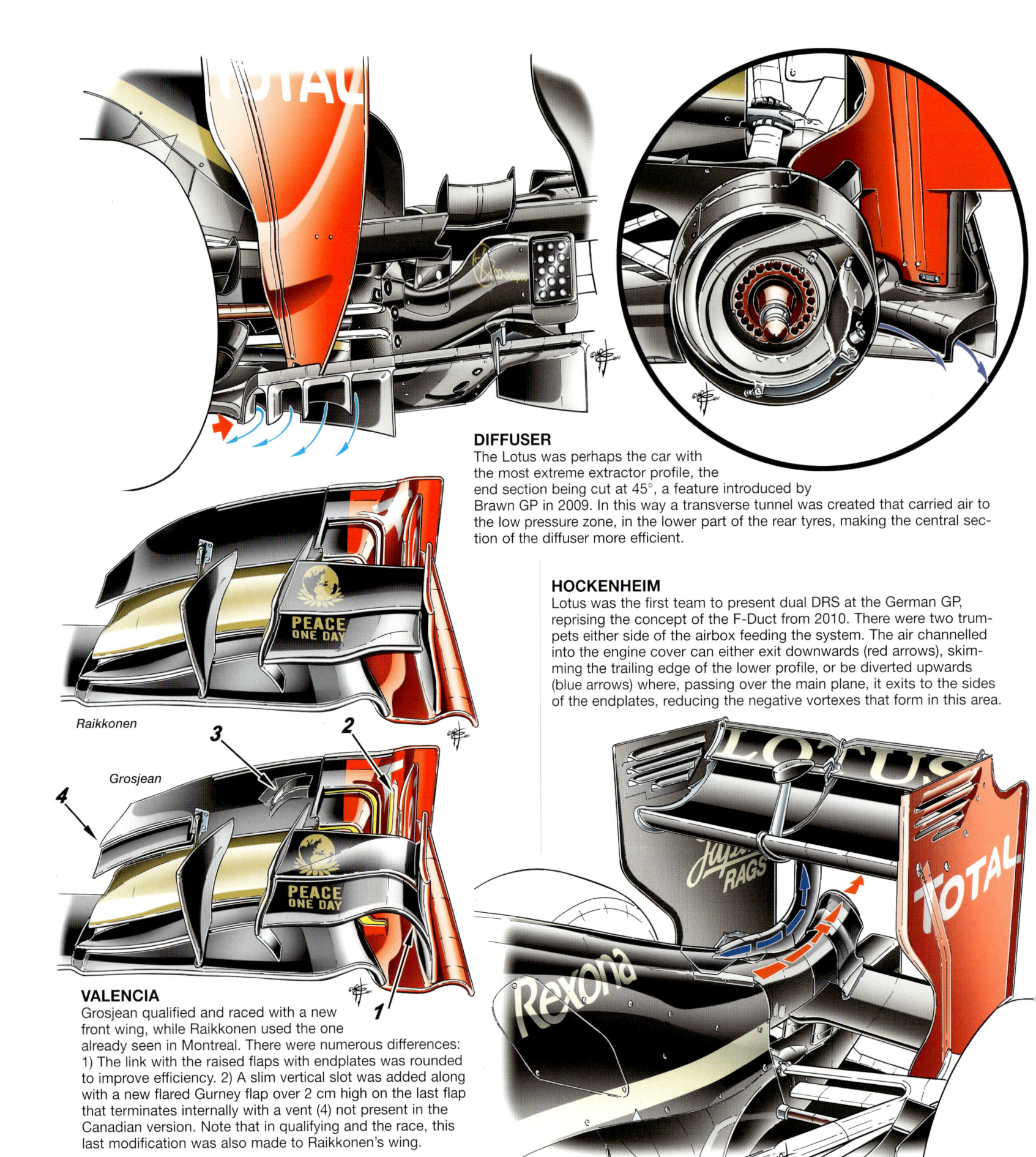

DIFFUSER
The Lotus was perhaps the car with the most extreme extractor profile, the end section being cut at 45°, a feature introduced by Brawn GP in 2009. In this way a transverse tunnel was created that carried air to the low pressure zone, in the lower part of the rear tyres, making the central section of the diffuser more efficient.

HOCKENHEIM
Lotus was the first team to present dual DRS at the German GP, reprising the concept of the F-Duct from 2010. There were two trumpets either side of the airbox feeding the system. The air channelled into the engine cover can either exit downwards (red arrows), skimming the trailing edge of the lower profile, or be diverted upwards (blue arrows) where, passing over the main plane, it exits to the sides of the endplates, reducing the negative vortexes that form in this area.

Raikkonen

Grosjean

VALENCIA
Grosjean qualified and raced with a new front wing, while Raikkonen used the one already seen in Montreal. There were numerous differences: 1) The link with the raised flaps with endplates was rounded to improve efficiency. 2) A slim vertical slot was added along with a new flared Gurney flap over 2 cm high on the last flap that terminates internally with a vent (4) not present in the Canadian version. Note that in qualifying and the race, this last modification was also made to Raikkonen's wing.

LOTUS
84

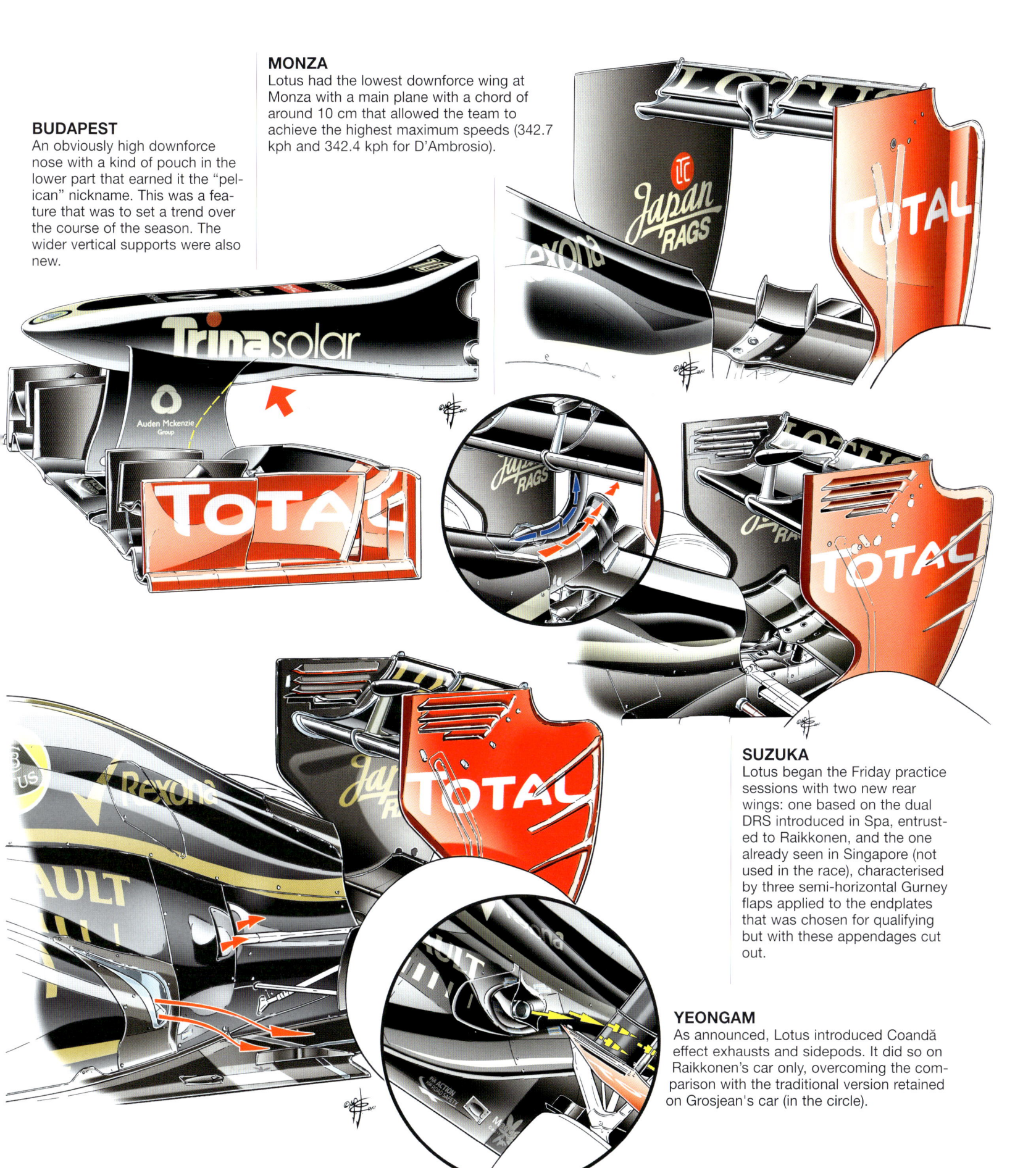

BUDAPEST

An obviously high downforce nose with a kind of pouch in the lower part that earned it the "pelican" nickname. This was a feature that was to set a trend over the course of the season. The wider vertical supports were also new.

MONZA

Lotus had the lowest downforce wing at Monza with a main plane with a chord of around 10 cm that allowed the team to achieve the highest maximum speeds (342.7 kph and 342.4 kph for D'Ambrosio).

SUZUKA

Lotus began the Friday practice sessions with two new rear wings: one based on the dual DRS introduced in Spa, entrusted to Raikkonen, and the one already seen in Singapore (not used in the race), characterised by three semi-horizontal Gurney flaps applied to the endplates that was chosen for qualifying but with these appendages cut out.

YEONGAM

As announced, Lotus introduced Coandă effect exhausts and sidepods. It did so on Raikkonen's car only, overcoming the comparison with the traditional version retained on Grosjean's car (in the circle).

LOTUS 85

MERCEDES

CONSTRUCTORS' CLASSIFICATION			
	2011	2012	
Position	4°	4°	=
Points	165	142	-23 ▼

Mercedes MGP W02
2011

Mercedes MGP W03

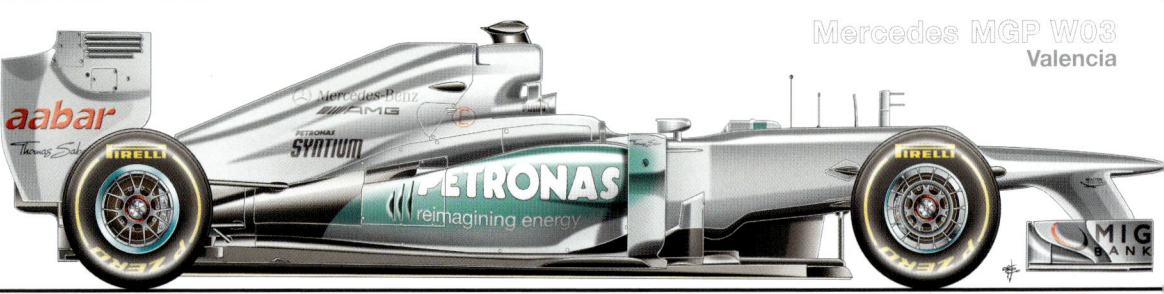

Mercedes MGP W03
Valencia

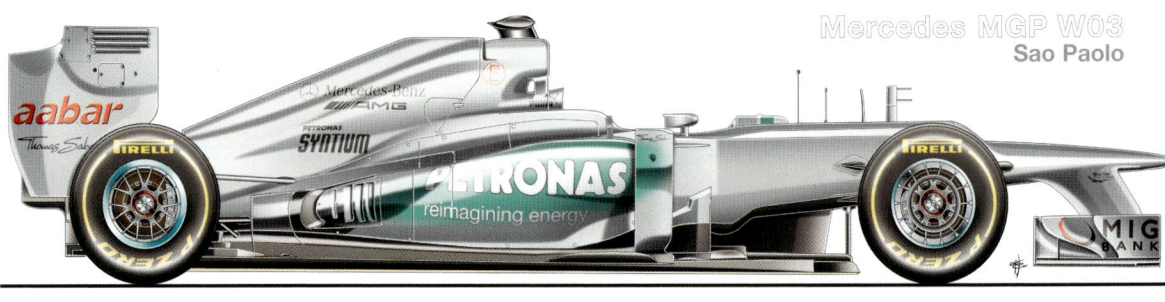

Mercedes MGP W03
Sao Paolo

Nico Rosberg's victory in the third race of the season gave the illusion that the 2012 championship would be really positive for Mercedes-Benz after the flop of the two previous seasons. Instead, the W03 was not a competitive car and was at risk of being overtaken by an optimum Sauber, which was only at a disadvantage because it had young drivers.

Even so, the W03 was a notable evolution of the W02, although the front F-Duct stratagem wasn't worth much, and was certainly not the winning device that the double diffuser became on the 2009 Brawn GP.

Discovered at the 2001 Grand Prix of Japan, in theory the development shouldn't have been approved seeing that, to all intents and purposes, it was a mobile aerodynamic device operated in a second phase by the driver. The request for clarification by Lotus, which had had its variable pushrod upright mount outlawed during the design stage, appeared to us to be a clear infraction of the regulations, even if less evident than the solution conceded to Ross Brawn.

In theory, both of them should have been prohibited for the same reason, but in the end that development turned into a boomerang for the Stuttgart company. It severely limited the car's aerodynamic development, both in relation to the front wing and its flaps and the rear wing's end plates, in which the hole was hidden. It was from there that the complicated passage of air between the front and rear began; it had to traverse the entire car to reach the front wing, as we saw in the New Developments and Controversies chapters.

But the front F-Duct did produce advantages, mainly in qualifying rather than racing, when the development sometimes turned out to be counter productive, causing increased understeer. Mercedes-Benz brought in its passive double DRS on the rear wing from the Grand Prix of Belgium, following the trend started by Lotus at the preceding German GP. As with others, Mercedes never used this technical development in racing, but only during Friday practice to gather data for transfer to the 2013 car project.

At mid-season, M-B also went from 50% to 60% scale wind tunnel models together in the handover of the aerodynamics department from Loic Bigois, who was taken on by Ferrari, to Mike Elliot, who came from Lotus.

All of which started an initial slow-down in the car's development. Strangely, Mercedes-Benz was one of the last teams to go for sidepods inspired by the Coandă effect, but it did so in Singapore with McLaren-type 'pods and exhausts, which were first tried out during private testing at Magny Cours.

On that occasion, we also saw a mini-fin on the engine cover, which was part of the experiment required by the Federation to better see the name of the driver. At the finale, the W03 dropped the McLaren-style sidepods and went back to its originals in an attempt to limit the greater degradation of the rear tyres associated with the new design. Degradation was still bad on the car despite the advantage – as per Lotus – of being able to use a hydraulic interconnection between the front and rear suspensions to ensure an optimum set-up, which was described in the 2011 Technical Analysis.

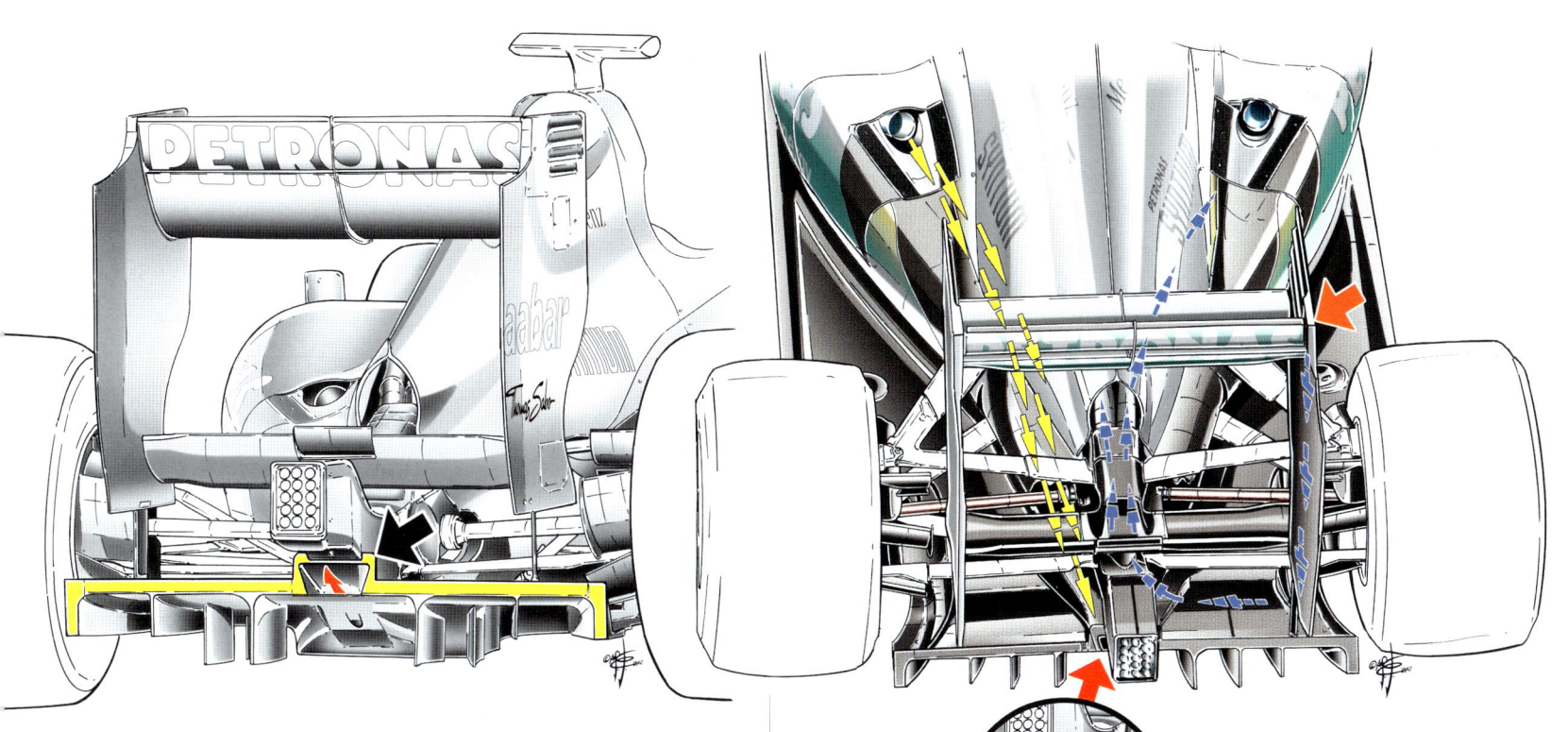

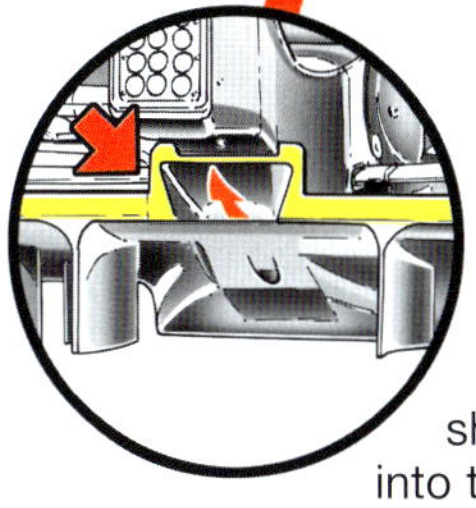

DOUBLE DIFFUSERS

The Mercedes-Benz W03 seemed like a car with good potential with many interesting developments, such as the double diffuser in the off-limits zone of the central 15 cm, which circumvented the height limitation imposed by the regulations. A development demonstrated right away during its track debut the day after the car's presentation.

EXHAUSTS AND FRONT F-DUCT

Mercedes-Benz didn't exploit the Coandă effect on its car to feed the diffusers' lateral channels. This illustration shows how the exhaust blew into the central area to augment the efficiency of the central double diffuser (yellow arrows). Blue indicates the air flow, which starts from the hole freed by the movement of the DRS to feed the front F-Duct, passing through the deformable structure behind the gearbox.

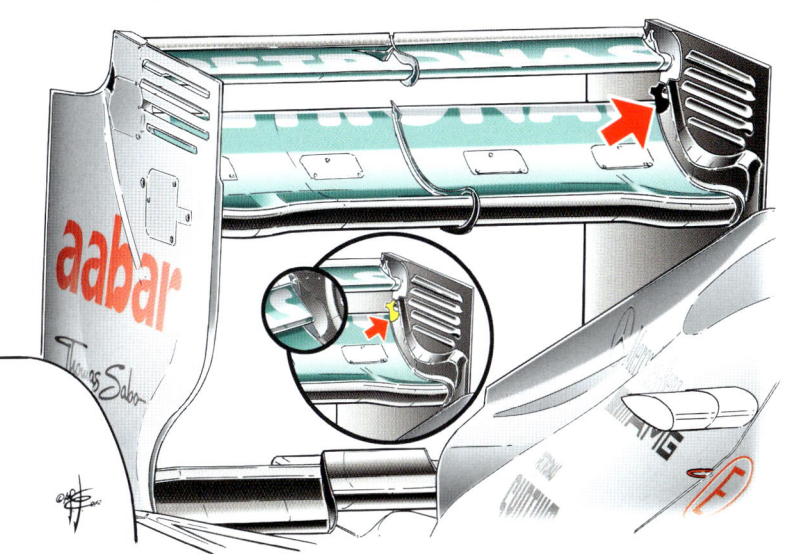

DRS

The most "generous" design of the mini-end plates at the sides of the rear wing's flaps was created in such a way that, with its rotation when the DRS came into operation, a hole was freed and that permitted air to enter, to feed the front F-Duct system.

SEPANG

The vents applied to the main plane of the front wing were discovered as early as the second race of the season in Malaysia due to Michael Schumacher going off the, which in practice thwarted all other efforts made in the pits to hide that feature. That confirmed the preview given at the 2012 GP of Japan. The only difference was that the narrow vents were double and not one per flap plane.

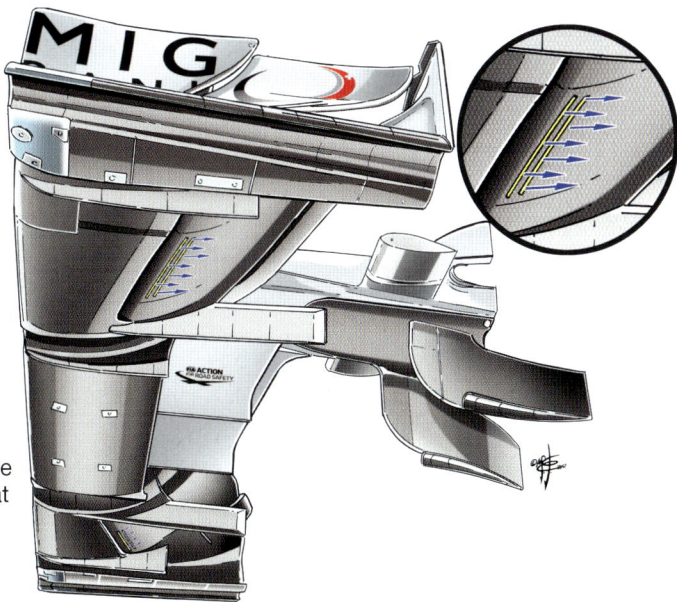

MERCEDES

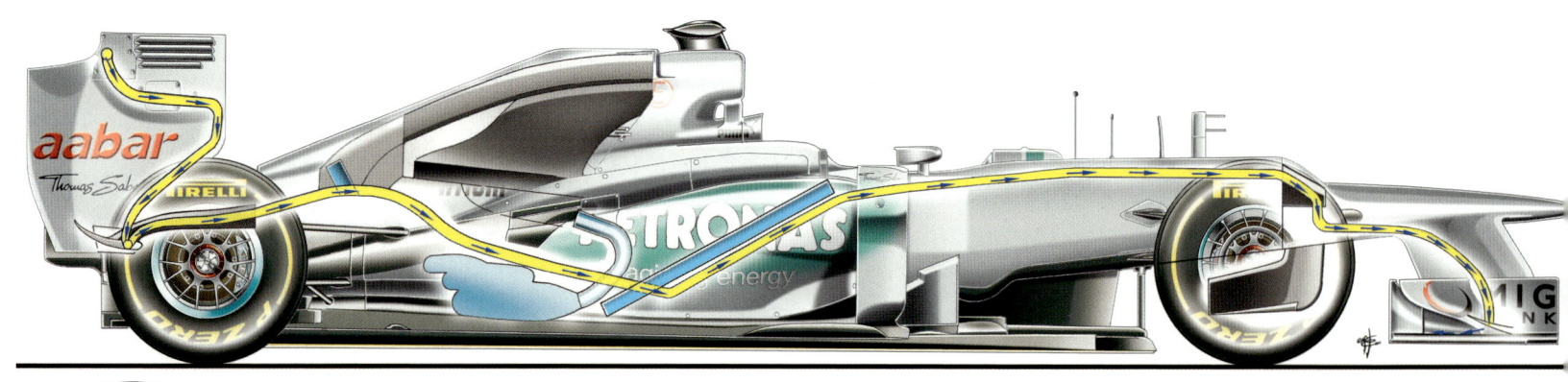

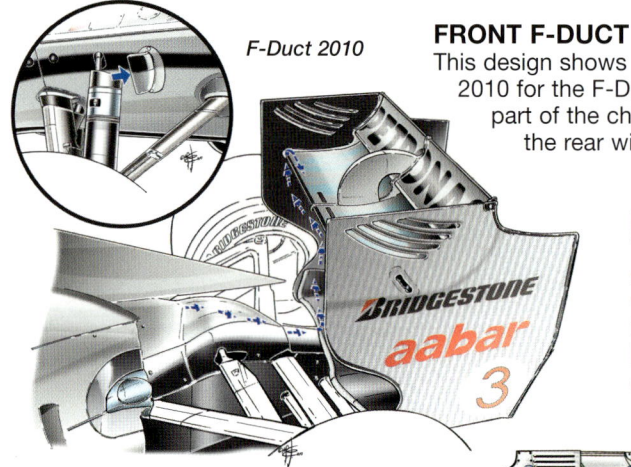

FRONT F-DUCT
This design shows the complicated passage of air inside the entire car, which inverts the layout used in 2010 for the F-Duct (above). That season, the air entered through two intakes at the sides of the front part of the chassis and took precisely the same route, but the other way around: from the front end to the rear wing.

F-Duct 2010

FRONT WING ENDPLATE
This illustration, taken from a 3D animation, shows the passage of air through the flows from the hole in the rear wing's end plates up to the front part of the chassis and then on to the front wing to make it "stall". In that way the loss of downforce was balanced at the rear, caused by the activation of the DRS. But it was only of use in qualifying.

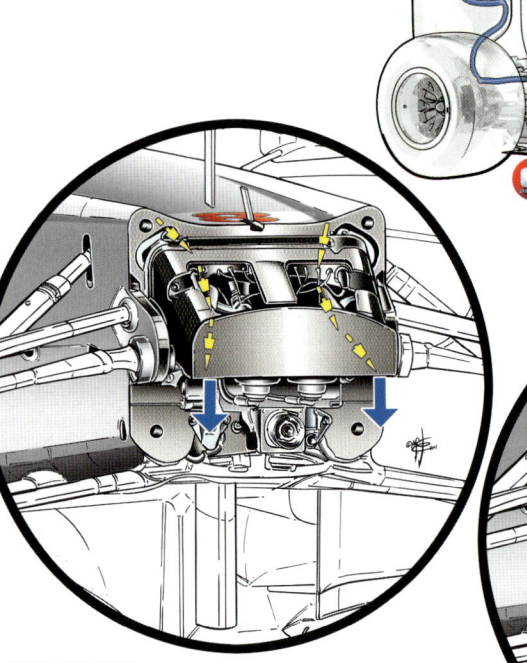

FLUID PIPES
It was almost impossible to see the fluid pipes (about 3-5 cm) that carried air towards the front wing supports without the carbon fibre covers, but after Malaysia the Federation banned all masking.
So here we reveal the sequence of details of the complicated front F-Duct system. The last illustration shows the small air flow management cylinders, with the principle of the air valves that had already been set up in 2010.

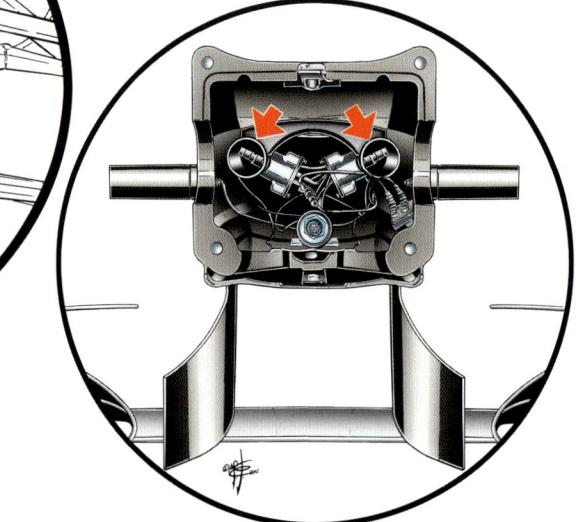

MERCEDES

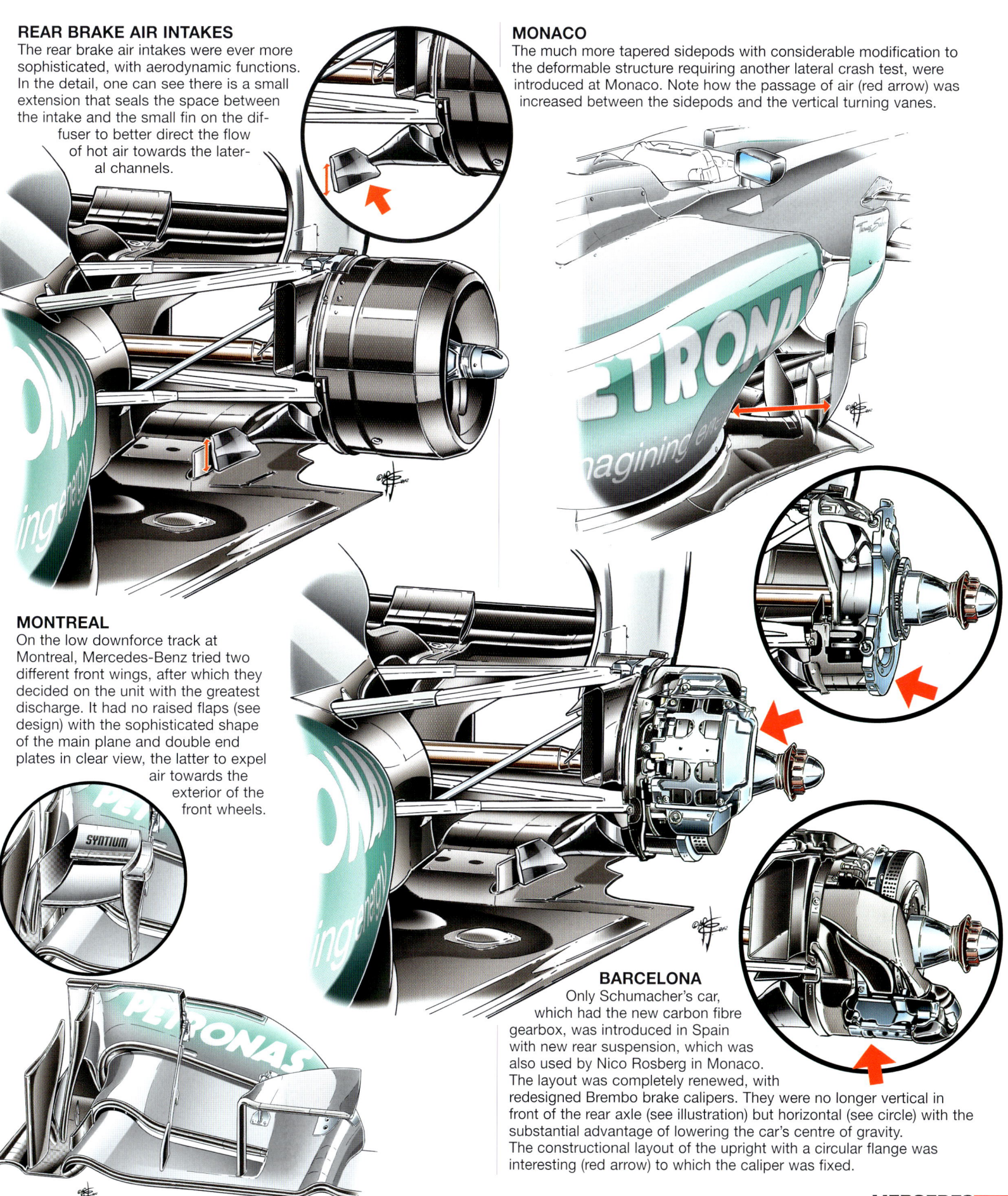

REAR BRAKE AIR INTAKES
The rear brake air intakes were ever more sophisticated, with aerodynamic functions. In the detail, one can see there is a small extension that seals the space between the intake and the small fin on the diffuser to better direct the flow of hot air towards the lateral channels.

MONACO
The much more tapered sidepods with considerable modification to the deformable structure requiring another lateral crash test, were introduced at Monaco. Note how the passage of air (red arrow) was increased between the sidepods and the vertical turning vanes.

MONTREAL
On the low downforce track at Montreal, Mercedes-Benz tried two different front wings, after which they decided on the unit with the greatest discharge. It had no raised flaps (see design) with the sophisticated shape of the main plane and double end plates in clear view, the latter to expel air towards the exterior of the front wheels.

BARCELONA
Only Schumacher's car, which had the new carbon fibre gearbox, was introduced in Spain with new rear suspension, which was also used by Nico Rosberg in Monaco. The layout was completely renewed, with redesigned Brembo brake calipers. They were no longer vertical in front of the rear axle (see illustration) but horizontal (see circle) with the substantial advantage of lowering the car's centre of gravity.
The constructional layout of the upright with a circular flange was interesting (red arrow) to which the caliper was fixed.

MERCEDES

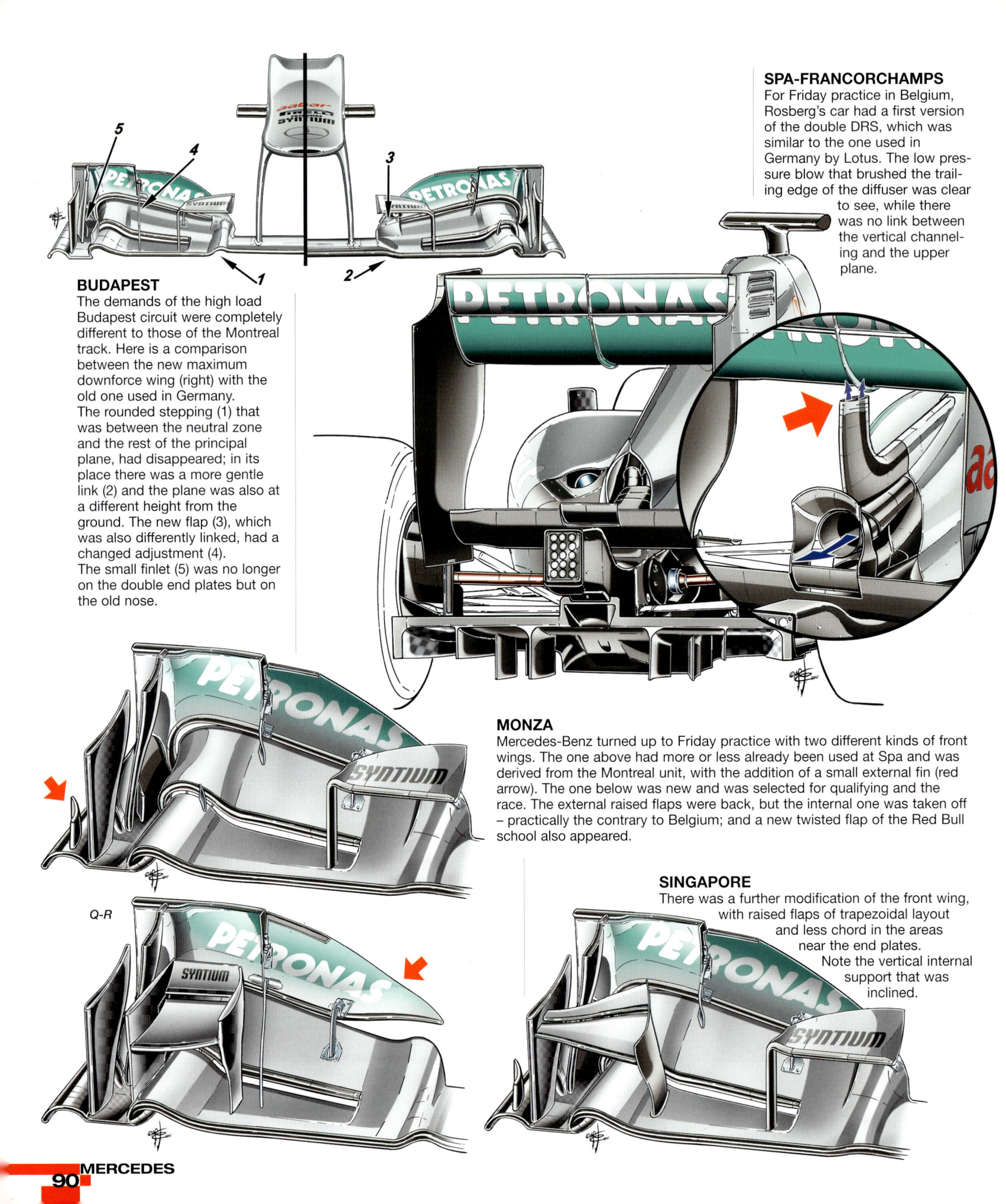

BUDAPEST
The demands of the high load Budapest circuit were completely different to those of the Montreal track. Here is a comparison between the new maximum downforce wing (right) with the old one used in Germany.
The rounded stepping (1) that was between the neutral zone and the rest of the principal plane, had disappeared; in its place there was a more gentle link (2) and the plane was also at a different height from the ground. The new flap (3), which was also differently linked, had a changed adjustment (4).
The small finlet (5) was no longer on the double end plates but on the old nose.

SPA-FRANCORCHAMPS
For Friday practice in Belgium, Rosberg's car had a first version of the double DRS, which was similar to the one used in Germany by Lotus. The low pressure blow that brushed the trailing edge of the diffuser was clear to see, while there was no link between the vertical channeling and the upper plane.

MONZA
Mercedes-Benz turned up to Friday practice with two different kinds of front wings. The one above had more or less already been used at Spa and was derived from the Montreal unit, with the addition of a small external fin (red arrow). The one below was new and was selected for qualifying and the race. The external raised flaps were back, but the internal one was taken off – practically the contrary to Belgium; and a new twisted flap of the Red Bull school also appeared.

SINGAPORE
There was a further modification of the front wing, with raised flaps of trapezoidal layout and less chord in the areas near the end plates.
Note the vertical internal support that was inclined.

MERCEDES

SINGAPORE

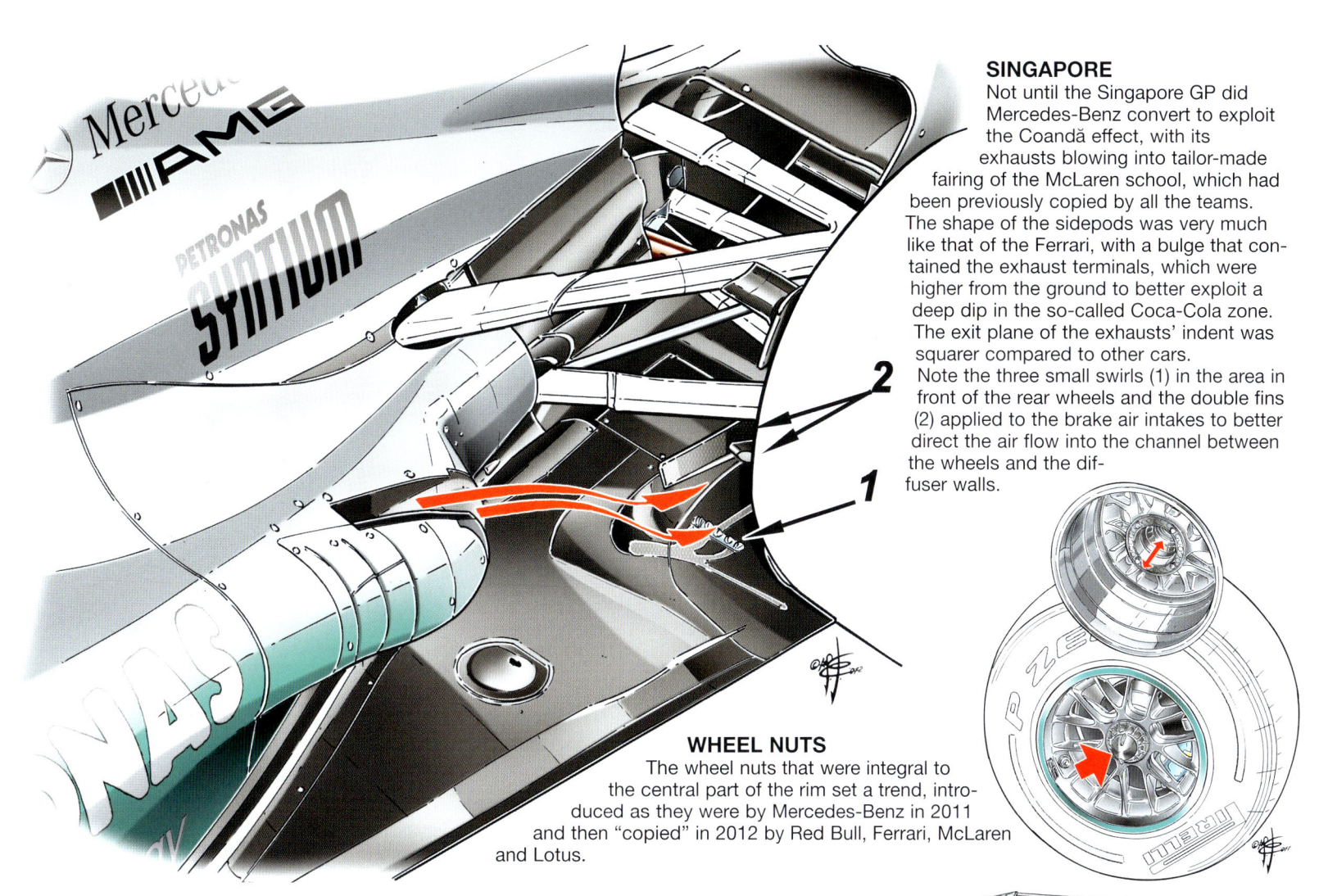

Not until the Singapore GP did Mercedes-Benz convert to exploit the Coandă effect, with its exhausts blowing into tailor-made fairing of the McLaren school, which had been previously copied by all the teams. The shape of the sidepods was very much like that of the Ferrari, with a bulge that contained the exhaust terminals, which were higher from the ground to better exploit a deep dip in the so-called Coca-Cola zone. The exit plane of the exhausts' indent was squarer compared to other cars.

Note the three small swirls (1) in the area in front of the rear wheels and the double fins (2) applied to the brake air intakes to better direct the air flow into the channel between the wheels and the diffuser walls.

WHEEL NUTS

The wheel nuts that were integral to the central part of the rim set a trend, introduced as they were by Mercedes-Benz in 2011 and then "copied" in 2012 by Red Bull, Ferrari, McLaren and Lotus.

INDIA

On the Friday morning, Mercedes-Benz once again tested the passive double DRS, an experiment useful in collecting data for 2013 given that the "passive" solution was not prohibited in the standard way, unlike the one operated by a DRS control. Its principal was similar to that of the Lotus and this was highly complicated to set up.

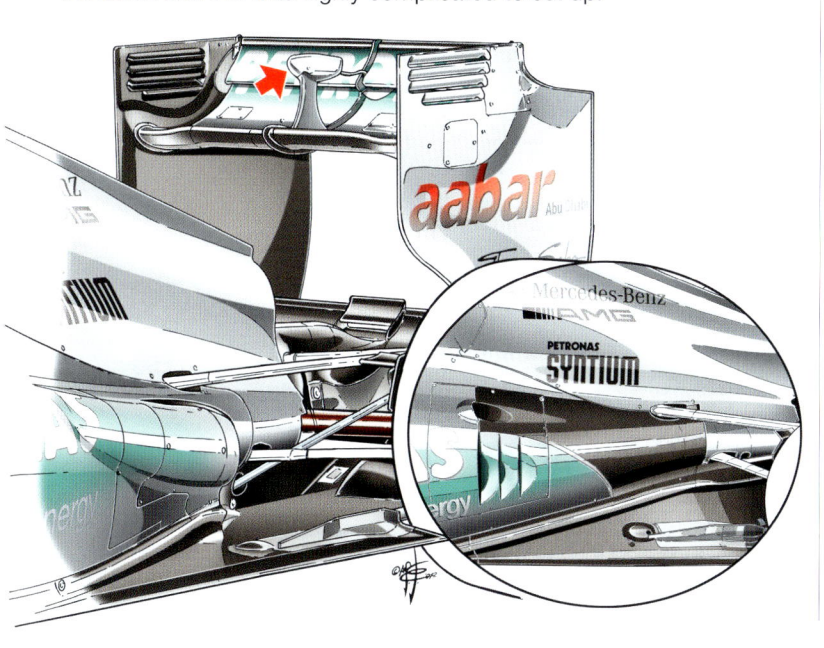

SAO PAOLO

The new DRS control made its debut in qualifying and the race, having been tested on the Friday in Austin, this time together with a body that had the original exhausts; they were preferred to those with the exit that exploited the Coandă effect. They created a crisis for the rear tyres, though; in practice, this was a car built for the collection of data for transfer to the 2013 project.

MERCEDES

SAUBER

CONSTRUCTORS' CLASSIFICATION			
	2011	2012	
Position	8°	6°	+2 ▲
Points	44	126	+82 ▲

The Sauber C31 was the revelation of the 2012 season, the car that more than any other set trends with the introduction of brand-new features that broke away from what had become the standard Formula 1 configuration, in particular the narrowing of the rear section of the sidepods with a Coke bottle shape that was originally introduced by McLaren way back in 1983 and had become a constant feature on all cars in more or less accentuated form. In truth, at its launch, the C31 was presented with a fairly conventional rear section, with the tapering of the sidepods recalling that seen on the previous car and an almost traditional exhaust position. However, from the very first track tests a surprising transformation was seen: in place of the Coke bottle shape the sidepods had a gently descending line similar to that on certain cars from the minor categories, with exhausts placed low down to exploit the Coandă effect that no less a team than Red Bull was to adopt. It should, however, be noted that in one of those strange coincidences that occasionally occur in F1, the wizard Newey had in all probability reached the same "conclusion" as Sauber even before the team took to the track with the new configuration, given that a Sauber-style version of the RB8 appeared as early as the second pre-championship test session. This meant that there would not have been sufficient time to copy such a sophisticated feature.
The new sidepod shape was by no means the only interesting novelty introduced by the group who had lost James Key to Toro Rosso over the winter.
The aperture in the nose that was inspired by the Ferrari F2008, albeit in a modern key, was unexpected if not wholly original. At the end of the 2008 season the Federation introduced restrictions that were so strict as to resemble to all intents and purposes a ban on this feature.
The new configuration of the step in the front section of the nose, imposed for safety reasons, has revived this idea that improves the aerodynamic efficiency of the front end and restricts the negative effects of the step itself.

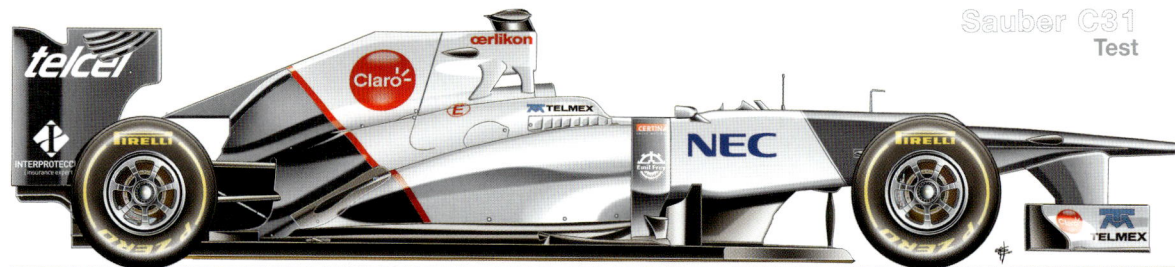

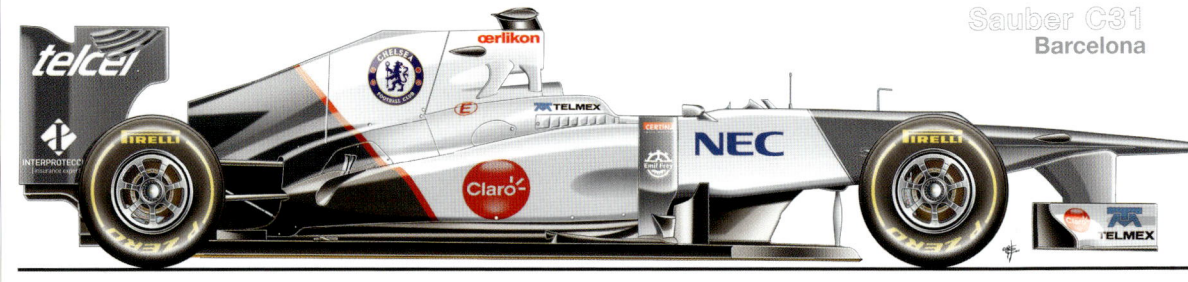

The vertical bridged vanes at the start of the sidepods also set a trend as did the brake ducts completely enclosed in the channel between wheel and chassis (a feature that had, however, been introduced some time earlier by Williams) which was adopted by Ferrari among others.
It should also be noted that the supply of both engines and gearboxes by the Maranello-based firm in the 2011 season had obliged the Swiss team to retain

the push-rod rear suspension configuration that only the F150 Italia still featured.
For the same reason, both cars had a kind of spacer between engine and gearbox housing the rear suspension pull-rod.
As well as being one of the most interesting cars of 2012, the C31 was also the one that permitted Sauber to enjoy the most competitive season in its recent history, conquering 6th place in the Constructors' Championship with no less than four podium finishes. Three factors ensured that its potential was even greater than that of the Ferrari: excellent race management of the Pirelli tyres which meant that a one-stop strategy could often be employed, maximum speed in fast corners and the efficiency of its DRS. These were all strengths that helped Sauber to fine results in Malesia, Montreal, Monza and Suzuka. There were three major evolutionary steps during the season: at the Spanish GP, those in Great Britain and Germany and in the two races in Singapore and Suzuka, with the introduction of new aerodynamic packages always bearing fruit.

SIDEPODS AND EXHAUSTS
Sauber was the leading player in the winter presentations, revolutionising the end section of the sidepods on its C31. The Coke bottle shape was out, with the sidepods descending slide-like, exploiting the Coandă effect and redirecting the flow of hot air from the exhausts towards the diffuser's lateral channels. An absolute novelty for F1 that, at the following Barcelona test session, was also seen on the "wizard" Newey's Red Bull. The red arrows indicate the thermo-tapes attached to check that the heat did not adversely affect the suspension arms while, at the bottom, they indicate two small vanes that prevent the flow from striking the tyres directly.

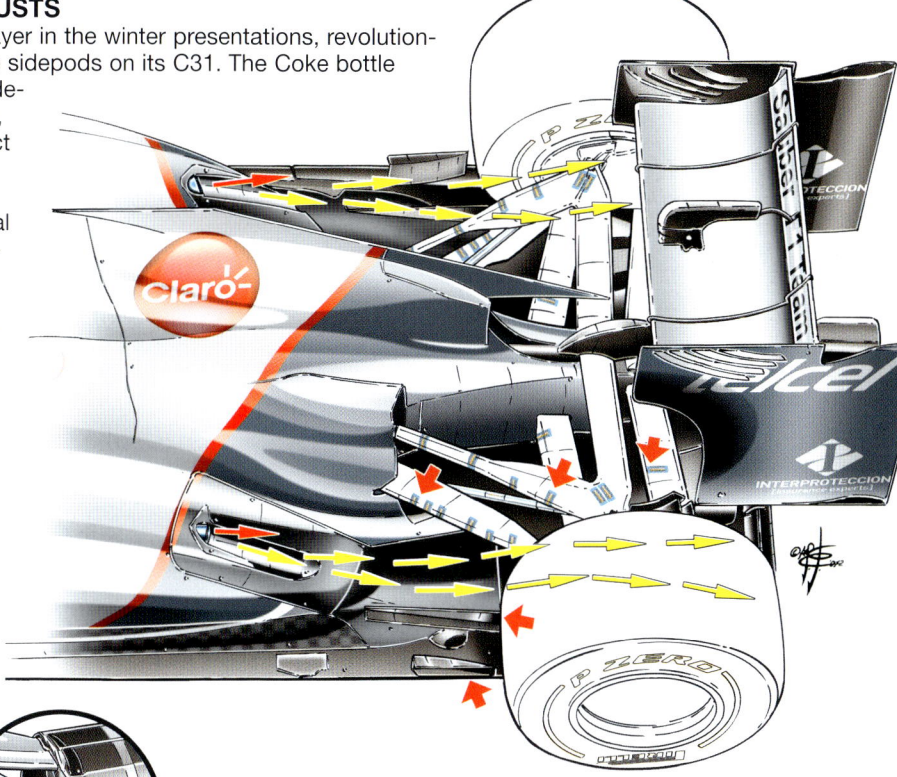

BRAKE DUCTS
Williams and Sauber introduced brake ducts that on certain circuits could be used without trumpet intakes on the internal part (insert). They therefore draw air from the restricted space between the carbonfibre "pans" and the wheel, with obvious benefits for the quality of the flow within the channel between wheel and chassis that is thus free of toxic turbulence.

NOSE APERTURE
These two drawings clearly show how the aperture in the nose of the Sauber was inspired by the feature adopted by Ferrari in 2008 (see the New Features chapter), clearly limited by the regulatory restrictions introduced by the Federation at the end of that season. The aperture had to be within 150 mm of the front axle (Art. 3.1.8). For this reason the ducting hidden within the nose inevitably had a strongly vertical configuration (highlighted in yellow). The passage of air between the lower part of the nose avoids the detachment of the fluid flow and therefore improves the efficiency of the air flow in the lower part of the car.

SAUBER

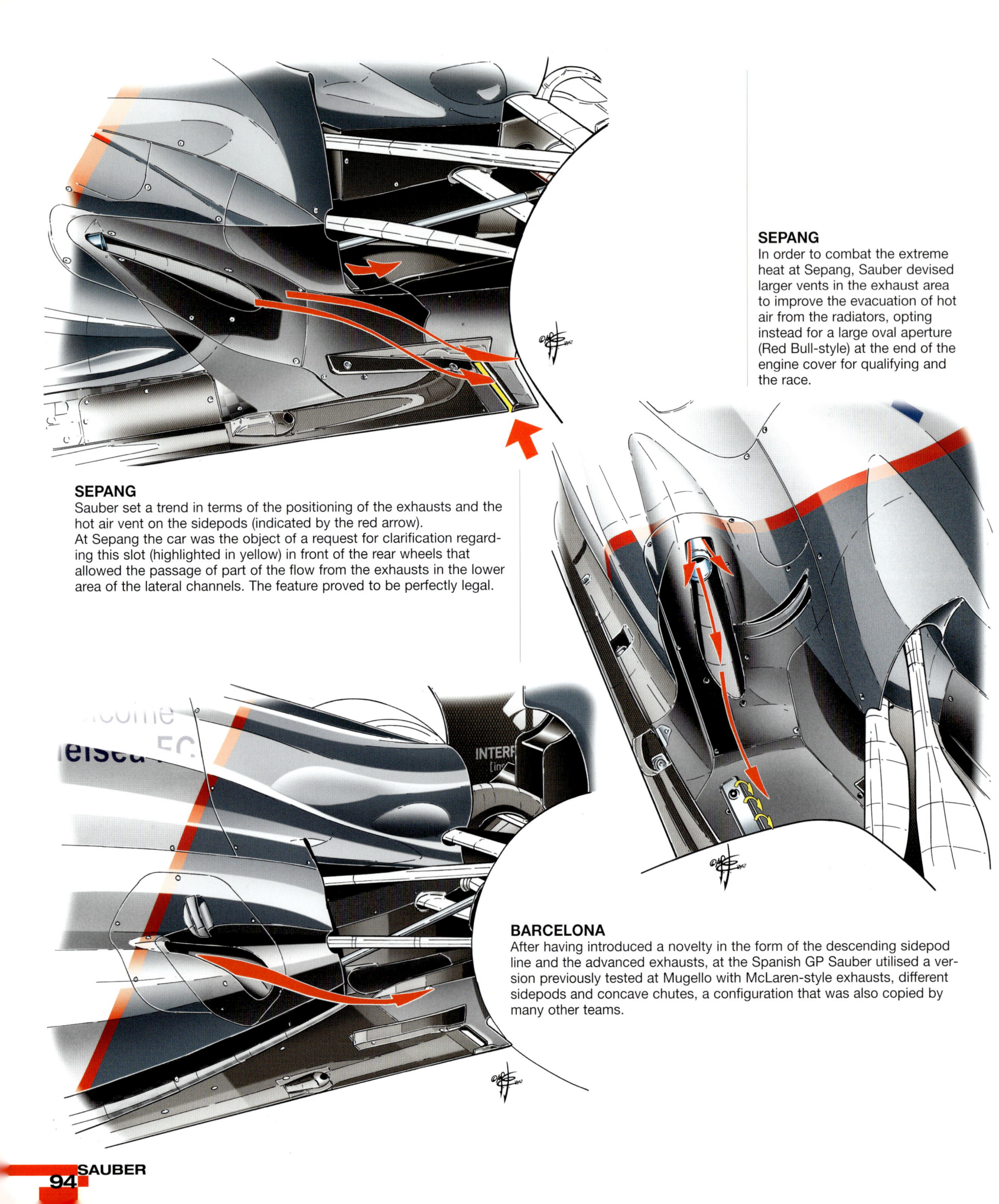

SEPANG
In order to combat the extreme heat at Sepang, Sauber devised larger vents in the exhaust area to improve the evacuation of hot air from the radiators, opting instead for a large oval aperture (Red Bull-style) at the end of the engine cover for qualifying and the race.

SEPANG
Sauber set a trend in terms of the positioning of the exhausts and the hot air vent on the sidepods (indicated by the red arrow).
At Sepang the car was the object of a request for clarification regarding this slot (highlighted in yellow) in front of the rear wheels that allowed the passage of part of the flow from the exhausts in the lower area of the lateral channels. The feature proved to be perfectly legal.

BARCELONA
After having introduced a novelty in the form of the descending sidepod line and the advanced exhausts, at the Spanish GP Sauber utilised a version previously tested at Mugello with McLaren-style exhausts, different sidepods and concave chutes, a configuration that was also copied by many other teams.

SAUBER

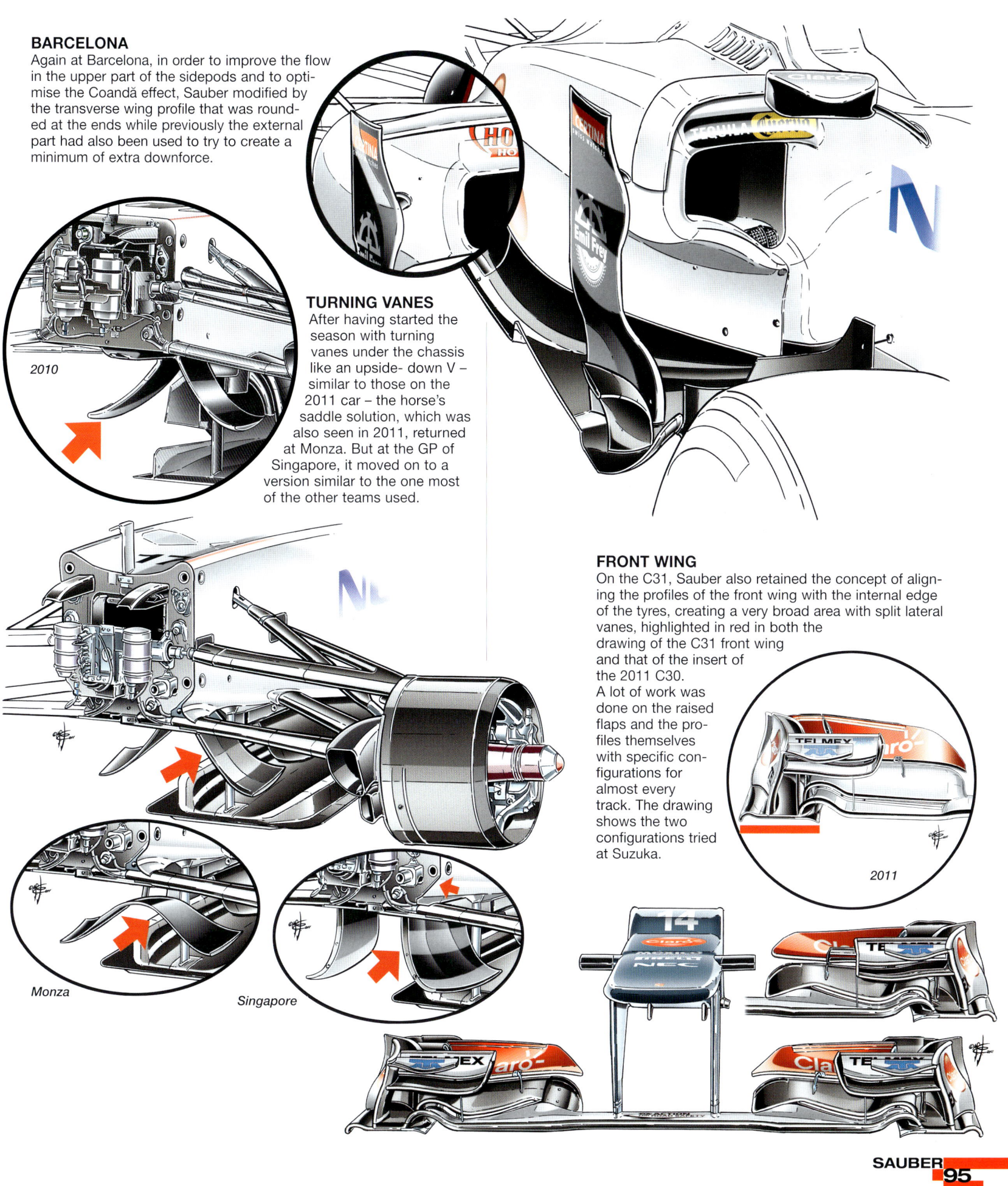

BARCELONA

Again at Barcelona, in order to improve the flow in the upper part of the sidepods and to optimise the Coandă effect, Sauber modified by the transverse wing profile that was rounded at the ends while previously the external part had also been used to try to create a minimum of extra downforce.

2010

TURNING VANES

After having started the season with turning vanes under the chassis like an upside-down V – similar to those on the 2011 car – the horse's saddle solution, which was also seen in 2011, returned at Monza. But at the GP of Singapore, it moved on to a version similar to the one most of the other teams used.

Monza

Singapore

FRONT WING

On the C31, Sauber also retained the concept of aligning the profiles of the front wing with the internal edge of the tyres, creating a very broad area with split lateral vanes, highlighted in red in both the drawing of the C31 front wing and that of the insert of the 2011 C30. A lot of work was done on the raised flaps and the profiles themselves with specific configurations for almost every track. The drawing shows the two configurations tried at Suzuka.

2011

SAUBER 95

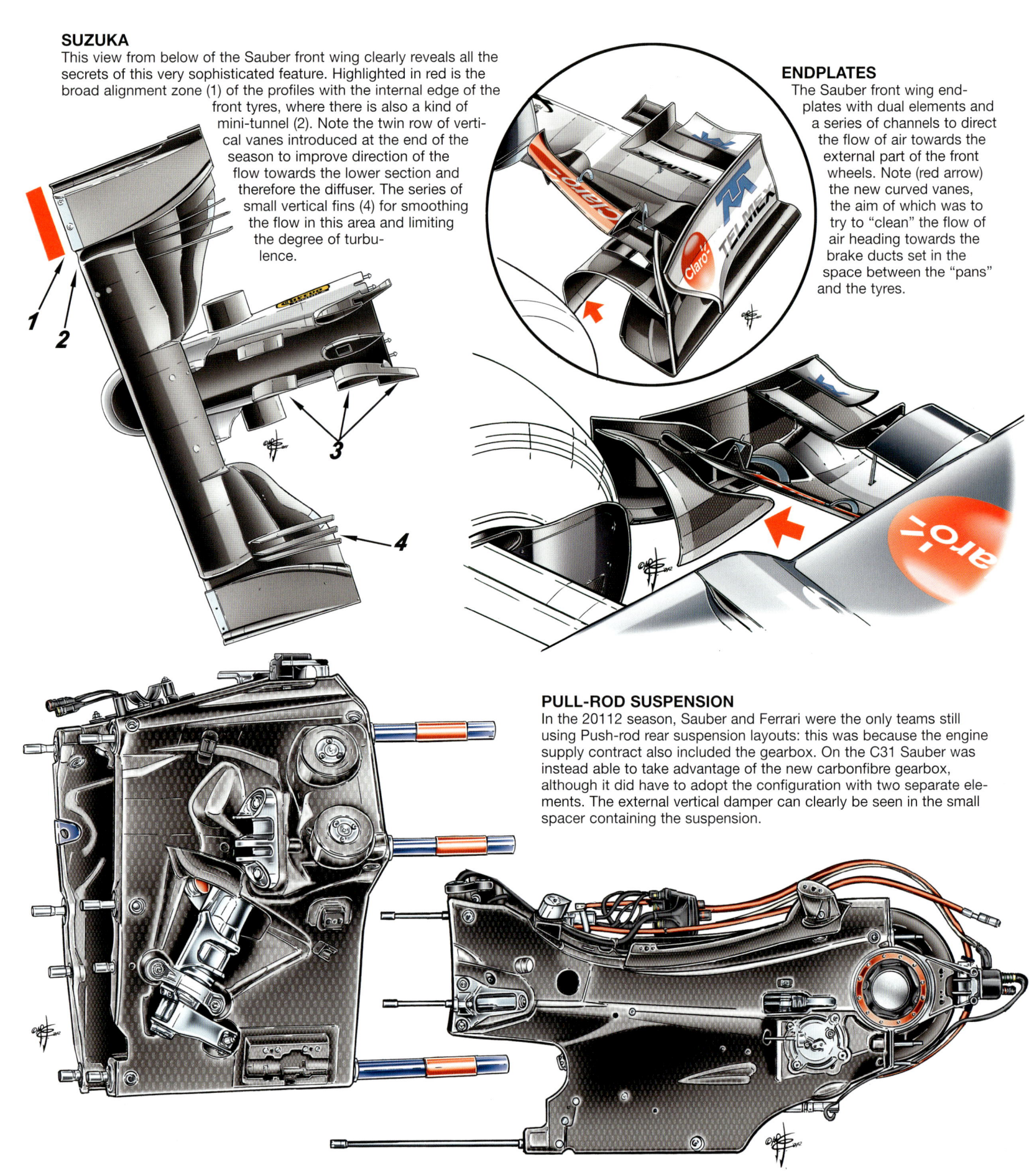

SUZUKA

This view from below of the Sauber front wing clearly reveals all the secrets of this very sophisticated feature. Highlighted in red is the broad alignment zone (1) of the profiles with the internal edge of the front tyres, where there is also a kind of mini-tunnel (2). Note the twin row of vertical vanes introduced at the end of the season to improve direction of the flow towards the lower section and therefore the diffuser. The series of small vertical fins (4) for smoothing the flow in this area and limiting the degree of turbulence.

ENDPLATES

The Sauber front wing endplates with dual elements and a series of channels to direct the flow of air towards the external part of the front wheels. Note (red arrow) the new curved vanes, the aim of which was to try to "clean" the flow of air heading towards the brake ducts set in the space between the "pans" and the tyres.

PULL-ROD SUSPENSION

In the 20112 season, Sauber and Ferrari were the only teams still using Push-rod rear suspension layouts: this was because the engine supply contract also included the gearbox. On the C31 Sauber was instead able to take advantage of the new carbonfibre gearbox, although it did have to adopt the configuration with two separate elements. The external vertical damper can clearly be seen in the small spacer containing the suspension.

SAUBER
96

FORCE INDIA

CONSTRUCTORS' CLASSIFICATION			
	2011	*2012*	
Position	6°	7°	-1 ▼
Points	69	109	+40 ▲

Despite dropping back one position in the constructors' championship, mainly caused by the major step forward by Sauber, the revelation of the year, Force India's 2012 season shouldn't be considered negative. Partly because the VM05, designed under the responsibility of Andrew Green, who replaced James Key after his move to the Swiss team, turned the page.

It was a project which, mechanicals apart, differed notably from its predecessors. Mercedes-Benz continued to supply engines and Kers as they did the gearbox, which was the same as that for McLaren. And the collaboration with the Woking team using its simulator continued, which enabled Force India to go to the circuits with set-ups ready for Friday practice.

As far as verification of the team's aerodynamics with the CFD system was concerned, Force India paid the price for having a department that was not yet up to those of the competition, opting to conduct verifications on-track with equipment during the early laps of the Friday mornings.

Another new factor was the arrival of Jacob Andreasson as head of the project, as he brought a new mentality to the team that had been the same for many years under Dominic Harlow's guidance.

The department of correlation between the car and tyre development was strengthened, if not created, first sacrificed by the aerodynamics department, which continued to be one of the strong points of the team.

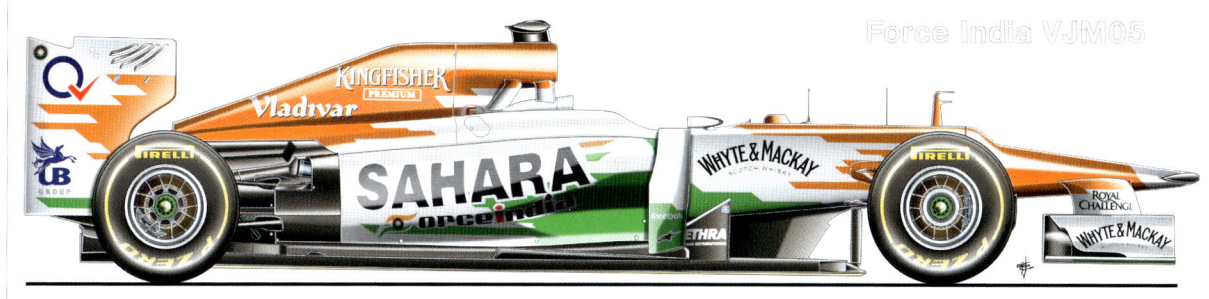

The unconventional disposition of the front brake callipers from the cars of previous years remained, fitted overhanging the front axle and often used by Force India with asymmetric brake air intakes, which were more or less open on one side compared to the other, to better manage temperatures inside the rims and, therefore, help the front tyres to quickly reach the correct temperature.

And it was precisely this characteristic that helped Force India in low ambient temperatures or rain, when there is obviously a greater need to have a quicker reaction from the front tyres, which normally reach an optimum state later than the rears. Development in exploiting the Coandă effect to partially recover exhaust blow slowed during the winter for fear that the solution they had come up with might not be considered legal.

And that was partly because the FIA had been most severe with extreme developments from Red Bull and Lotus in that sector. Only after the appearance of similar techniques on the Saubers and McLarens did Force India push to the full in that direction, arriving at the Mugello test with a method that later made its successful debut in the GP of Spain.

While having taken great care over the search for greater downforce, the VJM05 continued to be very fast on the straights, as confirmed by Paul Di Resta's fourth place in Monza qualifying and their fourth in the Singapore race. Compared to many other cars, the Force Indias didn't have excessively concave sidepods of reduced section all to the advantage of thermal dissipation, which didn't need to operate with the fairly inefficient apertures on the "hot" tracks.

On the aerodynamics front, Force India radically changed their philosophy in the design of the front wings, while the rear end brought in avant-garde developments, especially regarding the end plates.

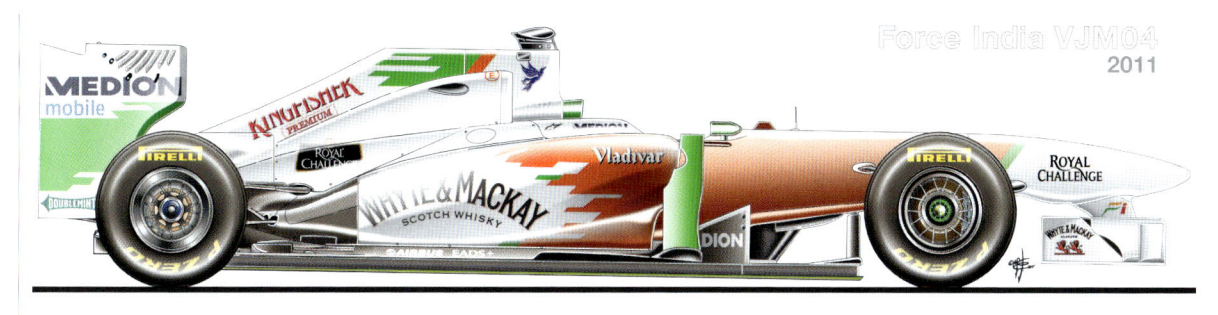

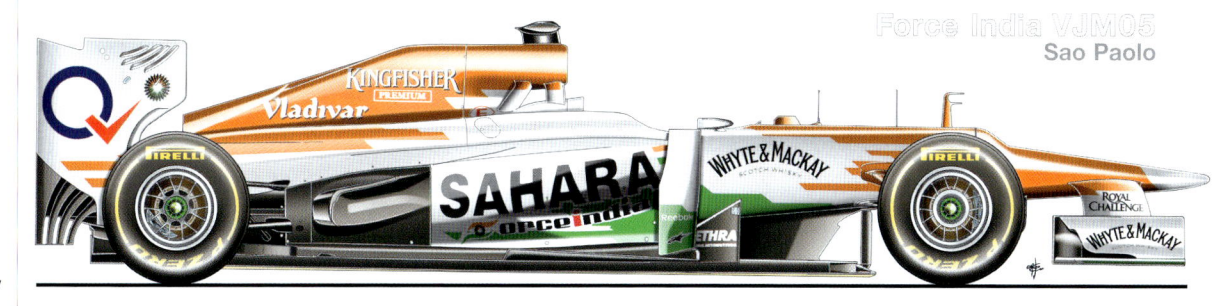

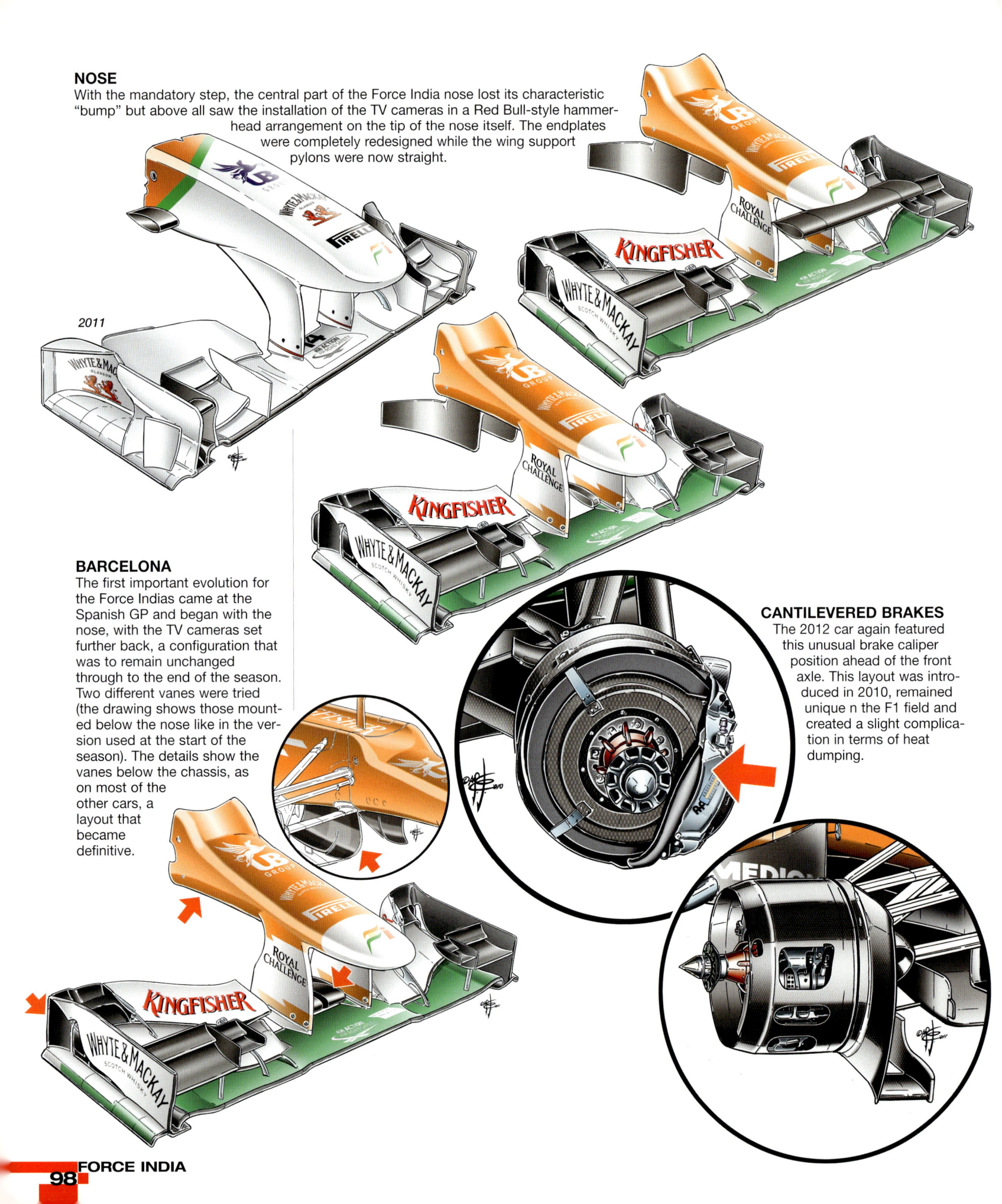

NOSE
With the mandatory step, the central part of the Force India nose lost its characteristic "bump" but above all saw the installation of the TV cameras in a Red Bull-style hammerhead arrangement on the tip of the nose itself. The endplates were completely redesigned while the wing support pylons were now straight.

2011

BARCELONA
The first important evolution for the Force Indias came at the Spanish GP and began with the nose, with the TV cameras set further back, a configuration that was to remain unchanged through to the end of the season. Two different vanes were tried (the drawing shows those mounted below the nose like in the version used at the start of the season). The details show the vanes below the chassis, as on most of the other cars, a layout that became definitive.

CANTILEVERED BRAKES
The 2012 car again featured this unusual brake caliper position ahead of the front axle. This layout was introduced in 2010, remained unique n the F1 field and created a slight complication in terms of heat dumping.

FORCE INDIA
98

EXHAUSTS
Force India began the season with exhausts blowing high up and in the central zone of the car to improve the efficiency of the rear wing. The "McLaren" version that exploited the Coandă effect arrived at the Spanish GP after testing at Mugello and was gradually refined over the course of the championship.

HOCKENHEIM
Force India copied the vertical slot in the endplates introduced that year by Williams. The team used two different main planes. The "fringe" in the lower part of the endplates was also new.

SILVERSTONE
There was further aerodynamic refinement for Silverstone with a new diffuser equipped with a small flap on the trailing edge. The drawing clearly shows the McLaren type exhausts introduced at the Spanish GP after private testing at Mugello.

FORCE INDIA

WILLIAMS

CONSTRUCTORS' CLASSIFICATION			
	2011	2012	
Position	9°	8°	+1▲
Points	5	76	+71▲

It was since Brazil 2004 that Williams had not won a Formula 1 race: while Maldonado's victory brought Sir Frank's team back to the winner's enclosure, it has to be pointed out that the 2012 season was remarkable for the face that six different cars proved capable of winning at least one race. This was by no means an underserved victory and the FW34 could easily have accumulated a greater points total and gained one if not two positions in the Constructors' Championship standings. This was thanks to a project led by Mike Coughlan and Mark Gillan, who revised and corrected the errors of the revolutionary FW33 and, above all, thanks to the replacement of the heavy and bulky Cosworth engine with the more compact and more powerful Renault. The French 8-cylinder unit was also less demanding in terms of heat dispersion, to the benefit of the sidepod section and, above all, the engine cover.
This finally allowed the designers to exploit the extreme lowline gearbox, the advantages of which had been nullified in 2011 by the greater volumes required by the previous power unit.
The team worked hard over the winter to improve reliability and quality control of individual components, a factor that in 2011 had created considerable difficulties. The two cars in the same garage frequently differed in terms of both mechanical and aerodynamic details.
The jewel in the Didcot team's crown was the Kers unit, fabricated entirely in-house to replace the standard component supplied by Renault. According to Mark Gillan, this feature provided very positive results.
The exploitation of the full power of the 8-cylinder Renault delayed the race-debut of the version with Coandă-effect exhausts tested at Mugello (ahead of the Spanish GP) but only introduced at the Chinese GP.
The engineers in fact preferred greater performance from the engine rather than making sacrifices to privilege hypothetical aerodynamic advantages provided by the Coandă effect that, unfortunately, would have required very different exhausts.
The aerodynamic department directed by Jason Sommerville was also very active and came up with a number of new and sophisticated features.
Two were trend setting: the brake ducts with no external trumpet (in the channel between wheel and chassis) and a vertical slot in the rear wing endplates that was also copied by other teams over the course of the season.
In contrast, the complicated front wing with a series of mini-tunnels at the edge of the main plane failed to attract any followers and proved to be a nightmare for the production department: around 9 weeks to build each wing.
The development of the car did not see the introduction of any major evolutionary packages, but rather detail modifications and features to better adapt the cars to the diverse demands of the various circuits, with a healthy ratio of in-house wind tunnel and CFD studies and track testing in the Friday morning practice sessions.

Williams FW33
2011

Williams FW34

Williams FW34
Barcelona

Williams FW34
New Dehli

LOWLINE GEARBOX

Williams retained the FW33's lowline gearbox for the 2012 season.
The profile drawing reveals by how much the differential was lowered. This led to an unusual angle of inclination (14°) of the halfshafts (3) that are usually fixed at around 7°.
Note the upper wishbone mounted directly on the titanium assembly supporting the rear wing.
The advantages on the 2012 FW33 were restricted by the notable volume of the engine cover dictated by the requirements of the 8-cylinder Cosworth, something that did not occur with the passage to the similarly configured Renault engine used in the FW34. The rear view shows how on the FW33 the end section of the bodywork (2) was already the lowest of all the cars in the 2011 season (2 cm lower than that of the RB7). The reduction in gearbox height initially obliged the mounting of the upper wishbone (1) on the wing support, a feature that was retained on the FW34. The pull-rod configuration (4) also helped to free-up the higher zone and improve the air flow in the area thanks to the low-set differential casing.

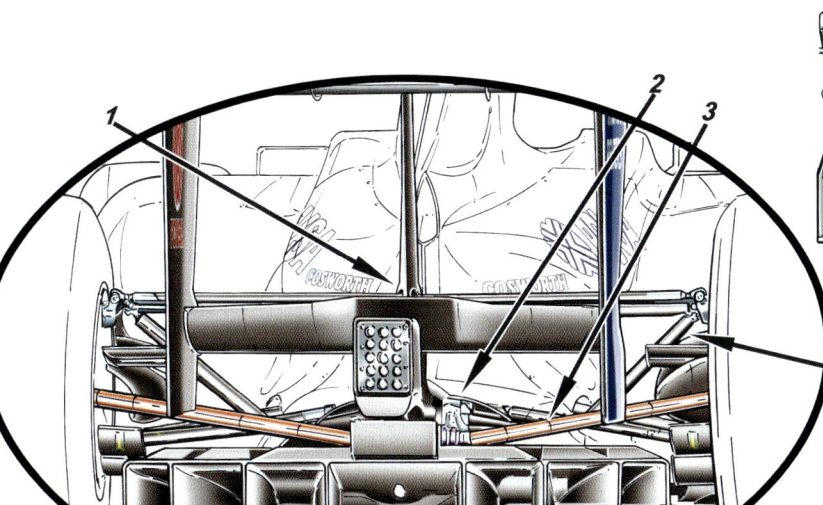

FRONT BRAKE DUCTS

Williams can claim credit for being the first team to introduce in the 2012 season brake ducts that no longer featured a trumpet within the channel between wheel and chassis.
The air enters the internal part of the large "pans", that is, in the space between the tyre and the brake duct, to the benefit of the quality of air flow in this area of the car. This feature caught on and was imitated by Sauber from the first tests.

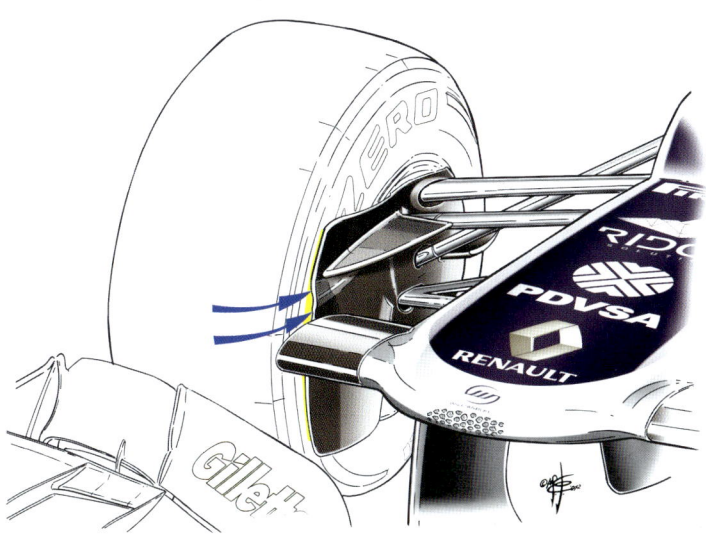

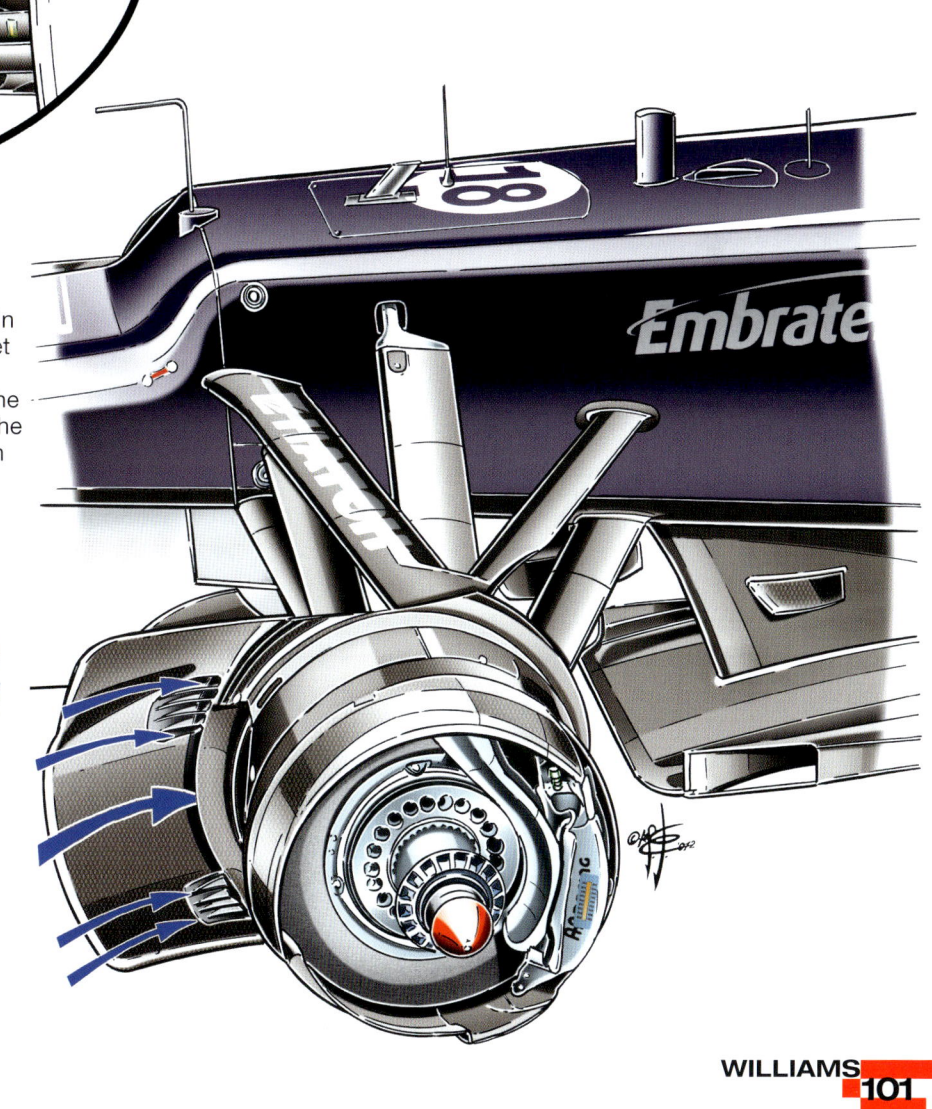

WILLIAMS 101

REAR BRAKE DUCTS

The rear brake ducts were no less sophisticated, designed as they were to create a seal with the lateral diffuser channels. In order to prevent any loss of efficiency, for the first time a vertical extension was introduced (highlighted in the detail), incorporated within the design of the duct that is subject to vertical oscillation when the car is moving. In this way a constant perfect seal is created with the small vertical fin attached to the underbody. An extreme design, albeit permitted by the regulations, that clearly also provided aerodynamic advantages.

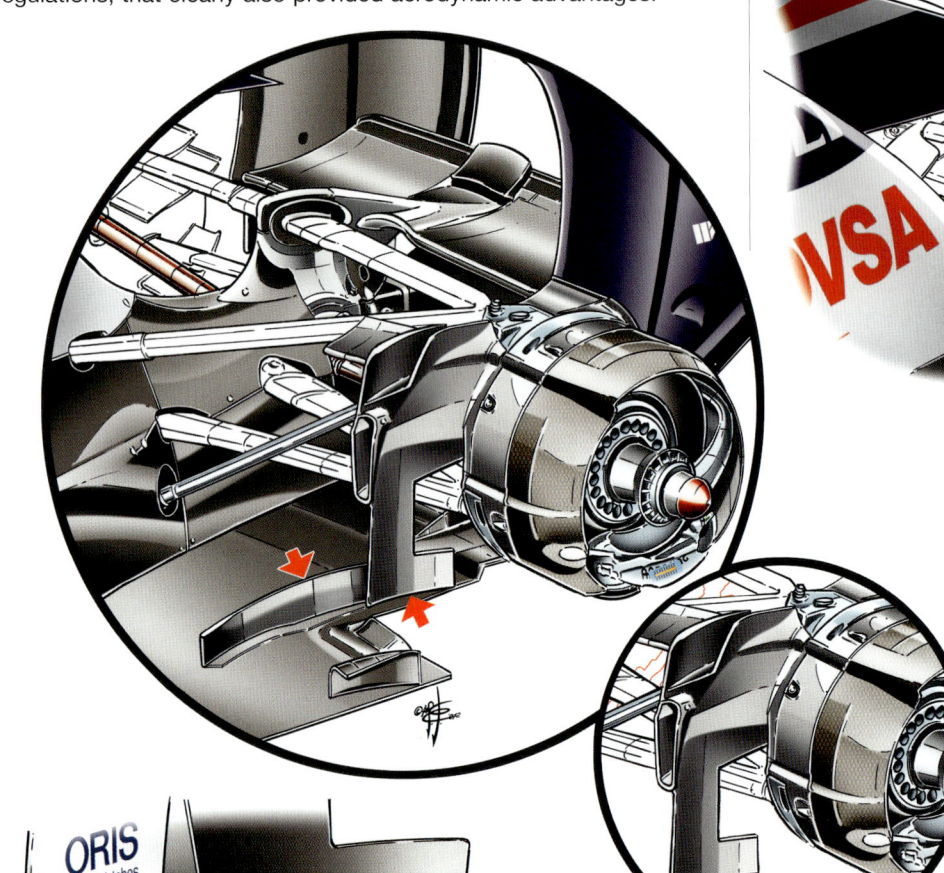

BARCELONA

Williams introduced a new rear wing at the Spanish GP, characterised by a new vertical slot to reduce drag on the straight. This feature was then taken up by other teams, starting with Force India. The winglet with a central cantilevered support was also unchanged having been seen previously but not used until the Spanish GP.

FRONT WING

The Williams boasted the field's most complex front wing, characterised by a series of mini tunnels in the area close to the endplates. A more extreme version of the concept introduced during the previous season. Around nine weeks were required to produce this wing.

WILLIAMS

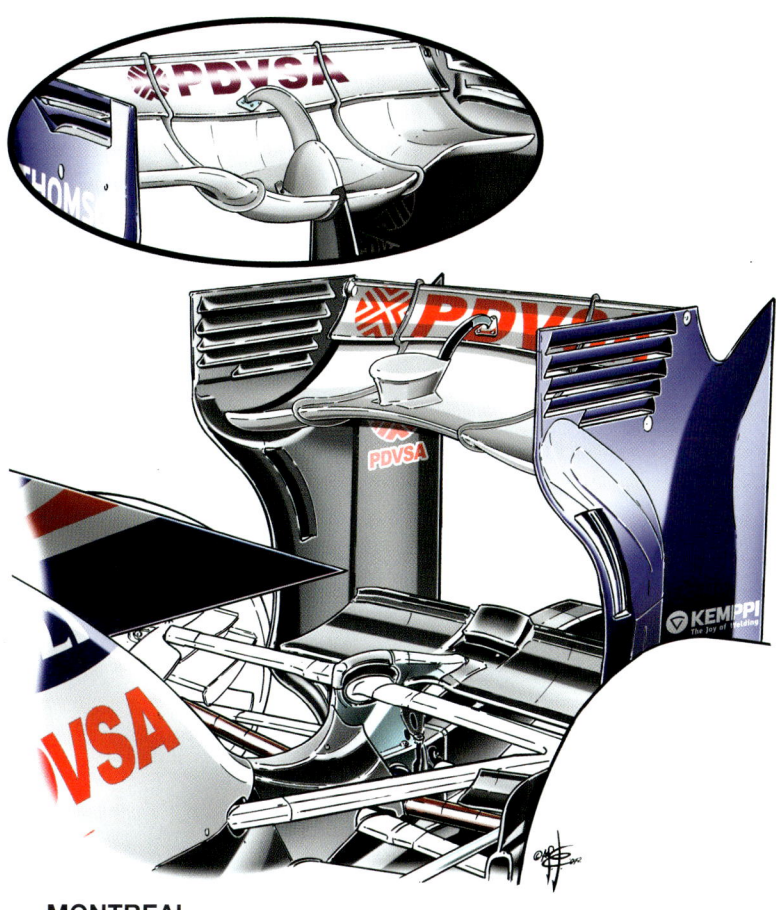

MONTREAL
Williams presented the most unusual of rear wings at the fast Canadian track, with a reverse dish that was in effect the opposite of the configuration tried in the 2011 season. In contrast with the situation the previous year, this new wing was used for both qualifying and the race.

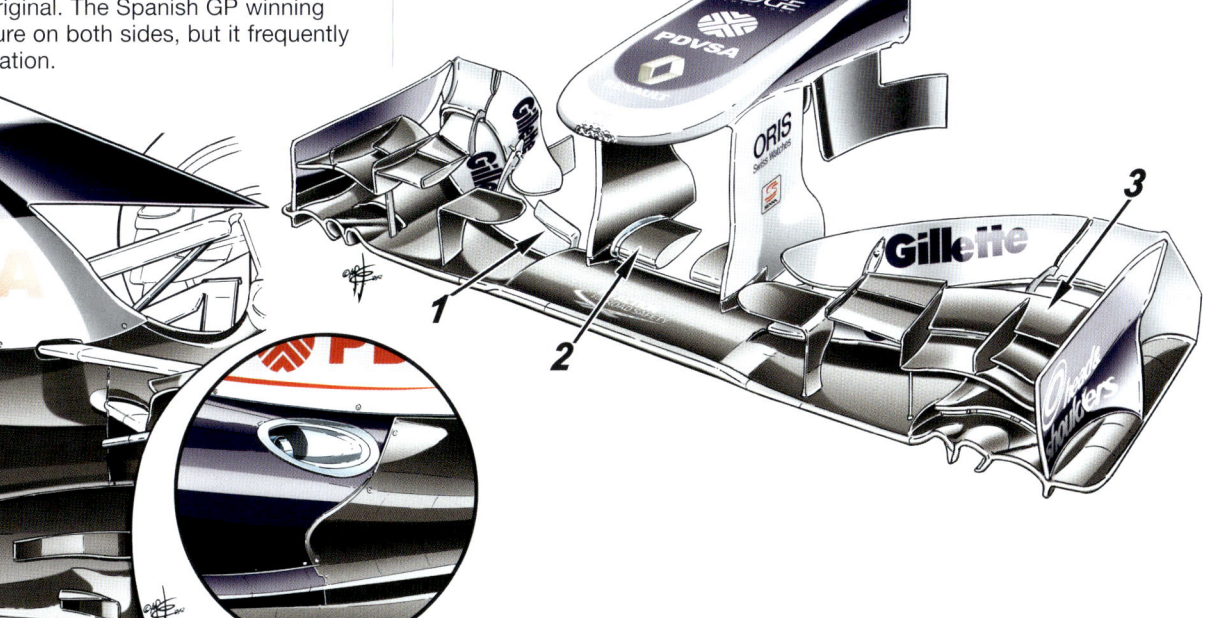

EXHAUSTS
Williams raced for almost the whole of the season with "traditional" exhausts, without exploiting the Coandă effect tested at the Mugello but only "used" in anger at the Korean G.P. The drawing shows the hot-track version rather than the original. The Spanish GP winning FW34 was equipped with this feature on both sides, but it frequently raced with an asymmetric configuration.

SPA-FRANCORCHAMPS
Fast-track wing used at both Spa and Monza. Naturally, at Monza the version with the main plane mounted in the lowest downforce configuration (yellow line) was used. This feature was not as extreme as that used by other teams.

HOCKENHEIM
Williams introduced a minor innovation in the form of this winglet (1) linked to the second flap on the front wing to better separate the flows in this area. The drawing depicts the version with the TV cameras shifted to the bottom centre (2) so as to form a continuation of the 50 cm neutral section even though, in qualifying and the race, the nose with hammerhead camera positioning was used. Slight modifications were also made to the raised flaps (3) that were designed to deflect the flow above the tyres.

WILLIAMS 103

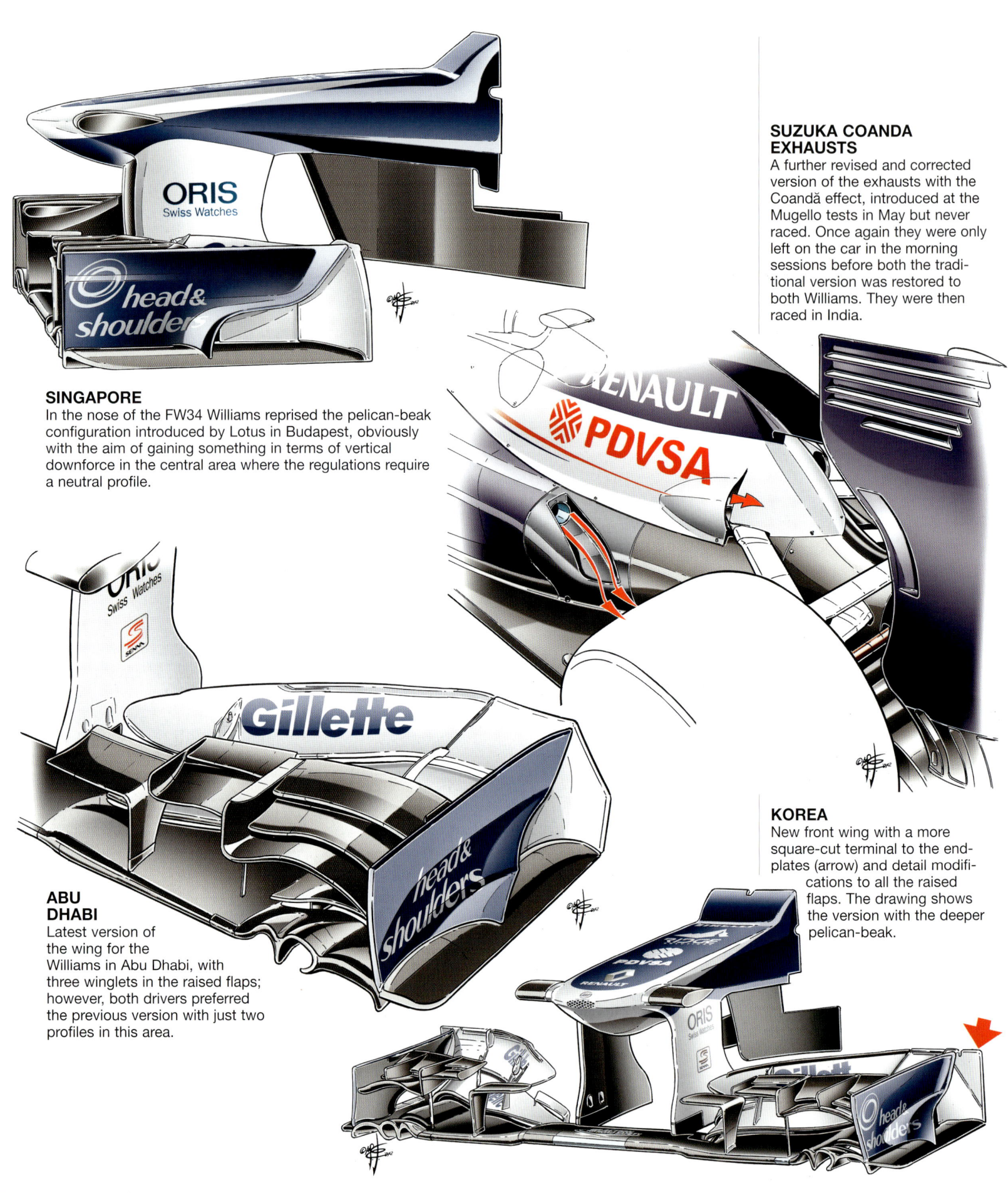

SUZUKA COANDA EXHAUSTS
A further revised and corrected version of the exhausts with the Coandă effect, introduced at the Mugello tests in May but never raced. Once again they were only left on the car in the morning sessions before both the traditional version was restored to both Williams. They were then raced in India.

SINGAPORE
In the nose of the FW34 Williams reprised the pelican-beak configuration introduced by Lotus in Budapest, obviously with the aim of gaining something in terms of vertical downforce in the central area where the regulations require a neutral profile.

KOREA
New front wing with a more square-cut terminal to the endplates (arrow) and detail modifications to all the raised flaps. The drawing shows the version with the deeper pelican-beak.

ABU DHABI
Latest version of the wing for the Williams in Abu Dhabi, with three winglets in the raised flaps; however, both drivers preferred the previous version with just two profiles in this area.

WILLIAMS

TORO ROSSO

CONSTRUCTORS' CLASSIFICATION			
	2011	2012	
Position	8°	8°	= ▲
Points	41	26	-15 ▼

For the 2012 season Toro Rosso again retained the raised sidepods on the STR7 that had been introduced the previous year to guarantee effective air flow to the rear of the car. This was a feature that was beneficial from a purely aerodynamic point of view, but which, in the end, conditioned the team's development work and fine-tuning.

The ST7 proved to be overly sensitive to height variations and the Faenza-based team then also suffered from the loss of its technical "wizard", the dynamic Giorgio Ascanelli after a dispute with the team principal Franz Tost. His replacement James Key took up his position at the Italian GP, recognising a certain lack of staff in the aerodynamic sector compared with his previous experiences at Sauber and, earlier, at Force India, direct rivals of the Red Bull "junior" team.

As in the 2011 season, Toro Rosso used the Ferrari engine and Kers unit, but not the transmission that had obliged Sauber to adopt the push-rod rear suspension system together with the F2012's gearbox casing. Increasingly differentiated with respect to the Red Bull, towards the end of the season the STR7 began to test the underslung front brake layout (retained on the Red Bulls in the 2012 season) in view of the 2013 season.

The vertical calipers were tried for the first time at the Belgian GP by Ricciardo only and then at Singapore by his teammate and finally at Abu Dhabi in the post-race tests.

Toro Rosso was competitive at the start of the season, reaching Q3 no less than three times and seeing Ricciardo starting from 6th on the grid at the Bahrain GP. The, over the course of the season, its development, while constant, was not as effective as that of its direct rivals.

The most important modification came in Canada with the McLaren-type exhausts, tested ahead of the Spanish GP at Mugello. These exhausts were then perfected at the Indian GP. The areas that saw the most work were the wings, both front and rear, with adaptations for almost all the races, the brake ducts which evolved Williams-style without the internal "trumpets", and the floor, this too in a number of steps.

Toro Rosso STR6 2011

Toro Rosso STR7

Toro Rosso STR7 Sao Paolo

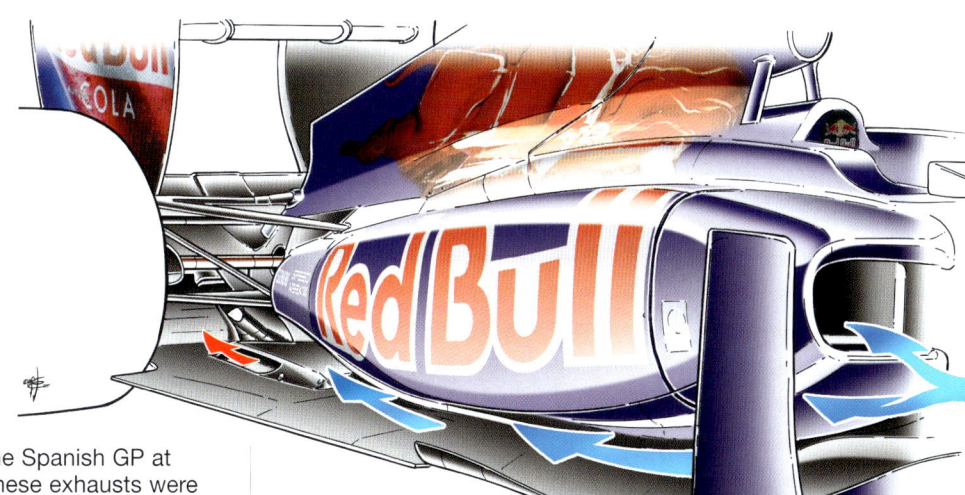

RAISED SIDEPODS
The STR7 also retained the Ferrari F192-type raised sidepods introduced by Giorgio Ascanelli in the 2011 season with an even more accentuated cutaway. In the long run this feature was not effective or at least partially retarded development of the car.

STR6 2011

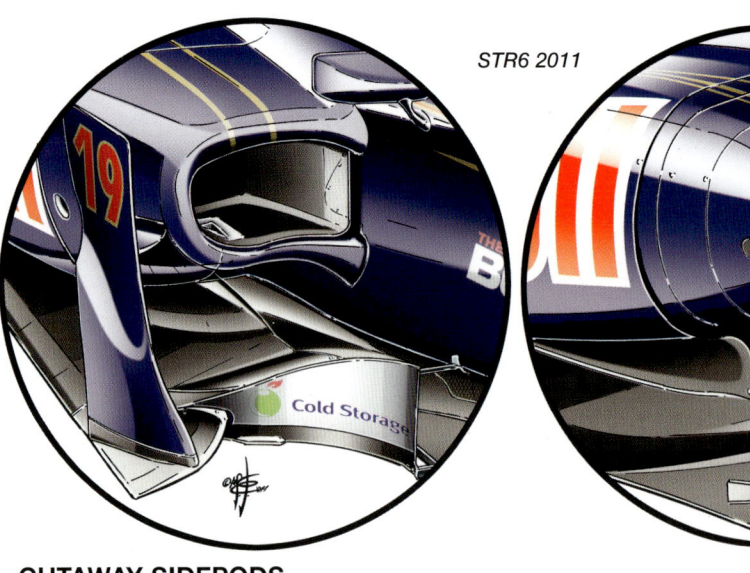

CUTAWAY SIDEPODS
The STR7 presented an even more accentuated cutaway than the 2011 car. The intake mouth was more square-cut and had an almost triangular section, while on the STR6 it was more rectangular. Note the incredible gap at the rear guaranteeing good air flow towards the rear axle.

VALENCIA
Valencia saw the introduction of mini-vanes in the upper part of the sidepods to redirect the flow towards the exhaust area, a feature introduced by McLaren at the Spanish GP. These fins were actually made in transparent plastic so as not to create visibility problems for the drivers.

SPA: BRAKE CALLIPERS
During the Friday morning's free practice at the Belgian GP, Vergne tested a new front suspension configuration characterised by a different brake calliper location a layout that recalled the one used by Red Bull at the Japanese GP in 2010. The vertical position permitted a certain reduction in weight for the same overall stiffness and improved cooling while, obviously, the horizontal position guaranteed a lower centre of gravity. The feature was tested above all in view of the 2013 car.

TORO ROSSO

SUZUKA
At the Japanese GP, the Red Bulls followed the trend for front brake ducts closed on the inside, introduced that year by Williams, followed by Sauber and then the rest of the field.

EXHAUSTS
Toro Rosso began the season with exhausts that were very similar to the original Red Bull configuration (then abandoned in favour of a Sauber-type layout). The terminal was located practically underneath the upper wishbone which effectively directed the flow and was therefore fitted with extensive heat shielding.

MONACO
Toro Rosso was the first team to follow Williams in the realization of a single central pylon for the winglet above the safety cell. Note also the conspicuously curved profile of the rear wing main plane.

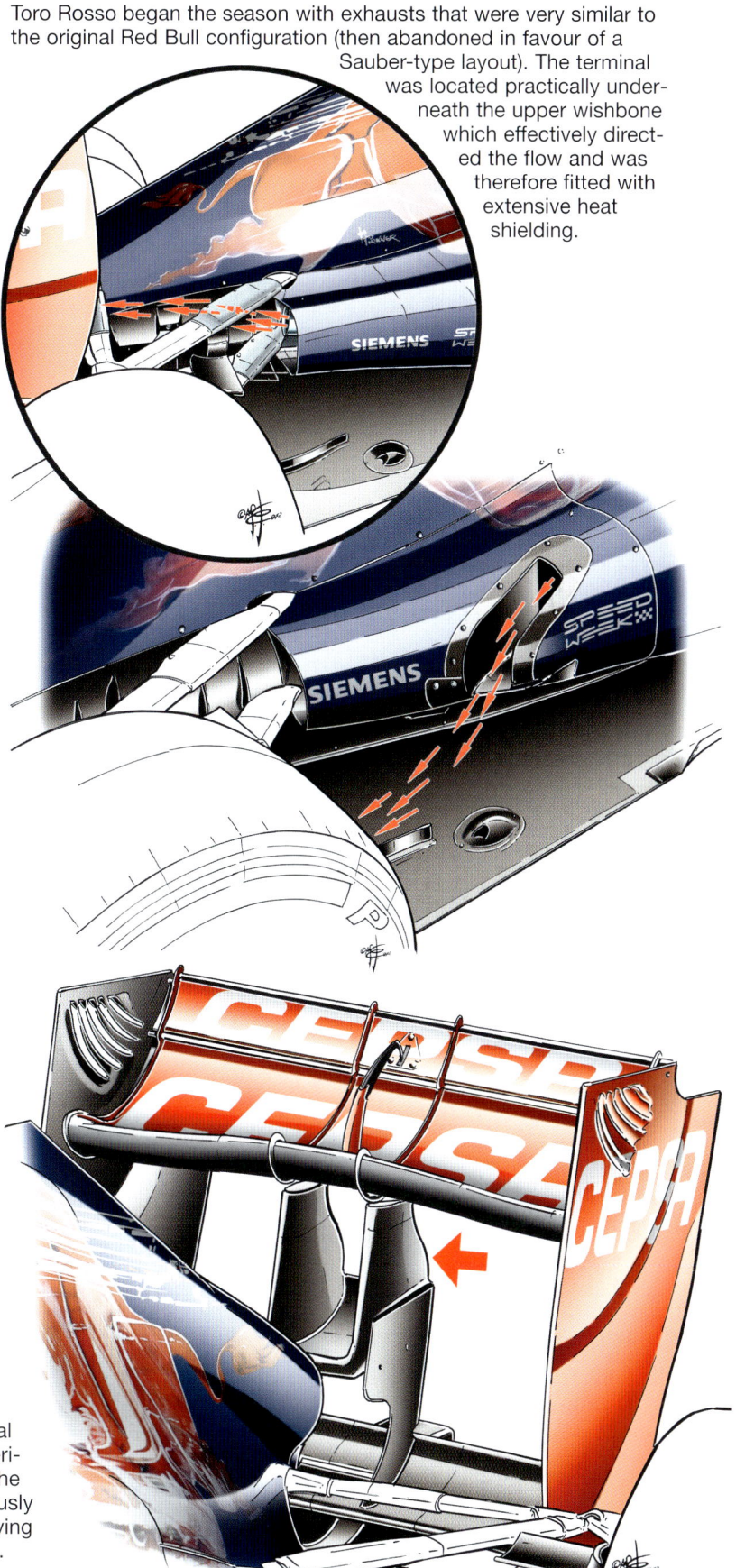

ABU DHABI
Toro Rosso used the post-race test session for young drivers to give dual passive DRS its first outing, an experiment conducted to gather data for the development of the 2013 car. Obviously the feature was never used in qualifying or the race at the following two GPs.

TORO ROSSO

Caterham • Marussia • HRT

Caterham

First among the "minor" teams, but still some distance from the "establishment", Caterham failed to progress as it had hoped in its second season in F1, despite the technical direction passing from Mike Gascoyne to Mark Smith, later assisted by the experienced John Illey.

Two significant novelties weighed against the reaching of this objective: the move from the Aerolab wind tunnel at Casumaro to the Williams facility and, above all, the change in headquarters. Only on two occasions did Kovalainen manage to get past Q1 (Bahrain and Valencia).

The new car retained the family look of the first Lotus T128, albeit with greater attention to detail and the fabrication of the components.

The most important technical novelties concerned the fitting for the first time of Kers, together with the Renault engine, which inevitably led to a longer wheelbase.

After having begun the season in a decidedly traditional configuration, partly in the interests of reliability, a development programme was initiated that was without doubt more significant than those of the team's two rivals.

The adoption of McLaren-type exhausts came at Silverstone, although it failed to bring immediate benefits in terms of performance.

Lotus T128 2011

Caterham CT01

Caterham CT01 Sao Paolo

SPLIT INTAKE
In 2011 Lotus, which became Caterham in 2012, and Force India had split engine air intakes, as on the 2010 Mercedes-Benz, respecting the section of the central structure as required by the regulations. However, the idea was dropped by both teams in 2012. The illustration shows the new oval intake on the Caterham.

108

Marussia

Marussia (ex-Virgin) also failed to move to the next level in its second F1 season despite the technical direction of the expert and pragmatic Pat Symmonds, who managed to progress the team as a whole with a car designed not only on the basis of CFD calculations but also developed in the wind tunnel, specifically the McLaren facility.
A collaboration that bore fruit. When evaluating the season it should be remembered that the Marussia (like HRT) was fitted with the less powerful Cosworth engine and did not enjoy the benefit of Kers, while Caterham not only had the stronger Renault engine but also Kers.
Nonetheless, the car still gave signs of significant progress with respect to the one realised under the direction of Nick Wirth.
The most important evolutionary package arrived at Spa.
The Coanda-effect exhausts were closer to the Red Bull rather than the McLaren type, with Sauber-style descending bodywork.

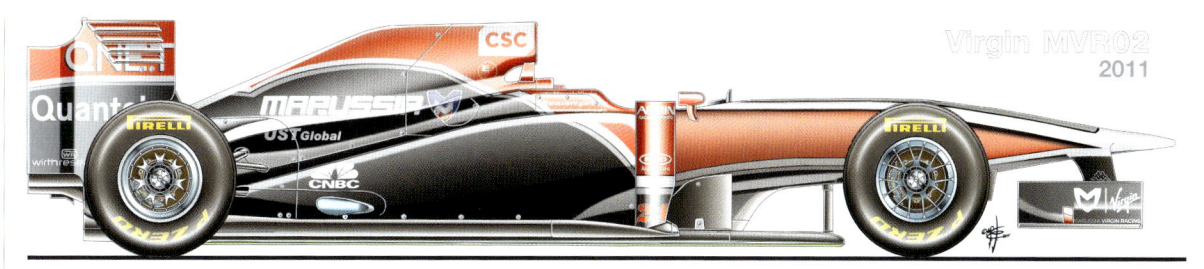

Virgin MVR02 2011

Marussia MR02

Marussia MR02 Sao Paolo

HRT

HRT's F1 adventure came to an end all too predictably as early as its second season.
The programme started out on the wrong foot, with the original project commissioned by Dallara hamstrung by budget issues and things then hardly improved despite the generous commitment of Luis Perez-Sala.
Without a true headquarters and with a designer (Geoff Willis) who had turned down the job in the November of 2011, HRT arrived at the first race without having participated in a single test session.
And this is something to think about, above all in terms of safety: a team that is about race in the first round of the World Championship without having covered a single kilometre should not be allowed onto the track. The season then went from bad to worse without a true development programme and above all with components that had reached their best before dates.

Obviously, in a situation such as this, the experience of a fine driver such as Pedro De La Rosa counted for nothing.

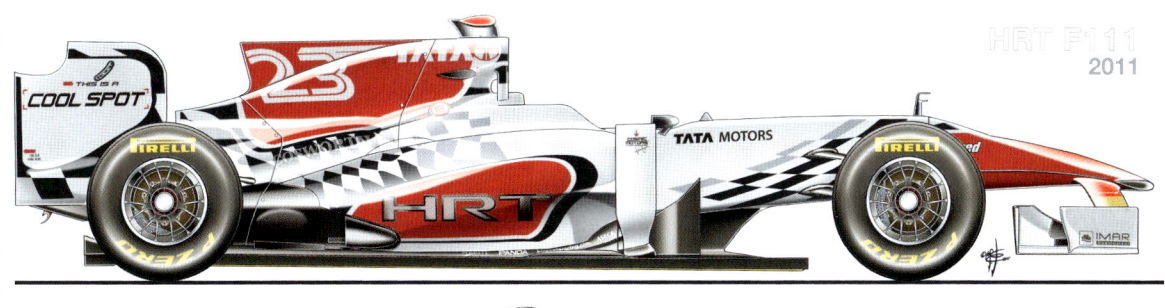

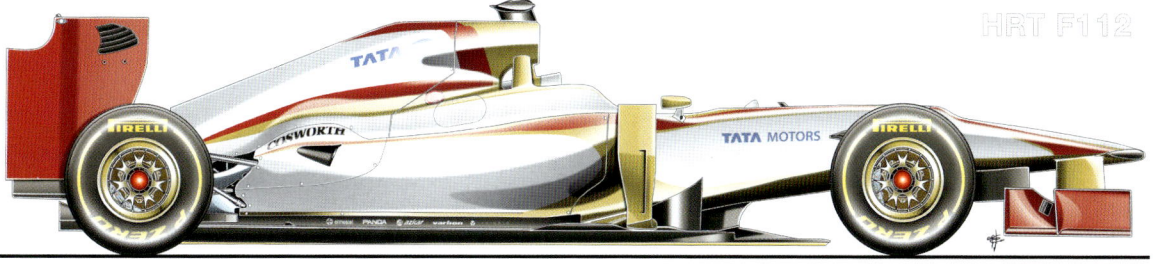

HRT F111 2011

HRT F112

CATERHAM • MARUSSIA • HRT

The 2013 SEASON

Pirelli TYRES

+200g.

+700g.

Pirelli introduced new tyres for the 2013 season (see the Regulations 2013 chapter) with a different structure and a metal band installed in place of the previous one in Kevlar, along with different compounds, with the aim of increasing tyre performance through an enlarged contact patch.
The combination of these structural modifications led to an increase in weight of 200g at the front and 700g at the rear.

CONTACT PATCH
The structural modifications increased the size of the contact patch, principally in corners, guaranteeing increased grip and therefore greater performance. The increased grip was the result of both the structural modifications mentioned and changes to the compounds, generally softer with respect to 2012, with the exception of the Super Soft, which was unchanged.
The drawing represents the increased size of the contact patch of the 2013 tyres (blue) compared with that of the 2012 covers (red).

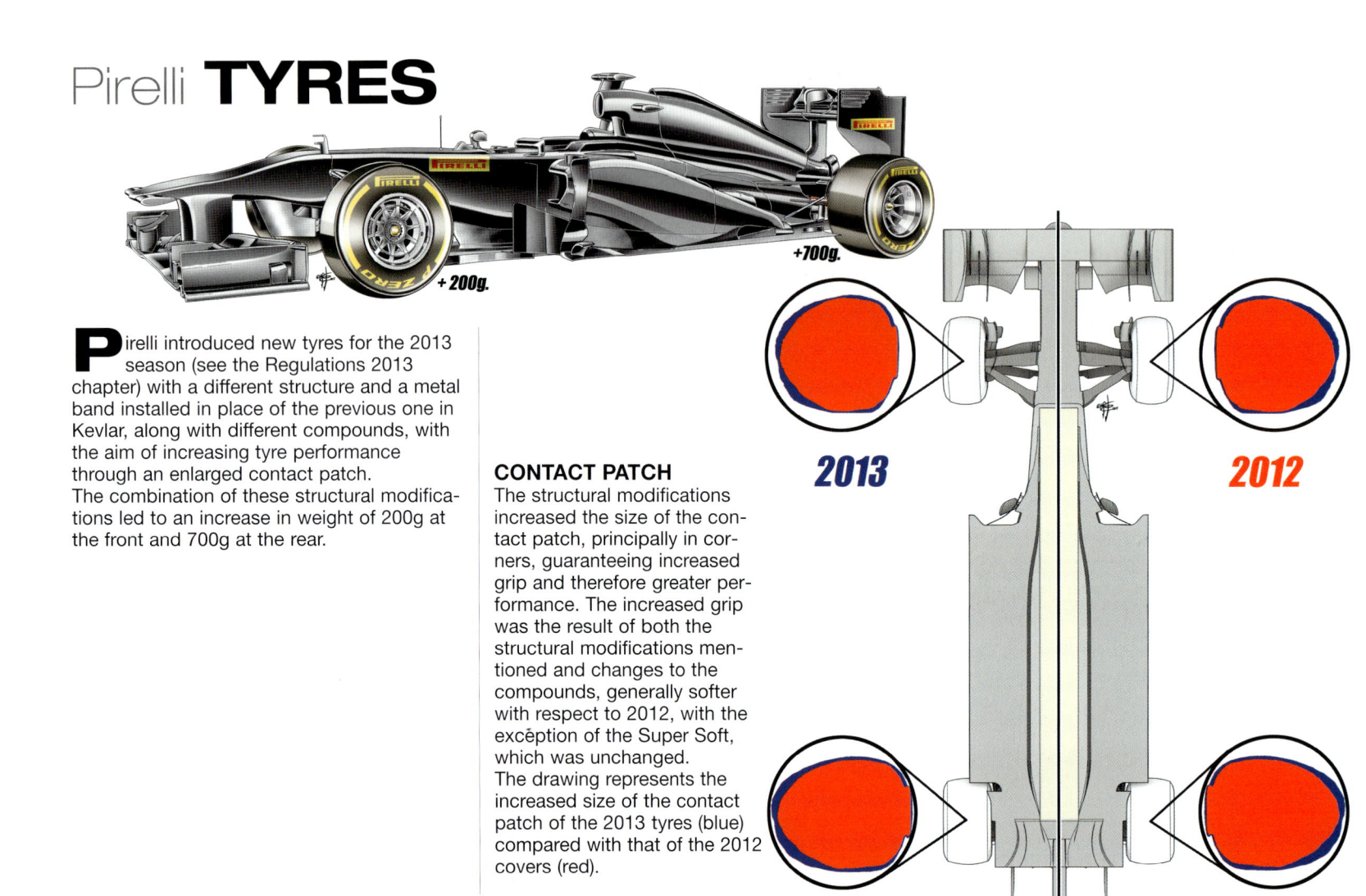

2013   **2012**

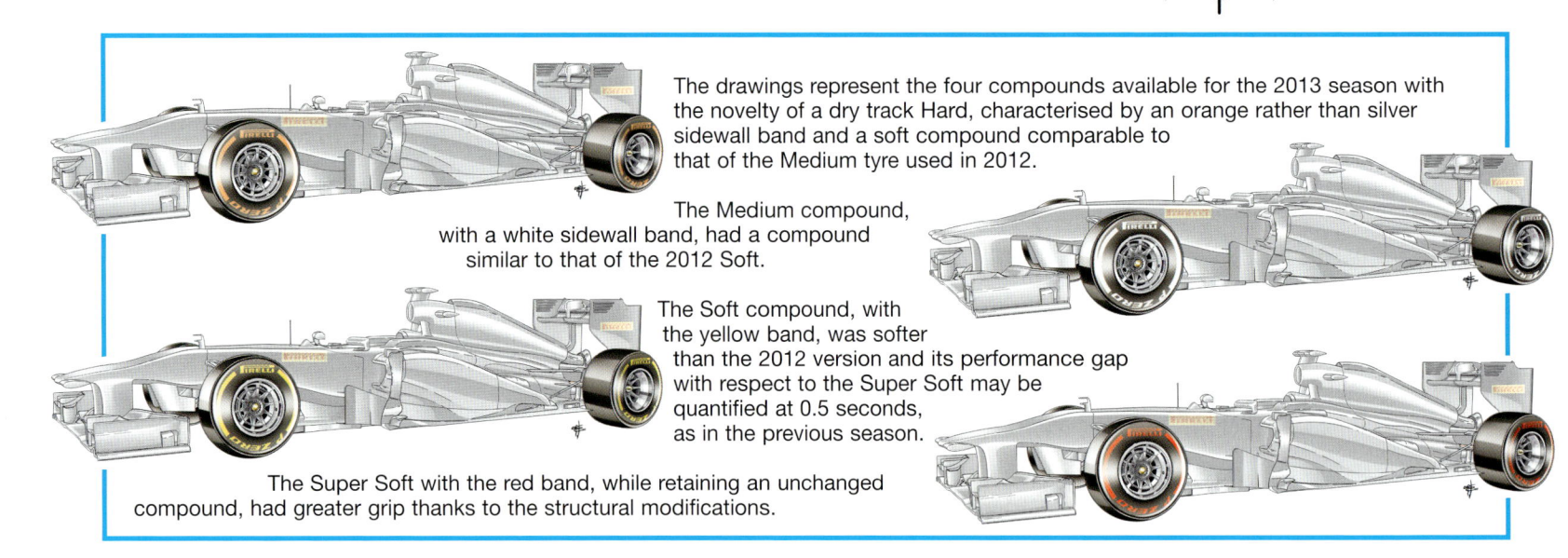

The drawings represent the four compounds available for the 2013 season with the novelty of a dry track Hard, characterised by an orange rather than silver sidewall band and a soft compound comparable to that of the Medium tyre used in 2012.

The Medium compound, with a white sidewall band, had a compound similar to that of the 2012 Soft.

The Soft compound, with the yellow band, was softer than the 2012 version and its performance gap with respect to the Super Soft may be quantified at 0.5 seconds, as in the previous season.

The Super Soft with the red band, while retaining an unchanged compound, had greater grip thanks to the structural modifications.

2013 REGULATIONS

The 2013 season was one based on technical stability in readiness for the major revolution that will take place in 2014. However, even if there were few new developments they were still rather significant. The most obvious was the chance to avoid the unattractive step on the car's nose, which had been much criticized in previous seasons. This time, the teams had the possibility of covering it with what the British call a vanity panel.
Take note that it was a possibility and not a duty; so some teams kept the step, among them Red Bull, Lotus, Sauber and Caterham and a kind of Mercedes. Obviously, below such a vanity panel there always had to be the structural part that respects the regulations for safety reasons, with a nose height limit of 550 mm, introduced in 2012. Remember that it was a rule associated with the need to limit driver injury in case of a T-bone collision between two cars.
And continuing the subject of safety, the 2013 technical regulations included strengthening the deformable structure for cockpit and roll bar lateral protection. In addition, all chassis had to pass the crash test imposed by the Federation before taking part in official events, including the pre-championship tests in Spain. One aspect that was not visible from the outside was the 2 kg increase in minimum weight that came into force to compensate for the identical increase in weight caused by the new Pirelli tyres, designed to guarantee greater F1 spectacle.
That number brought the same variation of values in weight distribution, in order to maintain the ratio that existed during the 2012 season. In the illustration, the sum of weights on the two axles was falls short by 7 kg in relation to the minimum weight and constituted eventual ballast for use when setting up the car.
Then there were two norms that considerably penalized the car's performance in 2013. The first regarded the introduction of a more severe control of front wing flexibility to avoid transverse plane flexing as well as on the longitudinal unit, with a tolerance that was halved, a considerable amount.
The second concerned the ban of using the rear wing flap aperture (DRS) to operate a second DRS at both the rear end – as did Red Bull from the GP of Singapore – and the front, which Mercedes-Benz used from the start of the season. But that wasn't enough: in the sports regulations, the use of the DRS in qualifying became the same as in the race at the express request of the drivers who, on more than one occasion, found themselves in dangerous situations in the exasperated search for the limit in qualification.
Those limitations should reduce the advantages that Red Bull enjoyed during qualifying in 2012, and it seemed clear by that time that the battle ground would move to the maximum exploitation of the double passive DRS, which made its first appearance in 2012 on the Lotus and Mercedes-Benz cars, but only to be tested for the 2013 championship and without ever using it during races.
Quite a poker game!

REGULATIONS 2013

The illustration shows the number of articles in the technical regulations in which the English text bears witness to possible disputes.

1) The Federation allowed the teams to cover the step on the 2013 car's nose with a so-called vanity panel of simple bodywork, so as not to create danger should an accident occur: but the structural part had to respect the 2012 rules.

2) More severe control over the flexibility of the front wing, with a 100 kg load applied to two different areas and also the longitudinal axis, with a tolerance reduced by half to just 10 mm of flexing.

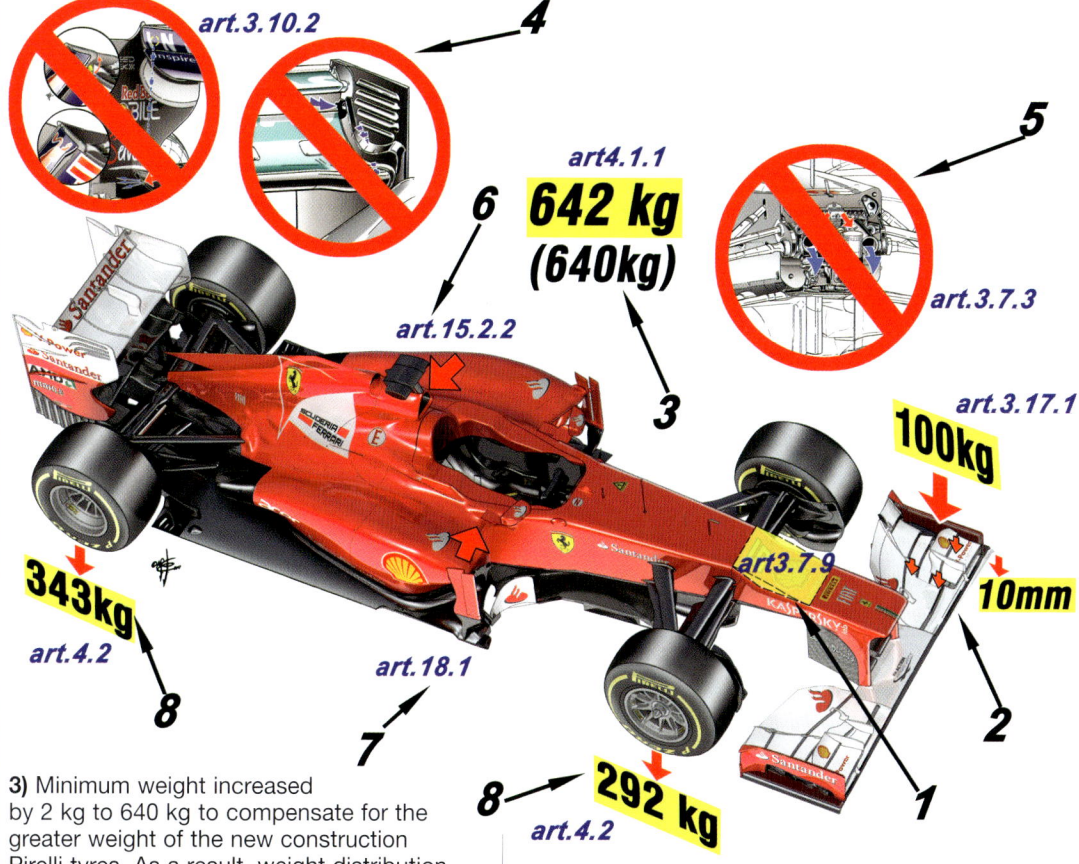

3) Minimum weight increased by 2 kg to 640 kg to compensate for the greater weight of the new construction Pirelli tyres. As a result, weight distribution was changed to 292 kg on the front end and 343 kg on the rear. The 7 kg difference between the two and the minimum weight became the value of eventual free ballast for use by the teams.

4) The double DRS operated simultaneously using apertures freed by the movement of the flap – the traditional DRS – was banned.

5) In the same way, the channeling that feeds the front F-Duct, such as that on the Mercedes, was banned.

6-7) Driver protection was improved, with a better roll bar and lateral anti-intrusion panels.

PIRELLI TYRES

To increase the footprint area and, therefore, available mechanical grip, Pirelli introduced new tyres for 2013. The cornering stiffness of the structure was reduced by about 10% to permit the tyre's greater deformation. At the same time, to avoid excessive "malleability" of the cornering force and, therefore, a loss of cornering performance, the under tread belt was made more rigid by adopting new geometry and adding reinforcing material. That resulted in a slight weight increase of 200 grams for the front tyres and 700 grams for the rears, adding about 2 kg more to the car's weight.

VANITY PANEL

Ferrari, McLaren, Sauber, Williams, Force India, Toro Rosso and Marussia completely masked the anti-aesthetic step, which was almost totally retained by Red Bull, Lotus and Caterham, while Mercedes-Benz chose partial masking. Adrian Newey took advantage of the step to introduce an upper slit to exploit the passage of air between the lower and upper parts of the car, as did Sauber in 2012.

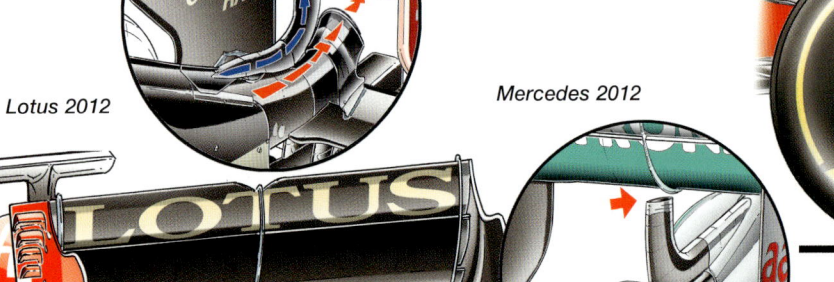

Lotus 2012

Mercedes 2012

FRONT WING FLEXIBILITY TEST

The severe limitation of front wing flexing introduced – at least in theory – during the last 2012 race and which became a harsh verification norm in 2013, had a major influence on cars. For the first time, the 100 kg load was applied at two points, both transversally and longitudinally, to avoid any kind of flexing but, and this was more important, the value of the flexing tolerance was reduced from 20 mm to 10 mm.

LOTUS

A passive double DRS was allowed, in other words the operation of the classic DRS without the direct or indirect intervention of the driver or as a secondary action.
Lotus were the first to bring in the system at the 2012 GP of Germany, followed by Mercedes in Belgium. Lotus continued with the device on the E21 in the pre-championship tests. Remember that this passive version, which is only operated by speed and air pressure, was never raced in 2012.

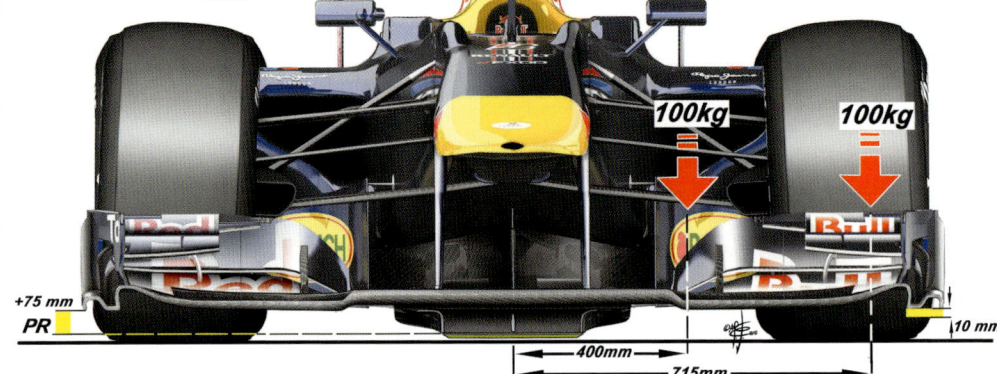

The 2013 **SEASON**
112

New DEVELOPMENTS

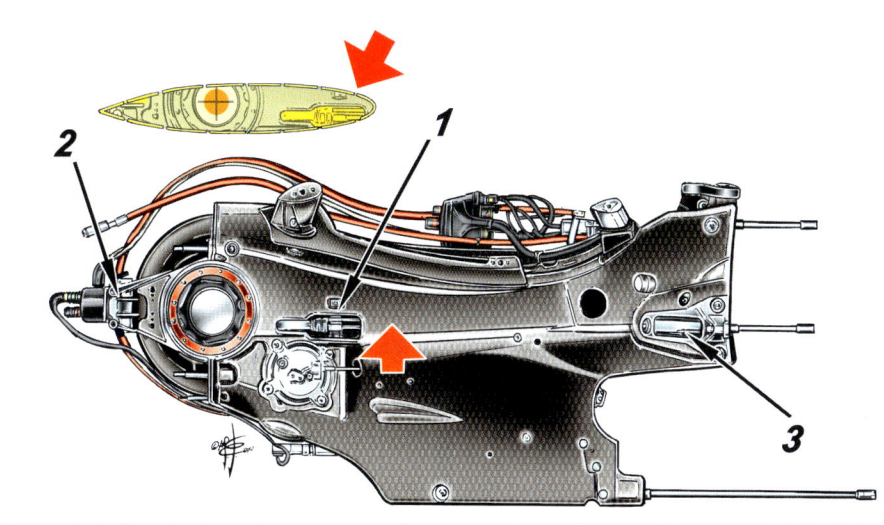

FERRARI: FAIRED DRIVE SHAFT

It was inevitable that the shrewd notion of Adrian Newey's to fair the 2012 RB8's drive shafts would turn into a 2013 fashion adopted by just about all the cars, starting with Ferrari. It was a real aerodynamic appendage that circumvented the ban on fairing the drive shafts by simply positioning the suspension's lower arms at drive shafts' height.

The regulation permits fairing the suspension arms with a ratio of 3.5 between the chord and the thickness of the plane, provided it is absolutely neutral. The toe-in link and the wishbone's rear lower arm were placed not only at the height of the drive shafts, but also close to them. The sum of the two fairing elements also included the drive shafts.

In the design of the F2012 gearbox (divided into two elements) one deduces that the lower wishbone was already located much higher during the previous season; that's why the lower wishbone mount had to be raised slightly (indicated by the arrow); all, obviously, without compromising the suspension's geometry.

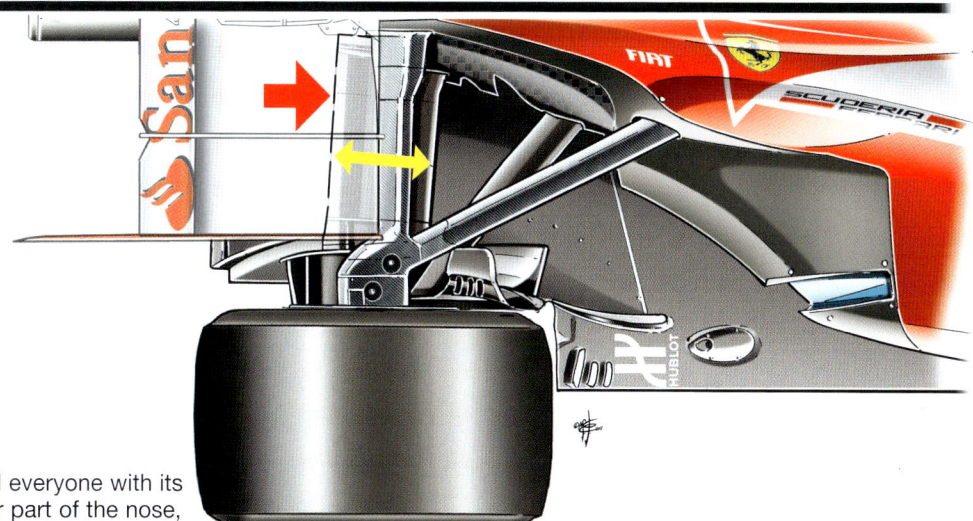

FERRARI HOLE

During pre-championship testing, Ferrari surprised everyone with its introduction of a hole in the chassis near the lower part of the nose, but without the air passing towards the upper part of the car as with, for example, the previous season's Sauber and the 2013 Red Bull. These two cars revived the concept of the air passing between the lower and upper parts of the nose a la Ferrari 2008 (see the 2012 New Developments chapter). But on the F138, it was not the passage of air for which observers presumed the hole was there to cool the electronic management system. The dubious aspects were almost immediately resolved, because this approach was dropped from the first race.

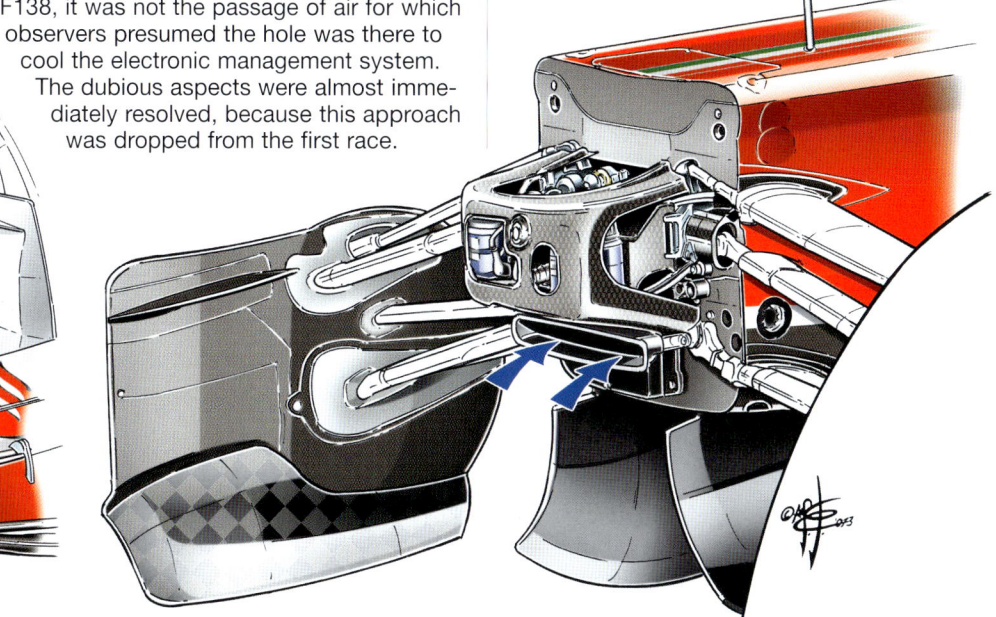

Sauber 2012

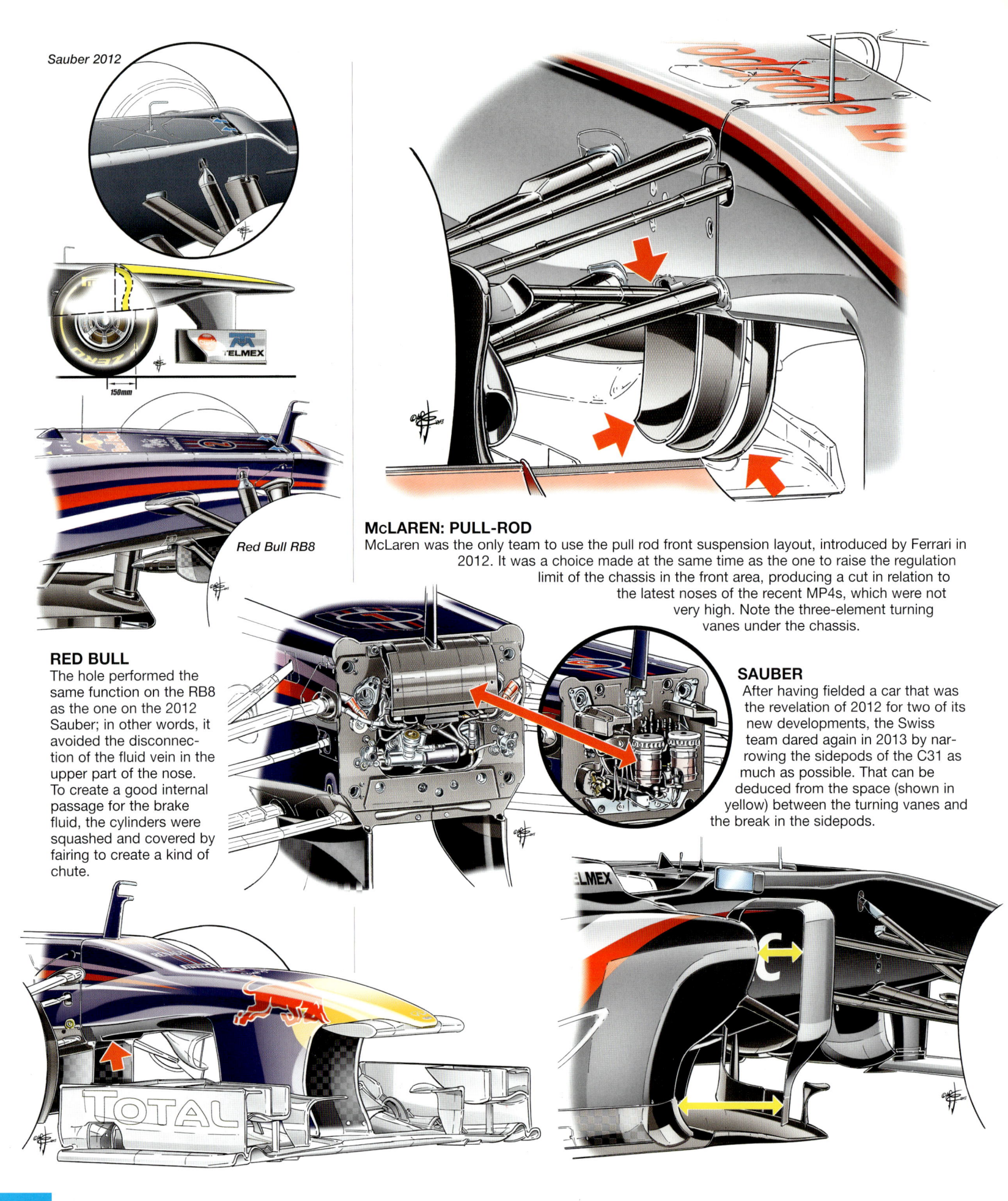

Red Bull RB8

McLAREN: PULL-ROD
McLaren was the only team to use the pull rod front suspension layout, introduced by Ferrari in 2012. It was a choice made at the same time as the one to raise the regulation limit of the chassis in the front area, producing a cut in relation to the latest noses of the recent MP4s, which were not very high. Note the three-element turning vanes under the chassis.

RED BULL
The hole performed the same function on the RB8 as the one on the 2012 Sauber; in other words, it avoided the disconnection of the fluid vein in the upper part of the nose. To create a good internal passage for the brake fluid, the cylinders were squashed and covered by fairing to create a kind of chute.

SAUBER
After having fielded a car that was the revelation of 2012 for two of its new developments, the Swiss team dared again in 2013 by narrowing the sidepods of the C31 as much as possible. That can be deduced from the space (shown in yellow) between the turning vanes and the break in the sidepods.

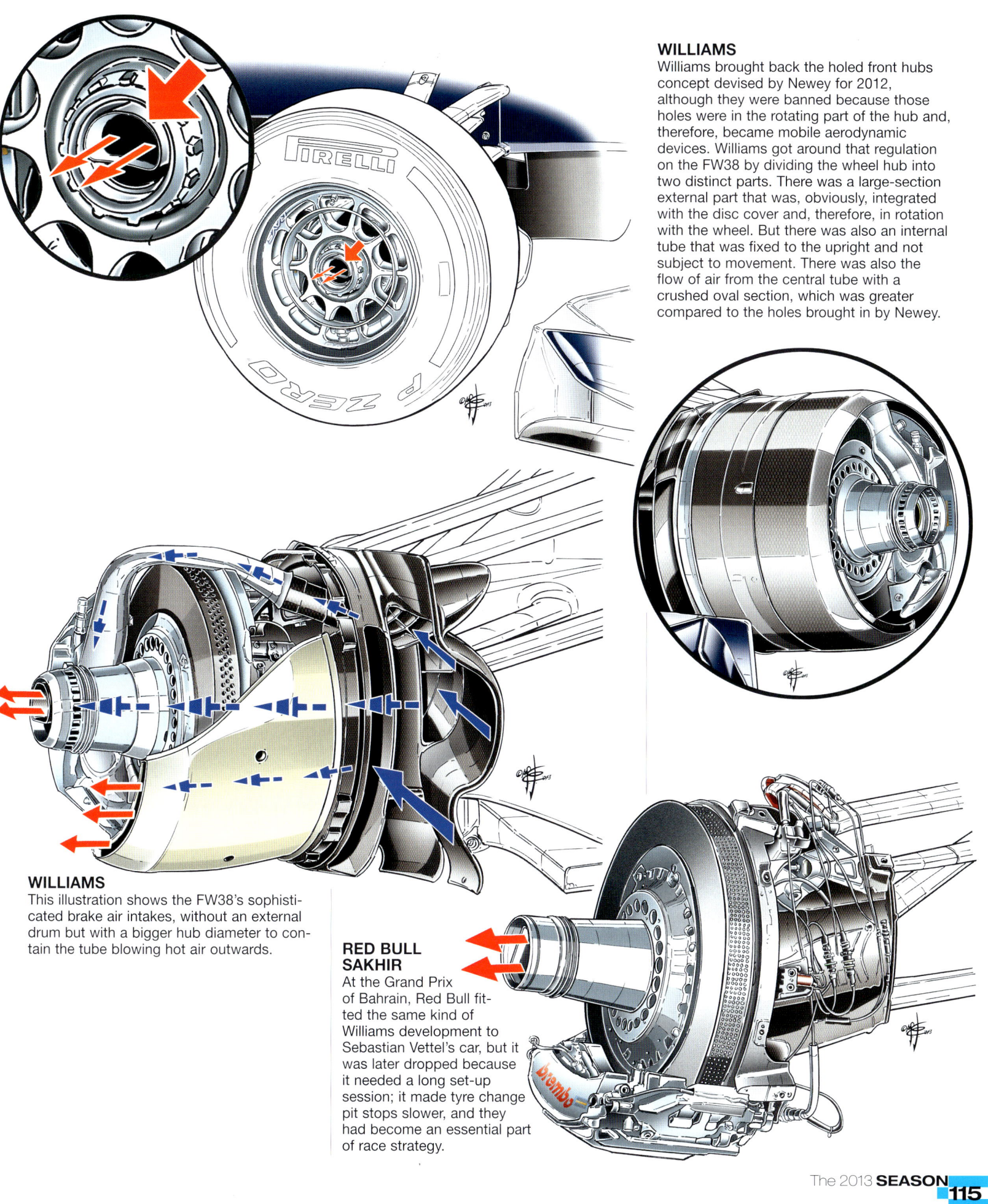

WILLIAMS

Williams brought back the holed front hubs concept devised by Newey for 2012, although they were banned because those holes were in the rotating part of the hub and, therefore, became mobile aerodynamic devices. Williams got around that regulation on the FW38 by dividing the wheel hub into two distinct parts. There was a large-section external part that was, obviously, integrated with the disc cover and, therefore, in rotation with the wheel. But there was also an internal tube that was fixed to the upright and not subject to movement. There was also the flow of air from the central tube with a crushed oval section, which was greater compared to the holes brought in by Newey.

WILLIAMS

This illustration shows the FW38's sophisticated brake air intakes, without an external drum but with a bigger hub diameter to contain the tube blowing hot air outwards.

RED BULL SAKHIR

At the Grand Prix of Bahrain, Red Bull fitted the same kind of Williams development to Sebastian Vettel's car, but it was later dropped because it needed a long set-up session; it made tyre change pit stops slower, and they had become an essential part of race strategy.

The 2013 SEASON 115

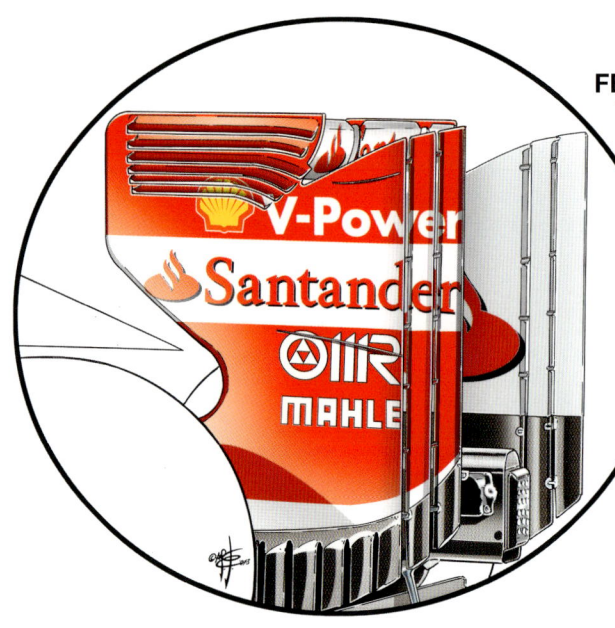

FERRARI-MINARDI

The aerodynamic development of the beam wing's end plate was completely new, even if something similar was introduced by Gabriele Tredozi on his 2005 Minardi. As well as the horizontal gills in the leading edge (taken from a wing tested at Suzuka, but never raced) and the fringes in the lower areas, there were two vertical blow holes near the terminal part of the end plates. It was a development that should have interacted well with the DRS and improve the beam wing's efficiency.

Controversies
2013

WILLIAMS AND CATERHAM IRREGULAR

Williams and Caterham were immediately admonished for their lack of respect for the exhaust opening regulation. Caterham's was obviously irregular, since it had a real fin inside the exhaust hole.
The Williams technicians had integrated the design of a turning vane in the single perimeter of the hole for the exhausts with the precaution of a cut to avoid the formation of a second hole.
Result: it was declared that neither development conformed, even before the start of the season.

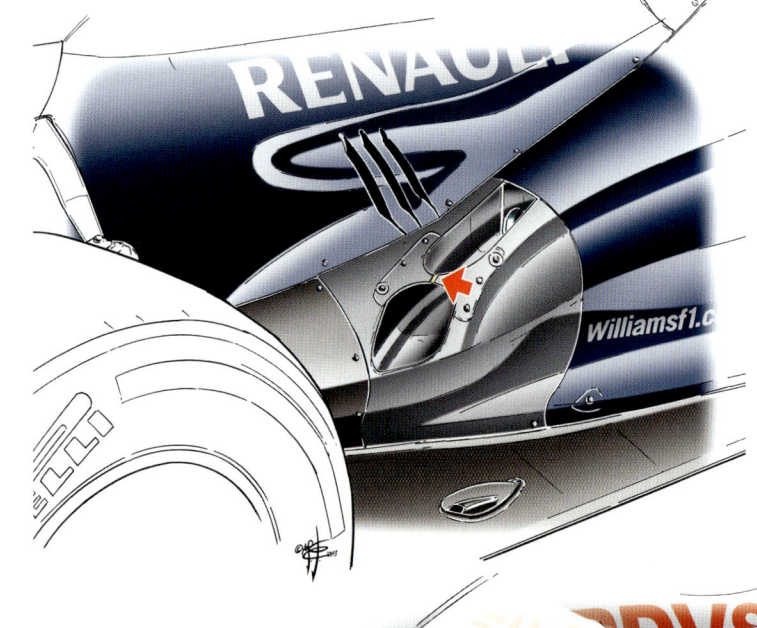

WILLIAMS REGULAR

Williams returned to normality by eliminating the small vane in the perimeter of the exhaust aperture and Caterham did the same.

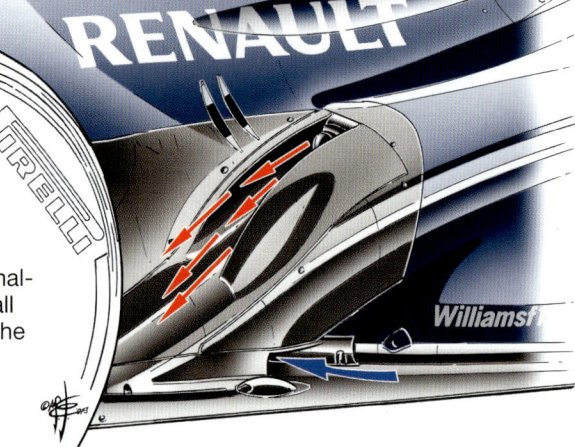

The 2013 SEASON

LOTUS

Immediately after the Malaysian GP, rubber caps that sealed the Lotus's front suspension mounts were the subject of clarification. But in the end, the team was able to retain that feature, which enabled it to eliminate even the slightest turbulence generated by conventional mounts.

SILVERSTONE: THE CASE OF THE TYRES

The 2013 Grand Prix of Great Britain will be remembered for its series of extraordinary tyre failures, especially the rears. It was a situation that originated from many factors, which came to the surface on the Silverstone circuit and will be examined in detail in the next edition. Here, we shall limit ourselves to spotlighting the predominant culprit, which was the steel ply used in the place of Kevlar. After invoking safety reasons, Pirelli was permitted to return to the 2012 tyre construction with 2013 tread compounds from the second race after Silverstone, in Hungary. It was a solution already requested before the British GP, but it was opposed by the teams as they had had difficulty fully exploiting the 2012 Pirelli tyres.

LOTUS AT SILVERSTONE

The front suspension of the Lotus was contested after a request for clarification from McLaren. The regulation stipulates that there should only be three suspension elements fitted to a single mount, but the E21 had four.

The strange thing is that this feature had been on the Lotus for no fewer than two seasons. This illustration shows the solution tested by the young drivers, with the push rod mount on the variable wishbone, depending on the load on the front end. The method was banned by the Federation before the start of the 2012 season. It was only two years later that the anomalous four anchorages were discovered: the two arms of the lower wishbone, the push rod of the suspension and the steering's tie-rod, which is at the same height on the Lotus as the lower unit.

LOTUS AT BUDAPEST

At the end of qualifying for the GP of Hungary, it was thought Romain Grosjean's Lotus didn't conform to Art. 3.17.5 due to the excessive flexibility of the T-tray, which could have 5 mm of tolerance with a thrust of 200 kg in three different points. The car showed evident signs of damage due to mounting the kerbs, but everything went back to normal.

The 2013 **SEASON** 117

2013 EVOLUTION

McLAREN
The McLaren half-shaft was also amply shrouded; note how the upper wishbone mounting plate effectively shifts towards the centre its anchorage point. Its shape meant that it became a small spoiler creating negative lift in the area permitted by the regulations.

FERRARI
In the comparison from above between the F2012 (top) and the F138 you can clearly see the depth of the chord of the wing (1) that covers the half-shaft and the sum of the fairings of the rear lower wishbone arm and the tie-rod. Note the upper wishbone mounting plate (2). There was a new vent at the top of the brake duct (3) acting as a downforce spoiler.

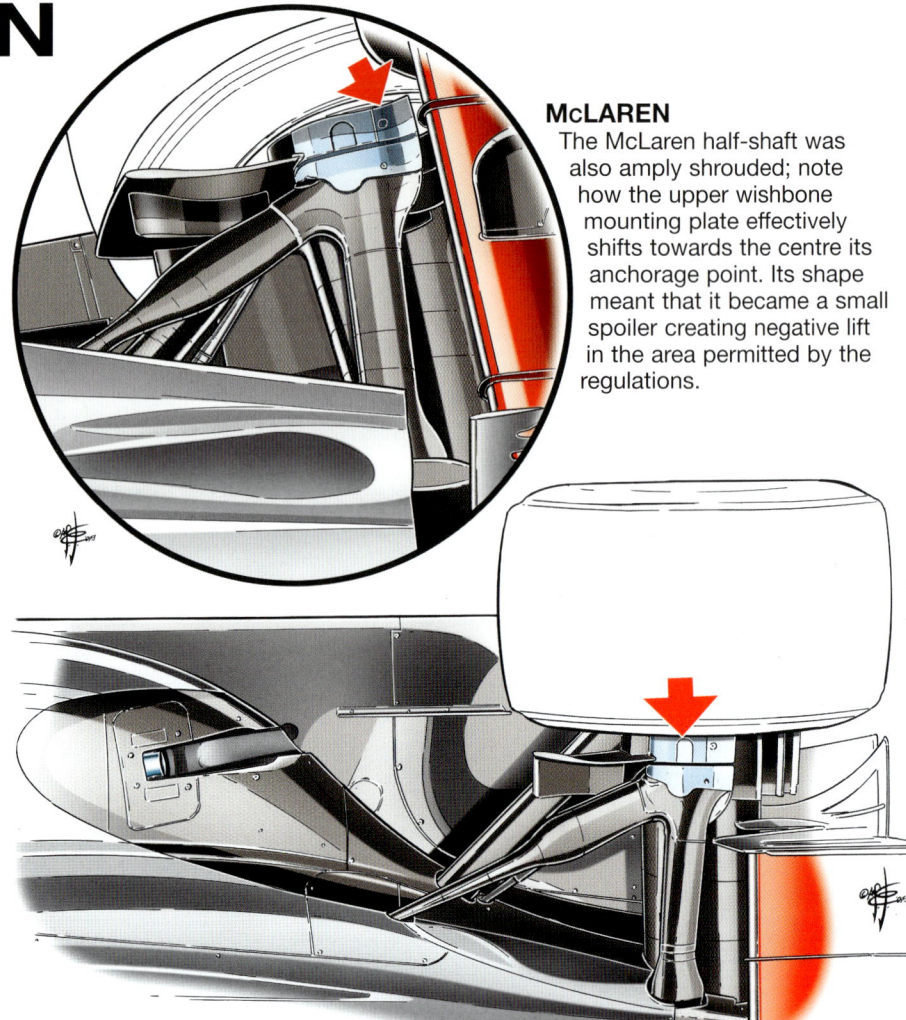

MERCEDES
Mercedes was the first team to present its 2013 edition front wing in the pre-season tests. It featured no less that four vents (1) where the old one had just two. The mini-flap (2) and the endplates with no vertical fin (3) were new.

LOTUS
In the previous season Lotus had been the last team (Japanese GP) to adopt the feature that exploits the Coanda effect in the exhaust area.
With the E21 it adopted the further refinement introduced by Red Bull: it presented in fact the same air passage in the lower part of the sidepods, in the area below the exhausts; these two were influenced by the RB8 school in both versions tested at Jerez ahead of the 2013 season.

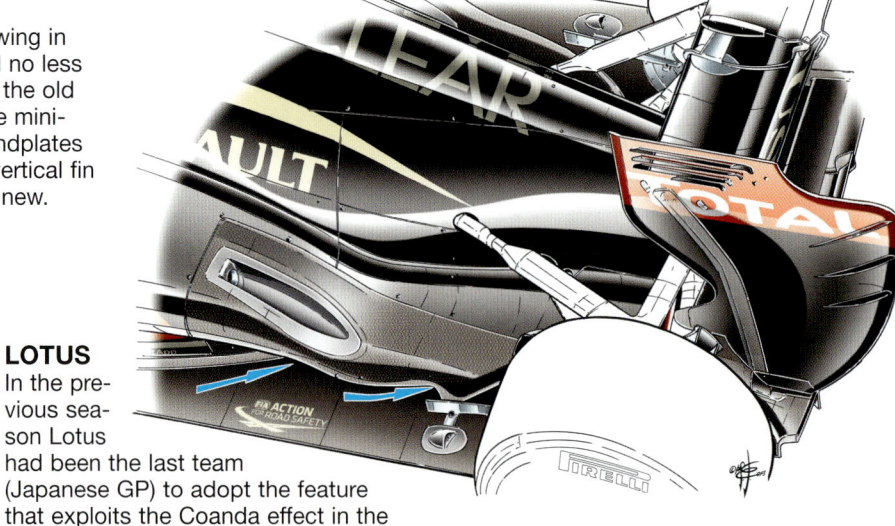

The 2013 SEASON

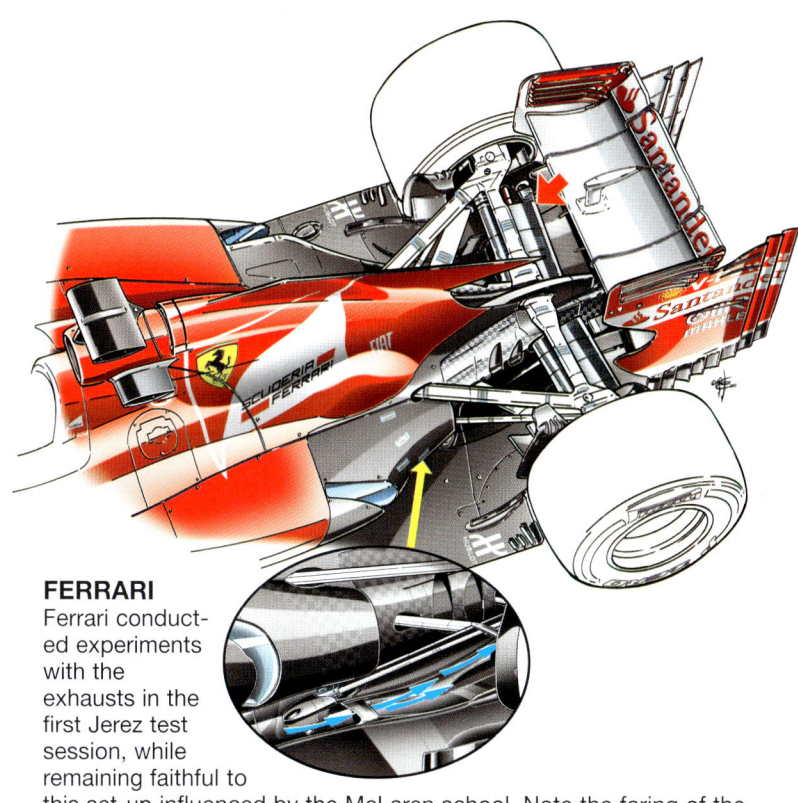

FERRARI

Ferrari conducted experiments with the exhausts in the first Jerez test session, while remaining faithful to this set-up influenced by the McLaren school. Note the faring of the half-shaft with a very deep chord (indicated by the arrow).
There was also a notable cutaway in the lower section with a kind of vast cradle between the stepped bottom and the gearbox fairing to which this small horizontal flap (in the oval) was added to prevent the detachment of the flow in this area.

LOTUS

From pre-season testing onwards, Lotus and Mercedes continued with the experiments with dual passive DRS begun in the second half of the 2012 season. The curious aspect was that Lotus abandoned its configuration (top) in favour of the one introduced by Mercedes in Belgium (to side) with the venting beneath the main plane. This passive "stall" solution not controlled by DRS proved to be very tricky to set up.

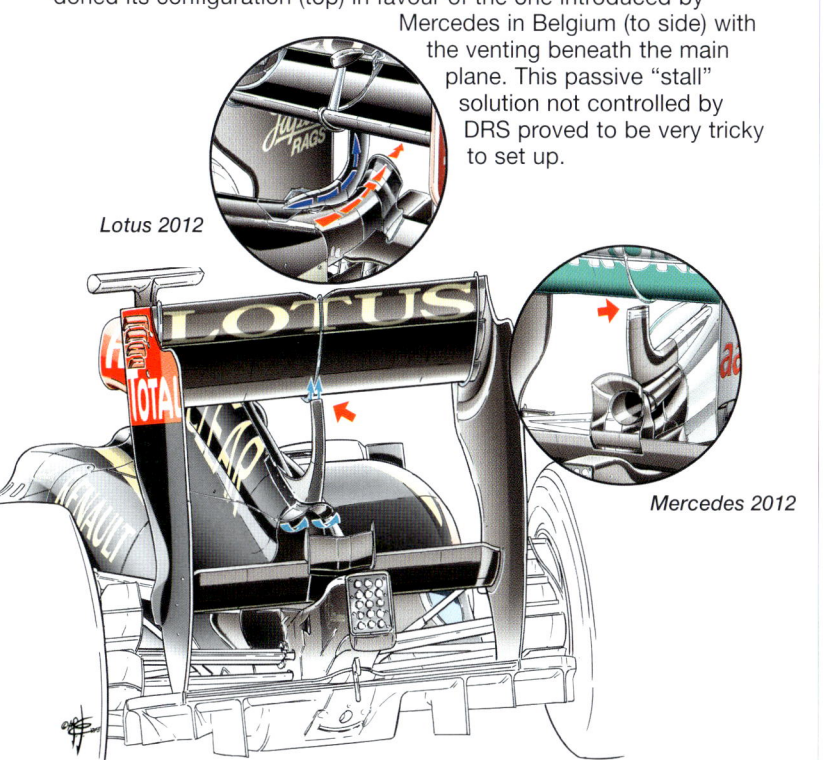

Lotus 2012

Mercedes 2012

RED BULL

On the RB9, Newey refined the sidepod configuration with an area upstream of the exhausts that was cutaway even deeper and equipped with a gap in the lower part to feed a vent (see the blue arrows) that in its turn fed the diffuser channels and the dual DRS tried in the last two days of the second Barcelona test. Note the fringes in the lower part of the wing endplates, practically identical to those introduced in the penultimate race of the 2012 season.

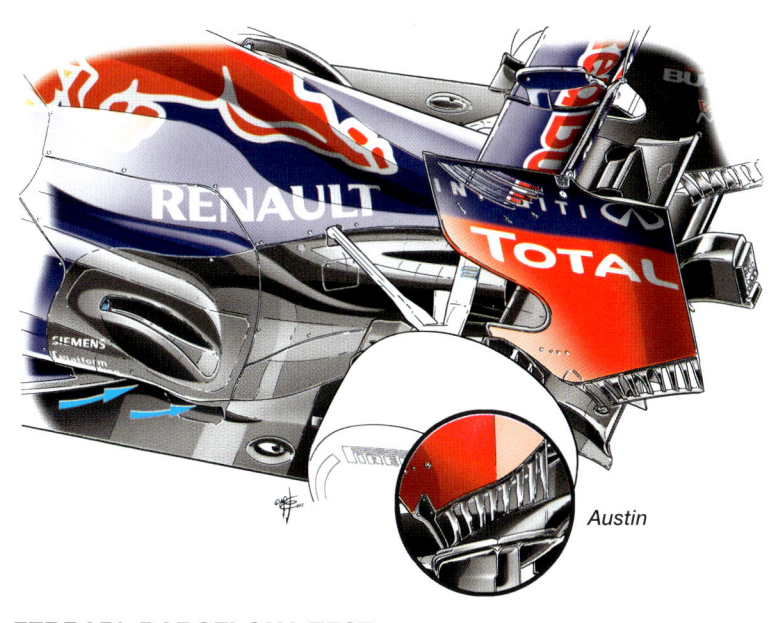

Austin

FERRARI: BARCELONA TEST

In the last pre-season test, Ferrari introduced new exhausts and new bodywork for the F138. The new configuration featured lower sidepod ends (see the yellow space) with the venting (1) therefore directed more towards the diffuser's lateral channels. The bodywork was also lower and more sloping as indicated by the two protuberances (2) required to cover

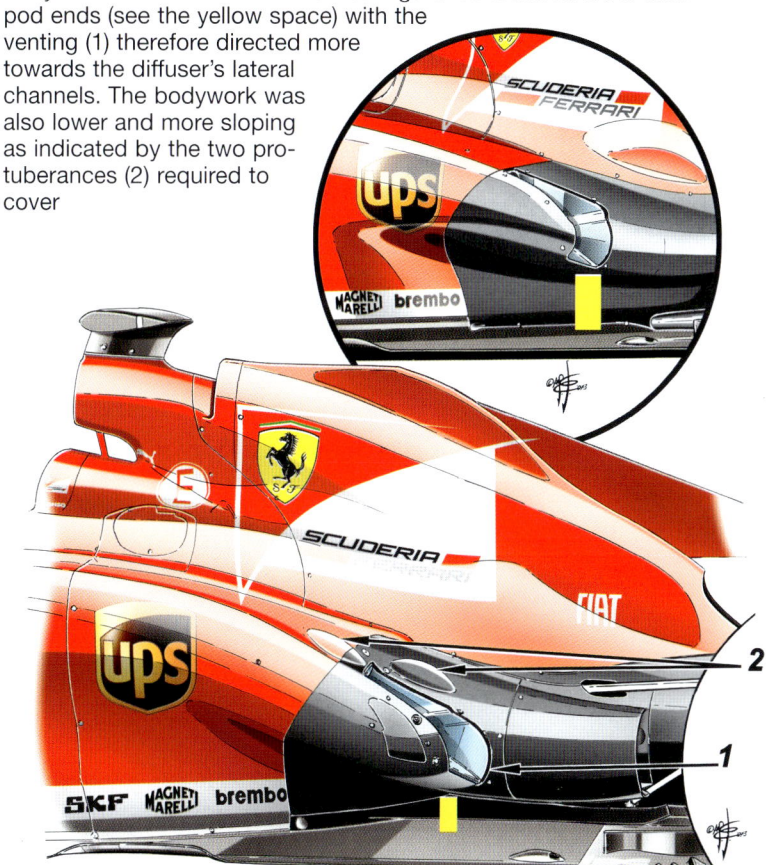

The 2013 **SEASON** 119

RED BULL

It was in Barcelona that both Ferrari and Red Bull introduced new wings. Both had two slots (1). The one on the RB9 also differed from the wing used previously in the Lotus-style rounded mount (2), with raised endplates on the flaps. The main plane also retained this feature (3), creating a mini-tunnel ahead of the endplate itself.

A feature that worked in synergy with the conspicuous longitudinal fins with which the underside of the profiles was equipped.

SAUBER MELBOURNE

In order to better channel the hot air from the exhausts, Sauber installed this long fin on the car, in the position where Ferrari had instead created a cutaway channelling the air to the starter hole and the central part of the diffuser.

FERRARI

From the first race in Australia the hole in both the chassis (visible in the circle) of the F138 and the lower part of the nose were eliminated. A decision that had exercised the various technical blogs on the specialist sites.

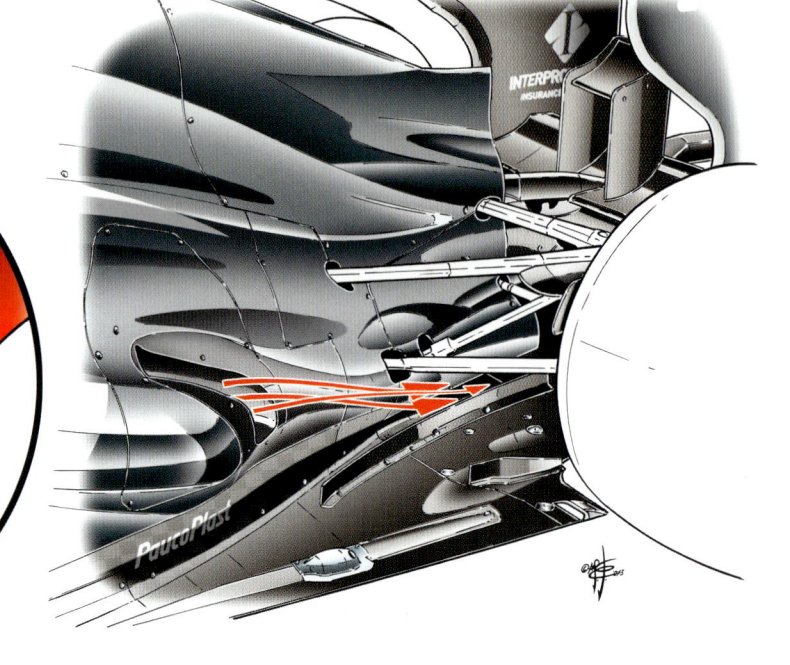

RED BULL

The new nose introduced in the last Barcelona test was not used, but the whole of the lower bodywork from the start of the sidepods was completely revised. These two drawings show the modifications made to the rear section. Inboard of the wheels, in place of the three vertical fins (one is hidden by the wheel in the insert) there was just one; the brake duct instead presented a generous extension forwards to channel the flow of hot air from the exhausts towards the lower part of the lateral channels.

Melbourne

LOTUS SEPANG

A lot of work was done on the front wing with a new configuration that differed from that used in Melbourne in the initial part of the endplate that presented a curled section in the top front part. It was used by both drivers.

The 2013 **SEASON**

FERRARI

In order to cope with the heat, Ferrari opened the small window provided for beneath the exhausts and longitudinally cut the end section of the engine cover.

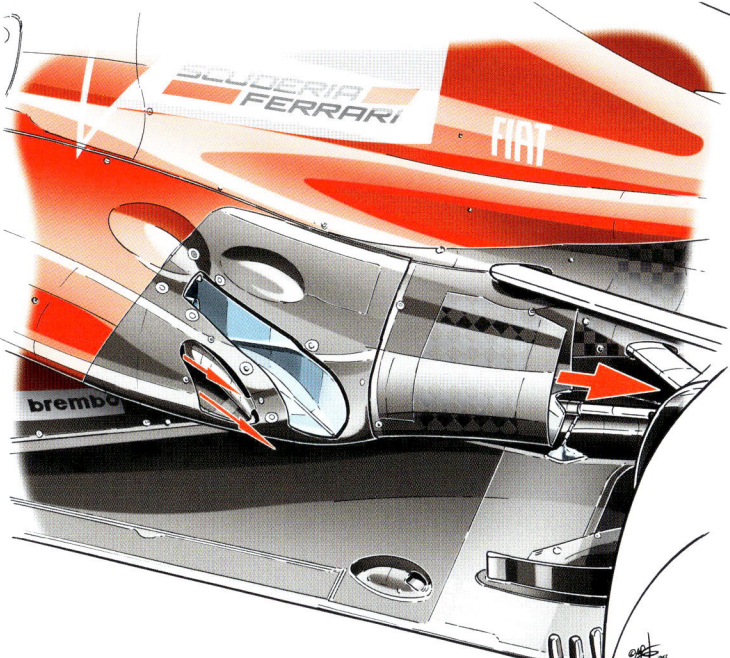

LOTUS SEPANG

A comparison between the exhausts used by Grosjean and the single set of new ones that were used by Raikkonen. The differences are clear: the exhaust zone presents a more accentuated humped protection as on the Red Bull, the ramp is steeper and short, as is the mouth in the lower part. In this way the section of the Coke-bottle zone is privileged with clear aerodynamic advantages.

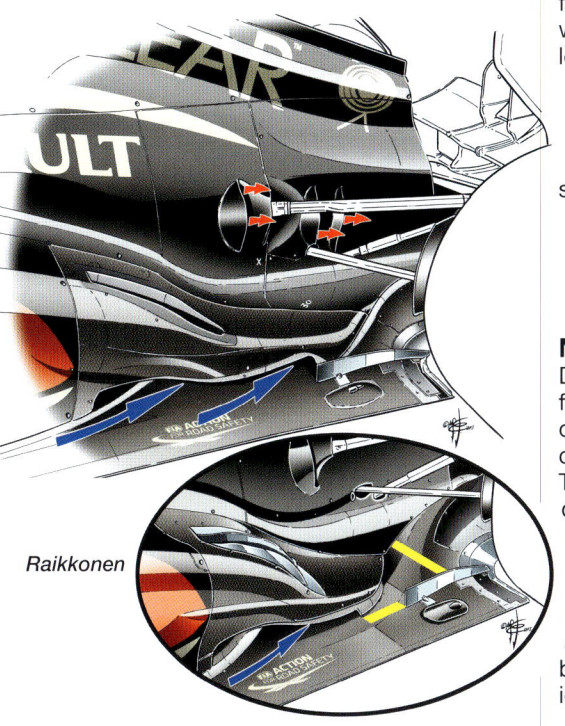

Raikkonen

MERCEDES: HYDRAULIC SUSPENSION

In this drawing originally made to illustrate the new twin vanes below the chassis introduced at Sepang you can see the hydraulic pipe used to recharge the W04's hydraulic suspension system prior to a test session; effectively, the same method was used to bleed the braking system. In the circle the old configuration with the vanes used in Melbourne.

LOTUS HYDRAULIC SUSPENSION

Almost a comparison with the layout used by Lotus, the hydraulic actuator that handles the balancing between front and rear axles was located in the left-hand sidepod. The drawing shows the bleeding operation pressurising the system.

McLAREN SHANGHAI

During the break after the first two races, the rear end of the MP4/28 was almost completely revised. The exhaust position was different and above all, the Coke-bottle area was redesigned. It should be noted that in the hurry the new area was not painted and remained plain carbonfibre, making it easy to identify the differences.

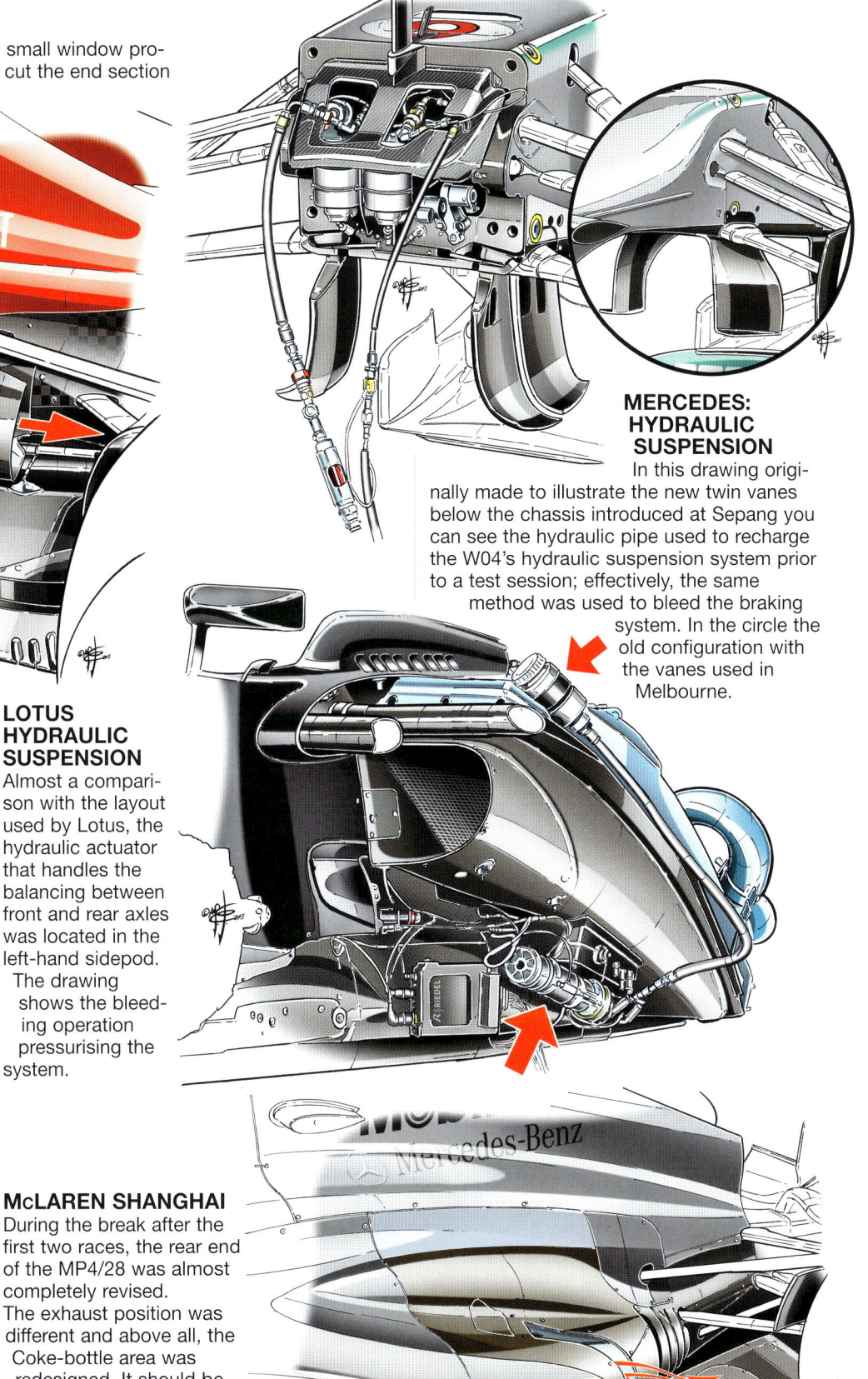

The 2013 **SEASON**

FERRARI SHANGHAI
For the first time Ferrari adopted brake shrouds that were open in the central area so as to allow the front tyres to get up to temperature more quickly. The air entering between shroud and tyre is not only expelled towards the outside but also inside the wheel rims where it helps increase the tyre operating temperature.

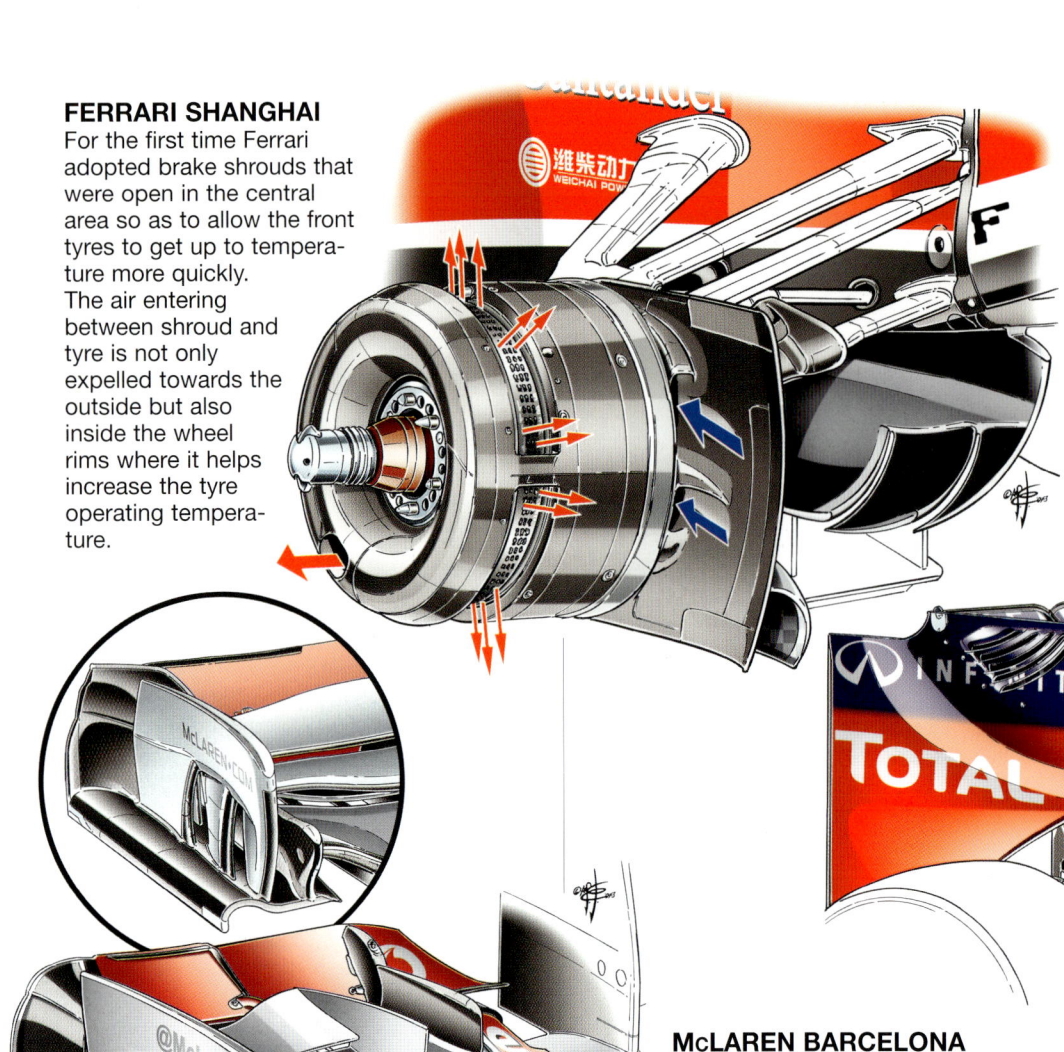

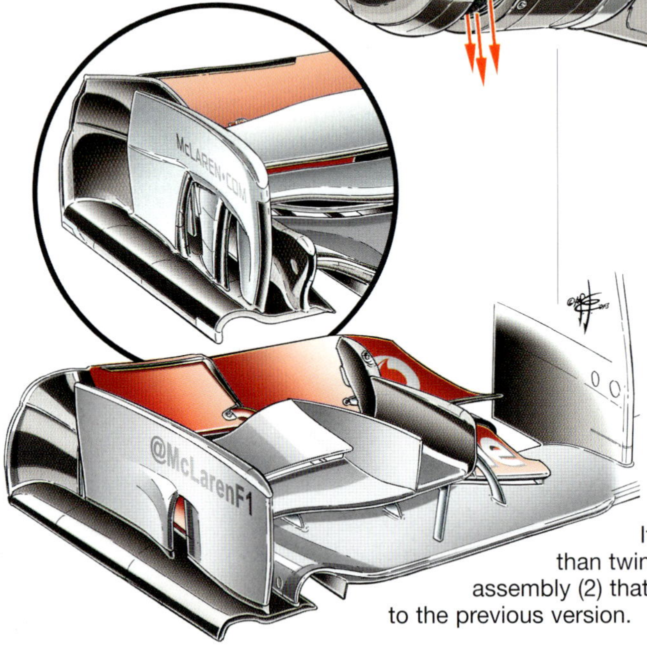

RED BULL SAKHIR
Red Bull underwent a laborious set-up procedure with no less than three different rear wings: on the Friday morning Webber used the high downforce (in the drawing) and Vettel the low downforce versions. In the afternoon, the German opted for a new high downforce wing with vertical endplates equipped with horizontal slots, then fitted to the Australian's car for qualifying and the race.

McLAREN BARCELONA
Perez alone briefly tested the new McLaren wing on the Friday. It was characterised by a single rather than twin endplate and a new raised flap assembly (2) that had also been simplified with respect to the previous version.

TORO ROSSO BARCELONA
There was a very important evolutionary step for the Toro Rossos at the Spanish GP, with the rear bodywork being completely revised and a feature that, albeit with certain original touches, resembled Red Bull's with the tunnel in the lower section feeding the diffuser's lateral channels. The exhausts were of course also new.

RED BULL BARCELONA
Two new front wings for Red Bull, of which the version with these vortex generators (2) was not used in qualifying, with the wing featuring this small vertical fin (1) in the trailing edge of the enw flap as its only novelty being preferred. The aim of these mini-appendages was that of preventing the blockage of the slots between one profile and the other.

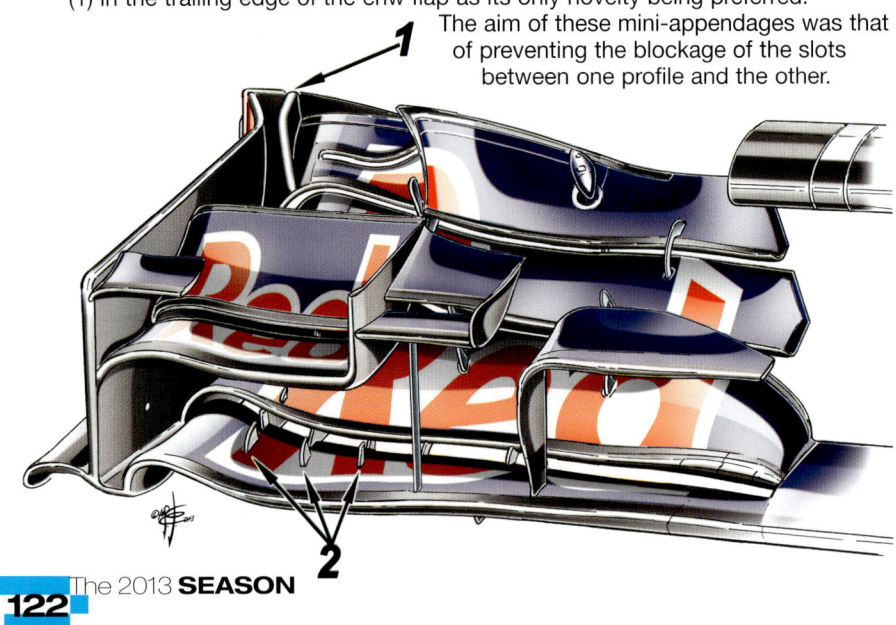

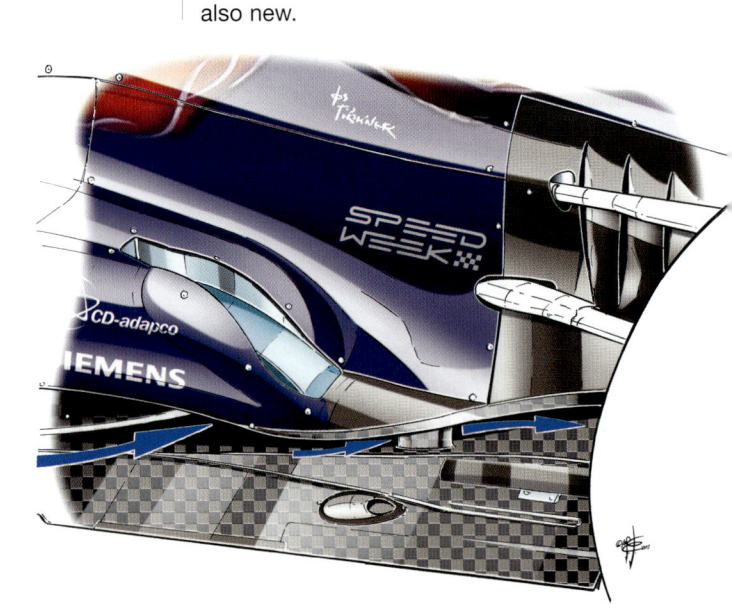

The 2013 **SEASON**

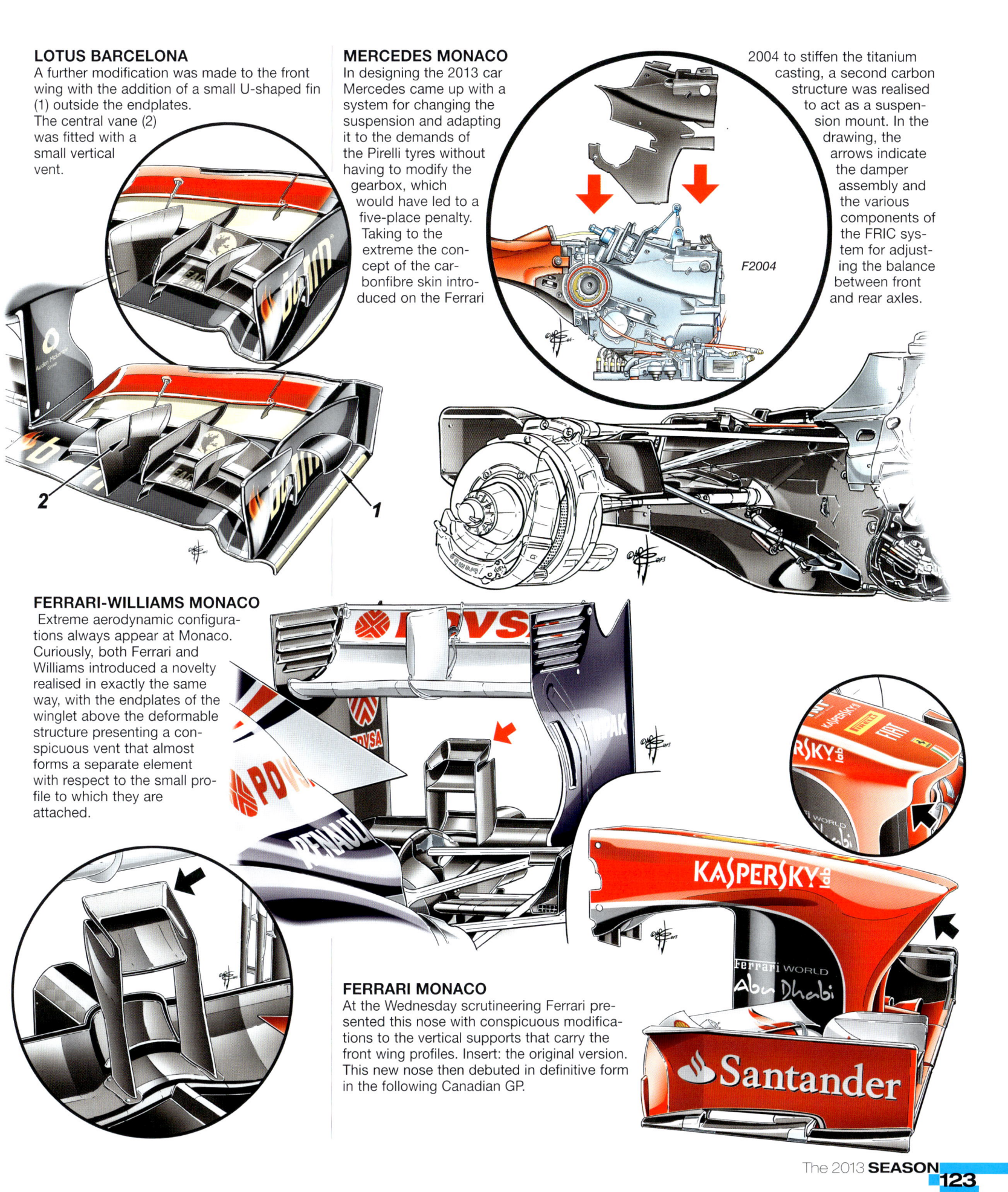

LOTUS BARCELONA
A further modification was made to the front wing with the addition of a small U-shaped fin (1) outside the endplates. The central vane (2) was fitted with a small vertical vent.

MERCEDES MONACO
In designing the 2013 car Mercedes came up with a system for changing the suspension and adapting it to the demands of the Pirelli tyres without having to modify the gearbox, which would have led to a five-place penalty. Taking to the extreme the concept of the carbonfibre skin introduced on the Ferrari 2004 to stiffen the titanium casting, a second carbon structure was realised to act as a suspension mount. In the drawing, the arrows indicate the damper assembly and the various components of the FRIC system for adjusting the balance between front and rear axles.

FERRARI-WILLIAMS MONACO
Extreme aerodynamic configurations always appear at Monaco. Curiously, both Ferrari and Williams introduced a novelty realised in exactly the same way, with the endplates of the winglet above the deformable structure presenting a conspicuous vent that almost forms a separate element with respect to the small profile to which they are attached.

FERRARI MONACO
At the Wednesday scrutineering Ferrari presented this nose with conspicuous modifications to the vertical supports that carry the front wing profiles. Insert: the original version. This new nose then debuted in definitive form in the following Canadian GP.

The 2013 **SEASON**

RED BULL MONACO
A new rear wing for the Red Bulls with the Williams and Force India-style vertical vent that allows it to be easily distinguished with respect to the version used in Spain of which it retained both the main plane and flap and the rest of the endplates.

FERRARI MONTREAL
On a track that is particularly hard on brakes and where the previous season it had adopted the William's style ducts with a smooth internal section, Ferrari reprised the trumpet ducts outside the shrouds. Note the space (highlighted in yellow) freed in the shrouds (in the circle the Monaco version) to facilitate the expulsion of hot air inside the wheels.

McLAREN MONTREAL
McLaren began the weekend in Canada with the brake ducts introduced at Monaco before switching to a version that was more open towards the outside so as to improve cooling of the discs which are particularly heavily stressed in Canada.

MERCEDES MONTREAL
On the fast Montreal circuit Mercedes introduced a new engine cover (top) that resembled that of the Ferrari due to the small fin created in this area. This engine cover was also slightly more tapering to improve the efficiency of the flow towards the rear wing.

FERRARI MONTREAL
The official debut of the new wing with the different supports that had not been used at Monaco.
The front wing assembly above all was new, in particular the raised flaps that were no longer connected to the endplates but had a curvilinear form that recalled the one used by McLaren two years ago. in the detail, the straight flap version retained through to the Monaco GP.

124 The 2013 SEASON

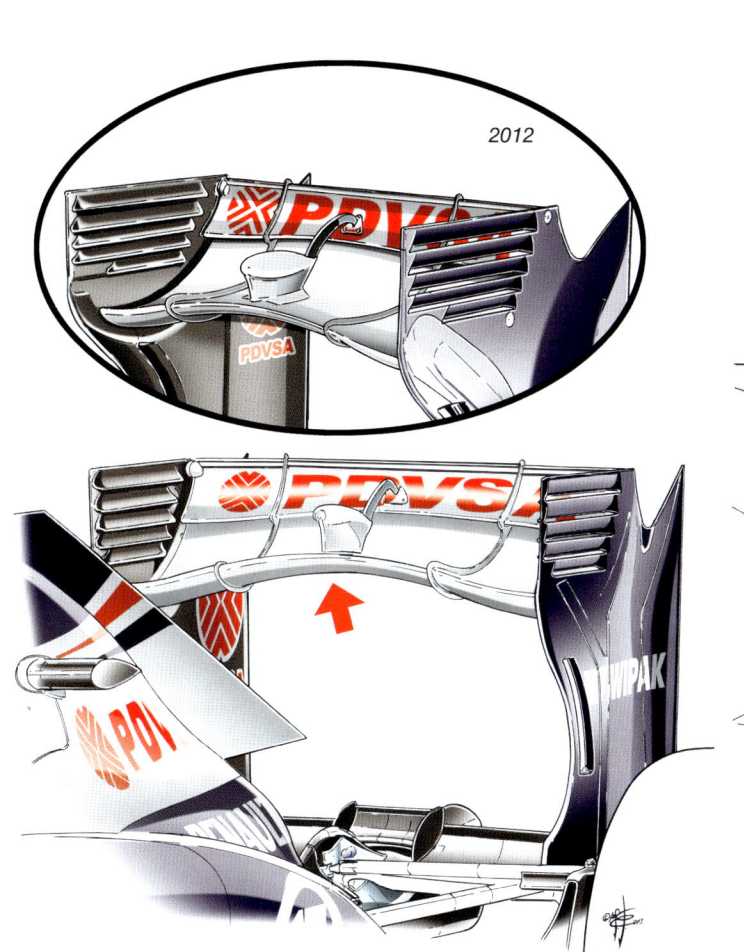

2012

FERRARI SILVERSTONE
A new rear wing for the Ferraris. It differed at the top in a return to the slots in the trailing edges of the flaps and above all in the vertical slot behind the wheels, introduced two years ago by Williams and then adopted by most of the other teams this season.

WILLIAMS MONTREAL
The prize for the most individual rear wing went to Williams, although it should be pointed out that this was the same dished wing used the previous year on the Canadian track.

LOTUS DDRS
As in the 2012 season, Lotus was the first team to experiment with dual passive DRS. It was also used in qualifying, but only to collect data. The large drawing shows the version tested before the start of the season. In practice, it reprised the Mercedes dual DRS concept from 2012, but without the link inside the rear wing profile. In the detail on the left, the version introduced on Raikkonen's car only.

RED BULL SILVERSTONE
Modified rear suspension geometry for the Red Bulls and above all new brake ducts with different internal finning; the shrouds were also modified with the mechanics checking to ensure that any contact with the wheel rims was avoided.

Mercedes 2012

The 2013 **SEASON**
125

LOTUS-MERCEDES NÜRBURGRING

Lotus and Mercedes revolutionised the flows inside the rear brake ducts, completely closing the shrouds towards the outside to prevent hot air exiting and creating detrimental turbulence. The flow of hot air was instead expelled internally, but in a precise area highlighted in the Lotus drawing, high up so as not to interfere with the numerous fins attached to the brake ducts.

MERCEDES NÜRBURGRING

A new nose for the Mercedes, different in all its details. The support pylons recalled those introduced by Ferrari, in part because the central area was higher from the ground and flatter. The new nose was also lighter which meant that the crash test had to be repeated ahead of the German GP.

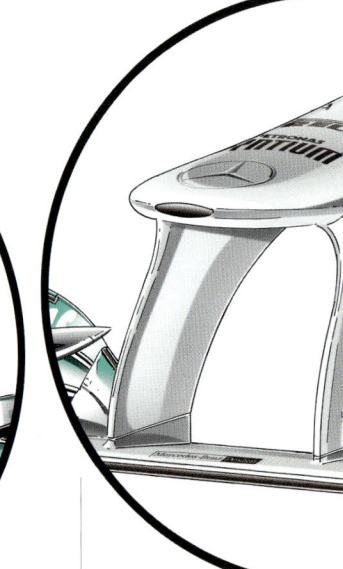

MERCEDES NÜRBURGRING

Mercedes gave the dual passive DRS its debut. The characteristic that distinguished it from the Lotus version, Mercedes's own 2012 device and the pre-season version was the presence of two new trumpet intakes in the engine cover feeding air passage which, in exploiting the same principle as the FDuct from 2010 "stalls" the rear wing's main plane.

The 2013 SEASON

SAUBER BUDAPEST
Sauber presented what was virtually a "B" version at the Hungarian GP. The drawing shows the new exhaust area, in practice a combination of the Red Bull and Toro Rosso configurations. As on these two cars, there was an air passage in the lower area that fed the central part of the diffuser.

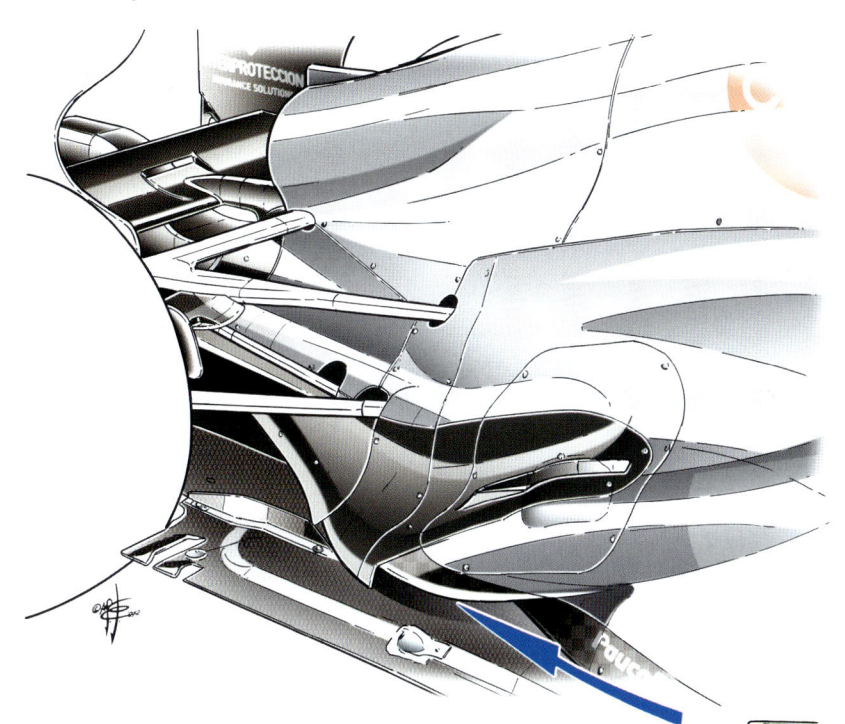

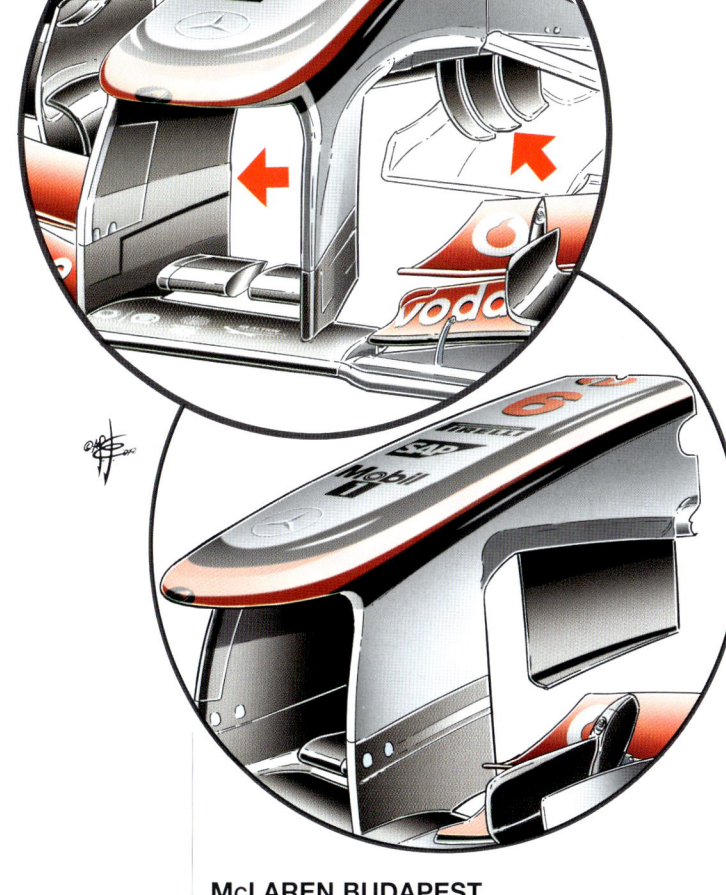

McLAREN BUDAPEST
New front aerodynamics for the McLarens (in the drawing above). The support pylons were winder and more inclined at the rear so as to work in synergy with the vanes below the chassis divided into three elements.
The previous version instead had narrower pylons combined with two square-cut, straight vanes applied to the lower part of the nose.

WILLIAMS BUDAPEST
Almost all the teams enlarged the Red Bull-style oval vents opening at the end of the engine cover. Williams took a different approach with numerous slots at the base of the fin in the engine cover itself in addition to the usual vents.

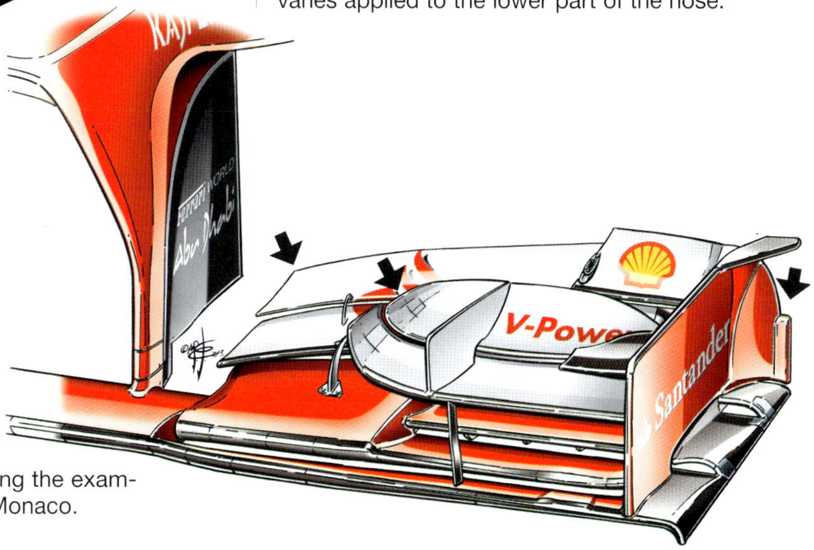

FERRARI BUDAPEST
New front wing for the Ferraris which differed with respect to the old one in the rounded and vented shape of the inside endplates of the raised flaps, following the example set by Williams at Monaco.

The 2013 SEASON
127

Giorgio Nada Editore
Editoria manager
Leonardo Acerbi

Editoria coordination
Giorgio Nada Editore

Graphic design and cover
Aimone Bolliger

Translation
Robert Newman
Neil Davenport

Contributors
Franco Nugnes (engines)
Gary Anderson (venting effects)
Ing. Giancarlo Bruno (tyres and suspensions)
Kazuhito Kasai (tyres table)

Computer graphic
Alessia Bardino
Elena Cerro
Camillo Morande
Gisella Nicosia
Paolo Rondelli
Marco Verna

3D Animations
Camillo Morande
Annunziata Generoso

Printed in Italy by
Grafiche Flaminia Srl
Trevi (PG)
september 2013

© 2013 Giorgio Nada Editore, Vimodrone (Milan, Italy)

ALL RIGHTS RESERVED
All rights reserved. Apart from any fair dealing for the purpose of private study, research, criticism or review, no part of this publication may be reproduced, stored in a retrieval system, or transmitted, by any means, electronic, electrical, chemical, mechanical, optical photocopying, recording or otherwise, without prior written permission. All enquiries should be addressed to:

Giorgio Nada Editore
Via Claudio Treves,15/17
I - 20090 VIMODRONE MI
Tel. +39 02 27301126
Fax +39 02 27301454
e-mail: info@giorgionadaeditore.it
www.giorgionadaeditore.it

Allo stesso indirizzo può essere richiesto il catalogo
di tutte le opere pubblicate dalla Casa Editrice.

Distribution
Giunti Editore Spa
via Bolognese 165
I - 50139 FIRENZE
www.giunti.it

Formula 1 2012-2013. Technical analysis
ISBN 978-88-7911-579-7